JAMES VI AND I

James VI and I: Kingship, Government and Religion brings together early career and established scholars with a range of approaches to the reign. Their original, research-based essays on a series of broad and interconnected topics invite us to consider Jacobean kingship afresh.

King James VI and I (1566–1625) was the first monarch to rule over the three kingdoms of Scotland, England and Ireland. His practice of kingship – which often so skilfully played upon, and navigated between, the contradictory expectations of his contemporaries – provoked lively debate in his day. Four hundred years after James's death, it still does. This book looks again at some of the hottest of the controversies that still define the historiography of the period. With chapters on James's personal reign in Scotland before 1603, his government of Ireland, corruption, peace-making, and the parliamentary and religious politics of his kingship in England, the contributing authors present new archival discoveries, and more familiar materials and problems are reassessed.

This edited collection is a stimulating resource for students and researchers of Stuart monarchy and early modern British and Irish history.

Alexander Courtney is an independent scholar and Assistant Head (Teaching and Learning) at The Perse School, Cambridge, UK. He is a Fellow of the Royal Historical Society and the author of *James VI, Britannic Prince: King of Scots and Elizabeth's Heir, 1566–1603* (2024).

Michael Questier is Hon. Chair in the Centre for Catholic Studies, Department of Theology, University of Durham, and the author and editor of several works on early modern political and religious history, including most recently *Dynastic Politics and the British Reformations, 1580–1630* (2019) and *Catholics and Treason: Martyrology, Memory, and Politics in the Post-Reformation* (2022).

JAMES VI AND I

Kingship, Government and Religion

Edited by Alexander Courtney and
Michael Questier

Routledge
Taylor & Francis Group

LONDON AND NEW YORK

Designed cover image: Detail of James VI & I, c. 1606 (oil on canvas). Critz, John de (1555-1641) (attr.to) / Flemish. Dulwich Picture Gallery, London, UK. © Dulwich Picture Gallery / Bridgeman Images.

First published 2025
by Routledge
4 Park Square, Milton Park, Abingdon, Oxon OX14 4RN

and by Routledge
605 Third Avenue, New York, NY 10158

Routledge is an imprint of the Taylor & Francis Group, an informa business

© 2025 selection and editorial matter, Alexander Courtney and Michael Questier; individual chapters, the contributors

The right of Alexander Courtney and Michael Questier to be identified as the authors of the editorial material, and of the authors for their individual chapters, has been asserted in accordance with sections 77 and 78 of the Copyright, Designs and Patents Act 1988.

British Library Cataloguing-in-Publication Data
A catalogue record for this book is available from the British Library

Library of Congress Cataloging-in-Publication Data
Names: Courtney, Alexander, editor. | Questier, Michael C., editor.
Title: James VI & I : politics, government and religion / edited by Alexander Courtney and Michael Questier.
Other titles: James VI and I
Description: Abingdon, Oxon ; New York, NY : Routledge, 2025. | Includes bibliographical references and index.
Identifiers: LCCN 2024046386 (print) | LCCN 2024046387 (ebook) | ISBN 9781032334691 (hbk) | ISBN 9781032334707 (pbk) | ISBN 9781003319764 (ebk) | ISBN 9781040318676 (adobe pdf) | ISBN 9781040318683 (epub)
Subjects: LCSH: James I, King of England, 1566-1625. | Great Britain--Kings and rulers--Biography. | Scotland--Kings and rulers--Biography. | Church and state--Great Britain--History--17th century. | Great Britain--History--James I, 1603-1625. | Scotland--History--James VI, 1567-1625.
Classification: LCC DA391 .J367 2025 (print) | LCC DA391 (ebook) | DDC 942.06/1092 [B]--dc23/eng/20241211
LC record available at https://lccn.loc.gov/2024046386
LC ebook record available at https://lccn.loc.gov/2024046387

ISBN: 978-1-032-33469-1 (hbk)
ISBN: 978-1-032-33470-7 (pbk)
ISBN: 978-1-003-31976-4 (ebk)

DOI: 10.4324/9781003319764

Typeset in Sabon
by SPi Technologies India Pvt Ltd (Straive)

CONTENTS

FIGURES

CONTRIBUTORS

Alexander Courtney is an independent scholar and Assistant Head (Teaching and Learning) at The Perse School, Cambridge. His biographical study of James in Scotland – *James VI, Britannic Prince: King of Scots and Elizabeth's Heir, 1566–1603* – was published by Routledge in 2024 and a second volume, covering James's life and kingship to 1625, is in preparation. He is a Fellow of the Royal Historical Society.

David Heffernan (independent scholar) is a historian of Tudor and Early Stuart Ireland. His books include *Debating Tudor Policy in Sixteenth-Century Ireland* (2018) and *Walter Devereux, First Earl of Essex, and the Colonization of North-East Ulster*, c. *1573–6* (2018). He has an edition of the Irish court-minutes of the Worshipful Company of Clothworkers, 1609–1676 forthcoming with the Irish Manuscripts Commission.

Peter Lake is University Distinguished Professor of History at Vanderbilt University. He is the author of twelve books, including *Moderate Puritans and the Elizabethan Church* (1982) and *Bad Queen Bess? Libels, Secret Histories, and the Politics of Publicity in the Reign of Queen Elizabeth I* (2015). He is Fellow of both the Royal Historical Society and the British Academy and has published widely on the religious and political history of post-Reformation England.

Kathryn Marshalek is a Postdoctoral Fellow in the Department of History at Vanderbilt University. Her research focuses on the European post-Reformation predicament: the destabilising force of persistent religious pluralism both within and between states after the legal and doctrinal Reformation of the mid-sixteenth century. She received her PhD from Vanderbilt in 2024. Her dissertation, 'Dynastic Politics and Religious Difference: English Catholics and the Crisis of the 1620s', explored how geopolitical circumstances at the start of the Thirty Years War allowed for English Catholics to call the existing religio-political settlement into radical question. Her work has been published in *Renaissance Quarterly* and *Historical Research*.

Thomas M. McCoog SJ commuted between the Jesuit Historical Institute (Rome) where he served as Editor of the *Archivum Historicum Societatis Iesu* and Editor-in-Chief of the Institute's publications and the Jesuit Provincial Archives (London) where he was archivist, for twenty years. His most recent monograph is *The Society of Jesus in Ireland, Scotland, and England 1598–1606: "Lest Our Lamp be Entirely Extinguished"* (2017). Currently he is co-editing (with Victor Houliston, Ginevra Crosignani and others) the complete correspondence of Robert Persons. He is a Visiting Research Fellow at Loyola University Maryland and Archivist of the former Maryland Province of the Society of Jesus.

Noah Millstone is Associate Professor in Early Modern History at the University of Birmingham and is the author of *Manuscript Circulation and the Invention of Politics in Early Stuart England* (2016) and oversaw the setting up of the *Manuscript Pamphleteering in Early Stuart England* database (http://mpese.ac.uk). He is the director of the Arts and Humanities Research Council-funded research network, *Europe's Short Peace, 1595–1620*.

Anthony Milton is a Fellow of the British Academy and Professor of History at the University of Sheffield. His publications include *Catholic and Reformed: The Roman and Protestant Churches in English Protestant Thought, The British Delegation and the Synod of Dort (1618–19), Laudian and Royalist Polemic in Seventeenth-Century England*, and (most recently) *England's Second Reformation: The Battle for the Church of England 1625–62*. He also edited volume 1 of *The Oxford History of Anglicanism*. Ongoing projects include a biographical study of the first earl of Strafford and a study of anonymous publications and their reception in early modern England.

Michael Questier is Hon. Professor in the CCS, Department of Theology, University of Durham. He has recently published *Dynastic Politics and the British Reformations, 1580–1630* (2019) and *Catholics and Treason: Martyrology, Memory, and Politics in the Post-Reformation* (2022).

Steven J. Reid is Professor of Early Modern Scottish History and Culture at the University of Glasgow. He has published widely on intellectual, religious and political culture in the reigns of Mary, Queen of Scots and James VI and I.

His most recent books include *The Early Life of James VI* (2023) and *The Afterlife of Mary, Queen of Scots* (2024).

David Chan Smith is Associate Professor of History at Wilfrid Laurier University, Canada. His major works include a study of seventeenth-century jurisprudence, *Sir Edward Coke and the Reformation of the Laws* (2014) and research on constitutional history, corruption and the moral economy of markets.

Andrew Thrush is the editor of The History of Parliament's Elizabethan House of Lords Section. He previously edited *The History of Parliament: The House of Commons 1604–1629* (2010) and *The History of Parliament: The House of Lords 1604–1629* (2021) and co-edited, with Richard Cust, *King James VI and I and His English Parliaments* (2011), Conrad Russell's posthumously published Trevelyan Lectures.

ACKNOWLEDGEMENTS

We would like to thank all the contributors to this volume for being so accommodating in bringing the project to a conclusion. We are also grateful to the very professional staff at Routledge, particularly to Laura Pilsworth, for their helpfulness in seeing the volume into print.

In several ways, the Elizabethan and Jacobean era remains one of the liveliest areas of debate and discussion in the whole of the early modern field of British studies, and it is in this context that we offer these essays to the field, hoping to stimulate further debate and discussion of James VI and I's practice of post-Reformation kingship.

ABBREVIATIONS

AAW   Archives of the Archdiocese of Westminster
ABSI   Archivum Britannicum Societatis Iesu
ARSI   Archivum Romanum Societatis Iesu
BL   British Library
BM   British Museum
CJ   Commons Journals
CSPI   *Calendar of State Papers, Ireland*
CSPScot   *Calendar of State Papers Scotland*
CSPV   *Calendar of State Papers, Venetian Series*
HMC   *Historical Manuscripts Commission*
JBS   *Journal of British Studies*
LJ   Lords Journals
McClure, LJC N. E. McClure (ed.), *The Letters of John Chamberlain* (2 vols, Philadelphia, 1939)
NLS   National Library of Scotland
NRAS   National Register of Archives for Scotland
NRS   National Records of Scotland
ODNB   *Oxford Dictionary of National Biography*
PiP, 1624   Proceedings in Parliament, 1624, available digitally on *British History Online*
PiP, 1625   M. Jansson and W. B. Bidwell (eds), *Proceedings in Parliament 1625* (New Haven, Conn., 1987)
SHR   *Scottish Historical Review*
TNA   The National Archives

NOTE ON THE TEXT

In the text, dates are given Old Style and, where appropriate in citing continental sources, Old Style/New Style but the year is taken to begin on 1 January. Unless otherwise stated, the place of publication of all works cited in this volume is London.

INTRODUCTION

Alexander Courtney and Michael Questier

Ever since the time itself, as it were, a range of commentators have offered their opinions about the monarchy of James VI and I – as indeed those who are so inclined have done about almost every monarchy and every political leader whose identity has become fused with the political system over which they preside. It would be surprising if it were any other way. Particularly in the early modern period, as Noah Millstone's essay in this volume points out, one of the principal concerns and tasks of diplomats was the remarking upon, and comprehending of, 'the preferences, tendencies and indeed the whole subject position' of those who exercised royal authority.[1] King James was as much a focus of observation and discussion as any other contemporary ruler.

To take just one well-known instance, we can cite the early character sketch of James, composed by Albert Fontenay in August 1584. Despatched to Edinburgh that summer as an envoy for James's mother Mary, Fontenay reported to the captive queen's secretary, Claude Nau, that the then eighteen-year-old king of Scots was 'with respect to his age, the chiefest of the princes who has ever been in the world'. Swift in apprehension and serious in judgement, the young king was of lively and piercing sharpness in disputation, 'whether upon matters of religion or any other topic', so Fontenay claimed, and more learned in 'languages, sciences and affairs of state ... than any in his realm'. Besides these admirable virtues of James's 'miraculous spirit', the envoy noted in him 'only three things' that could have bad consequences for 'the maintenance of his state and government': James's poor understanding of his financial and military weakness; his lack of discernment in his 'love' for, and subsequent stubbornness in sticking with, those he favoured, despite the opposition of 'all his subjects'; and his being 'too lazy ... and too much given over to his pleasure, and principally to the chase'.

DOI: 10.4324/9781003319764-1

In time, of course, reports such as this were reviewed and recycled by others, increasingly at a distance, in accounts which claimed to set out a coherent general understanding of the reign. In this process, though, the often tabloidesque quality of snippets of these contemporary observations was replicated in such a way as to obscure what was problematic, or indeed sophisticated, observationally and polemically, about those original reports. A favourite source for biographers of James, Fontenay's account – often somewhat carelessly translated from its original French – seems to present the reader with the familiar picture of the clever-clever king, the spendthrift *roi fainéant*, besotted with unpopular favourites and addicted to hunting.[2]

As often as not, more careful readings and contextualisation tend to undercut the apparent take-away messages of such documents – revealing a king who is more complex and politically adroit than perhaps first appears. James had graced Fontenay with privileged access at the hunt and in his cabinet, but in so doing he had controlled and restricted his interactions with this Frenchman, and had started playing mind games with him. Though Fontenay remarked on James's acuity, the envoy's own critical faculties seem to have been partially blunted by James's performances. For example, he witnessed James engage in 'several disputes on religion' in the privacy of his chambers, during which the king took to defending Catholic theological positions. James gave Fontenay the impression that his personal beliefs could be accommodated to Catholic doctrines – 'faith is dead without works, there is no predestination' – and also 'promised' that he would 'hang two or three' Protestant ministers 'to serve as an example' to bring others in the Kirk of Scotland to heel. Rather than take these words as instances of diplomatic signalling, as performances designed to appeal to their particular audience, Fontenay appears to have been so charmed by James that he accepted such royal statements at face value: '[the king] believes and maintains always what seems to him to be most true and just'.[3] While Fontenay recognised that James never once asked him anything personal about his mother Mary, 'neither about her health, nor her living conditions, nor her servants … nor about anything of the like', he still came away with the impression that James 'loves her and honours her greatly in his heart'. Yet, as we know, in the autumn following this letter, James broke off negotiations with Mary. This king, 'too lazy and little concerned about his affairs', was evidently not so indolent that he could not run rings around this envoy.[4]

Now, Fontenay's words about James in 1584 are not wholly misleading and some of his observations could apply broadly to aspects of James's character in much later adult life. After all, James really did love hunting. But, as Steven Reid writes below, James was 'a chimeric king'. He was, from his emergence from minority to the very end of his life, a creative and agile political player, a master of dissimulation. The 'many versions' of him which we might observe were 'to a greater or lesser degree, consciously performative', adapted (more or less successfully) to the needs of the moment.[5] Across his long reign, one of the longest in European history, and in his kingship over multiple kingdoms, his priorities changed, his freedom of manoeuvre grew and shrank. His enthusiasm for certain projects waxed and waned; new problems surfaced and old ones returned. Religious and diplomatic 'settlements' were seldom long settled. What we would now call the king's identity – in reference to what we can glean of his religious beliefs and in the nature of his personal relationships (including but not limited to his sexuality) – was no more fixed or susceptible to easy categorisation.[6] When we examine anew the sources and problems of his life and reign, the experience can therefore be, as Professor Reid puts it, 'disruptive' of established narratives.[7] We are not looking, therefore, for some catch-all, holistic view, some interpretative approach or formula that can (re)package him and the complexities of his long reign neatly and simply.

I

We do think, however, that the reign of King James remains subject, here and there in the literature, to a sometimes artificial push-me-pull-you interpretational contest over his reputation. (He is, of course, far from unique in this respect. Richard III, Mary Stuart, Charles I and James VII and II, to name just some, have their modern-day champions and detractors.) But, for whatever reason, the reign of the first Stuart king of England and Great Britain seems to trigger almost viscerally pronounced opinions and reactions among those who study this aspect of early modern monarchy, court politics and government.

There has, for example, long been a sense that the Stuart monarchy, when it came to England, was an intrusive entity, undermining the standards and set positions established during the previous reign. That is a case that has been made concerning the structure of the Stuart court in England.[8] In matters concerning the Church, the alleged lodestone of religious moderation in England is taken as the obvious pattern for what should happen in the rest of the British Isles, and the claim is that the new king's approach to such matters disturbed and disrupted the English Church.

Wallace MacCaffrey's retrospective on the reign of Elizabeth, published in 1992, is still a good guide to persistent tendencies in the literature concerning the shift from Tudor to Stuart. Here, for example, Elizabeth's natural conservatism, setting the tone of her court and government, becomes a self-fulfilling political virtue, allegedly serving as a guarantee of political stability. The 'queen made the appointments' in government, 'and even ... the routine details of service remained a matter for her decision'. 'Ambassadors abroad, the deputy and council in Ireland, commanders in the field, and ministers at court made no move without royal knowledge and royal approval' – except, presumably, when they did, for instance, when deciding to decapitate an imprisoned Scottish queen; or when they were, apparently, looking to set up an interregnum regime completely against Elizabeth's instincts and wishes.[9] That natural conservativism was visible in the queen's authority over the Church. In matters of religion, the queen was 'pragmatic and principled', not least in insisting that 'there was to be no more change'. Although some of the queen's subjects continued to argue about religion, this did not prevent Elizabeth from being the 'nursing mother to the Church of England'.[10] Perhaps she was; and the English Church did undoubtedly steer clear of aspects of the European Protestant Reformation. But that is not quite the same thing as unchanging stability.

Although MacCaffrey's narrative allows that Elizabeth's 'paradoxical blend of wilfulness and indecisiveness ... posed problems for the queen's councillors', it seems that, even in circumstances created by her own failure of decision-making, 'at least she listened to' those councillors. The last of the Tudors had an uncanny knack of securing the allegiance of her most important subjects – that is, by 'arousing a sense of conscious loyalty to her own person and securing the confidence of the governing classes in her ability to lead. To this end she bent all her considerable gifts of personality'. Moreover, 'within the political core – court and council – her blend of royal wilfulness and princely graciousness assured unquestioned mastery of the inner elite'.[11] The implication is that her successor was not able to do this.

If by 'governing classes' one in fact means the small number of people immediately around the Tudor queen, then there was indeed an almost astonishing continuity of personnel, who hung together almost to the end. But there has been a claim that this is connected with the emergence of a more modern, and impliedly progressive, mode of government. 'For this generation at least, English government made a significant turn away from the dynastic past towards the still distant future of the early modern bureaucratic state'.[12] Again, the inference is that Jacobean monarchy was, after 1603, a reversion to a less progressive mode of royal government.

In these and other respects, one often senses that one is supposed to conclude that, after 1603, underlying guarantors of stability were cut away, and that the rot set in as the experience and counsel available from the surviving stalwarts of the Elizabethan establishment were removed by death. Nor is this completely wrong-headed – in the sense that clearly contemporaries did witness a kind of generational shift in, for example, the passing of high-ranking Elizabethan councillors and officials, such as the earls of Dorset and Salisbury during the years up to 1612. The assumptions of the late Elizabethan period, heavily influenced by years and years of trying to make war against the house of Austria, were obviously disrupted and up-ended by the onset of peace. Stable or not (actually, not) the Jacobean settlement was inevitably going, to some, to look rather different to what preceded it. But in several respects, this compare-and-contrast approach often appears to be based on artificial either/or distinctions.

II

Now, clearly, some of the cruder verbalisations of Tudor-perspective accounts of Stuart rule in England and across the British Isles have long been subject to criticism. This was certainly the case in Jenny Wormald's much-cited piece laid before students of early modern British politics over forty years ago, when she asked whether James VI (before 1603 in Scotland) and James I (after 1603 in England) were 'two kings or one?'[13] Why was it that James VI, a king of 'very remarkable political ability ... and conspicuous tenacity ... assuredly the most successful of his line in governing Scotland', was routinely portrayed in English scholarship as the 'mumbling', 'timid', 'slobbering drunkard' and 'pedantic buffoon', James I?[14]

Wormald challenged the latter view as a distortion, derived (at least in part) from Sir Anthony Weldon's 'brilliant and deeply biased' caricature of the king. Through her positive account of James's long experience and skilfulness as king in Scotland before 1603, and by presenting these as assets in his government of England, Wormald was inviting English historians to take James more seriously. She argued that the crises and controversies of early seventeenth-century English politics and government could not be explained satisfactorily by trotting out questionable lines about the failings and foibles of a foreign king who could not compare to the supposedly towering achievements of Gloriana: 'when in doubt about what caused the problems of Jacobean England, the answer may not be James I'.[15]

For Wormald, reassessment of James VI and I's kingship involved reflection not just upon him and certain well-worn and dubious sources about him; it involved critical thinking about the wider context in which he came to operate after 1603 – about English political culture, English religious divisions, English parliamentary practices and anti-Scottish prejudices, and the structural problems of the English state (its dwindling revenues, the mounting costs of war and the onward creep of corruption). These inherited problems were, for Wormald, the true sources of dysfunction and disappointment in this remarkably shrewd Scottish king's English reign. In other words, Wormald's essay presented a version of James VI that was calculated to disrupt established narratives of the reign of James I – and likewise, for good measure, a number of assumptions about the reign of Elizabeth I.[16]

With none of this would (most of) the contributors to this volume disagree. By taking James seriously and in context, and by seeking to understand his kingship and its significance afresh, Wormald was opening up, not closing down, discussion of the question.

But, at the same time, there is a risk of certain kinds of judgement becoming part of an equal-and-opposite version of the world in which a diametrically contradictory account of the reign seems to take on a life of its own. This has been the case with a number of issues in the early modern historical canon – for example, the (perception of the) medieval Church either as a sink of corruption and spiritual aridity or, on the other hand, the zenith of all human religious achievement; the English Reformation as either a moderate and consensual establishment of a distinctively English mode of worship, or as a Reformed full-on continental style of Protestant change of religion; and the English/British civil war/s as either merely a rebellion or, on the other hand, an epoch-defining revolution.

In other words, genuinely exciting claims can become part of a (sometimes inflexible) new historiographical orthodoxy. This was certainly the case with the Wormaldian moment, if one can call it that. At the time that the 'Two Kings or One?' topic started to attract attention, the new 'revisionist' mode of political analysis was in the ascendant, and its challenge to the perceived and actual anachronisms of 'Whig' history was taken, by some, as self-evidently true. We think, here, primarily of the *oeuvre* of Professor Conrad Russell, and its headline-grabbing mantras about the status/crisis of parliaments, about the demilitarisation of the English state, about the effects of financial instability and inflation (the 'functional breakdown'), and the instability of multiple monarchies. For Russell, religion was the red mist of avoidable division which, propagated through miscommunication and misunderstanding, made possible the kind of violent oppositional politics that should have been absent from the English political arena – in which there were no necessarily entrenched structures of ideologically driven division – certainly no absolute division between 'court and country', or between 'crown/government and opposition', at least in any modern sense.[17]

III

Into this model, a new perception of the first Stuart king of Great Britain could easily be assimilated. Even without merely lionising James Stuart, here there was plenty of material to refute Whig shibboleths about gradually increasing entrenchment of political opposition, and about the, in some sense, inevitability of future civil strife, and the emergence of a new world order, driven by deep underlying causes that contemporaries could not fully grasp.

But, as Peter Lake has argued, the sharper the delineation of the difference between the new and the old, the more inevitable were the 'false oppositions and dichotomies' and the 'self-serving polemical claims doomed to generate far more heat than light'. The end result of a good deal of early Stuart revisionism was a determination 'not so much to qualify or controvert but simply to invert the central contentions of what had calcified, in myriad textbooks and undergraduate essays, as conventional ("Whig") orthodoxy'.[18]

Still, despite revisionism's occasionally journalistic tendencies and moments, it provided a new basis for discussing post-Reformation monarchy. As Lake argues, it freed the 'domain of the political from a whole series of determinisms, of petty inevitabilities, of tacitly assumed we-already-know-thats' made up of traditional narratives and various sorts of social, economic and cultural causes – and, by doing this, 'revisionism rendered the political interesting again'. For 'the first time probably since Gardiner, the politics of early Stuart England had become an open-ended subject for research'.[19]

In turn, this allowed for new approaches towards early Stuart monarchy and the court, up to and concentrating on the person of the king. While the anti-revisionist response was fairly straightforward, that is, in the form of a return to past/Whiggish certainties,[20] there emerged here a more nuanced post-revisionist project. The first stand-out publication here was the volume of essays entitled *Conflict in Early Stuart England*, in which the contributors took issue with arguably crude headline-snatching claims in and derived from Russell's work, but still took the revisionism seriously enough to engage with it.[21]

It is in this context and spirit that the essays in this present volume are framed. Without covering every topic that is potentially relevant here, the volume does its best to construct new platforms for talking about the political impacts of the reign of King James across the three kingdoms of the British Isles. In Russell's work, the problems associated with the government of multiple monarchies were given a new prominence. James's determination to argue for a 'perfect' union could no longer be taken as simply the arrogance of an ignorant foreigner. Not that this rendered his views uncontroversial. As Andrew Thrush's contribution to this volume reminds us, the fact that James may have been, in some constitutional-law context, correct in his analysis of what was at issue did not make the topic less provocative. In fact, Dr Thrush's essay demonstrates exactly how far this was a high-stakes game in which everyone was aware of how much turned on the outcome – that is, on what construction of the recent accession publicly came out on top.

One of the functions of the debate about the Union was, of course, to determine who, at court, had access to the monarch, and on what terms. The broader revisionist project had already tried to make the court a respectable subject again for historians of politics. David Starkey, who was associated with Russell's seminar at the Institute of Historical Research in the 1980s and early 1990s, had, with his volume *The English Court* (1987), sought to refute the modernisation thesis of Elton's *Tudor Revolution in Government*, in which far-sighted bureaucrats such as Thomas Cromwell got on with the real business of ruling the kingdom, even while public attention was focused on the often-lurid news coming out of the court. For Starkey, the real political action was and remained at the court – at Whitehall and other royal palaces, rather than in the ramshackle spaces of Westminster that formally housed the departments of state and the law courts. What really informed the high politics of the period was, therefore, the structure of the court and what happened there – its rituals, modes of organisation, who had access to which rooms, who could lobby for favours of various kinds, and so on.[22] In this volume, Steven Reid's review of the importance of the workings of the Scottish court in the period before 1603 is a reminder of how central this topic remains – problematising issues that we sometimes think have been entirely settled, and pointing out that still-unused archives (in this case for James's early reign in Scotland) offer answers to the relevant questions.

The court was, with, of course, venues such as parliament, the location for the exercise of the royal voice – both in person and through print. As Kevin Sharpe said some time ago, 'literary and cultural critics have made us more aware of the inextricable interrelationship of discourse and power', in the sense that 'speaking, writing, [and] discursive performances … not only reflect social arrangements and structures of authority' but 'are themselves acts of authority'.[23] Alex Courtney's essay in this volume on James's Scottish writings and the contexts of their publication up to 1603 is a reminder of the king's distinctively 'logocentric' political style. Lori Anne Ferrell wrote a monograph nearly thirty years ago on how far the king's rhetorical interventions were designed to exert his authority.[24] In the context of recent scholarship, Professor Ferrell's intervention looks even more prescient now than it did then. The Hampton Court Conference was just one instance of this royal use of discourse – a version of what James had done during his Scottish reign before 1603.[25]

James's rule in England was peppered with instances of his presiding, discursively, over controverted issues. Some of those occasions were relatively informal, such as the confrontation, in front of the king, between John Howson and George Abbot in 1615.[26] In 1622 there were disputations at court, in front of the king, that involved a Jesuit (John Percy) and Church of England clergymen (including William Laud).[27] The reassembling by Peter Lake, in this volume, of the clash at the end of the reign between representatives of Lambeth Palace and of Durham House over what was technically a fairly minor licensing issue shows how the king was, via the language of contemporary theology, still using words in order to engage and control those kinds of political interest groups.

Kathryn Marshalek's essay in this volume shows the king performing the same kind of role in more formal public settings, at court and in council, during the period in 1624–1625 when he was being lobbied over the emerging dynastic alliance that would see Stuart royal authority projected into the future. Here we have a kind of macro-level version of the same kind of pitch-making that Professor Lake's essay on the Edward Elton/William Crompton licensing case describes.

Although reviewers may remark on the number of essays here that deal with 'religion', we follow in the post-revisionist tradition of a very broad understanding of that term. At its most restricted, this topic has been taken to be almost coterminous with various kinds of regulatory issues inside the Church of England. But at its maximum and more interesting extent, it has always allowed students of the period to unpick a number of other questions – principally concerning the power relationships between different actors holding public office in the Church and in (the rest of) the local and national state. Here was the principal contemporary language for the discussion of the extent and limits of royal authority. In this volume these questions are addressed primarily by Peter Lake, Anthony Milton and Thomas McCoog. Professor Milton revisits the issue of how far James could be believed when he professed to be a tolerant ruler. As with all the other essays in this volume, context is the crucial determinant of what the king meant when he presented himself in such terms. What one had here was less a matter of tolerance as such (in anything like the modern sense) but, rather, a debate about under what circumstances latitude should be allowed to certain interests and individuals. Dr McCoog's account of the regularisation of the structures of the Society of Jesus in post-Gunpowder plot England, and of how far those who were of a Catholic tendency could integrate themselves into the new Stuart polity, is one of the contexts for that debate about tolerance and about who exactly might expect to be comprehended in the Stuart polity. There is an obvious link here with the (one might think, extraordinary) events at the end of the reign when English Jesuits, with other Catholic clergymen, temporarily seemed to enjoy de facto tolerated status and became mixed up in the politics of the Spanish Match and its successor dynastic arrangement with the French court.[28]

This volume seeks, therefore, further to probe the topic of how far there was a stable post-Reformation settlement of religion in England.[29] No essay here deals explicitly with the major politics/religion controversy on which the king himself actively published, that is, concerning the new oath of allegiance, of 1606, incorporated into statute as one of the regime's responses to the Gunpowder business.[30] But the wonderful research of Matthew Growhoski has shown how subtle and deliberate was the process whereby the king's work was disseminated to foreign audiences. Here the king entangled a number of constituencies in a debate about what his subjects might and might not say about the, in some sense absolute, rights of kings, a debate which picked up on the slew of literature generated by the recent wars of religion in France.[31]

Of course, the purely personal element in politics remains elusive. Our accounts of such interactions between this and that person often depend heavily on the nature of difficult and scattered sources. Perhaps the most visible, though still complex, instance of the king engaging the public, actually a range of publics, was the long-drawn-out process which led up to the accession in March 1603 but which extended into the months and years after that event.

We do not have an essay here dealing exclusively with the accession. But Robert Cross's Princeton PhD dissertation has described how its aftermath saw a number of challenges to what passed for the status quo in late Elizabethan England, in particular by reference to the implications of the peace with Spain. Professor Cross argues that in the negotiations necessary to bring this about, James was not the cipher that some have taken him to be. James unleashed a creative chaos in which certain people who were previously out were brought in, enabling the king to escape the potentially asphyxiating effects of having to accommodate himself entirely to the Elizabethan establishment.[32] The obvious case here is Henry Howard, meteorically promoted after James took the English crown. He was an overtly conformist Catholic. Howard's presence on the privy council was of huge advantage to a king wishing to escape the popular political implications of aspects of English puritanism, just as James had wrenched himself free in Scotland from aspects of Scots Presbyterianism. It is possible to argue that, in England, Howard fulfilled a role not dissimilar to the one that George Gordon, earl and subsequently marquess of Huntly played in Scotland.[33]

IV

And yet, and yet. Even if James understood the practical business of the politics of representation, and could engage rhetorically, at a variety of levels, with different and often antagonistic interest groups, the contemporary mutterings about royal malfeasance have never gone away – because of his alleged laziness, his apparent inability to understand the value of money, and his failure to address the acid corrosiveness of (permitting) corruption in high places. This volume does, therefore, address the claim that there were gaping shortfalls between the rhetoric and what actually happened – between, say, initiatives for reform and the actual woeful reality of debt and peculation.

Once again, though, we stress the need for the avoidance of an absolute either/or approach. In part this is because, inevitably, many of the complaints about the king's inattention to business, and absences from London, were themselves ways of articulating frustration at lack of access to the king.[34] Not that one needs merely to posit a model of royal efficiency, probity and consistency, which, in any case, would be difficult to do. As David Heffernan's chapter amply demonstrates, there were times when the very necessary task of restructuring aspects of landholding in Ireland had James's full attention, and there were times when it apparently just did not.

This, however, remains an area for scholarly discussion. David Smith's contribution expands the contemporary account of what corruption might be taken to be – taking it as an 'interpretative lens' which allows us to construe 'Jacobean ideas about rulership'; but this mode of analysis, he insists, cannot be limited to the confines of the court, just as it cannot be restricted to one kingdom in the British Isles, or even just to issues of office-holding/finance.[35] In matters of money, and this is hardly something unique to the early modern period, financial stability and sustainability are actually a function of credit; and so the exercise of royal authority in this, as much as other regards, was directly associated with the credibility more generally of the line that the king, in his own person, took over issues in which the public – even a variously constituted general public – had a voice and a stake.

Russell's influential *Parliaments and English Politics, 1621–1629* offered a number of perceptive comments about the extent of corruption in Jacobean, and in fact all early modern, government. As Russell argued, concerning the debates in parliament over patents and monopolies in 1621, 'considering the story of the patents as a whole, we cannot say that right was all on one side'.[36] In the post-Reformation, royal government had extremely bureaucratic aspects (as anyone who has waded through chancery and exchequer records can testify) but there were very few paid bureaucrats to carry out royal policy. When it came to the personnel available to enforce the king's will, either there was government by gratuity, or no government at all. Equally, what some people saw as corrupt – one flagrant instance was the apparently subverted statute law concerning recusancy – did not seem thus to others.[37] Here, the ways in which contemporaries perceived political corruption – for example, as set out in the crude stereotyping used in verse libels and manuscript separates – are representative enough of real issues; but, as Lake has argued, although there was a growth in the use of libels to attack the regime, these were 'phenomena … of a distinctly Elizabethan provenance; products … of the long succession and accession crises that did so much to shape the politics of the post-Reformation in late sixteenth-century England'.[38]

In line with recent post-revisionist accounts, therefore, we argue for engagement with a wide spectrum of contemporary public and political opinion about the way that royal government was conducted. This seems especially appropriate for the controversies in the early 1620s. While Thomas Scott might have accurately expressed the fury of a certain kind of critic of the late Jacobean court, there were others who, while sharply observing the turn of the times, did so from a very different set of perspectives. Faced with the prospect of the Spanish Match in the early 1620s, Richard Verstegan produced an almost perfect inverted version of Scott's account of the effects of peace and war on the court and the country, and the political and religious health of the nation, trading off and appealing to, it would appear, clusters of opinion, both Catholic and conformist, that saw the world that way.[39]

By the later 1610s and early 1620s, indeed, some of those who had been completely politically tainted and unacceptable in earlier times (particularly, here, a range of people who defined themselves primarily as Catholics) were now regarded by the king as capable of being integrated into the Stuart polity. Indeed, depending on the turn of events (especially in the later 1610s and the 1620s), the issue of who was being loyal and who was being seditious was something that could alter with disconcerting speed. Towards the end of the reign, the direction of travel of royal (foreign) policy disrupted the ideological checks and balances which contemporaries observed at the start. This forced even moderate Calvinists into forms of opposition to the king. While scholars have, as Lake says, 'pointed out the obvious advantages which would have accrued to the English Church and crown from a Grindalian or Leicestrian accommodation with the forces of moderate puritanism and popular anti-popery', this path was rejected by 'three very different monarchs' (Elizabeth, James and Charles) and one of them, that is, James was 'a Calvinist intellectual'. Here, James was part of a much longer tradition of political debate and practice than is sometimes recognised, and was engaging with a range of constituencies that do not always show up in supposedly mainstream accounts of the period.[40]

V

There have been several essay collections on James's reign in the past fifty years and the 1625–2025 quatercentenary will see a number of biographical studies of him as well.[41] And yet formulae that have so long been part of the furniture seem to reappear almost effortlessly. In popular history, we can still find him depicted today as 'the wisest fool', whose 'lavish life' in Scotland and England can be boiled down into a tale of 'romantic attachments', 'soft spots' and 'lust' for a succession of 'lovers'.[42]

By contrast, in a recent attempt to cover the first part of his reign in England, Susan Doran depicts James more favourably and yet still, when weighed in the balance with (a version of) Elizabeth, he is found wanting: 'Elizabeth was frugal, James profligate; Elizabeth's speeches were terse, James's orations longwinded … Elizabeth was praised for her interactions with her subjects, unlike James who was perceived as inaccessible. Elizabeth wooed her House of Commons, whereas James often adopted a confrontational stance'. Unlike under Elizabeth, 'there is no evidence that policies were thrashed out in council' and 'while James did not deny the importance of counsel, he was evidently loath to take it'. Unlike Elizabeth, he paid only 'lip service to [the] expectation' that a monarch acted 'on conciliar advice'. Whereas she 'relied' upon the advice of 'experts' in her council, 'the same cannot be said of James': he 'went his own way', turning to 'more congenial voices in his bedchamber'. James was, admittedly, 'one of the most intelligent of England's monarchs and took the business of kingship seriously'. 'Regime change in 1603 … did not result in a radical break with the past'; but he was nevertheless a 'foreign king' whose reign in England would be 'blight[ed]' because of his 'policies and style of government'.[43]

But this depends to some extent on which contemporary voices one chooses to credit. It is quite true that some of his future English subjects regarded James with suspicion – and may even have regarded him as 'devious, duplicitous and capable of treachery'.[44] But it is a different matter entirely to argue that he was handicapped 'by the general perception of him as weak and untrustworthy' or that he spent his time playing catch-up in order to repair the damage to his 'reputation in England' as the result of his political blunders, or that he was disadvantaged by his 'unreliability in religion'.[45]

It is, in fact, equally easy to construct an account of the reign in which, for example, James was bountiful, and Elizabeth was tightfisted; and in which Elizabeth was largely confined in her later years to her Thames Valley houses, whereas James presented himself to his subjects more widely, both in person and through the print publication of his own words. In such an account it would be possible to narrate Elizabeth's retreat into the bunker as she silenced her House of Commons on topics she defined as *arcana imperii*, whereas James, used as he was in Scotland to engaging personally in political and theological debate and to trying to win round sceptics and opponents, on some topics at least tried to do the same in England.[46] Here, again, Elizabeth's council was narrow, whereas James's was broad; or, at least, to the consternation of those, in both Scotland and England, who wanted to narrow down and dominate his counsels and court in their own interests, James had his own agenda. He had long preferred to rule as a 'universal king', preserving his authority and political independence by drawing into his service loyalists of varied confessional preferences.[47] In Scotland before 1603 and in England afterwards, he employed different combinations of counsellors depending upon their expertise and the nature of the business in hand. It can be argued that this too preserved his independence and constituted an approach to kingly government that, even *if* it differed from Elizabethan practices, was neither informal nor *ipso facto* less legitimate.[48] James was undoubtedly, in England, a 'foreign king', but the case can be made that he had taken great pains over the preceding decades to prepare the ground for the accession, in his well-publicised and carefully crafted critiques of radical Presbyterians in the Kirk of Scotland and the Scottish nobility's blood feuding, and he had presented himself to his future English subjects as a reassuringly anti-Scottish claimant.[49] Facing the dire fiscal consequences of the predecessor regime's conservatism and deep-rooted practices of entrenched corruption, Jacobean government was characterised by efforts at reform, though these were fitful and controversial.[50] Is it so clear that (one particular version of) the practices of Elizabethan queenship are the measure of excellence against which to judge the kingcraft of her successor?

No one denies, of course, that new regimes tend to be controversial. Moreover, after a long-running succession/accession crisis, in which the identity of the successor did not become absolutely clear until near the end, it was inevitable that there would be winners and losers, and, as night follows day, perceptions of double-dealing and betrayal. Dr Thrush's essay here on the struggle over the Union is a reminder about how much was still at stake after the accession took place. The surviving newsletters sent abroad by a range of separatist Catholic clergy (who all reckoned that, by their own lights, they were loyalists) are a reminder, often week by week, of exactly how much had not been settled by the arrival of the new king.[51]

But historical claims that this was, in essence, accidental – the result of a Scottish king's failure, as it were, to get the English privy conciliar memo – are simply unconvincing, that is, without sources that explicitly make that case. It is true that the political honeymoon period for James, in England, was relatively short. Nor is it completely wrong for Professor Doran to argue that during the brutal post-accession factional battles, which saw spectacular winners and losers, 'it did not take long for criticisms of James to emerge', and that 'even before the coronation, his obsessive hunting and debasing of knighthoods were provoking hostile comments', while the 'arrival of a large contingent of Scots in London' led to 'a discontent that was to haunt the early years of the reign'.[52]

Still, to imply that this was the default position of all observers and commentators is assumed rather than proved. Here, the insinuation is that a combination of royal incompetence and ignorance meant that within a few months the 'mood' of the 'country' had turned 'fractious', and that 'puritans' and 'Catholics' had taken to campaigning, and 'Protestants' were deeply unhappy, certainly about the 'Catholics', as if this was something that could have been avoided by a more prudent monarch.[53] Equally, at the Hampton Court Conference, James apparently should have acted as an 'impartial mediator', should have exercised 'chairmanship' to manage the meeting, but failed to do this through his 'idiosyncratic' and 'opinionated' interventions.[54]

Such accounts are rather at odds with narratives that can be traced back at least to Simon Adams's magisterial thesis on the politics of the Protestant cause, and which demonstrate that the thorny aspects of Protestant-centred politics had their origins deep in Elizabeth's reign – and that James was acting deliberately and energetically to negotiate this and other difficult aspects of his political inheritance in England.[55]

It is obvious from the foregoing that we do not think that Jacobean monarchy is in imminent danger of being de-problematised. The collective aim in this volume is certainly not to articulate, univocally, a positive version of James VI and I, but rather to consider afresh several aspects of Jacobean kingship, in the light of recent scholarship and by sharing archival discoveries and reinterpretations of more familiar materials. Many more chapters might have been included, had limitations of time and space, and the availability of contributors, not dictated otherwise. As any reader with knowledge of this period will understand immediately, in no sense is this collection comprehensive and we do not pretend otherwise. Nevertheless, we hope to encourage further thinking and different perspectives on James VI and I and the politics of his kingship. If these essays prove 'disruptive' of established narratives of the complex of topics that constitute the field(s) of Jacobean and Stewart/Stuart monarchy, then that will be all to the good.

Notes

1 See below, p. 176.
2 TNA, SP 53/13, fos 128ᵛ–9ᵛ. For biographical uses of Fontenay's account, see D. H. Willson, *King James VI & I* (1956), pp. 53–4; P. Croft, *King James* (Basingstoke, 2003), pp. 19–20; S. Veerapen, *The Wisest Fool: The Lavish Life of James VI and I* (Edinburgh, 2023), pp. 83–8. Fontenay's line – 'il ayme indiscretement et opiniastrement en despit de tous ses subjects' – is regularly misconstrued as a comment critical of James's sexuality – for example, M. B. Young, *King James and the History of Homosexuality* (revised edn, 2016), p. 25; Veerapen, *Wisest Fool*, p. 87–8 ('the king's indiscreet and obstinate love'). Fontenay was in fact making a political comment about James's 'love' (that is, his favour) towards figures at court, such as the then earl of Arran; he was not passing judgement about 'love' in the sense of physical attraction – 'indiscretement' meaning 'lacking in discernment' and not 'indiscreetly' or 'illicitly'.
3 TNA, SP 53/13, fos 129ʳ, 123ᵛ (Fontenay to Mary, 15 August 1584).
4 TNA, SP 53/13, fos 128ᵛ, 129ʳ.
5 S. J. Reid, ch. 1, below, pp. 36–7.
6 For recent, divergent and thought-provoking works addressing James's sexuality or queerness, see S. J. Reid, below, pp. 30–1, 37–8; N. Malcolm, *Forbidden Desire in Early Modern Europe: Male-Male Sexual Relations, 1400–1750* (Oxford, 2023), pp. 273–6; L. R. Hinnie, 'Queering the Castalian: James VI and I and "Narratives of Blood"', in A. Kennedy and S. Weston (eds), *Life at the Margins in Early Modern Scotland* (Woodbridge, 2024), pp. 194–209.
7 See below, p. 32.
8 See, for example, N. Cuddy, 'The Revival of the Entourage: the Bedchamber of James I, 1603–1625', in D. Starkey (ed.), *The English Court from the Wars of the Roses to the Civil War* (1987), pp. 173–225.
9 W. MacCaffrey, *Elizabeth I: War and Politics, 1588–1603* (Princeton, 1992), p. 543.
10 MacCaffrey, *Elizabeth*, p. 550, 552.
11 MacCaffrey, *Elizabeth*, pp. 545, 546, 548.
12 MacCaffrey, *Elizabeth*, p. 549.
13 J. Wormald, 'James VI and I: Two Kings or One?', *History* 68 (1983), pp. 187–209.
14 Wormald, 'Two Kings or One?', pp. 187 (quoting Gordon Donaldson, Wallace Notestein and Lawrence Stone), 188, 191.
15 Wormald, 'Two Kings or One?', pp. 191, 198.
16 Wormald was, to some extent, building on an earlier line of discussion in, for example, M. L. Schwarz, 'James I and the Historians: Towards a Reconsideration', *Journal of British Studies* 13 (1974), pp. 114–34, trading off, *inter alia*, Gordon Donaldson's work. See also M. Lee, Jr., 'James I and the Historians: Not a Bad King after All?', *Albion*, 16 (1984), pp. 151–63; R. Houlbrooke, 'James's Reputation, 1625–2005', in *idem* (ed.), *James VI and I: Ideas, Authority, and Government* (Aldershot, 2006), pp. 169–90.
17 C. Russell, 'Introduction', and 'Parliament and the King's Finances', in *idem*, *The Origins of the English Civil War*, pp. 1–31, 91–116; *idem*, 'Parliamentary History in Perspective, 1604–1629', *History* 61 (1976), pp. 1–27; *idem*, 'The British Problem and the English Civil War', *History* 72 (1987), pp. 395–415; the latter two essays reprinted in *idem*, *Unrevolutionary England 1603–1642* (1990), and see also the other essays in that volume; and see also *idem*, *Parliaments and English Politics, 1621–1629* (Oxford, 1979).
18 T. Cogswell, R. Cust and P. Lake, 'Revisionism and its Legacies: the Work of Conrad Russell', in T. Cogswell, R. Cust and P. Lake (eds), *Politics, Religion and Popularity in Early Stuart Britain: Essays in Honour of Conrad Russell*

(Cambridge, 2002), pp. 1–17, at pp. 13–14 (we quote from the sections of the introduction written by Professor Lake). For this kind of either/or approach, cf. Kevin Sharpe's *Personal Rule of Charles I* (New Haven and London, 1992) with, for example, David Cressy's *Charles I and the People of England* (Oxford, 2015).

19 Cogswell, Cust and Lake, 'Revisionism', pp. 7–8.

20 T. Rabb and D. Hirst, 'Revisionism Revised: Two perspectives on Early Stuart History', *Past and Present* 92 (1981), pp. 55–99; for Russell's response, see C. Russell, eds R. Cust and A. Thrush, *King James VI and I and his English Parliaments: The Trevelyan Lectures Delivered at the University of Cambridge 1995* (Oxford, 2011), ch. 10.

21 R. Cust and A. Hughes (eds), *Conflict in Early Stuart England* (London, 1989), esp. the essay by Thomas Cogswell ('England and the Spanish Match'); see also Peter Lake's review of C. Russell, *The Causes of the English Civil War* and *idem, The Fall of the British Monarchies, 1637–1642*, and *idem, Unrevolutionary England*, in *Huntington Library Quarterly* 57 (1994), pp. 167–97.

22 Starkey, *The English Court from the Wars of the Roses to the Civil War*.

23 K. Sharpe, 'The King's Writ: Royal Authors and Royal Authority in Early Modern England', in K. Sharpe and P. Lake (eds), *Culture and Politics in Early Modern England* (1994), pp. 117–38, at p. 117.

24 L. A. Ferrell, *Government by Polemic: James I, the King's Preachers, and the Rhetorics of Conformity, 1603–1625* (Stanford, CA, 1998).

25 M. H. Curtis, 'Hampton Court Conference and its Aftermath', *History* 46 (1961), pp. 1–16; M. Questier, *Dynastic Politics and the British Reformations, 1558–1630* (Oxford, 2019), pp. 153, 179–80.

26 N. Cranfield and K. Fincham (eds), 'John Howson's Answers to Archbishop Abbot's Accusations at his "Trial" before James I at Greenwich, 10 June 1615', *Camden Miscellany Volume XXIX* (Camden Society, 4th series, 34 1987), pp. 319–41.

27 T. Wadkins, 'The Percy–"Fisher" Controversies and the Ecclesiastical Politics of Jacobean Anti-Catholicism, 1622–1625', *Church History* 57 (1988), pp. 153–69.

28 K. Marshalek, 'Putting the Catholics Back In: The "Rise of Arminianism" Reconsidered', *Historical Research* 97 (2024), pp. 238–58; *idem*, 'An Unsettled Religious Settlement and the Crisis of the 1620s: English Catholics, Anti-Popery, and the Spanish Match, 1622–4' (forthcoming in *English Historical Review*); M. Questier, *Stuart Dynastic Policy and Religious Politics, 1621–1625* (Camden 5th series, 34, Cambridge, 2009).

29 For the Reformation in Scotland and James's rule there before 1603, see S. J. Reid, ch 1 below, pp. 22–5. We should point out that, although this volume does not address James's managerial reforms in the Scottish Church after 1603, the work of Alan MacDonald and Laura Stewart reminds us that we must avoid Anglocentric approaches when dealing with James's policy in this respect; see, for example, A. R. MacDonald, 'James VI and I, the Church of Scotland, and British Ecclesiastical Convergence', *Historical Journal* 48 (2005), pp. 885–903; L. Stewart, 'The Political Repercussions of the Five Articles of Perth: A Reassessment of James VI and I's Religious Policies in Scotland', *Sixteenth Century Journal* 38 (2007), pp. 1013–36; L. Stewart, '"Brothers in Treuth": Propaganda, Public Opinion and the Perth Articles Debate in Scotland', in Houlbrooke, *James VI and I: Ideas, Authority, and Government*, pp. 151–68.

30 J. P. Sommerville, 'Jacobean Political Thought and the Controversy over the Oath of Allegiance' (PhD, Cambridge, 1981).

31 M. Growhoski, 'The Secret History of a "Secret War": John Barclay, his *Satyricon*, and the Politicization of Literary Scholarship in Early Modern Europe, 1582–1621' (PhD, Princeton, 2015), chs 8–11 passim.

32 R. Cross, 'To Counterbalance the World: England, Spain, & Peace in the Early 17ᵗʰ Century' (PhD, Princeton, 2012).

33 R. Grant, 'George Gordon, Sixth Earl of Huntly and the Politics of the Counter-Reformation in Scotland, 1581–1595' (PhD, Edinburgh, 2010); and see Anthony Milton, ch. 5, below p. 127.

34 As Dr Courtney has argued, there is a case for seeing royal government in the early seventeenth century as more like medieval royal regimes and courts rather than as a failed attempt to achieve 'modern' bureaucratic efficiency that we associate, often as an article of faith rather than on the basis of fact, with 'good' government: A. Courtney, 'Court Politics and the Kingship of James VI & I, c. 1615–c. 1622' (PhD, Cambridge, 2008), *passim*, esp. at pp. 4–6, 9, 95, 97. See also P. Croft, 'Can a Bureaucrat be a Favourite? Robert Cecil and the Strategies of Power', in J. H. Elliott and L. Brockliss (eds), *The World of the Favourite* (1999), pp. 81–95; C. Perry, 'The Politics of Access and Representations of the Sodomite King in Early Modern England', *Renaissance Quarterly* 53 (2000), pp. 1054–83.

35 See ch. 4 below, pp. 95–9.

36 Russell, *Parliaments and English Politics*, p. 103.

37 M. Questier, 'Sir Henry Spiller, Recusancy and the Efficiency of the Jacobean Exchequer', *Historical Research* 66 (1993), pp. 251–66.

38 P. Lake, '"Free Speech" in Elizabethan and Early Stuart England', in R. Ingram, J. Peacey and A. Barber (eds), *Freedom of Speech, 1500–1850* (Manchester, 2020), pp. 63–97; P. Lake, 'Constitutional Consensus and Puritan Opposition in the 1620s: Thomas Scott and the Spanish Match', *Historical Journal* 25 (1982), pp. 805–25; see also A. Bellany, '"Rayling Rymes and Vaunting Verse": Libelous Politics in Early Stuart England', in K. Sharpe and P. Lake, *Culture and Politics in Early Stuart England* (Basingstoke, 1994); *idem, The Politics of Court Scandal In Early Modern England: News Culture and the Overbury Affair, 1603–1660* (Cambridge, 2002); T. Cogswell, 'Underground Verse and the Transformation of Early Stuart Political Culture', *Huntington Library Quarterly* 60 (1997), pp. 303–26.

39 Lake, 'Constitutional Consensus'; A. F. Allison, 'A Group of Political Tracts, 1621–1623, by Richard Verstegan', *Recusant History* 18 (1986), pp. 128–42; see also P. Lake and M. Questier, 'Thomas Scott, Richard Verstegan and the Public Politics of News Management' (forthcoming).

40 P. Lake, *Anglicans and Puritans?: Presbyterianism and English Conformist Thought from Whitgift to Hooker* (1988), p. 249.

41 See esp. A. G. R. Smith (ed.), *The Reign of James VI and I* (1973); J. Goodare and M. Lynch (eds), *The Reign of James VI* (East Linton, 2000); S. Clucas and R. Davies (eds), *The Crisis of 1614 and the Addled Parliament: Literary and Historical Perspectives* (Aldershot, 2003); G. Burgess, R. Wymer and J. Lawrence (eds), *The Accession of James I: Historical and Cultural Consequences* (Basingstoke, 2006); M. Kerr-Peterson and S. J. Reid (eds), *James VI and Noble Power in Scotland 1578–1603* (Abingdon, 2017); J. Wormald, ed. M. Kerr-Peterson, *James VI & I: Collected Essayes by Jenny Wormald* (Edinburgh, 2021); and see also Houlbrooke, *James VI and I: Ideas, Authority, and Government*.

42 Veerapen, *Wisest Fool, passim*.

43 S. Doran, *From Tudor to Stuart: The Regime Change from Elizabeth I to James I* (Oxford, 2024), pp. 259–60, 283, 465–76; *idem*, 'A Foreign King on the English Throne', *History Today* (June 2024), pp. 42–51.

44 S. Doran, 'Polemic and Prejudice: A Scottish King for an English Throne', in S. Doran and P. Kewes (eds), *Doubtful and Dangerous: The Question of Succession in Late Elizabethan England* (2014), pp. 215–33, at p. 228.

45 Doran, 'Polemic and Prejudice', pp. 224–5, 226–7.

46 On the other hand, it can be argued that political methods which James had deployed to great effect in Scotland did not necessarily work in an English parliamentary context: for example, see A. Thrush, *The House of Commons 1604–1629: Introductory Survey* (Cambridge, 2010), pp. 345–7.

47 A. Courtney, *James VI, Britannic Prince: King of Scots and Elizabeth's Heir, 1566–1603* (Abingdon, 2024), esp. pp. 64–5, 144, 166, 210, 240; K. Fincham and P. Lake, 'The Ecclesiastical Policy of King James I', *Journal of British Studies* 24 (1985), pp. 169–207.

48 See, for example, Courtney, *James VI, Britannic Prince*, pp. 223, 235 n. 119, 241–2; *idem*, 'Court Politics and the Kingship of James VI & I, c. 1615–c. 1622' (PhD, Cambridge, 2008), ch. 3.

49 See Courtney, below, ch. 2, pp. 55–6, 60.

50 See D. C. Smith, below, ch. 4, pp. 101–12.

51 See M. Questier (ed.), *Newsletters from the Archpresbyterate of George Birkhead* (Camden 5th series, 12, Cambridge, 1998).

52 Doran, 'A Foreign King', pp. 42–9.

53 Doran, 'A Foreign King', p. 50.

54 Doran, 'A Foreign King', p. 51; Doran, *From Tudor to Stuart*, p. 162.

55 S. Adams, 'The Protestant Cause: Religious Alliance with the West European Calvinist Communities as a Political Issue in England, 1585–1630' (DPhil, Oxford, 1973).

1

ONE KING, AND MANY

New Perspectives on James's Personal Reign in Scotland, c. 1578–c. 1603

Steven J. Reid

In her seminal article 'James VI and I: Two Kings or One?', Jenny Wormald noted that the elements that made James a success as ruler of Scotland prior to 1603 – his willingness to debate, his frank and informal courtly style, his readiness to avoid war – served both to his advantage and as a source of tension in his dealings with the English political community after 1603.[1] Despite Wormald's contention that James's tenure in England should not be viewed separately from his years in Scotland, and that he should be regarded as one king rather than two, Michael Questier has suggested that James was perhaps 'not one king but three', if we treat his years in Scotland as a single period and split his English reign in two.[2] James's relative smoothness in managing the cultural transition of his court at his accession, coupled with his notable early successes in domestic and foreign religious policy, contrast sharply with the period after 1615 when various factors, including the rise of George Villiers, the Palatinate and Spanish Match crises, and James's failure to call parliaments regularly pushed his later reign into an era of decline.[3] Godfrey Davies, writing an assessment of James's character as far back as 1941, proposed an even more complex structure of four periods of James's life. He further subdivided the Scottish reign into two periods – the period from James's birth until the end of the Ruthven Raid in the summer of 1583, and the personal reign thereafter, when James gradually extended his authority over Scotland until his removal to England in 1603.[4] This chapter focuses on Davies's second period, the reign of the young adult James, an era for which there has been extensive research into discrete aspects of politics, culture and society, but where there is still much to do to create a holistic picture of the king himself and his court.

DOI: 10.4324/9781003319764-2

There have been several studies of James's adult Scottish reign as part of combined reassessments of his life, chief among them Alexander Courtney's recent biography to 1603 which situates him expertly within the context of post-Reformation Europe and the English succession, the short narrative of James's reign completed by Jenny Wormald, and recent popular studies by Alan Stewart and Steven Veerapen. Alongside these sit the review of James's historiographical reputation by Ralph Houlbrooke, and the critical reassessments of James's court and politics made by Marc L. Schwarz, Maurice Lee and Michael B. Young.[5] In a Scottish context, the most impactful recent reassessment remains the collection of essays co-edited by Julian Goodare and Michael Lynch, which outlined a series of 'black holes' in our understanding, several of which were in part addressed by themselves and in doctoral research by their students.[6] These included the politics of James's minority and rise to power, particularly where his childhood ended and his adult reign began; the narrative of the struggle for control of the Kirk in the 1580s and 1590s, and the actual amount of power held by the radical Presbyterian faction during this period; how far James's relations with his nobility broke with the old model of late-medieval Stewart 'laissez faire' monarchy, and was replaced by a growing centralised state; the extent to which James's chronic indebtedness complicated or hampered this process; the role of the court as a political tool used by James; and how far James himself consciously cultivated an 'imperial' image, both in his writings and actions. This chapter explores what progress has been made over the past two and a half decades in addressing these voids, what has been learned as a result, and what new questions have been generated by subsequent research. It also looks at James within a Scottish archival context and offers thoughts on how underused manuscript material might significantly reshape our view of James as a young adult king, particularly in relation to his court.

I Filling in the 'Black Holes' of James's Reign in Scotland: Progress and Remaining or New Challenges

A basic query raised by Goodare and Lynch was when James actually assumed power, an act they believed did not fully occur until late 1586, when the signing of the Anglo-Scottish league in the summer of that year and the immediately ensuing trial of Mary forced James to take a public position on continued support for his mother or safeguarding his relationship with Elizabeth.[7] Taking 1586 as James's first full entry into independent political decision-making, when he would have been aged twenty, would suggest that he did so extremely late by the standards of his Stewart predecessors, who, from James II onwards, assumed power at various points between the ages of fifteen and nineteen. It would also suggest that James was little more than a passive player in the six coups and counter-coups that took place at court between

1578 and 1585, which in several instances saw varying restrictions placed on James's personal freedom.

A recent reappraisal of James's childhood and rise to power, focussing primarily on archival primary material alongside the well-established narratives found in sources such as the English State Papers, and histories written by James Melville of Halhill, David Calderwood and others, has suggested that James was actively involved in political life and alliance-building from just shy of his twelfth birthday.[8] Moreover, the entire period of James's 'long apprenticeship' between 1578 and 1585 shows that he was thoroughly consistent in the pursuit of two key political aims – bolstering his own authority (and thus protecting himself from internal threats) wherever possible, and pursuing his claim to the English succession. In March 1578 James assented to ending formally the regency of James Douglas, earl of Morton, and (from a technical perspective at least) to taking adult rule upon himself. James did this at the behest of his kin and friends the earls of Atholl and Argyll who had a deep-seated enmity towards Morton. While James had little personal liking for the regent, he was already at this stage in his very young life attempting to create a series of balanced factions at court, in this case an alliance of Stewart kin which he supported against the predominant Douglas-Erskine power bloc, which included James's young friend John Erskine, the earl of Mar, as James's notional custodian at Stirling Castle. While this coup was short-lived, and ended disastrously when a group of Mar's and Morton's allies violently seized control of Stirling Castle, James quickly learned that it was paramount to temporise and adapt to rapidly changing political circumstances if he wished to survive.

However, this experience did not diminish James's desire to create a strong Stewart kin-based alliance around himself. To this end he was actively involved in the recruitment of Esmé Stuart, sieur D'Aubigny, from France as the most suitable heir for the Lennox earldom, then in danger of passing to James's English cousin Arbella Stuart. While James expected D'Aubigny's arrival, and intended for him to act as a political counterweight to his pro-English nobility, he was not prepared for the deep personal love that quickly developed in him for his elder kinsman. This grew to such an extent that James became oblivious to the widespread political opposition mounting against his favourite. The regime established by Lennox and his ally, Captain James Stewart of Ochiltree (who seized the earldom of Arran for himself), alienated many of the Scottish nobility for its excessive spending, predatory seizure of lands, goods, and financial exactions, and for its sympathetic stance towards Catholics and France. James's enthusiastic and public support of Lennox, who was arguably the first courtier to treat him with the service and reverence that James felt was his right as a monarch, made him a clear target for the coalition of nobles, led by the earl of Gowrie, who seized James in the Ruthven Raid. One of their immediate priorities was to remove Lennox from

Scotland permanently; in this they succeeded and he died in France the following year. Although the Raid saw James placed under house arrest and forced to sign a humiliating series of household financial reforms, it was also the decisive moment when James moved to assume adult power. James used the leverage gained by visiting French ambassadors concerned for his welfare to divide the Ruthven lords and to build a coalition of nobles willing to support him when he escaped from his captors at Falkland in late spring 1583.

James would restore Captain James Stewart to power quickly after his escape, and Stewart would act as the leading figure of daily government both in the privy council and in the urban centres of Edinburgh and Stirling over the next two years. Yet his main policies were all clearly enacted at James's will, and followed consistent patterns aligned with his interests going back to 1578. These included persecuting the former Ruthven lords, upholding royal authority against all perceived enemies including the outspoken Scottish Kirk, and aggressively pursuing James's claim to the English throne while rejecting Elizabeth's frequent attempts to direct James's domestic policy. James learned a bitter lesson from his experience with Lennox, and thereafter ensured that his leading agents in government could be the focus for ire and opposition rather than himself, and that he did not personally get too close to them. Thus, when a wide coalition of the disaffected noble lords marched to remove Arran from power in November 1585, James calmly met them at Stirling and readily acceded to their wishes, in marked contrast with the dogged support that he had provided for Lennox.

Goodare and Lynch both noted that the older view of religious life in Jacobean Scotland was too coloured by the highly partisan source collections and histories compiled by Calderwood, James Melville, John Row and others, which portrayed the Presbyterian Kirk as a well-established and popular movement increasingly persecuted by James. Even as recently as the late twentieth century, the historiography was as divided along confessional lines as these partisan narratives, with authors such as James Kirk maintaining that the Scottish Kirk had been fully Presbyterian from its inception, responding to Gordon Donaldson's narrative of episcopal and moderate survival within reformed Church structures.[9] Major reassessments of the development of the Kirk by Alec Ryrie and Alan MacDonald, coupled with a turn towards cultural and local studies of the impact of reformed worship led by Margo Todd and others, have confirmed that the process of reform was in fact far more contingent and contested, and that there were strong trends of moderation and continuity across the sixteenth century. Alec Ryrie's portrayal of the origins of the Scottish Reformation as a political 'revolution' against French hegemony that had a strong religious undercurrent, and which caused a sharp legal break with Scotland's Catholic past followed by a gradual assimilation of a reformed culture, is a convincing one.[10] The period of change in which this transformative effect took hold is open to debate, but a scholarly consensus has emerged that this took more than half a century to embed. Margo Todd's landmark study of Kirk session cultural practice confirmed that by the early 1600s a broad picture of adherence to reformed discipline was discernible in urban centres across Scotland.[11] However, evidence for earlier adoption is sparse and fragmentary, and regional and local studies in areas ranging from Fife to the Highlands have shown that only a skeletal disciplinary framework existed by the 1580s, with semi-skilled readers handling the bulk of clerical duties in most parishes.[12] As Bess Rhodes has revealed, the most intensely debated issues in the first half century of the Kirk's existence were not details of worship, but the need to understand who controlled ecclesiastical land and its revenues.[13] Ironically, given the reformed faith's focus on worship in the vernacular, the biggest change was in Latinate culture, where one of the great pillars of reformed humanism – facility with Latin and Greek – was only carried to Scotland on the backs of the reformed intelligentsia after 1560.[14] That element of the renaissance came to fruition in James's reign and is arguably the key to his own literary bent, schooled as he was by George Buchanan, one of the greatest humanists of the age. It is also the reason why the literary culture which marked out James's reign as a golden age for neo-Latin poetry was inextricably linked with reformed scholars.[15] As Alan MacDonald has shown in his history of the Jacobean Kirk, James's relationship with the Church was highly contingent on political considerations, such as his signing of the King's or Negative Confession in 1581 to appease critics of Lennox, or granting the Presbyterian 'Golden Act' in 1592 in response to sustained criticism of his leniency towards George Gordon, earl of Huntly and the other so-called 'Catholic earls' who rebelled against Chancellor Maitland's role in government from 1589 onwards.[16] However, as Alexander Courtney has recently argued, James was intent on both managing the new currents of popular religious opinion that emerged in the wake of the Reformation, and on directing the development of the Kirk itself.[17] James did attempt to restore episcopacy and a hierarchy of top-down and royally-controlled authority during his later personal reign in Scotland. This included support for Patrick Adamson as archbishop of St Andrews and his 'chief oratour' in Kirk affairs in the 1580s, the promulgation of the 'Black Acts' of 1584 which limited clerical freedom to meet and preach and which required ministers to swear an oath of obedience to their ordinary or superior on pain of loss of stipend, and his seizure of control of the General Assembly following the 'Tolbooth Riot' of December 1596. The majority of ministers were willing to accept a moderate and royally controlled settlement, seen most visibly in the lack of anger at the flight of many of the leading radical ministers in the Kirk in early 1584 and the relative willingness of most to subscribe their oath of obedience.[18] The gap between Presbyterian rhetoric and reality has been shown to be equally wide in revisionist assessments of the character of Andrew Melville, who was politically weaker and far more fallible as a leader and university reformer than previous generations have suggested. Melville was a gifted poet and theologian, and an intellectual whose ideas for curricular reform had long-lasting impact at the College of St Mary in St Andrews and at the University of Glasgow.[19] However, he was in fact only one figure among several in a radical minority within the Kirk, a group that was far more challenged by nobles, other moderate ministers, and the average denizens of Scottish burghs hauled before the Kirk sessions than the writings of men such as Thomas M'Crie and David Hay Fleming would suggest. Recent research into the life and career of Patrick Adamson has offered an equally contrasting view to established notions surrounding leading figures in the early Jacobean Kirk.[20] Adamson was a scholar and minister who followed the same intellectual paths in Scotland and at the best reformed universities on the Continent as Melville, and was arguably a more gifted poet and polemicist, whose intellectual circle included Buchanan (his patron on his return to Scotland in 1570) and the celebrated French humanist Adrien Turnèbe. On his return to Scotland, Adamson consciously chose to forge a career as a churchman in service to the crown, first as chaplain to the regent, Morton and then from 1576 as archbishop of St Andrews. Adamson was shrewd and pragmatic, and could see that the essential landed and fiscal structures of the archbishopric still existed in post-Reformation Scotland. He exploited these fully for the benefit of himself and his family, but he also undertook serious administrative work for James, including the leadership of subscription to the oath of obedience in the territories under his jurisdiction, presentation of candidates to the ministry across the same area, involvement in the work of parliament and the privy council, and a diplomatic embassy to England. He would not have chosen such a path if he did not feel that a moderate and royally-controlled episcopal hierarchy under James was not only desirable but also viable.

As the idea of James in perpetual conflict with an entrenched reformed Kirk has given way to a narrative of a king gradually assuming headship of a more moderate ecclesiastical polity, older notions of James's domestic governance, and particularly his relations with his nobility, have shifted along similar axes. Maurice Lee, Gordon Donaldson and Julian Goodare have all suggested that the closing decades of the sixteenth century were the beginning of a Stewart 'revolution in government', drawing heavily on the thesis pioneered in the context of Tudor England by G. R. Elton.[21] Lee believed that James's chancellor Maitland of Thirlestane set out early in the king's adult reign to curb local noble power and establish a centralised 'Stewart despotism' through industrial-scale legislation at a series of parliaments (most notably on the occasion of the king's twenty-first birthday in 1587). Acts included making landlords responsible for the behaviour of their tenants and the king the central arbiter in local feuds, restoring order and hierarchy to parliamentary proceedings, and annexing the temporal income from major ecclesiastical benefices to the crown.[22] Maitland also used an enlarged and strengthened privy council and College of Justice, and the inclusion of lairds as another estate in parliament as represented by shire commissioners from 1587, to mount a strong central challenge to the power of nobles such as Huntly and Bothwell, who both identified Maitland as the source of their grievances when they rose in rebellion at various points between 1589 and 1592.[23]

Lee's thesis was expanded and modified by the extensive body of work on state formation, government and finance in James's reign by Julian Goodare. Goodare noted that the sweeping economic and social changes at work in the late sixteenth century created a period 'where it is still often difficult to describe how politics worked ... or how much the king himself was at the controlling centre of politics'.[24] In this regard, James's reign saw high inflation and increasingly sophisticated credit networks to which even the crown became subject, the rapid change of parliamentary and conciliar power structures, and the increasing professionalisation of local and regional bureaucracy, law and commerce. Yet by almost every conceivable measure, Scotland's government became more centralised and recognisably 'modern' over the course of James's adult reign. The privy council, established only in 1545, became the central executive body with the capacity to conduct business independently on the king's behalf, as when James was away hunting and when he visited Denmark in 1589–1590, while a permanent exchequer to oversee the various financial departments of the royal government was gradually established from the 1580s onwards.[25] Attempts were made to enforce a state monopoly on political violence through the creation of a permanent royal guard in the same period, followed by the increased purchasing of weapons and pressure on landholders and towns alike to provide military musters in the name of the royal government between 1595 and 1601.[26] Alongside the significant expansion in the volume of legislation passed by parliament came growth in the frequency and cost of taxation, which became regularised by the end of the sixteenth century, and the systematic improvement of crown income gathering from customs duties, royal land management, and charter and seal fees.[27] For a country moving towards apparently absolutist state tendencies there seems to have been surprisingly little room for the figure of the king himself.[28] For Goodare, the crown was not the source of the monarch's authority, but merely 'the vehicle for the issuing of orders in that person's name in such a way that they carried effective legal force'.[29] As such, James's ability to make decisions and set policy was arguably limited by how far he could influence the consensus generated by the privy council, which was increasingly confident in its own power and in (for example) its maintenance of records to justify its authority. The huge body of research carried out into Scottish parliamentary history over the past two and a half decades in the wake of the *Records of the Parliaments of Scotland*, particularly by Alan MacDonald, has further confirmed that the legislative agenda at parliament was not rigorously controlled by the king through its steering group, the Lords of the Articles, but could be influenced.[30] Each parliamentary session was host to a wide range of lobbying meetings, where interest groups ranging from the nobility to burgh commissioners would meet to shape responses to legislation and to devise petitions for their own interests.[31]

A monarch's ability to govern strongly, whether enforcing political decisions at the local or regional level, or showcasing magnificence at court, required finance. In this regard James's power was highly subject to others. James was probably the only Scottish monarch to be chronically indebted,[32] but was able to make use of an emerging credit market in the 1580s and 1590s, and could effectively set the terms for interest and repayment. This included less than scrupulous schemes such as forcibly depositing part of his wedding dowry with the town of Edinburgh and then demanding regular interest payments, and then – in the most spectacular case – becoming massively indebted to the Edinburgh goldsmith Thomas Foulis and failing to repay the agreed interest or total sum over several decades, which ultimately left Foulis significantly worse off.[33] James's own adult court incurred considerable and ever-increasing deficits from 1579 and throughout the 1580s, which saw modest improvement in the 1590s.[34] However, a string of hived-off debts allocated to crown officers who had been responsible for James's finances remained, rising in total from £150,000 in 1582 to over £400,000 by 1599. These were only gradually paid off after 1603, when he could access the far larger revenues of the English crown.[35]

Goodare argued that the nobility were an integral part of this new absolutist framework, and rather than being independent actors and judicatories in their own localities with infrequent connection to the court they were now 'incorporated' into this new structure as 'cogs in a state machine'.[36] However, the view that noble power diminished significantly in James's adult reign, or that James departed from traditional forms of their usage to exercise his authority, has been significantly rebutted by Keith Brown and other scholars. Building on an ongoing debate between Maurice Lee and Jenny Wormald, Brown's studies of blood feud, the exercise of noble power, and the lived experience of the Scottish nobility recognised that the Jacobean elite faced significant social and economic upheaval, including rampant inflation, the increasing role of central law courts to resolve disputes over kin-based violence, and changing behavioural patterns as a result of Protestantism and growing literacy.[37] Yet James still valued and upheld the role of his nobility in their respective local spheres, and Brown believed their role in political life remained largely unchanged until the era of the Covenant. Similarly, Ried Zulager found that in terms of social background and education, many of James's new administrative servants, previously described by Lee as akin to the rising French bureaucratic elite known as the *noblesse de robe*, actually followed recruitment patterns going back to the reign of James IV, and were granted their roles as a form of social clientage, usually with the support of noble patrons.[38] The idea that parliament became the supreme source of legislative authority in this period and was able effectively to suppress noble dissent has also been challenged. While it certainly was the most important legal body in terms of passing new statutes, James far more frequently used conventions of estates as a form of informal consultation and governance, which have been described as a forum for 'elite political contact to sort out routine problems'.[39]

Case studies have also shown how James's personal relationships with nobles, ranging from his intransigent rebel kinsman Francis Stewart, fifth earl Bothwell, to James's friend and Catholic intriguer George Gordon, fourth earl of Huntly, followed traditional lines of power. Bothwell and John Maxwell both challenged James's authority directly in a series of rebellions between 1587 and 1595, and in both cases were treated as traditional threats to the crown with armed musters against them.[40] Bothwell also repeatedly used the established method of directly targeting the king's person, in a series of daring night-time raids at Falkland and Holyrood, to achieve his political aims. However, these assaults, which in one case saw James surprised in his chamber, broke with older examples as Bothwell immediately submitted to the king and sought his mercy, rather than aiming to hold him fully captive. As Alexander Courtney has argued, Bothwell was clearly unable to effect sustainable political change using this tactic when the king was a secure adult ruler.[41] However, the very fact that Bothwell attempted this at all shows how much significance key nobles still invested in James's personal role in the function of government, even with rapid advancement in new governmental structures. While it has been suggested by Steven Veerapen that James's relationship with the earl of Huntly was one of unrequited sexual and emotional love on the king's part, surviving evidence suggests that the two men enjoyed a strong personal friendship and mutually advantageous political relationship.[42] Huntly's network of contacts with Catholic intriguers on the Continent provided James with a means to conduct informal diplomacy at arm's length, while Huntly was given considerable latitude to manage both his own political affairs and to act on the crown's behalf as a lieutenant, most notably in his murder of James Stewart, the 'bonny earl' of Moray. In these cases, James's personal relationship with these men – his profound distrust of Bothwell following the latter's betrayal of James during the Ruthven Raid, and his deep loyalty to Huntly as a man who had remained loyal to his mother's cause – had a significant disruptive effect on national politics.

Yet, as with the Kirk, there was, as Miles Kerr-Peterson has shown in his study of George Keith the fourth earl Marischal, an as yet unstudied body of nobles whose interests lay more in the locality than the court, and who rarely engaged with that separate and often culturally distant sphere.[43] Marischal was rich enough that he simply did not need to concern himself with politics, being able to stay at any point along the east coast in one of his many residences whenever he felt the need to travel, and using his wealth to support the crown – for example, by serving as proxy for James at the conclusion of James's marriage in Denmark in 1589 – when it suited. Marischal was also wealthy enough to found an eponymous university in Aberdeen, was an active patron of ministerial posts in his locality and contributed to church repair, and engaged in bitter and quite personal disputes with his own family, especially his younger second wife, that had a highly disruptive effect on local politics in the north-east. These examples suggest that the idea that the nobility were recruited *en masse* into a central governmental sphere neglects the very important continuities in their wielding of power at the local level. As the most recent collection of essays on noble power in James's reign has argued, James continued to view the nobility through a *laissez faire* lens in much the same way as his predecessors did, and (his acerbic comments on their feuding in *Basilikon Doron* to the contrary) relied on them as an essential extension of his will in the locality, serving the vision of universal kingship in which he ardently believed.[44] A fuller prosopography of the nobility actively engaged in political life and at court during James's reign would give us a much better sense of how this ideal worked out in practice.

Paradoxically, the policy towards the Highlands and Isles, Borders, and coastal boundaries along the Irish Sea which developed during James's personal reign in Scotland was one where processes of state-formation and centralisation were most apparent, and yet where James's own personal views and guiding influence can arguably be seen most clearly.[45] These three regions were increasingly viewed by the king as an interconnected issue.[46] James was keenly aware of the fact that the Borders would become the 'middle shires' of his kingdom should he succeed Elizabeth, and the establishment of the Anglo-Scottish league in 1586 gave further impetus to ensuring the region was pacified so that transport and communication could pass easily along a variety of routes. James put considerable personal effort into this process prior to leaving Scotland, including dealing with a large-scale uprising by Lord Maxwell in 1588, starting to establish a network of new burghs of barony in the region, and personally undertaking progresses to dispense royal justice in the 1590s.[47]

James's policy towards the Highlands and Islands was more variegated and 'scatter-gun' prior to 1603 in its approach, but the fact that there was a developing policy is in itself important, as James started to engage actively with an area of his kingdom that had last been the subject of systematic royal interference in the reigns of James IV and V.[48] Like these two kings, James initially tried a range of traditional policies to exert crown influence in the region that reflected his desire to work with his nobility, beginning with military intervention and commissions of lieutenancy led by men including Colonel William Stewart of Houston, the earls of Bothwell, Huntly and Argyll, and the duke of Lennox.[49] Although an act was passed in the parliament of 1581 making reference to the Highlands, it was only from the parliament of 1587 onwards that legislation to bring these areas within the established zone of Stewart control emerged.[50] This included making clan chiefs accountable for the behaviour of their tenants in 1587, the establishment of dedicated councils to discuss border and Highland issues, approval for the creation of three new burghs in Lochaber, Kintyre and Lewis in 1597, and the legal requirement in the same year that chiefs show their titles to the central government or face forfeiture.[51] The 'plantation' of Lewis in 1598 by a group of men known as the Fife Adventurers was James's first attempt at forcibly settling and 'civilising' an area of the Highlands, and was a significant departure from earlier approaches. However, the motivations for taking this action were clearly personal to James. The rich herring fisheries in the Minch basin and the potential for an enhanced collection of rents and other duties from the region offered him a much-needed source of finance, and a successful venture here would send a message to his potential English subjects that similar schemes would work in Ireland.[52] As Alison Cathcart notes, James's extensive education had also ingrained in him the core tenets of civic humanism and the idea of the Highlands as a rude and barbarous region to be tamed, particularly the outer isles.[53] While the plantation at Lewis would fail spectacularly despite multiple attempts between 1598 and 1609, the general principle of 'civilising', firstly by plantation and then closer integration, was a personal one that James would hold on to throughout his life.[54]

New analyses of James's reign are at last engaging with the impact that gender had on the court, both in terms of the way that James presented himself within a series of masculine constructs as an essential display of power, and in the ways that women negotiated the court's cultural space. Anna of Denmark has been shown in a sequence of biographical and cultural studies to be anything but the vapid and weak queen of previous histories.[55] Her direct role in Scottish political life has been evidenced in a series of studies by Maureen Meikle, ranging from her role in the negotiations for her dower lands when she first arrived in Scotland through to her intercessory role at court in both domestic and foreign affairs and her direct influence on James's financial policy through the appointment of the Octavians in 1598.[56] Anna brought subtle but dangerous influence to bear against Maitland in the early 1590s during their disputes over the rights to Dunfermline Abbey, and in the leverage she exerted over James in their bitter and highly damaging dispute over the upbringing of Prince Henry in the traditional system of fostering.[57] The most important recent scholarly intervention in studies of Anna has been the work of Jemma Field, whose examination of the material and social culture associated with the queen and of her role as James's consort has revealed the extensive network of familial and political connections she wielded, and her central impact on tastes and fashions at court, particularly in a post-1603 context.[58] Anna was the most important of a series of women who exercised a strong influence over James, ranging from his foster mother Annabella Murray (still alive in 1603), to Annas Keith the countess of Argyll who played a key role in James's initial rise to power, and Elizabeth Stewart countess of Arran, who at the high point of her career in 1584 controlled Edinburgh Castle and allegedly held her own legal courts.[59] Henrietta Stewart, the countess of Huntly, would be as important as her husband in wielding 'soft power' at court, particularly when Huntly was forced into exile as a result of his rebellions against Maitland's place at court and the family's political and territorial survival rested on Henrietta's intercessions with the king and queen.[60] These women, and many others at the court, are urgently in need of further study.

One of the most important, yet arguably unanswerable, questions relating to James as a young adult is why the clear preference for emotional and physical intimacy with male favourites seen in his earlier and later life seems to diminish markedly in the later 1580s and 1590s. Recent searches in archives to find new evidence of the nature of James's relationship with Lennox have turned up frustratingly little material, and what has emerged has strengthened the view that this relationship was as much political and transactional as it was intimate.[61] Despite this, the overall weight of evidence across James's life, particularly in his last two decades, amply confirms that he was attracted to other men, though how he articulated that has to be framed against his mental world and not ours. James would not self-identify as queer, gay or bisexual, and he clearly thought of himself not in terms of sexual preference, but first and foremost in his power relations with others as a patriarchal head of household and father, not just to his immediate family but to his nation. However, as Randolph Trumbach and others have suggested, there is considerable evidence of a cultural dynamic in other areas of late medieval and early modern Europe, ranging from Florence to the Islamic Mediterranean, where same-sex acts were permissible within specific and highly structured contexts and co-existed alongside an entrenched masculinist hardline religious culture.[62] It is entirely plausible that in his bedchamber James would have actively engaged in a pederastic dynamic with other men when he was younger and taken on a penetrative role when he was older. One glaring issue that stands against this is the public aggression and severity of treatment towards confirmed acts of sodomy and bestiality seen in fragmentary evidence within the Kirk session records, most infamously in the burning of two young men for sodomy in 1570, and which is reflected in James's own denunciation of sodomy as a sin as grave as witchcraft in *Basilikon Doron*.[63] Yet the curious lack of persecution for same-sex acts in the Kirk session records, which, if covert, would cause far less social damage than the unwanted pregnancies often caused by adulterous heterosexual liaisons, may indicate a similar dichotomy in Scottish culture. However, the noticeable silence on this issue, despite repeated investigations by scholars, makes this no more than a tantalising hypothesis.

Even allowing for this speculation, the evidence for James's interest in same-sex relationships during his adult reign in Scotland is even more fleeting than in his teenage years. At present, his relationship with the favourite Alexander Lindsay, the 'minion who lies in his bed chamber', remains impossible to substantiate more fully, as does the unfounded suggestion that Patrick, Master of Gray was another early lover.[64] Much has been made of James's considerable reluctance to marry, captured most succinctly in his own open letter to the people of Scotland when he fled in the autumn of 1589 to retrieve Anna from Oslo, where he noted that he would delay his marriage much longer if it was not for people considering him to be 'bot a barren stock, whose weakness bred disdain'.[65] Yet James devoted considerable time and energy to choosing his bride, weighing up carefully whether the Danish match or an alliance with the much older Catherine of Navarre would bring the greatest benefits to Scotland, and praying and thinking hard on what he knew was a serious issue.[66] When poor weather stopped Anna's travel to Scotland, James made arguably the most reckless and bold decision of his life in leaving Scotland in the hands of an interim council led by the earl of Bothwell and the teenage duke of Lennox to collect her, showing a concerted will to make this happen. Moreover, reflecting a few years after his marriage in the *Basilikon Doron* on how his son should choose a wife, James showed clearly that Anna was an essential element of his success, both as a partner in his royal household, in perpetuating his family and lineage, and in the role of queenship at court.[67] The issue of how exactly James balanced his own internal preferences and desires with external performances of display and power rooted in heteronormative masculinity and patriarchy is thus highly complex, but also essential to examine and embed in new accounts of his personal reign in Scotland.

II Towards a Reassessment of James's Court: Underused Archival Sources for the Scottish Personal Reign

We now turn from surveying secondary literature on James and his reign to consider underutilised manuscript material, predominantly in Scottish national and private archives. Despite recent forays into this corpus, the range of material remaining unexplored is substantial and has the capacity to reshape our understanding of politics and daily life at James's court. A useful illustration is the Bowes-Lyon collection held by the family of the earls of Strathmore and Kinghorne at Glamis Castle, which proved to be central evidence in this author's study of the early life of James VI. I first came across the unpublished Bowes-Lyon papers during a search in the National Register of Archives for Scotland (NRAS) electronic catalogue, the full version of which can only be accessed internally at the National Records of Scotland (NRS) search room.[68] The Bowes-Lyon collection contains the papers of Sir Robert Bowes, the chief English ambassador in Scotland in the early years of James's reign, and his brother Sir George Bowes, governor of Berwick. They are part of a much larger collection of Bowes family papers that initially resided at Streatlam Castle but now, after a brief dispersal following their accidental auction in the 1920s, have nearly all been repurchased and are kept at Glamis.[69] Many of the Bowes papers have been calendared or edited for publication, both as texts within the *Calendar of State Papers* and as stand-alone collections of letters.[70] However, one volume, prosaically entitled 'Scottish Affairs', appeared from the catalogue not to have been printed, and in the autumn of 2019 I paid a visit to the archive to examine it.[71] What I found was a collection of over forty letters between George Bowes and a series of paid English agents and spies in and around the Scottish court, including Archibald Douglas, David Hume the minister of Oldhamstocks, and the anonymous '40', narrating events in Scotland over the course of 1579 in considerable detail. These ranged from the expected arrival of Esmé Stuart at court, which was revealed in this correspondence to have been planned with considerable forethought and with James's full knowledge, through to the suspected death by poisoning of the earl of Atholl and the public outcry associated with this, including an account of his very public funeral procession.

Why these papers were not thought worthy of inclusion in the *Calendar* is unclear, but they transformed the view I had of this pivotal year in James's life.[72] More broadly, the story of writing *A Long Apprenticeship* was itself one of constant disruption, as each set of manuscript sources examined seemed to change or upend what I thought I knew about James, and where that evidence might fit the established narrative. A similarly 'disruptive' process can be observed at work in Alexander Courtney's new biography of James's life in Scotland, and in the recent discovery of a series of ciphered transcripts of Mary's letters between 1578 and 1585 by a code-breaking team led by George Lasry in the French national archives. It is clear there is still much to be done from the archival point of view in relation to James, a fact that is quite remarkable given his importance as a British monarch, but is perhaps unsurprising given the relative lack of active scholars until very recently working on the Scottish reign.

Key sources for James's personal reign in Scotland include the Register of Deeds at the National Records of Scotland, which contain contracts, loans and credit agreements linked to key actors in and around the court, and manuscript multi-volume chronicles compiled by Edinburgh burgesses including John Monypenny, the doctor Patrick Anderson, and the Johnston family, which provide corroborative and incremental detail on the basic narrative of James's life in Scotland, often with additional transcripts of documents and letters, that rival the rich historical narratives written by David Calderwood or James Melville of Halhill.[73] Personal correspondence in private hands is another underused source, both in terms of letters mentioning figures and events at James's court and letters to and from James himself, which can shed considerable light on his epistolary relationships with other men. As well as the collection at Glamis, another key series of papers originally belonging to the countess of Argyll, Annas Keith, and now held by the earls of Moray at Darnaway Castle, contains detail relating to the Stewart kin networks around James.[74] The NRS Gifts and Deposits (GD) collection and the NRAS internal electronic catalogue record over 420 separate items in a simple search for letters relating to James, many of which are unprinted.[75] These include diplomatic correspondence sent by the king, such as the confirmation of the ambassadorial credentials of Patrick, Lord Gray sent to Sigismund, Prince of Transylvania and Moldavia in 1597; single letters and small series of correspondence sent to local landowners, such as the laird of Abercairny; and holograph letters sent to key political allies in James's adult life, including John Erskine, earl of Mar and John, Lord Hamilton.[76] However, perhaps most important are the NRS 'E' series of financial, treasurers' and household accounts, which are entirely unpublished for the period 1581–1603, and which comprise over 1,600 folios in total. The treasurer's accounts contain discrete sections in both Latin for the 'charge' of income to the royal household from customs, fees and other sources, and in Scots for the 'discharge' of funds spent by the crown on daily living costs, a range of household staff and pensioners, and messengers. The core record series is also enhanced by a range of supplementary and miscellaneous accounts, including various draft bills for reforming the household and its staff, accounts for specific household expenditure such as the maintenance of the king's hounds, and for the household and wardrobe of Queen Anna.[77]

These records underpinned the summary narrative of the evolution of James's court and household produced in a pioneering thesis by Amy Juhala, but they still have much to tell us about James's own use of soft power and display and broader political life at court, an area highlighted as a desideratum in Michael Questier's recent call for a re-assessment of James.[78] As well as details of expenditure, they include monthly accounts of all letters and proclamations distributed from the court by 'officeris, boyis and utheris travelland in the kingis ma[jes]ties effairis'.[79] These entries allow us to see who the regular correspondents were in James's domestic network; how the court distributed proclamations, muster notices and parliamentary and council summons both to private individuals and in public at market crosses and in other urban spaces; and the depth and scale of communication campaigns triggered by emergencies such as the uprisings by Bothwell and the Catholic earls, showing how seriously the court took these crises.[80] The accounts also allow us to do interesting things with the standard biographical model, as their granular detail gives us exceptional insight into James's daily lived experience, ranging from the money he spent on hobbies and décor to the exact amount of linen cloth he regularly bought for cleaning himself on his 'stule of eiss'.[81] There are several key questions these records allow us to ask: how did the court interact with the 'revolution in government' at work in late sixteenth-century Scotland? How did James wield his court and the people in it as a political tool? How did James himself perform within this courtly space? To what extent did the culture of his court follow or break with that of his predecessors? And what was daily life like at the last Stewart court in Scotland? What follows sketches out some dimensions of James's courtly activity, drawn from account entries in the transitional period between the fall of Arran in November 1585 and James's marriage to Anna in 1589, and the period around the baptism of Prince Henry in 1594.

Firstly, it is clear from the treasurer's accounts that the court was an essential political tool for James, and for most of his personal residence hunting was its biggest performative element. Hunting was the reason for James's first unsupervised excursion from Stirling in June 1579, a fact commemorated in verse by Patrick Hume of Polwarth's *Promine*. In the aftermath of the Ruthven Raid, James regularly used the hunt as a space in which to discuss Anglo-Scottish relations with Edward Wotton and other visiting English agents, free from the oversight of other officers of the court.[82] As Nicole Cumming has found in her recent doctoral thesis, hunting remained a central part of James's court ritual throughout his time in Scotland, though the intensity with which he did this dipped noticeably in the early 1590s as he established a household and family with Anna.[83] The basic costs of James's kennel of hounds alone – including their feed, bedding, coal in the winter for housing, leashes, and livery – amounted to several thousand pounds per year. Frequent payments were also made for the maintenance of James's hunting hawks, including the fashioning of hoods and bells for each bird.[84] James incurred regular monthly costs for hunting apparel, ranging from frequently replaced 'sockis and bute heidis' to keep his feet warm and dry while on the hunt, through to payments for spears painted by Adrian Vanson, 'certane boltis to his hienes cursbow', and to 'ane wyf in dalkeyt for making of ane cadge [cage] for taking of the fox'.[85] Both aspiring courtiers and the officers of government adapted to accommodate James's passion for the hunt. Many nobles, lairds and foreign interests (including Elizabeth) sent gifts of horses and dogs to James in attempts to win favour, while the privy council frequently relayed messengers and decisions to and from James with fresh hunting hounds moving between different royal residences.[86]

More broadly, animals were a perpetual interest of James, with creatures ranging from badgers and otters to large wild cats being delivered to his menagerie at Holyrood. These animals were kept in appalling conditions, with larger animals being manacled to the walls with little freedom of movement, and the lions proved a particular source of difficulty due to the expense associated with feeding them.[87] These animals also formed a part of performance at James's court, particularly as a display of his strength. It is well known that James tried to use one of the royal lions in the pageantry at Stirling Castle as part of Henry's baptismal celebrations, paying over £257 for the horses and men to transport it and providing the lion's keeper with grey cloth worth £21 to create a suitable set of clothes for the occasion.[88] However, the conditions in which the lion was kept suggest why it was so unwilling to comply.

Dress and textiles played a significant role at court, and the importance of fashion for the later Stewart monarchs has been explored in exceptional depth by Maria Hayward.[89] James was no different to his later British counterparts in spending significant quantities on dress, and he also knew how to use it to make a political statement. A key case in point was the spending of several hundred pounds recorded in March 1587 to Robert Abercromby for 'the furnessing of the dule clais' or black mourning garb for James, his pages and lackeys, and other members of the court serving staff, which included apparel down to socks and saddle coverings.[90] The visual impact of this would have left onlookers in no doubt that James was grieving for his mother and wanted this publicly witnessed. However, the fact that in the preceding month James spent £50 in commissioning 'ane Irland man for ane cairt of genelogie', presumably to outline his claim to the Irish throne as a form of leverage in case his right to succeed Elizabeth was challenged as a result of Mary's execution, shows how pragmatic and calculated a performance this was.[91] Textiles were also important in the early relationship James forged with his son Henry, with the first mentions of the infant prince in the accounts in February 1594 noting that Abercromby had been sent four dozen elns of linen worth £64 and a dozen elns of 'plaiding verie fyne for the use of his ma[jes]ties darrest sone' worth £18.[92] James also spent an extraordinary amount on dressing key figures both at court and in Henry's life for his baptism, including 1,000 merks (£666 13s 4d) to James's former nurse Helen Little and her two daughters for clothes, with a further £200 being paid to Richard Gray.[93]

Unsurprisingly, a central focus of the treasurers' accounts is the recording of ad hoc spending and purchases. While these individual transactions are often small, collectively they reveal important patterns about James's use of money as a form of courtly display. As the 1580s wore on and James and his court became increasingly mature and peripatetic, so too did regular evidence of James carrying cash for miscellaneous gifting and expenditure. A standard way of doing this was by providing drinksilver for servants and messengers who did James service, whether in returning lost hounds and hawks to him, bringing him gifts from their own noble and lairdly masters, or even for providing the king with small kindnesses, such as the fifty shillings paid by James 'to ane man [tha]t brocht russer berries at sindrie tymes fra Ballinbreich'.[94] Like his grandfather and great-grandfather, the young king also clearly enjoyed games of chance, and these offered another means for the king to entertain himself and engage socially with members of the court. This passion was particularly apparent in December 1587, when James spent more than £220 'to play at the cairtis' in a single month, and in March 1588 he ordered a bespoke green cloth costing £14 to cover the table when he played.[95] James also regularly provided alms as a form of courtly largesse. In addition to continuing the tradition of payments of a gown and purse to poor elderly men equivalent to the number of his age on his birthday, as he did to twenty-one individuals in June 1587, James dispersed broad casual alms when the court was on the move, as recorded in a summary entry of £400 in April 1588.[96] Bespoke individual payments and gifts were also used pointedly and politically, both to consolidate relationships with individuals and visitors at the court and to send public messages to Elizabeth and other European monarchs. James continued the annual royal practice of providing gold rings and jewellery as New Year gifts to favourites and key members of the court, spending almost £2,000 on commissions with the goldsmiths Michael Gilbert and Thomas Foulis in January 1587.[97] In June 1587 James made a gift of £40 'to Iudeth frensche woman being ane auld servande of his ma[jes]ties motheris',[98] and across the year made even larger payments to visiting French scholars and poets including £100 to Jean de Mayerne and £320 to attendants in the train of Guillaume de Salluste du Bartas. In July 1587 James also gifted a subsidy of £266 13s 4d to William Burgoyne 'and his brether yrland men strangeris for ayd help and support being banisched men'.[99] Such visible support for Irish exiles and visiting Frenchmen would have reminded Elizabeth that James had a range of diplomatic friendships beyond England and that he could interfere in her domestic politics by providing succour to Irish rebels. However, James also gave alms to support religious exiles not affiliated with England, as he did over a number of years for a series of refugees fleeing the war-torn kingdom of Hungary who were now 'captives by the Kirk'.[100] Although James has a deservedly terrible reputation for managing large-scale expenditure, it is clear that he knew how to disperse small-scale payments with maximum return in terms of political impact.

III Conclusion: One Monarch, Many Kings – The Young James in Scotland

As noted at the start of this chapter, James VI and I was a chimeric king, who appears to historians in markedly different ways depending upon which era of his life they focus. These many versions were all, to a greater or lesser degree, consciously performative on the king's part, though by the end of his life James was arguably revealing more of his own true personal desires and feelings in his increasingly open and public relationships with his male favourites. The image of the young adult king has been brought into focus here, and the James who ruled over Scotland in the decades immediately before 1603 was markedly different from his earlier and later selves. In terms of domestic policy and governance, the consensus underlying recent historiography is that James was a king participating in and affected by broader cultural and social change triggered in large part by the Reformation, but who also directly shaped the direction of travel in these spheres. He was neither an absolutist in training, driving forward a revolution in government and a programme of untrammelled mastery over the Kirk, nor was he an impotent cipher for broader centralising processes in state development and national religious change. The young king was shrewd, well-versed in political statecraft by his early teens and, like his Stewart predecessors, he remained a key figure of authority whom the political elite wished to court or control, even as late as the 1590s. Like many of the developments in Scottish politics and culture in the century after the Reformation, the continuities in James's personal practice of monarchy and kingcraft arguably outweighed sweeping changes.

This chapter has also briefly touched upon the potentially disruptive image of James that awaits us if we turn to examine more fully domestic archival sources in Scotland, especially the accounts of the household and James's own epistolary network. A full prosopography of the cast and characters of James's court, derived from this source base, would allow us to reconstruct the daily activity and political role of the court in exceptional detail, how different social classes and genders navigated this space, and the myriad ways in which James used courtly culture and 'soft power' to effect change and consolidate his power. Following his marriage to Anna and the establishment of his family, James was more conscious than at any other time in his life of the need to act – and to be seen to act – as a husband, patriarch and father, both to his own household and to the nation. This James engaged personally with his own newly created family more than he ever would again, while conversely the period is notable for the near-complete absence of male favourites like Lennox, Robert Carr or George Villiers, who each held deeply intimate relationships with James that directly affected politics at court. Fully exploring James's expenditure and gift-giving will reveal hidden details of his own personal interactions at the Scottish court, and examining more closely the relationships James had with key figures like John Erskine earl of Mar and John marquess of Hamilton will tell us how he interacted with other men where there is not a clearly visible driver of sexual or homosocial intimacy in their relationship. On the surface, most of these relationships were structured far more along lines of mutual interest and support, ranging from aligned political aims to a shared interest in hunting, than they were on grounds of love or sex, but they were none the less important to James. While the young adult James clearly deployed a range of masculinities to achieve his political ambitions, it is clear that this 'patriarchal' version of James was arguably the most self-consciously performative instantiation of himself that he put forward publicly over the course of his long reign. This version of James arguably arose – and was well fitted – to meet the unique challenges of running a troubled and divisive Scotland in the closing years of the sixteenth century, but gradually disappeared from view after his arrival in England.

Notes

1 I am grateful to Professor Roger A. Mason and colleagues in the University of Glasgow's Scottish History Work in Progress Reading Group for helpful comments and suggested revisions to this chapter. J. Wormald, 'James VI and I: Two Kings or One?', *History* 68 (1983), pp. 187–209.

2 M. C. Questier, 'The Reputation of James VI and I Revisited', *Journal of British Studies* 61 (2022), pp. 949–69 [quote at p. 952].

3 A. Courtney, 'Court Politics and the Kingship of James VI & I, c. 1615–c. 1622' (PhD, Cambridge, 2008).

4 G. Davies, 'The Character of James VI and I', *Huntington Library Quarterly* 5 (1941), pp. 33–63.

5 *ODNB, sub* 'James VI and I' (article by J. Wormald); A. Stewart, *The Cradle King: The Life of James VI and I* (2003); S. Veerapen, *The Wisest Fool: The Lavish Life of James VI and I* (Edinburgh, 2023); A. Courtney, *James VI, Britannic Prince: King of Scots and Elizabeth's Heir* (Abingdon, 2024); R. Houlbrooke, 'James's Reputation, 1625–2005', in *idem* (ed.), *James VI and I: Ideas, Authority, and Government* (Aldershot, 2006), pp. 169–90; M. L. Schwarz, 'James I and the Historians: Toward a Reconsideration', *Journal of British Studies* 13 (1974), pp. 114–34; M. Lee, Jr, 'James I and the Historians: Not a Bad King After All?', *Albion* 16 (1984), pp. 151–63; M. B. Young, 'James VI and I: Time for a Reconsideration?', *Journal of British Studies* 51 (2012), pp. 540–67. Other useful biographical studies include D. M. Bergeron, *Royal Family, Royal Lovers: King James of England and Scotland* (Columbia, MI, and London, 1991); and C. Bingham, *James VI of Scotland* (1979).

6 J. Goodare and M. Lynch (eds), *The Reign of James VI* (Edinburgh, 2000); quote from J. Goodare and M. Lynch, 'James VI: Universal King?', in the same volume, pp. 1–31, at p. 5. For attempts to tackle some of the questions they posed, see R. Grant, 'George Gordon, Sixth Earl of Huntly and the Politics of the Counter-Reformation in Scotland, 1581–1595' (PhD, Edinburgh, 2010); A. L. Juhala, 'The Household and Court of King James VI of Scotland, 1567–1603' (PhD, Edinburgh, 2000); and C. Sáenz-Cambra, 'Scotland and Philip II, 1580–1598: Politics, Religion, Diplomacy and Lobbying' (PhD, Edinburgh, 2003).

7 Goodare and Lynch, 'James VI: Universal King?', p. 4.

8 For what follows, see S. J. Reid, *The Early Life of James VI: A Long Apprenticeship, 1566–1585* (Edinburgh, 2023).

9 J. Kirk, 'The Development of the Melvillian Movement in Late Sixteenth Century Scotland' (PhD, Edinburgh, 1972); G. Donaldson, *Scotland: James V–James VII* (Edinburgh, 1965), chs 8–11; *idem, The Scottish Reformation* (Cambridge, 1960); *idem, Reformed by Bishops: Galloway, Orkney and Caithness* (Edinburgh, 1987).

10 A. Ryrie, *The Origins of the Scottish Reformation* (Manchester and New York, 2006).

11 M. Todd, *The Culture of Protestantism in Early Modern Scotland* (New Haven and London, 2003).

12 See for example J. McCallum, *Reforming the Scottish Parish: The Reformation in Fife, 1560–1640* (Farnham, 2010); for further details, see S. J. Reid, 'Cultures of Calvinism in Early Modern Scotland', in B. Gordon and C. Trueman (eds), *The Oxford Handbook of Calvin and Calvinism* (Oxford, 2021), pp. 220–37.

13 B. Rhodes, *Riches and Reform: Ecclesiastical Wealth in St Andrews, c.1520–1580* (Leiden, 2020).

14 S. J. Reid, 'A Latin Renaissance in Reformation Scotland? Print Trends in Scottish Latin Literature, c. 1480–1700', *SHR* 95 (2016), pp. 1–29.

15 S. J. Reid and D. McOmish (eds), *Corona Borealis: Scottish Neo-Latin Poets on King James VI and his Reign, 1566–1603* (Glasgow, 2020).

16 A. R. MacDonald, *The Jacobean Kirk, 1567–1625: Sovereignty, Polity and Liturgy* (Aldershot, 1998).

17 Courtney, *James VI, Britannic Prince*, chs 5–7.

18 A. R. MacDonald, 'The Subscription Crisis and Church-State Relations, 1584–1586', *Records of the Scottish Church History Society* (1994), pp. 222–55.

19 S. J. Reid, *Humanism and Calvinism: Andrew Melville and the Universities of Scotland, c. 1560–1625* (Farnham, 2011); E. R. Holloway III, *Andrew Melville and Humanism in Renaissance Scotland, 1545–1622* (Leiden, 2011); R. A. Mason and S. J. Reid (eds), *Andrew Melville (1545–1622): Writings, Reception and Reputation* (Farnham, 2014).

20 A. R. MacDonald, 'Best of Enemies: Andrew Melville and Patrick Adamson, c. 1574–1592', in J. Goodare and A. A. MacDonald (eds), *Sixteenth-Century Scotland: Essays in Honour of Michael Lynch* (Leiden, 2008), pp. 257–76; J. McCallum, '"Sone and Servant": Andrew Melville and his Nephew, James (1556–1614)', in Mason and Reid, *Andrew Melville*, pp. 201–14; D. G. Mullan, 'Patrick Adamson', in his *Episcopacy in Scotland: The History of an Idea, 1560–1638* (Edinburgh, 1986), ch. 4; S. J. Reid, *Challenging the Scottish Reformation: Patrick Adamson, Archbishop of St Andrews, c. 1574–1592* (forthcoming).

21 Lee, *John Maitland of Thirlestane*; Goodare, 'A Stewart Revolution in Government?', in *idem, The Government of Scotland, 1560–1625* (Oxford, 2004), ch. 12; Gordon Donaldson did not use this specific term, but his view of an 'Eltonian' shift is clear in 'King James's Peace', in his *Scotland: James V–James VII*, ch. 12.

22 RPS 1587/7/1–156, especially 18, 26–7, 67.

23 J. Goodare, 'The Admission of Lairds to the Scottish Parliament', *English Historical Review* 116 (2001), pp. 1103–33; Grant, 'George Gordon'; R. G. Macpherson, 'Francis Stewart, 5th Earl Bothwell, c. 1563–1612: Lordship and Politics in Jacobean Scotland' (PhD, Edinburgh, 1997).

24 Goodare and Lynch, 'James VI: Universal King?', p. 11.

25 Goodare, *The Government of Scotland*, chs 5 and 6, p. 289; *idem*, 'The Octavians', in M. Kerr-Peterson and S. J. Reid (eds), *James VI and Noble Power in Scotland, 1578–1603* (Abingdon, 2017) pp. 176–93.

26 Goodare, 'Warfare', in *idem, State and Society in Early Modern Scotland* (Oxford, 1999), ch. 5 (esp. pp. 145–50), pp. 293–4, 309.

27 J. Goodare, 'Parliamentary Taxation in Scotland, 1560–1603', *SHR* 68 (1989), pp. 23–52; Goodare, 'Finance', in *idem, State and Society*, ch. 4.

28 Goodare, 'Personal Monarchy', in *idem, The Government of Scotland*, ch. 4.

29 Goodare, *The Government of Scotland*, pp. 87, 289–90.

30 G. H. MacIntosh and R. J. Tanner, 'Balancing Acts: The Crown and Parliament', in K. M. Brown and A. R. MacDonald (eds), *The History of the Scottish Parliament, volume 3: Parliament in Context, 1235–1707* (Edinburgh, 2010),

pp. 1–30, esp. pp. 16–20; A. R. MacDonald, 'Deliberative Processes in Parliament, c. 1567–1639: Multicameralism and the Lords of the Articles', *SHR* 81 (2002), pp. 23–51; *idem*, 'Consultation and Consent under James VI', *Historical Journal* 54 (2011), pp. 287–306.

31 A. R. MacDonald, 'Voting in the Scottish Parliament before 1639', *Parliament, Estates and Representation* 30 (2010), pp. 145–61; *idem*, 'Uncovering the Legislative Process in the Parliaments of James VI', *Historical Journal* 84 (2011), pp. 601–17; *idem*, *The Burghs and Parliament in Scotland, c. 1550–1651* (Farnham, 2016).

32 J. Goodare, 'The Debts of James VI of Scotland', *Economic History Review* 62 (2009), pp. 926–52, at p. 949; *idem*, 'A Balance Sheet for James VI of Scotland', *Journal of European Economic History* 38 (2009), pp. 49–91.

33 Goodare, 'Debts', pp. 934, 939; *idem*, 'Thomas Foulis and the Scottish Fiscal Crisis of the 1590s', in W. M. Ormrod, M. Bonney and R. Bonney (eds), *Crises, Revolutions and Self-Sustained Growth: Essays in European Fiscal History* (Stamford, 1999), pp. 170–97.

34 Goodare, 'Debts', pp. 930–1.

35 Goodare, 'Debts', p. 946.

36 J. Goodare, 'The Nobility and the Absolutist State in Scotland, 1584–1638', *History* 78 (1993), pp. 161–82; Goodare, *State and Society*, p. 37.

37 K. M. Brown, *Bloodfeud in Scotland 1573–1625* (Edinburgh, 1986); *idem*, *Noble Society in Scotland: Wealth, Family and Culture from Reformation to Revolution* (Edinburgh, 2004); *idem*, *Noble Power in Scotland from the Reformation to the Revolution* (Edinburgh, 2011). For the debate, see J. M. Brown [Wormald], 'Scottish Politics 1567–1625', in A. Smith (ed.), *The Reign of James VI and I* (Basingstoke, 1973), pp. 23–39; M. Lee, 'James VI and the Aristocracy', *Scotia* 1 (1977), pp. 18–23; J. Wormald, 'New Men for Old', *Scotia* 2 (1978), pp. 70–6.

38 R. R. Zulager, 'A Study of the Middle-Rank Administrators in the Government of King James VI of Scotland, 1580–1603' (PhD, Aberdeen, 1991). See also Goodare, *The Government of Scotland*, p. 287.

39 MacDonald, 'Consultation and Consent under James VI'; Goodare, *The Government of Scotland*, p. 41.

40 Macpherson, 'Francis Stewart'; *idem*, 'Francis Stewart, Fifth Earl Bothwell, and James VI: Perception Politics', in T. Brotherstone and D. Ditchburn (eds), *Freedom and Authority: Scotland c. 1050–c. 1650: Historical and Historiographical Essays Presented to Grant G. Simpson* (East Linton, 2000), pp. 155–64; K. Brown, 'The Making of a "Politique": The Counter Reformation and the Regional Politics of John, Eighth Lord Maxwell', *SHR* 66 (1987), pp. 152–75.

41 Courtney, *James VI, Britannic Prince*, ch. 6.

42 Veerapen, *The Wisest Fool*, pp. 114–15; Courtney, *James VI, Britannic Prince*, ch. 5; Grant, 'George Gordon'; *idem*, 'Friendship, Politics and Religion: George Gordon, Sixth Earl of Huntly and King James VI, 1581–1595', in Kerr-Peterson and Reid, *James VI and Noble Power in Scotland*, pp. 57–80.

43 M. Kerr-Peterson, *A Protestant Lord in James VI's Scotland: George Keith, Fifth Earl Marischal (1554–1623)* (Woodbridge, 2019).

44 Miles Kerr-Peterson and Steven J. Reid, 'Introduction', in Kerr-Peterson and Reid, *James VI and Noble Power in Scotland, c. 1578–1603*, pp. 1–11, at p. 9.

45 The best single account of James's highland policy before 1603 is Alison Cathcart's 'Clanship and Commerce: Plantation in a North Channel Context', in her *Plantations by Land and Sea: North Channel Communities of the Atlantic Archipelago, c. 1550–1625* (Oxford, 2021), pp. 216–52. See also A. MacCoinnich, *Plantation and Civility in the North Atlantic World: the Case of the Northern Hebrides, 1570–1639* (Leiden, 2015), esp. ch. 3; A. I. MacInnes, 'Crown, Clans and Fine: The "Civilising" of Scottish Gaeldom, 1587–1638', *Northern Scotland*

13 (1ˢᵗ Series), pp. 31–55; J. Goodare and M. Lynch, 'The Scottish State and its Borderlands, 1567–1625', and M. Lynch, 'James VI and the "Highland Problem"', in Goodare and Lynch, *Reign of James VI*, pp. 186–207, 208–27; D. Gregory, *The History of the Western Highlands and Isles from A.D. 1493 to A.D. 1625* (London and Glasgow, 1881 edition), chs 5–6.

46 MacInnes, 'Crown, Clans and Fine', p. 31; Goodare and Lynch, 'The Scottish State and its Borderlands', pp. 187–8.

47 Goodare and Lynch, 'The Scottish State and its Borderlands', pp. 194, 201–5.

48 Lynch, 'James VI and the "Highland Problem"', pp. 216–20 (quote at p. 216). As Aonghas MacCoinnich notes, 'crackdowns from Edinburgh were nothing new, but the way in which James VI kept up a sustained pressure on the Highlands from 1587 onwards was': MacCoinnich, *Plantation and Civility*, p. 337.

49 A commission led by Bothwell was planned in 1588–9 but never occurred: MacCoinnich, *Plantation and Civility*, pp. 103–4; Cathcart, *Plantations*, pp. 228, 246.

50 'Addition to the acts made against notorious thieves and sorners of clans', 29 November 1581: www.rps.ac.uk, 1581/10/35.

51 MacInnes, 'Crown, Clans and Fine', pp. 32–4; Cathcart, *Plantations*, p. 241. It would be over two decades before the three towns – Fort William, Campbeltown, and Stornoway – were fully established.

52 Lynch, 'James VI and the "Highland Problem"', p. 212.

53 Cathcart, *Plantations*, pp. 241–5.

54 For the development and legacies of this policy, see A. I. Macinnes, *Clanship, Commerce and the House of Stuart, 1603–1788* (East Linton, 1996); J. Goodare, 'The Statutes of Iona in Context', *SHR* 77 (1998), pp. 31–57; M. MacGregor, 'The Statutes of Iona: Text and Context', *Innes Review* 57 (2006), pp. 111–81; A. Cathcart, 'The Statutes of Iona: the Archipelagic Context', *Journal of British Studies* 49 (2009), pp. 4–27.

55 For an example of older views of Anna, see E. C. Williams, 'The Birth of Prince Henry 1594', in *idem*, *Anne of Denmark, Wife Of James VI of Scotland: James I of England* (1970). In addition to the discussion of Jemma Field's works below, see also L. Barroll, *Anna of Denmark, Queen of England: a Cultural Biography* (Philadelphia, 2001).

56 M. M. Meikle, '"Holde her at the Oeconomicke rule of the House": Anna of Denmark and Scottish Court Finances, 1589–1603', in E. Ewan and M. M. Meikle (eds), *Women in Scotland c. 1100–1750* (East Linton, 1999), pp. 105–11; M. M. Meikle, 'Anna of Denmark's Coronation and Entry into Edinburgh, 1590: Cultural, Religious and Diplomatic Perspectives', in Goodare and MacDonald, *Sixteenth-Century Scotland*, pp. 277–94; *idem*, 'Once a Dane, Always a Dane? Queen Anna of Denmark's Foreign Relations and Intercessions as a Queen Consort of Scotland and England, 1588–1619', *The Court Historian* 24 (2019), pp. 168–80; C. A. Fry, 'Diplomacy and Deception: King James VI of Scotland's Foreign Relations with Europe (c. 1584–1603)' (PhD, St Andrews, 2014); Courtney, *James VI, Britannic Prince*, ch. 8.

57 D. Stevenson, 'And They Did Not Live Happily Ever After', in *idem*, *Scotland's Last Royal Wedding: The Marriage of James VI and Anne of Denmark* (Edinburgh, 1997), pp. 63–76.

58 J. Field, 'Dressing a Queen: The Wardrobe of Anna of Denmark at the Scottish Court of King James VI, 1590–1603', *The Court Historian* 24 (2019), pp. 152–67; *idem*, *Anna of Denmark: The Material and Visual Culture of the Stuart Courts, 1589–1619* (Manchester, 2020); *idem*, 'Anna of Denmark: Daughter, Wife, Sister, and Mother of Kings', in A. Norrie, C. Harris, J. L. Laynesmith, D. R. Messer and E. Woodacre (eds), *Tudor and Stuart Consorts: Queenship and Power* (2022), pp. 211–29.

59 R. Grant, 'Politicking Jacobean Women: Lady Ferniehirst, the Countess of Arran and the Countess of Huntly, c. 1580—1603', in Ewan and Meikle, *Women in Scotland*, pp. 95–104.

60 Grant, 'Friendship, Politics and Religion', pp. 57–80.

61 Reid, *The Early Life of James VI*, ch. 4; Courtney, *James VI, Britannic Prince*, ch. 3.

62 R. Trumbach, 'Renaissance Sodomy, 1500–1700', in M. Cook (ed.), *A Gay History of Britain: Love and Sex between Men since the Middle Ages* (Oxford, 2007), pp. 45–75.

63 King James VI and I, *Basilikon Doron*, in J. P. Somerville (ed.), *King James VI and I: Political Writings* (Cambridge, 1994), pp. 1–61, at p. 23; P. Maxwell-Stewart, '"Wild, Filthie, Execrabill, Detestabill, and Unnatural Sin": Bestiality in Early Modern Scotland', in T. Betteridge (ed.), *Sodomy in Early Modern Europe* (Manchester, 2002), pp. 82–93.

64 Veerapen, *The Wisest Fool*, p. 87; *ODNB, sub* Lindsay, Alexander, first Lord Spynie (article by R. Macpherson).

65 'The King's declaration in his own hand of the reasons for his resolution of going to Norway', *Register of the Privy Council of Scotland*, first series, IV, 1585–92, pp. 427–30.

66 Stevenson, *Scotland's Last Royal Wedding*.

67 King James VI and I, *Basilikon Doron*, pp. 38–41.

68 For the public online catalogue, see https://www.nrscotland.gov.uk/record-keeping/national-register-of-archives-for-scotland.

69 For the history of the papers, see C. M. Newman, 'The Bowes of Streatlam, County Durham: A Study of the Politics and Religion of a Sixteenth Century Northern Gentry Family' (PhD, York, 1991), pp. 15–17; B. L. Horn and F. J. Shaw, 'Bowes Bound Correspondence and Papers', in *Archives* 14 (1980), pp. 134–40.

70 Excerpts, particularly of royal letters from across the NRAS885/5/ volumes were published in Sir Cuthbert Sharp, *Memorials of the Rebellion of 1569* (1840). NRAS885/5/Volume D was printed by the Surtees Society as *The Correspondence of Robert Bowes of Aske, Esquire, the ambassador of Queen Elizabeth in the court of Scotland* (1842) and in excerpted form in *CSPScot*, VI.

71 NRAS885/5/Volume 9.

72 One hypothesis for this would be because the letters are addressed primarily to George Bowes and not to the English court.

73 NLS, Adv. MS 33.7.25, Adv. MS 35.4.2, Adv. MS 35.5.3.

74 NRAS217.

75 Of these, 79 are only visible on the internal NRAS catalogue, accessible on site at Register House.

76 NRAS4320/4/9/1/12 (James to Segismund, Prince of Transylvania, Moldavia, 6 June 1597); NRS, GD24/5/57/15, 17, 18, 21 (letters from James to the Laird of Abercairny, 1588–1592); GD124/10/65 James to the earl of Mar, 1594, where he bitterly complains 'of the misgouvernement of the cuntrey'); NRS, GD406/1/10433 (James to Lord Hamilton, 6 July 1595, noting Hamilton is 'now mair occupyet in bigging than in halking' and that he is keeping his hunting dogs for a longer period).

77 NRS, E21/65; E22. The E22 series also includes a number of receivers' accounts for the court, while E23 includes vouchers agreeing to expenditure that should be receipted within the main account. Household reform accounts for James's adult reign begin at E34/33.

78 Juhala, 'The Court and Household of James VI'; Questier, 'The Reputation of James VI and I Revisited'.

79 NRS, E21/65, fo. 124ᵛ (March 1587).

80 As well as a considerable increase in dispatches at the time of each uprising, the accounts also sometimes record additional narrative details, such as in February 1594 when a messenger boy was paid 40s for travelling from Stirling to Angus with a closed letter to Sir James Lindsay and 'a directioun to prepare the castell of Sanctandrois ffor the resait of the earle of Huntlie' (NRS, E21/70, fo. 93ᵛ).

81 James bought 4 elns of Holland cloth for this purpose in early 1587 (NRS, E21/65, fo. 138ᵛ) and 6 in March 1588 (NRS, E21/66, fo. 103ʳ).

82 Reid, *The Early Life of James VI*, ch. 10.

83 N. Cumming, 'Hunting, Dominion and the Natural Order in Early Modern Scotland: A Case Study of the Court of James VI, c. 1579–1603' (PhD, Strathclyde/Glasgow, 2024).

84 For example, NRS, E21/66, fos 75ᵛ–6ʳ (August 1587).

85 NRS, E21/66, fo. 75ᵛ (£6, crossbow bolts, August 1587); fo. 92ʳ (26s 8 d for cage, 43s 4d for spears, December 1587).

86 For example, letters sent with the king's buck hounds from Falkland to Glamis and Erskine of Gogar [NRS, E21/66, fo. 84ʳ]. For gifts, see Reid, *The Early Life of James VI*, ch. 10.

87 A household reform bill from April 1585 (NRS, E34/38) made specific reference to a need to provide significant compensation to 'the puir man quha had the lyoun in keiping'. A range of small payments were made to the animal keepers at various points, for example in March 1588 when £10 was awarded to the lion keeper (NRS, E21/66, fo. 103ʳ).

88 NRS, E21/70, fos 120ʳ–1ʳ.

89 M. Hayward, *Stuart Style: Monarchy, Dress and the Scottish Male Elite* (New Haven, 2020).

90 NRS, E21/65, fos 120ʳ–3ᵛ.

91 NRS, E21/65, fo. 115ᵛ. I am grateful to Drs Martin Macgregor and Aonghas MacCoinnich for this observation.

92 NRS, E21/70, fo. 92ᵛ.

93 NRS, E21/70, fos 106ᵛ [Little], 111ᵛ [Gray].

94 NRS, E21/66, fo. 66ᵛ.

95 These payments, both made in December 1587, consisted of two angel nobles at £8 13s 4d and 'fourscoir crownis of the sone' at £213 6s (NRS, E21/66, fo. 92ʳ⁻ᵛ); NRS, E21/66, fo. 103ʳ (green cloth, March 1588). In August 1587, James also made the unusual purchase of sixteen pairs of 'greit tarres cairtis' costing £10 13s 4d in total (NRS, E21/66, fo. 76ʳ).

96 NRS, E21/66, fos 66ᵛ–7ʳ, 107ᵛ.

97 £1956 13s to be exact, recorded in April 1588 (NRS, E21/66, fo. 106ᵛ).

98 NRS, E21/66, fo. 67ʳ.

99 NRS, E21/65, fo. 138ʳ (April 1587, Jean Mayerne, £100); NRS, E21/66, fo. 79ʳ (September 1587, £320 to attendants of Du Bartas); NRS, E21/66, fo. 75ʳ (July 1587, William Burgoyne, £266 13s 4d).

100 NRS, E21/66, fo. 67ʳ (June 1587, £53 6s 8d 'to certane pure ungariane strangeris); NRS, E21/70, fo. 92ʳ (February 1594, £200 'to certaine pure strangeris ungarianis captives by the kirk').

2

TO 'READ A PERFECT KING INDEED'

James VI's Printed Writings, c. 1584–1603

Alexander Courtney

On 18 July 1583, the presbytery of Edinburgh despatched a delegation of ministers to the seventeen-year-old James VI, whose court was then at Falkland. To their dismay, late in the previous month James had escaped from the Ruthven Raiders. Having thrown off the tutelage of those Anglophile and Presbyterian-favouring lords, the young king (so these ministers thought) would benefit from stern admonition. He must 'beware of innovations in court' and remember who his true enemies were – papists and not godly brethren like themselves. The interview started badly. James needled his clerical guests with an impish assertion of his royal authority: 'I am catholick King of Scotland ... and may choose anie that I like best to be in companie with me'. At the king's deliberately provocative use of this c-word, some of the ministers 'were not weill pleased'. But then one of their number, the Dunfermline minister David Ferguson, intervened to restore calm: 'No, brethrein', Ferguson called out, 'he is universall king, and may make choice of his companie as David did in the [101st] Psalme'.

Ferguson's sudden intervention to gloss the king's words positively and cross-reference them to the Old Testament cannot be ascribed to a flash of exegetical inspiration. Before the meeting convened in the king's cabinet, Ferguson had had sight of James's own verse translation of Psalm 101:

> thy mercy will I sing & justice eik
> with musik will I prayse jehova great
> I will tak he[e]d the richteous path to seik
> ...
> within my house quhich hallowed is to thee
> myne eyes upon no wikkid thing shall roule

DOI: 10.4324/9781003319764-3

...
all godles men (thay shall) from me depairt
I will not know no evill nor wikked thing ...

These words had apparently persuaded Ferguson that James was prayerfully meditating upon the example of the biblical King David; James's piety should thus be encouraged with gentle words rather than hectoring. And so, despite some further awkward exchanges between the king and his guests, the anticipated ministerial tongue lashing did not materialise. James subsequently eased the delegation from his presence with a typically unctuous display of royal charm, wafting them homeward with 'faire speeches', having 'layed his hands upon everie one of them'.[1]

This is the earliest demonstration of the potential of James's writings to disrupt opposition, to persuade and appease. We also encounter here a challenge, shared by contemporaries and historians, of how to interpret this king's words. Can we, like David Ferguson, read James through his writings? The late Kevin Sharpe saw in James's poetry, including his manuscript verse translations of the Psalms, 'rich ... evidence of [James's] values and ideals': 'Poetry for James ... was a meditation with himself and God', according to Sharpe, and poems like James's rendition of Psalm 101 provide the 'purest crystal' into the king's 'conscience'.[2] By contrast, Jane Rickard warns against thinking of James's writings as straightforwardly autobiographical: 'his texts contruct the king as much as they reveal him', she argues; his writings were 'to a large extent the product of his interest in the ability of art to manipulate and deceive', 'a means of expressing and enacting his political power'.[3]

James's playfulness and authorial artifice in presenting a version of his private self for political advantage are certainly what can be read through this episode at Falkland in July 1583. For the manuscript draft of James's Psalm 101 poem survives. This pious reflection upon a king's commitment to godly living at the head of a godly household was written, unbeknownst to David Ferguson, on the reverse of a quite different kind of poem – a sonnet to Bacchus on the topic of vomitous blind-drunkenness:

O michtie sunne of Semele the faire
o bachus ...

...

quho with thy power blindithes the sicht
to sum, to utheris thou the eirs hes deafed,
fra sum thou takis the taist, sum smelling richt
dois laike, sum tuiching, sum all five bereaved
are of thee. The greit alexander craved
thy mercy oft; oure maister poet now
is warrd be thee; we smaller then sall leve it

to strive with thee. Then on his tombe I vow
sall be 'heir lyis quhom bachus be his wine
hes trappit first & maide him rander sine'.

Compared with the manuscript Psalm 101, this sonnet is drafted in a bolder, more rumbunctious version of James's italic script. He invokes the god of wine, whose capacity to deprive man of each and every sense has overpowered ('warrd') his drinking partner, the 'maister poet' Alexander Montgomerie. James swears over Montgomerie's prostrate body that he shall inscribe upon the poet's tomb how Bacchus had ensnared ('trappit') Montgomerie and forced him to 'rander' – meaning both to surrender and to 'discharge'. Perhaps it was with a sore head that James turned the page of this sonnet and – in a softer, more deliberate hand – wrote his more solemn vows unto the God of Jacob, that he would 'tak heed the richteous path to seik'.[4] In this instance, therefore, James's poetry is not the 'purest crystal' through which to espy his soul. In Bacchanalian sonnet and hangover psalm we see him only dimly, as it were, from the bottom of the brimful glass.

The gulf between the young James's night-before antics and his morning-after piety may amuse or, I suppose, appal the reader. But it is his poetry's subsequent *use* that is more remarkable, revealing as it is of what would become his political style. The disclosure of the Psalm 101 translation to David Ferguson in the intimacy of the king's chambers was surely deliberate, James's intent being to reassure and wrongfoot the Edinburgh presbytery's delegation with privileged evidence – in his own hand, no less – of his private devotions, his soundness in religion and hence the legitimacy of his godly kingship. By reading his Psalm 101 translation in this context, we catch a glimpse of James as a delightfully (and shamelessly) inventive political tactician, whose written word could be a potent weapon.

Less outrageous instances of his using his compositions in poetry and prose to advance his political ends could be multiplied. We find him in December 1585, for instance, appealing to Queen Elizabeth by sending her a copy of his handwritten and robust response to Presbyterian objections to the 'Black' Acts of 1584. Through this, he both evidenced his solidarity with the English queen in 'uphold[ing] ever a regal rule' against puritanical challenges and also sought to reassure her of his reliability as a diplomatic ally, by ending the piece with a call to arms in both kingdoms against 'the commoun enemie', Spain.[5] Another approach was to share copies of his verse enclosed with his letters. Though addressing a love sonnet to Elizabeth was a less successful tactic – she did not even acknowledge its receipt – as Sebastiaan Verweij has shown, James nurtured personal relations with his leading subjects through such poetical gifts and epistolary exchanges. With a sonnet to Lady Jean Douglas in 1589, for example, James advanced the suit of his favourite Alexander Lindsay for her hand.[6] Indeed, his personal, holograph letters are in themselves strongly suggestive of James's ability and character as a king and writer. In a superb essay on his personal letters, Grant Simpson demonstrates how varied and impressive they are in style and rhetorical construction: James's letters reveal 'a writer … highly conscious of the person whom he is addressing, and of the effect he wants to achieve'.[7]

This chapter, however, examines one important and distinctive strand of James VI's king-craft as it developed in Scotland: his public self-presentation in print. To borrow Lori Anne Ferrell's phrase, by 1603 James's use of 'splendidly logocentric' methods of publicity was a long-established trait.[8] One such method was to present his published word as a window into his 'honest' or 'inwarde intention'. If, in James's formulation, 'it is the tongues office to be the messenger of the mind' and if 'writing … is nothing els, but a forme of Enregistrate speech', then the writings of a king could convey to readers 'true pictures of [his] mind'.[9] As both king of Scots and likely (but not uncontested) heir to Elizabeth's throne, James used several of his printed works to represent himself to readers on both sides of the border, to defend his authority at home and promote his dynastic right in England. While the pieces focused upon here cannot be treated as straightforward evidence of the king's actual self or conscience, they are richly revealing of their author's political style and capabilities. After considering briefly how and why James developed into the 'most writerly of British monarchs',[10] the presentation of the king's self in his early printed works (from *The Essayes of a Prentise* to *His Majesties Poeticall Exercises*) is explored, before we look more closely at the most innovative and effective of these 'mirrors' of the king's 'inwarde intention', *Basilikon Doron*.

I Private Delight and Public Pitch Making

It was noted in 1586 that, while hunting was James's 'great delight', 'his private delight' was 'in enditing poesies, &c. In one or both of these commonly hee spendeth the day'. The same observer commented that, to enjoy these pursuits, the king preferred 'to withdraw him self from places of most accesse and company to place of more solitude and repast, with very small retinue'.[11] Throughout his life, James was happiest when in the midst of a small household 'family' of companions where he could attend to the chase and literary pursuits.

It was in such an environment that he had been brought up and educated at Stirling Castle from his infancy to adolescence. Too often misunderstood as a relentlessly traumatic experience that left him physically and psychologically 'hobbled', James's childhood at Stirling was rather the making than the breaking of him. Early witnesses to that included the Presbyterian divines Andrew Melville and his nephew James, who saw the eight-year-old James at Stirling in 1574. They watched with 'grait mervell and estonishment' as the boy king walked hand-in-hand with his guardian the countess of Mar and spoke sagely 'of knawlage and ignorance'. For James Melville, the little James VI was 'the sweitest sight in Europe that day, for strange and extraordinar gifts of ingyne [mental acuity], judgment, memorie and langage'.[12] The Melvilles were not alone in being impressed by James's 'marvallous' and 'strainge' eloquence as a child. James's studies with his tutors George Buchanan and Peter Young made of him 'the Patterne' of 'learning and judgement', wrote the English diplomat Thomas Randolph in 1579 – a line that might savour of mere sycophancy were it not also reflected in Randolph's less positive description of the king two years later: 'Though hee bee younge, yet ... he wanteth neither wordes, nor awnsers to any thing I can saye unto him'.[13]

The mixed notes of admiration and frustration in those last words of Thomas Randolph point to another aspect of James's character and capacities: his education at Stirling made of James a prince bold and often virtuosic in spinning a verbal yarn. From his youth onwards, James's contemporaries, particularly those aware of how difficult it was to pin him down in discussion, commented on his talent for dissembling: for 'playne dissimulation ... hee is In theis his tender yeres better practized than others fourtie yeres elder than hee'.[14] As a child, James loved study and that equipped him with more than mere book learning in 'literature and religion': he developed the creative, persuasive, part-playing and argumentative skills of an expert in rhetoric and dialectic, that striking verbal facility that his sceptical observers called 'dissimulation'.[15]

Those 'strange and extraordinar gifts' of the 'ingyne' and the gab, inculcated under Buchanan and Young in the 1570s, were further honed in the early 1580s. It was then, as Steven Reid states, that James 'began to explore in earnest the passion for literature and writing which became such a marked feature of his royal identity'.[16] Between 1579 and 1585, poets present at court and enjoying varying measures of James's favour included Patrick Hume of Polwarth, Alexander Montgomerie, Thomas Hudson and William Fowler. Montgomerie was, as the above evidence of the king's drinking and verse-making session with him indicates, a close companion at this stage. The relationship of 'literary tutelage' between the two is suggested by James's hailing of Montgomerie as 'maister poet' while calling himself a mere 'prentise' in the 'divine art of poesie'.[17]

From 1584 onwards, James VI not only delighted privately in the composition of 'poesies &c.'; he made the public circulation of his writings in print central to his king-craft. In so doing, he was responding inventively to two broad sets of political conditions: the Scottish Reformation's transformative impact upon political culture and his status as the genealogically best-placed but contestable candidate to succeed to Elizabeth I's throne. These conditions – which, fortunately for the reader, can only be sketched very briefly here – challenged James throughout his personal reign in Scotland with a series of complex and inter-connected problems and crises. In tackling those challenges, the publication of James's writings would play an important role, as he sought through them to present 'true pictures of [his] mind' into his readers' hands and therby to defend the legitimacy of his rule, both in the present in Scotland and for the future in England.

Firstly, and as Karin Bowie argues, the Reformation 'created situations in which oppositional groups found it useful to mobilise opinion at large and the crown found it necessary to devote effort to the management of opinions'.[18] In Scotland, as elsewhere, this profoundly changed how politics was conducted. Reformation, for both opponents and proponents of reform, involved efforts to persuade elites and, ideally, whole communities to advance and enact visions of godliness for society, and to reject what threatened the realisation of those visions. Hence, integral to 'the post-Reformation condition', to borrow Peter Lake's words, was 'public politicking and pitch making', to generate, appeal to and mobilise public opinion and support.[19] James's own tendentious account of the Scottish Reformation in his *Basilikon Doron* (1599) picks up on the social depth, intensity and violence of political engagement stirred by such 'popular' politicking during the regency of his grandmother Mary of Guise and onwards:

> the reformation of Religion in Scotland being made by a popular tumult & rebellion ... some of our fyerie ministers got such a guyding of the people at that time of confusion, as ... having (by the iniquitie of time) bene over-well baited upon the wrak, first of my Grand-mother, and syne of my own mother; & after usurping the liberty of the time in my long minoritie, ... [they hoped] in a popular governement by leading the people by the nose, to beare the sway of all the rule.[20]

Godly activism (or, as James termed it here, 'popular tumult & rebellion') was stirred by written words, in print and manuscript publications, as well as through other forms of media and communal practice. Through libellous pasquils, ballads, pamphlets and proclamations, through the spreading of rumour and the singing of psalms, through sermons, solemn public fasts, the subscription of bands and swearing of covenant oaths, people were moved and engaged. These methods (and more) served to extend the social and emotional reach of attempts to activate public commitment for the renewal and defence of Kirk and commonweal – or, as James VI preferred to say, 'leading the people by the nose'.[21]

James's account of post-Reformation public politicking by 'fyerie ministers' further alleges that there never rose faction in the time of my minority, nor trouble sen-syne, but ['fyerie ministers'] were ever ... quarrelling me (not for any evill or vice in me) but because I was a King, which they thoght the highest evil: & because they wer ashamed to profes this quarrel, they were busie to looke narrowlie in al my actiones; and I warrant you a moat in my eye, yea, a false reporte was matter ynough for them to worke upon ...[22]

As we shall see, James's claims about 'fyerie', 'Puritane' ministers were articulated with a particular polemical agenda in mind; however, they were not outlandish. In 1580–1600, whenever radical Presbyterian ministers and their lay backers disapproved of his court and counsels, accusations circulated in sermon and libel that he had, for instance, 'declynit to Papistry', that he had been 'enticed' into a 'dissolute life' by the 'licentious companie' he kept, or even that he had been 'bewitched' by his 'profane counsellers', and that he must repent and set his 'affection on good things, and godly men', lest he be 'ruitted out' like Jeroboam or Ahab.[23] The opportunist rebel fifth earl of Bothwell recognised the power of such discourse to 'alienat the hearts of the people' from the king. Posing as their 'maist loving broder in Christ', Bothwell cast 'little Pamphilett[s]' among the congregation at St Giles's Kirk, through which he appealed to the 'godlie wisdoms' of the people and ministers of Edinburgh to view him as one whose care was 'for the welfare of Religion'. Besides cloaking himself in this rhetoric of 'penitencye' and enmity towards papists, for good measure Bothwell also accompanied his attacks on the court in 1592–1594 with verse libels defaming the king as 'a bougerer ... that left his wife all the night *intactam*'.[24] James thus had a clear incentive to intervene in the public sphere, so as to counter what he construed (quite reasonably) as anti-monarchical misrepresentations of his moral character.

James's claim to the English throne provided a second, and connected, reason for him to publish his writings, given that public representations of him as corruptly declining towards 'papistry' under the influence of 'profane' counsels, 'French courses' or 'Spanish factionares' – or (from the opposite perspective) as being under the 'populer power' of rabble-rousing Presbyterian ministers – could have a bearing upon his chances of succeeding Elizabeth. His lineal descent from Henry VII via Margaret Tudor, and the imminent demise of Henry VIII's line with the childless Elizabeth meant that James VI's character and kingship and the course of religion in Scotland were not matters of peripheral interest for English politics in the decades before 1603.[25] Critiques of James's kingship in Scotland mattered for his prospects in England not least because his critics at the radical end of the Scottish Kirk had, at times, powerful support in England. James's apparent softness towards Catholics, most notably his favour towards the earl and countess of Huntly in the late 1580s and 1590s, raised some people's hackles in both kingdoms. Could his commitment to Protestantism be trusted? Might he be converted to Catholicism? Moreover, both advocates and adversaries of 'further reformation' in the Church of England had stakes in what sort of king James VI was and might yet become. Did he represent the glittering promise (or the hair-raising prospect) of thoroughgoing, hot Protestant reform across the British Isles? What could be expected of him, were he to succeed Elizabeth? Whose confessional-political agenda would benefit from his accession? By representing himself through his writings, James could respond to such questions, although it was neither in his power nor necessarily in his interests to settle matters unambiguously. As Richard McCabe has put it, 'In England James needed to be, if not quite all things to all men, as many things to as many men as possible'. The task of assuaging fears and courting backers for his claim was, therefore, a delicate one, demanding great tactical subtlety and authorial skill.[26]

II 'Vertew, Godlines and Learning': James VI's Early Writings

James's print publications in Scotland between 1584 and 1603 encompassed poetic, homiletic and didactic works in varied forms. Two volumes were compilations of poetry, *The Essayes of a Prentise, in the Divine Art of Poesie* (1584) and *His Majesties Poeticall Exercises at Vacant Houres* (1591), the first of which also included prose 'rewlis' for the writing of Scots verse. The two *Meditatiouns* (1588 and 1589) were sermon-like commentaries on passages of Scripture. Two more books were intended to instruct readers, respectively, in the 'truth' of the diabolical nature of witchcraft and of the subject's duty of obedience: *Daemonologie* (1597/8), in the form of a dialogue, and *The True Lawe of Free Monarchies* (1598), a political treatise addressed directly to the reader. The last of his Scottish printed writings, *Basilikon Doron* (first printed in 1599), was in the form of private instruction for his son, a mirror-for-princes advice book. Each of these royal publications was part of wider efforts of public communication and persuasion that responded to particular political conjunctures in Scotland and also, usually (though not always), to the needs of James's English diplomacy.[27]

Their variety of form and the detail of their contents notwithstanding, the earlier of these works – *The Essayes of a Prentise, His Majesties Poeticall Exercises* and the two *Meditatiouns* – were quite simple in their representational intent: through them, and often via other texts that can be associated with them, James depicted himself as a godly prince. That is not to suggest that these works were banal or uncontroversial. They were *livres de circonstance*; it was in order to make conscious and targeted political and/or diplomatic interventions that they fashioned him as a virtuous and learned exemplar of Protestant piety (without, perhaps, defining that too closely) and as conscientious in his attention to the duties of his divinely-ordained office. When James's leading counsellor Arran wrote to William Cecil to send him a copy of James's *Essayes of a Prentise* in December 1584, he summarised that intent nicely: 'I have heirwith Imparted to your Lordship his hienes first pruif and prentissage in poesie/ Be the reiding quherof your Lordship will persave a gude Inclinatioun in his Majestie to do weill'.[28] Contemporaries in both Scotland and England understood that self-fashioning core message of James's published works – and some, at least, saw through it. 'For all the King's great professyng of religion he loving huntyng better', commented William Knollys in 1585. Another Englishman remarked in 1591 upon general murmuring among Scots against their king, 'for his carles guyding & governement, as uncredible writing'. Patrick Galloway, one of the king's own household ministers, surely had more in mind than just James's declarations of godliness in print, but his overall sentiment is comparable: in November 1596 he complained to James's face 'That the kirk gott but faire words and promises without effect, and the [Kirk's] enemeis gott the deid and effect'.[29]

The Essayes of a Prentise, James's first foray into print-form publicity, was the centrepiece of a royal campaign responding to radical Presbyterian challenges at home and seeking to win over support in England. Most commentary on *The Essayes* has focused on just two of its elements – 'Reulis and cautelis to be observit and eschewit in Scottis Poesie', the first stylistic guide to the writing of Scottish vernacular poetry, and 'The tragedie called Phoenix', an allegorical poem on the fate of the royal favourite overthrown by the Ruthven Raid, Esmé Stuart d'Aubigny, first duke of Lennox. However, the majority of the text consists of pieces that reflect on James's devotions and the application of his learning to godly exercises, presenting an image of the king that was reinforced for readers in other books also published at that time by the king's printer, Thomas Vautrollier.[30] James's 'The Uranie', for instance, translates from the poetry of French Huguenot Guillaume de Salluste du Bartas. Urania, the Christian muse, leads the poet from 'subjects base' to praise of the Holy Trinity and the witness of the Bible: James hereby entones his will to 'consecrat' his 'eloquence … | To sing the lofty miracles and fair | Of holy Scripture'.[31] Just as he had achieved on a miniature scale with his Psalm 101 translation in July 1583, so here James steered the reader towards interpreting his verse as autobiographical. Not only was James meant to benefit from a literary association with Du Bartas and his Protestant credentials, but he prefaced the poem with a sketch of his own devotional reading practices, writing that he had 'oft revolved, and red over … the booke and Poems of … du Bartas … perusing [that is, thoroughly reading] them, with a restles and lofty desire, to pre[s]s to attain to the like vertue'.[32] The same theme, of James's edifying literary piety, can be seen in his poem 'Psalme CIIII' ('To Jehova I all my lyfe shall sing, | To sound his Name I ever still shall cair') as well as in his 'Poeme of Tyme', expressing his wish that 'we sould bestow' the precious gift of time 'In doing weill, that good men may commend us' and as would most please 'our heavenly King'.[33]

Other books printed in 1584–5 by Vautrollier and, like *The Essayes*, sold in both Edinburgh and London, conjure a similar image of James as a shining example of a prince of virtuous intentions and godly learning. Thomas Hudson, one of James's English viol players, published his translation of another poem by Du Bartas, *The Historie of Judith*. Hudson's preface relates how James commissioned Hudson's translation while 'discoursing at Table' with his servants, 'after [his] accustomed & vertuous manner'.[34] Likewise Patrick Adamson, archbishop of St Andrews, wrote in his *Declaratioun of the Kings Majesties Intentioun*, also printed by Vautrollier in January 1585, that by 'reiding and heiring the word of God ... our King is ane Theologue, and his hart replenishit with the knawledge of the heavenly Philosophie ... ane King of great expectation [in respect of his] vertew, godlines and learning, and daylie incresse of all heavenly sciences'.[35] Besides his Protestant piety, *The Essayes*, *Judith* and Adamson's *Declaratioun* all gave some emphasis to James's 'birthricht' that had 'destinate and provydit great kingedomes' to him, announcing a desire to make James and his virtuous learning better known in 'Brittain'.[36]

The image peddled in these works, of James VI as virtuous Protestant poet-king, responded to the 'propaganda war' that was then being waged against the Scottish court by Presbyterian opponents of the 'Black' Acts of May 1584 and of the earl of Arran's ascendancy. Around twenty such ministers, including Andrew Melville, Walter Balcanquhall, John Davidson and Patrick Galloway, were given refuge in England, from where they conducted their campaign. In thunderous sermons in London's pulpits and a deluge of letters and pamphlets, they declaimed against James and his 'blind godlesse court, overflowing with all kinde of sinne and impietie'. His heart had been 'carie[d] away ... from the cheefe professors and mainteaners of the Gospell, to runne course direct against religioun ... and standing of himself in good estate of kinglie honour, bodie and soule'. The Acts of May 1584 had, they contended, made of James a 'new Pope' to tyrannise over the Church and let in 'Heresie, atheisme, and Papistrie'.[37]

The Elizabethan regime's tolerance towards such activities, along with the support enjoyed in England by Scottish noble exiles who opposed Arran, ran counter to James's interests both at home in Scotland and in relation to his claim to succeed Elizabeth. By the autumn of 1584, this situation had developed into a significant crisis in Anglo-Scottish diplomacy, the English having received intelligence of Jesuit ambitions to secure James's conversion to Catholicism and of the king's continued (though desultory) entertainment of Mary Queen of Scots' scheme, through 'association' with her son, to secure her release from captivity and her return to Scotland. In October, as *The Essayes* was going into print, William Cecil Lord Burghley and Sir Francis Walsingham drew up the 'Bond of Association' to resist and kill any person (including, in theory, James) who might benefit from Elizabeth's assassination.

Created to coincide with the arrival in London of Patrick, Master of Gray as James's ambassador, the Bond robustly signalled to the King of Scots that he needed to make good on his promises to maintain 'solyde amyty' with Elizabeth and to 'defend hyr agenste all hyr ennymys'. For James, 'solyde amyty' would require Elizabeth to protect him from the provisions of the Bond of Association, silence the fugitive ministers and move the rebel Scottish nobles away from the border, where their presence threatened his security. For their part, Elizabeth and her leading counsellors required James to abandon the 'association' scheme or any other trafficking with Mary – a repudiation of his mother that James communicated to Elizabeth via the Master of Gray's embassy.[38] At this critical juncture in Anglo-Scottish diplomacy and Kirk politics therefore, *The Essayes*, Hudson's *Judith* and Adamson's *Declaratioun* were intended to rebut the propaganda of opponents of Arran and of the 'Black' Acts, and also to provide reassurance to Elizabeth, her counsellors and, indeed, a wider English public that James VI had a 'gude Inclinatioun ... to do weill', as Arran wrote to Burghley on the covering letter accompanying his gift copy of *The Essayes*.

A need, then, to respond to hot Protestant criticism of his kingship in Scotland went hand in hand with James's desire to protect his interests in England. One Scots Presbyterian critique urged him, for instance, to 'give experiment of his godlie and vertuous education' so that 'the sentence of the propheit may be verefeit in him saying, that kyngis should be nuritouris of trew religione'.[39] His printed writings might be understood by his readers, so he hoped, as such an 'experiment', in the sense of a lively testimony or experience. In his publications of 1588–1591, James sought similarly to appeal to Protestant opinion in both kingdoms. His *Fruitfull Meditatioun ... of the 20 Chap[ter] of the Revelatioun*, published in October 1588, milked the opportunity of the Armada's defeat to trumpet again his godly credentials as, in the words of its title page, 'maist christiane King ... and chief defender of the treuth'. In an elision of the kingdoms of Scotland and England into 'this Ile', the 'native countrie' of 'warriouris in ane camp and citizens of ane belovit citie' assailed by the papal 'Antichrist', he pointed beyond the present defensive league with Elizabeth to his own claim to succeed her and to the resulting union of the kingdoms as a common Protestant, patriotic and providential enterprise.[40] In the spring of 1589, around the time of his defeat of the Catholic earl of Huntly's rebellion at the Brig o' Dee, he published *Ane Meditatioun upon the ... first buke of the Chronicles of the Kingis*, which reinforced its message 'as ane witnes of [James's] upricht meaning in the caus of Christ' with a royal sonnet at its close, celebrating the deliverance of God's people in 1588.[41] Like *The Essayes*, James's second volume of poetry, *His Majesties Poeticall Exercises at Vacant Houres* (1591), was designed to convey an image of a king of impeccable piety. The book's conceit, announced in its title and preface, is that its content was merely thrown together in haste, the product of what little time James could snatch for leisure from his devoted application to the 'great and continuall ... fasherie' of government. The reader is invited thereby to believe that James's few 'vacant houres' are spent in the translation of Huguenot devotional poetry (in this case 'The Furies' by Du Bartas) or in the composition of a poetic account of the 1571 defeat of the 'cruell Turks' at Lepanto. The latter refigures this Catholic victory over 'infidells' and 'Pagans' as evidence of how God would surely favour Protestants more and 'revenge [the] cause' of those who worshipped Christ 'Aright'.[42]

III *Basilikon Doron*, Anti-Puritanism and the Succession

Verbal posturing as a godly prince, occasionally seasoned with anti-Spanish and anti-popish inflections, was of some assistance when James needed to persuade Elizabeth of his 'cousin-like zele' or to turn pulpits to his praise. In the later 1590s, though James's printed writings did not represent a clean break from his earlier uses of print, they were shaped, however, by new topical concerns. In *Daemonologie* (1597/8) and *The True Lawe of Free Monarchies* (1598), James's printed writings took on a more polemically anti-Presbyterian character in response to fresh domestic challenges from radical opposition within the ministry. Following an attempted insurrection by radical Presbyterians at Edinburgh on 17 December 1596, James set about increasing royal authority over the Kirk and the restoration of bishops.[43] While the majority of ministers were reluctant to defy the king in the aftermath of the failed coup of 17 December, James's efforts to curb radical Presbyterianism did stimulate another wave of criticism in the form of 'despitefull letters' that were 'cast dayly in the Kinges palace' and several ministerial 'Apologies' that, in their complaints against 'persecutioun' and their denunciations of James as 'an avowed enemie' to the religion whose 'heart is alienated from ... Jesus Christ', were less than apologetic.[44]

Daemonologie and *The True Lawe of Free Monarchies* were published in that polemical context. Though he had most likely written *Daemonologie* in 1590–1591, when he participated in the North Berwick witch hunt at that time, James's decision to publish it came only in 1597 (or possibly early 1598), when James found it politically convenient to portray himself, in contrast to the claims advanced by his Presbyterian critics, as a watchful godly magistrate and enemy to the 'detestable slaves of the Devill, the witches'.[45] As with the publication of *Daemonologie*, James's *True Lawe of Free Monarchies* can be understood as a topical work. It refutes arguments that can be found in the works of George Buchanan, for instance, by denying that monarchy was elective and that the monarch was subject to censure by the kingdom's estates and could be legitimately and violently resisted for tyrannical acts. But Buchanan (to whom James's text does not refer directly) was long dead. James's choice to answer such arguments in print in 1598 makes topical sense as a response to the 'apologies', libels and sermons of 1596–8, the radical works of 'our seditious preachers in these daies … that busied themselves most to stirre up rebellion under cloake of religion', as James puts it.[46]

It was, however, in *Basilikon Doron*, the last of his Scottish printed works, that James enacted afresh and most fully his strategy of writing as revelation of the self. This too is an anti-Presbyterian text, though one that, I argue, was crafted and circulated mainly with the English succession in mind. Though he had long been attentive to English opinion of him and his claim, in the later 1590s James was especially alert to developments that could harm his prospects as Elizabeth's successor. The English Jesuit Robert Persons had, in 1595, published a wide-ranging attack on James's claim, in *A Conference About the Next Succession to the Crowne of Ingland*, and advanced as an alternative claimant the Infanta Isabella Clara Eugenia, Philip II's daughter. Among Persons's arguments was the contention that James VI should not be welcomed among the English on the grounds of religion. This was not simply because he was not Catholic but because he practised a different 'religion' to that 'which in Ingland is mainteyned'. Persons invited English conformist Protestant readers to consider 'what the state of religion is in Scotland at this day' and then to conceive what might happen if James VI, who was 'content to yeld' to the 'exorbitant and populer power of his ministers' in Scotland, became king in England. The consequences would be 'the woorst and most dangerous' for the Church and for the wider social and political fabric of the kingdom. Persons's polemical move here was so clever because it was of a piece with anti-puritan works by defenders of the Elizabethan religious settlement and of episcopacy in the Church of England. For several years English anti-puritans, such as Thomas Nashe, Matthew Sutcliffe and Richard Bancroft, had held up the Scottish Kirk as a horror show of 'confusion' and 'barbarisme', and depicted its 'rayling, libelling, and lying' ministers as 'Puritanes' whose 'Presbiteriall Discipline' was a means to disturb the state by stirring popular, anti-monarchical 'disorder'. Persons's work made explicit what could only be inferred from the anti-Scottish strand in the anti-puritanism of Bancroft and his allies: that James VI, whether through his inability or unwillingness to assert royal (and episcopal) authority over the Kirk, was an enabler of dangerous schismatics and so an unsafe prospect as Elizabeth's successor.[47]

Persons's *Conference* displeased James as soon as he read it in late 1595. It was only from 1598–1599 onwards, however, that James saw the necessity to answer Persons in a more determined fashion. At this time, James feared that his claim was threatened in England by several developments, namely the fall from favour of his supporter at Elizabeth's court, the earl of Essex, and the apparently improved prospects for a peace between England and Spain after the Franco-Spanish settlement in the Treaty of Vervins. The rival claim of the Spanish Infanta Isabella, as trumpeted by Persons, might, in such conditions, gain greater traction. Hence, between 1598 and 1601, multiple pamphlets were published in print and manuscript to defend James's claim and to counter the arguments of Persons's *Conference* by publicising the genealogical superiority of his claim over others, by warning English readers of the dire consequences of a disputed succession, and by answering allegations that James's foreign birth and religion were impediments to his title. James contributed to this campaign with his own pen, returning again to his strategy of self-representation.[48]

On one level *Basilikon Doron* was meant to function as a book of advice for James's four-year-old heir Henry, a guide for his 'godlie and vertuous education' and his future 'duetifull administration of that great office' of kingship which God had laid upon him. Yet, from the first, the book was meant to work for James himself: it both holds up for Prince Henry a 'mirrour' in which he would 'reede | How to become a perfite King indeede', and in that same 'mirrour' other readers may espy a 'worthy' image of James.[49] Despite the book's ostensible form as a private communication between father and son, James's intention was always that it would be read much more widely and would therefore have public political significance.[50] At the very start of James's draft manuscript of *Basilikon Doron*, there are hints of his carefully choosing his register to pull off that public-though-'private' balancing act, as he crossed through different versions of the book's opening words of address. Natural but too informal for wider consumption was his first attempt: 'To harrie'. The more formal but too distant 'To oure dearest sonne' was abandoned as soon as James had rounded out the 'o' of 'oure'. 'To Henrie my dearest sonne & naturall successoure' was just right to seem intimate enough for the public eye.[51]

That *Basilikon Doron* was made to *appear* private was integral to its publicity value: it purported to draw back the curtain of the king's mind for the reader and to vouchsafe to them what he really thought, to provide, as it were, the inside story of Stewart kingship. As two modern editors have so nicely put it, *Basilikon Doron* has 'the allure... of representing, however fictively, the immensely attractive spectacle of the king's private self'.[52] When he acceded to the English throne, James prefaced the bestselling 1603 edition with much the same argument: as the book was 'first written in secret', so 'it must be taken of al men, for the true image of my very minde'. The privacy and secrecy of the text was a sham, a deliberate ruse to stoke curiosity about its content and what that would reveal about its author. For the conceit that this was a private, secret text to work, its existence as a secret had to be *known*. It was, therefore, no coincidence that, uniquely among James's printed works of the 1580s and 1590s, this was the one that was trailed by rumours for months before it went to press (in a suspiciously well-publicised 'secret' edition of seven copies only), and which was then selectively leaked in the months that followed.[53] The English diplomatic agent in Edinburgh George Nicolson, who was informed about the book even while James was still drafting it in the autumn of 1598, acquired some sort of copy as early as February 1599, and later that spring word spread (not inaccurately) about its content and how James had therein 'bitterly defamed' ministers, was intent upon overturning the Kirk's Presbyterian 'discipline' and praised the service of those who had been loyal to his mother.[54] *Basilikon Doron* was never really a private text – it was always intended for circulation.

Advice books (or 'mirrors') for princes lent themselves to dull sententiousness and James indeed has much to say here on 'the love of vertue and hatred of vice'; yet the reader of *Basilikon Doron* is struck by the liveliness, or *lifelikeness*, of its style. In the words of one of its prefatory sonnets, the book holds up to the prince (and to any other reader) 'a mirrour *vive* and faire, | Which sheweth the shaddow of a worthy King'.[55] This 'vive' image of James is conjured through the text's fluid, conversational style. The text is repeatedly lightened by witty illustrations. James's advice to Henry on clothing demonstrates this well. 'Be ... moderate in your rayment', he declares; make choice of 'proper, cleanlie, comelie and honest' clothes; remember that garments 'ought to be used according to their first institution by God ... to hide our nakednesse and shame ... to make us more comelie ... to preserve us from the injuries of heate and colde'. But these basic moralising arguments are amplified in a lively and playful manner:

> Be ... moderate in your rayment; neither over superfluous (like a deboshed waister) nor yet over-base (like a miserable pedder)[56]; not artificiallie trymmed and decked (like a Courtizane:) nor yet over sluggishlie clothed (like a Cuntrie-clowne) not over lightly (like ... a vaine young Courtier) nor yet over gravelie (like a Minister:) but in your garments bee proper, cleanlie, comelie and honest .... But to returne to the purpose of garments, they ought to be used according to their first institution by God .... If to hide our nakednesse and shamefull partes, these naturall parts ordeyned to be hidde, should not then be represented by anie formes in the cloathes, as the great filthy Baloppes[57] do (bearing the pensel of PRIAPUS) .... And if they should preserve us from the injuries of heate and colde ... although it be praise worthie and necessarie in a Prince to be *patiens algoris & aestus*[58], when he shal have adoe with warres upon the feeldes: yet I thinke it meeter that ye goe both clothed and armed, nor naked to the battle; excepte ye would make you light for away-running ...[59]

In its joking similes at the expense of prostitutes, pedlars, courtiers and ministers, in its comical condemnation of the codpiece as overblown phallic display, and in its wry suggestion that a prince could appropriately go to battle stark naked in order to flee the field faster, we see that *Basilikon Doron* owes rather more to Horatian satire, in its liveliness and humour, than to pedantic sermonising on princely virtues.

The 'vive'-ness of the text is also conveyed in its passages of arresting candour. The strength of James's literary construct in *Basilikon Doron*, of this conceit of intimacy and straight-talking, is that the reader is thereby drawn in, encouraged to think that the text represents faithfully what James sincerely believed, including his statements on the piety, justice and virtuous living required of kings. The author who, in an ostensibly private text, unguardedly reveals what he 'really' thinks of radical Presbyterians – 'vain proud puritanes', 'verie pestes in the Church and common-weill of Scotland ... breathing nothing but sedition' – may seem by the same token rather more credible when he declares that the king must 'first of al things, learne to know and love ... God' and 'frame all [his] affections to follow precisely the rules' of Scripture.[60] A work wholly made up of such pious truisms would have been much less lifelike – the candid outspokenness of the text lends some credibility to those passages which are more conventional. Likewise, the presentation of a few self-criticisms – acknowledging his 'misthriving in money matters', for instance, and an over-inclination to mercifulness when 'severe justice' was required – meant that precepts for his son which otherwise might have savoured too much of hypocrisy might start to take on another flavour, as the honest expressions of someone experienced in rule and striving to live up to the moral obligations of Christian kingship.[61] The image of 'James VI' conveyed by *Basilikon Doron* is far from a warts-and-all portrait, but it is crafted so as to seem a realistic representation 'of a worthy King'. Only through a book that was ostensibly private in form, lifelike in style and apparently guileless in content could a king as committed to virtue as this 'James VI' appear at all convincing.

The text is dotted with passages designed to dispel the 'preoccupied conceits' that people had formed of James since the early 1580s.[62] Had he 'declined' towards 'papistry' in his religion? *Basilikon Doron*'s 'First Booke' ('Anent a Kings Christian Duetie towards God'), answers: 'I was never ashamed to give accounte of my profession, how-so-ever the malitious lying tongues of some have traduced me: & if my conscience had not resolved me, that al my Religion was grounded upon the plaine words of the Scripture, I had never outwardly avowed it'. 'I am no Papist', he affirms.[63] Was he, as Persons had insinuated, dangerously 'Puritan' in his religion? James's text is, in his own later words, ten times more bitter towards 'Puritans' than it is towards 'Papists', and *Basilikon Doron* commits James and his son to the re-establishment of episcopacy and royal authority over the Kirk.[64] If James is, then, no friend to 'Puritans' in Scotland, what of his religion? Is he 'indifferent' in religion for his own political interest? The king's declaration that 'al that is necessarie for salvation is contayned in the Scripture', the evidence of his knowledge of Scripture, his enjoining of his son to daily personal prayer, his repeated references throughout the text to 'conscience' that must not be offended and to kingship as 'calling', 'charge' or 'office' (that is, as divinely-ordained duty for the right administration of which God will call the king to an account), all suggest that James's is a conscientious vision of Christian kingship.[65] What of rumours that his consort is Catholic? James's advice to Henry suggests otherwise (without quite denying it): 'beware to Marie any but one of your owne Religion; for how can ye be of one flesh and keepe unitie betwixte you, being members of two opposite Churches?'[66] Is his succession to the English throne really acceptable, given English prejudices against 'barbarous' Scots and his own countenancing of links between the 'wild' and 'unciuil' Gaels of his kingdom and the rebels of Ulster? In *Basilikon Doron* some reassurance might be found, where he crows about his latest project, beginning with the Isle of Lewis from the summer of 1598, of 'planting Colonies' among the 'barbares' of the Isles whom he means to 'roote... out', planting 'civilitie in their roomes'.[67] Indeed, when we place such remarks alongside his complaints about the Scottish nobility's 'fectless arrogant conceite' of their power and their 'barbarous feides [feuds]' as well as the strong denunciations of Scottish Presbyterians, it appears that James was representing himself through *Basilikon Doron* as the Scottish and yet also, for a range of English readers, reassuringly anti-Scottish candidate for the English throne.

The leaks of this ill-kept secret of a text stoked curiosity about the book (and about the king behind it) ahead of more widespread and overt future publication. Moreover, in what was yet another difficult phase in James's relations with Elizabeth, when he was especially keen to win powerful backers in England, some carefully managed 'pre-releasing' of the book was opportune. James Sempill of Beltries, who helped James prepare the book for printing in 1599, was (surely not coincidentally) despatched as an envoy to London in August that year. What he lacked in first-hand experience of diplomacy, he made up for in familiarity with the text. His surviving letters to James from London that autumn show how diplomatically valuable his knowledge of *Basilikon Doron* was. Sempill found that the buzz around James's book was helpful for his task in making useful connections at Elizabeth's court: 'The more secret your Majesties buik be kept, the more it will it be suted heir, and be ane occasioun of acquenting me with... the best sort'. Some worried that James's book might show that he 'declyneth from religion'. Sempill claimed to have assuaged such concerns, answering such enquirers 'to their great contentement'. Others pressed him for a view of the whole text. The English lord chamberlain, Hunsdon, sent to Sempill one night to entreat 'a pleasour ... to show him [James's] last buik privelie'. Archbishop Whitgift of Canterbury was likewise keen to read it, approaching Sempill cautiously through 'some of his, who deale indirectly'. Knowing the book's anti-Presbyterian contents, Sempill was sure that 'It wold pleas him well inough'.[68] It was surely no coincidence that, during Sempill's stay in London, Andrew Melville and some of his colleagues, to whom also choice extracts from the book had leaked, sought to have its 'Anglo-pisco-papisticall conclusiones' (that is to say, James's condemnation of Presbyterian 'paritie' as inimical to monarchy and his commitment to both episcopacy and a form of royal supremacy over the Kirk) censured in the Synod of Fife. This timely row with radical Presbyterians, swiftly contained by ordering the arrest of one of the offending ministers, was just the ticket for a King of Scots keen to signal his reliability as a future Supreme Governor of England's episcopalian Church.[69]

Basilikon Doron's public-private form served James's interests perfectly. For those English readers who gained privileged early access to the text, it confirmed or encouraged a favourable impression of the man who had the strongest lineal right to be their next king: as one wrote in commendation of this 'long desired booke', it manifested the king's 'soundnes in religion, wisdome by experience, and excellency of learning: So, as for giftes of the minde, I thinke verily (judging by this and other rare workes) that there hath not benne the like king, since Solomon'.[70] Furthermore, the controversy provoked by some of the leaked features of the book was not necessarily unwelcome to James either. His favour to former supporters of Mary Queen of Scots was hardly news and, though some in England and Scotland disapproved, for many others James's 'universal' acceptance of loyal service from wherever it came was a positive feature of his kingship. He was not shy of confrontation with those whom he now habitually called 'puritan' ministers, but the vehemency of James's anti-puritanism could plausibly be denied while the work remained, technically, 'un'-published. To that end, James reassured supporters of his claim among the godly in England with a much-copied letter circulated among them at that time: urging recipients to make known James's intentions to other 'honest subjects in England, that sincerelie professe the onlie true religioun', he declared 'on the princelie word of a Christian king' that he would 'mainteane and continue' the 'professioun of the Gospell' once he succeeded to the English throne, and that he would not 'suffer or permitt anie other religioun to be professed ... within the bounds of that kingdome'.[71] Nevertheless, the leaking of anti-puritan invectives from *Basilikon Doron* could bolster his appeal to several other constituencies, both domestic and foreign, Catholic as well as Protestant. Bishop Bancroft and Archbishop Whitgift would have agreed enthusiastically with James's characterisations of the Scottish Reformation as 'made by popular tumult and rebellion' and of Presbyterian 'Paritie' as disorderly, confused and (shockingly) 'Democratik'. Such statements, by the same token, answered Robert Persons's charge that James, as one 'content to yeld' to the 'exorbitant and populer power' of Presbyterian ministers, was a danger to the Church of England.[72]

Basilikon Doron appears, then, to have been designed neither as a private, personal document, 'written for refreshment and for pleasure', nor merely as a mirror for princes.[73] Those were James's literary conceits which shaped the form of the text but they did not constitute its purpose. Archbishop John Spottiswoode's later assessment of both James's achievement and his intent in *Basilikon Doron* is more compelling: 'Certain it is, that all the discourses that came forth at that time … for maintaining his right to the crown of England, prevailed nothing so much as did this treatise against which such exceptions had been taken'.[74] *Basilikon Doron*, in other words, was an English succession tract, skilfully packaged and vividly composed as the intimate reflections of the King of Scots upon his kingship and teasingly pre-published to stir interest in the text and its author. A new English edition was prepared for publication long in advance of Elizabeth's last illness, so that it was on sale in London in late March 1603, with up to 16,000 printed by the following month. *Basilikon Doron*'s immense popularity in 1603 is not sufficient to prove Spottiswoode's contention as to the book's effectiveness – perhaps, as Jenny Wormald suggests, it was bought as an accession souvenir, like a coronation mug.[75] Yet, compared to all the voluminous English succession tracts written in this period, this was the most subtle, clever and entertaining intervention in the debate. The book's form, content and early publication history reveal James at the height of his powers of literary invention and political craft.

IV Conclusion

As has long been recognised, James VI engaged energetically in publicity politics. He had, as Karin Bowie persuasively argues, a 'commitment to proactive persuasion', using the 'cachet of a royal author' as one innovative means to influence opinion.[76] Through his printed works, he moved beyond suppression of critiques and libels, articulating his own arguments in response and creatively representing himself to readers in Scotland and England. In the most sophisticated of his writings, *Basilikon Doron*, he produced what has been described as 'surely one of the best pieces of political propaganda ever engineered' – a judgement with which I am not inclined to disagree.[77]

James's willingness, his enthusiasm even, to use his writings to represent himself and, by that means, to go toe-to-toe with opponents in the public sphere and to mobilise opinion in his cause – what did that signify for his kingship before and after 1603? Of course, James's repeated turns on paper were not wholly convincing when compared with his actions. We have seen some evidence of complaint about his 'uncredible writing' and 'faire words … without effect'. It was precisely because observable circumstances could suggest otherwise that James chose to publish works which insisted upon his Protestant piety, his commitment to his office (to do justice and defend true religion), and therefore also his reliability as an ally to Elizabeth or, indeed, as the future Supreme Governor of the Church of England. James's engagement in this sort of publicity has also been characterised as somehow unseemly, in contrast to Elizabeth who sensibly 'kept her thoughts to herself'. 'Instead of standing apart from political and theological controversies, as Elizabeth had often done, James entered their midst', writes Susan Doran. James thereby 'eroded some of the mystique surrounding monarchy, which probably explains why no other European early modern monarch had been or was to become a published author'.[78]

In response to this last point, we might wonder whether the reason that most monarchs did not write and publish as James VI did was because, intellectually, they were not up to the task! With tongue removed from cheek, assessments of James VI and I that take Elizabeth I's political style as normative, or that replicate opinions articulated in some parts of her servants' archives, can only ever present one side of what was a more complex reality. James could not afford to be aloof. He faced far, far greater challenges in Scotland than Elizabeth ever did as queen in England. The history of his Scottish reign, from the declaration of his majority in 1578 to 1603, is punctuated by multiple court coups, noble rebellions, seditious assemblies and tumults, all of which he, in person, endured, faced down and survived. No royal 'mystique' offered him its numinous protection. From the plush safety of her well-guarded Thames Valley palaces, Elizabeth could (and frequently did) lecture him on how he ought to do as she did, 'play the King' and just stamp his (by which she presumably meant her) authority on his kingdom.[79] Would that Elizabeth had 'kept her thoughts to herself'. James knew better. His experience of Scottish politics taught him from early on that he needed to engage, to persuade, to pitch for support from one party while not terminally alienating others. The same applied in relation to his claim to the English throne. His claim was contested and developments in Scotland were attended to and commented upon by friends and enemies of that claim. Management of opinion was sensible and James's own writings carried weight in that effort by making a version of himself known among his future subjects. Should he really, then, just have lain back and thought happy thoughts of England instead?

By offering up to readers a construct of virtuous, pious and just kingship, by allowing them to 'read … the perfect king indeed', James VI's writings gave contemporaries a measure against which to judge him, his self-professed standards to which they might refer to move, or rebuke, him. That, after all, is the sense of the complaint of 1591 that contrasted his 'uncredible writing' and his 'guyding & governement'. At the start of his reign in England, petitioners and panegyric poets welcomed him, quotes to hand, mirroring back to him his own presentation of his kingship and thereby offering him counsel as well as compliments.[80] Towards the end of his life, bitter criticism of his government was articulated in pamphlets and verse libels that, in parts, also held up the familiar lexicon of his written discourse on good kingship as a stick with which to beat him.[81] One could interpret such lively political, and polemical, engagement with James's writings as evidence of how 'perilous' it was for a king to write as James did. For Kevin Sharpe, James VI 'came to the English throne with a belief that he needed not simply to *be* sacred authority but to *argue for* it'; the king's 'conviction [was] that his writings and words were essential representations of majesty' and yet that that disposition to publish undercut the 'mystery' of kingship. Through his writing, Sharpe argues, James 'stimulated discussion and exchange ... and so reduced representation ... to verbal and political contest'.[82]

Such arguments have merit. It is worth stating, however, that contemporaries dissatisfied with a prince's government were not short of discourses to turn to for inspiration: James's critics did not need to refer to his words in order to decry the injustice, corruption, impiety or, indeed, tyranny that they perceived in his rule.[83] Moreover, an interpretation that assumes that 'sacred authority' and 'majesty' ought to have been uncontested and that 'verbal and political contest' was a failure, a 'reduction', presents (as James himself might have put it) a fine picture of 'a King in Divinity'.[84] Yet in practical terms the exercise of power *was* contested and it is far from clear that such thinking presented *the* answer to the 'discussion and exchange', to the 'verbal and political' contestation of legitimacy and authority that James, in common with other early modern monarchs, faced. James knew, as he put it in *Basilikon Doron*, 'That a King is as one set on a skaffold [that is, a stage], whose smallest actions & gestures al the people gazingly do behold' and that, therefore, how the king presented himself publicly mattered: 'the people who seeth but the outwarde parte, will ever judge of the substance by the circumstances, & according to the out warde appearance ... will conceive preoccupied conceits of the Kings inwarde intention', and such 'conceits' themselves bred 'Contempt, the Mother of Rebellion and disorder'. James's writings were a distinctive means to represent his 'inwarde intentions' to the gazing world. That he established and defended his authority in Scotland before 1603, acceded then peacefully to the English throne and twenty-two years later died not on a 'skaffold' but in his bed suggests that his 'demystifying' writings were not so problematic.[85]

Notes

1 D. Calderwood, *The History of the Kirk of Scotland*, ed. T. Thomson (8 vols, Wodrow Society, Edinburgh, 1842–9), III, pp. 717–19; Bodleian Library, Oxford, MS Bodley 165, fo. 58ᵛ. On the Ruthven Raid of August 1582 and James's escape in late June 1583, see S. J. Reid, *The Early Life of James VI: A Long Apprenticeship 1566–1585* (Edinburgh, 2023), ch. 7; A. Courtney, *James VI, Britannic Prince: King of Scots and Elizabeth's Heir, 1566–1603* (Abingdon, 2024), pp. 60–5, 70–2. Calderwood's text refers to 'the 110th Psalme' – clearly an error of transcription, as it is Psalm 101, not 110, that refers to the king's choice of companions.

2 K. Sharpe, 'Private Conscience and Public Duty in the Writings of James VI and I', in K. Sharpe, *Remapping Early Modern England: The Culture of Seventeenth-Century Politics* (Cambridge, 2000), pp. 151–71 at pp. 167, 169.

3 J. Rickard, *Authorship and Authority: The Writings of James VI and I* (Manchester, 2007), pp. 3, 9, 18. For another very fine modern work on several of James's printed writings, see A. Stilma, *A King Translated: The Writings of King James VI & I and their Interpretation in the Low Countries, 1593–1603* (Farnham, 2012).

4 Courtney, *James VI, Britannic Prince*, pp. 76–7; Bodleian Library, MS Bodley 165, fo. 58^{r-v}; *Dictionaries of the Scots Language* (dsl.ac.uk) – *sub.* 'Rander, Render' and 'Trap, *v*'. I have added punctuation to the Bacchus sonnet and expanded 'the' to 'thee' for clarification's sake.

5 Courtney, *James VI, Britannic Prince*, pp. 87–9.

6 S. Verweij, *The Literary Culture of Early Modern Scotland* (Oxford, 2016), pp. 64–71.

7 G. G. Simpson, 'The Personal Letters of James VI: A Short Commentary', in J. Goodare and M. Lynch (eds), *The Reign of James VI* (East Linton, 2000), pp. 141–53, at p. 145.

8 L. A. Ferrell, *Government by Polemic: James I, the King's Preachers, and the Rhetorics of Conformity, 1603–1625* (Stanford, 1998), pp. 8, 168.

9 J. Craigie (ed.), *The Basilicon Doron of King James VI* (2 vols, Scottish Text Society, Edinburgh 1944–50), I, pp. 19, 62, 162, 180, 182, 184.

10 N. Rhodes, J. Richards and J. Marshall (eds), *King James VI and I: Selected Writings* (Aldershot, 2003), p. 1.

11 D. Laing (ed.), *Original Letters of Mr John Colville 1582–1603* (Bannatyne Club, Edinburgh, 1858), pp. 315–16.

12 G. R. Kinlock (ed.), *Diary of Mr James Melvill, 1556–1601* (Bannatyne Club, Edinburgh, 1829), p. 38. On James's childhood at Stirling, see Courtney, *James VI, Britannic Prince*, ch. 2, esp. pp. 23–31.

13 TNA, SP 52/26/1, fo. 64^r (Killigrew to Walsingham, 30 June 1574); NLS, Advocates MS 15.1.6, fo. 27^r (Randolph to Buchanan, 15 May 1579); BL, Harleian MS 6999, fo. 66^r (Randolph to Hunsdon, 14 February 1581). The claim that George Buchanan regularly subjected James VI to beatings at Stirling is founded on misinterpretations of later sources: see Courtney, *James VI, Britannic Prince*, pp. 28–9.

14 BL, Harleian MS 6999, fo. 194^r (Hunsdon to Walsingham, 6 June 1581).

15 On James VI's education and how this empowered him: A. Pollnitz, *Princely Education in Early Modern Britain* (Cambridge, 2015), ch. 6, esp. pp. 274–82. See also Simpson, 'Personal Letters', p. 143: 'One key to understanding [James's] personality may lie in the fact that he was an intellectual .... The "hothouse" style of education imposed upon James as a child was certainly intended to develop his intellect, and it did so, mainly to his benefit'.

16 Reid, *Early Life of James*, pp. 282–3.

17 Reid, *Early Life of James*, pp. 283–7. Professor Reid sees the period of the Ruthven Raid (August 1582 to June 1583) as 'an enforced break from any literary activity' for James; however, the Treasurers' Accounts seem to indicate that James's English violers, including the poets Thomas and Robert Hudson, remained in attendance and payment was made to the poet 'Rob Stevin', possibly an alias for Alexander Montgomerie, in September 1582: NRS, E22/5, pp. 156, 253, 267 (Sarah Carpenter's digital transcriptions of these entries are available at https://reedprepub.org/royal-court-of-scotland/).

18 K. Bowie, *Public Opinion in Early Modern Scotland, c. 1560–1707* (Cambridge, 2020), p. 4.

19 P. Lake, 'Publics and Participation: England, Britain, and Europe in the "Post-Reformation"', *Journal of British Studies* 56 (2017), pp. 836–54, at pp. 837 and 848.

20 Craigie, *Basilicon Doron*, I, p. 74. 'Syne' = 'next', 'thereafter'.

21 Bowie, *Public Opinion in Early Modern Scotland*, throughout, but see esp. pp. 89–104 (on bands and covenant oaths), 143–54 (on pasquils, pamphlets, broadsides, rumours etc.). On covenanting, see also J. E. A. Dawson, 'Bonding, Religious Allegiance and Covenanting', in J. Goodare and S. I. Boadman (eds), *Lords and Men in Scotland and Britain, 1300–1625: Essays in Honour of Jenny Wormald* (Edinburgh, 2014); J. E. A. Dawson, 'Covenanting in Sixteenth-Century Scotland', *SHR* 99 (2020), pp. 336–48.

22 Craigie, *Basilicon Doron*, I, p. 76.

23 E.g. Courtney, *James VI, Britannic Prince*, pp. 53, 56–9, 61, 75–6, 79, 80, 87, 135, 154, 179.

24 Calderwood, *History*, V, pp. 150–6, 171; TNA, SP 52/48, nos 24, 81.

25 Cf. L. Hutson, *England's Insular Imagining: The Elizabethan Erasure of Scotland* (Cambridge, 2023).

26 R. A. McCabe, 'The Poetics of Succession, 1587–1605: The Stuart Claim', in S. Doran and P. Kewes (eds), *Doubtful and Dangerous: The Question of Succession in Late Elizabethan England* (Manchester, 2014), pp. 192–211, at pp. 202 and 203.

27 On 'public diplomacy', including the use of printed literature, to engage foreign audiences and support diplomatic activities during the early modern period, see H. Helmers, 'Public Diplomacy in Early Modern Europe: Towards a New History of News', *Media History* 22 (2016), pp. 401–20; T. A. Sowerby and J. Craigwood (eds), *Cultures of Diplomacy and Literary Writing in the Early Modern World* (Oxford, 2019).

28 BL, Lansdowne MS 42, fo. 13^r; S. Verweij, '"Booke, go thy wayes": The Publication, Reading, and Reception of James VI/I's Early Poetic Works', *Huntington Library Quarterly* 77 (2014), pp. 111–31, at pp. 115–16.

29 TNA, SP 52/38, no. 101; SP 52/47, no. 102; Calderwood, *History*, V, pp. 454–5.

30 J. Corbett, 'The Prentise and the Printer: James VI and Thomas Vautrollier', in K. J. McGinley and N. Royan (eds), *The Apparelling of Truth: Literature and Literary Culture in the Reign of James VI* (Newcastle, 2010), pp. 80–93; G. Sargent, 'Happy Are They That Read and Understand: Reading for Moral and Spiritual Acuity in a Selection of Writings by King James VI and I' (PhD, Glasgow, 2013), ch. 3, 'Reading for Moral Investment: *The Essayes of a Prentise* and Thomas Hudson's *Judith*'.

31 James, *Essayes*, sigs D^r, F^r. On James and Du Bartas, see P. Auger, 'Translation and Cultural Convergence in Late Sixteenth-Century Scotland and Huguenot France', in Sowerby and Craigwood (eds), *Cultures of Diplomacy*, pp. 115–28; P. Auger, *Du Bartas' Legacy in England and Scotland* (Oxford, 2019), esp. ch. 2 ('History of a Friendship: James VI and Du Bartas').

32 James, *Essayes*, sig. C3^r.

33 James, *Essayes*, sigs N3^r–N4^r, O2^r.

34 G. de Salluste du Bartas, *The Historie of Judith in Forme of a Poeme*, transl. T. Hudson (Edinburgh, 1584), *STC* 21671, sig. A2^r.

35 Patrick Adamson, *A Declaratioun of the Kings Majesties Intentioun and Meaning Toward the Late Actis of Parliament* (Edinburgh, 1585), *STC* 21949, sig. A2^r.

36 Adamson, *A Declaratioun*, sig. A2^v; James, *Essayes*, sigs A^v, C3^r; *Judith*, transl. Hudson, sig. A4^v.

37 A. R. MacDonald, 'The Subscription Crisis and Church-State Relations 1584–1586', *Records of the Scottish Church History Society* 25 (1994), pp. 222–55, esp. pp. 231–3; *idem, The Jacobean Kirk, 1567–1625* (1998), pp. 26–7; Courtney, *James VI, Britannic Prince*, pp. 70–5, 80.

38 Courtney, *James VI, Britannic Prince*, pp. 80–1, 82–3.

39 NLS, Advocates MS 29.2.8, fos 134ʳ–5ʳ (Anon., 'Advertisement for the kyngis majestie', n.d. [summer 1583]).

40 James VI, *Ane Fruitfull Meditatioun ... of the 20 Chap. of the Revelatioun in Forme of ane Sermone* (Edinburgh, 1588), STC 14376, sigs B2ʳ–[4ʳ].

41 James VI, *Ane Meditatioun upon ... the XV Chapt. of the First Buke of the Chronicles of the Kingis* (Edinburgh, 1589), STC 14380, sigs. A2ʳ, [B4ᵛ]. This work is sometimes read as anti-puritanical, but see Courtney, *James VI, Britannic Prince*, pp. 113–14.

42 James VI, *His Majesties Poeticall Exercises at Vacant Houres* (Edinburgh, 1591), STC 14379, 'The authour to the reader' (sig. [A]2ᵛ) and 'The Lepanto' (sigs [H]3ʳ, [L]3ᵛ–[L4ᵛ]).

43 For the events of 17 December 1596 and their significance, see J. Goodare, 'The Attempted Scottish Coup of 1596', in J. Goodare and A. A. MacDonald (eds), *Sixteenth-Century Scotland: Essays in Honour of Michael Lynch* (Leiden, 2008), pp. 311–36; J. Goodare, 'The Scottish Presbyterian Movement in 1596', *Canadian Journal of History* 45 (2010), pp. 21–48.

44 MacDonald, *Jacobean Kirk*, pp. 74–82; Courtney, *James VI, Britannic Prince*, pp. 178–9.

45 James VI, *Daemonologie, in Forme of a Dialogue* (Edinburgh, 1597), STC 14364, preface, sig. 2ʳ; Courtney, *James VI, Britannic Prince*, pp. 178–82. See also J. Goodare, 'The Scottish Witchcraft Panic of 1597', in J. Goodare (ed.), *The Scottish Witch-Hunt in Context* (Manchester, 2002), pp. 51–72; P. G. Maxwell-Stuart, 'A Royal Witch Theorist: James VI's *Daemonologie*', in J. Machielsen (ed.), *The Science of Demons: Early Modern Authors Facing Witchcraft and the Devil* (Abingdon, 2020), pp. 165–78.

46 James VI, *The True Lawe of Free Monarchies* (Edinburgh, 1598), STC 14409, sig. C3ᵛ; Courtney, *James VI, Britannic Prince*, pp. 183–8. For other accounts of the arguments of *The True Lawe* and its context, see J. H. Burns, *The True Law of Kingship: Concepts of Monarchy in Early Modern Scotland* (Oxford, 1996), pp. 225–42; R. A. Mason, *Kingship and the Commonweal*, ch. 8 ('James VI, George Buchanan, and *The True Lawe of Free Monarchies*'); P. Lake, 'The King (The Queen) and the Jesuit: James Stuart's *True Law of Free Monarchies* in Context/s', *Transactions of the Royal Historical Society* 14 (2004), pp. 243–60.

47 Courtney, *James VI, Britannic Prince*, pp. 166–8.

48 On publications defending James's claim in 1598–1601, see S. Doran, 'Three Late-Elizabethan Succession Tracts' in J.-C. Mayer (ed.), *The Struggle for the Succession in Late Elizabethan England: Politics, Polemics and Cultural Representations* (Montpellier, 2004), pp. 91–117. For James's heightened concerns about the defence of his claim in the years from 1598 onwards, see Courtney, *James VI, Britannic Prince*, pp. 195–6, 211–14.

49 Craigie, *Basilicon Doron*, I, pp. 3, 6. References are to the printed 1599 version, reproduced in Craigie's parallel texts edition, unless otherwise specified. The following section is adapted from the account provided in Courtney, *James VI, Britannic Prince*, pp. 204–11.

50 For this view see also McCabe, 'Poetics of Succession', p. 206. Cf. J. Wormald, 'James VI and I, *Basilikon Doron* and *The Trew Law of Free Monarchies*: The Scottish Context and the English Translation', in L. L. Peck (ed.), *The Mental World of the Jacobean Court* (Cambridge, 1991), pp. 36–54, at pp. 48–9.

51 BL, Royal MS 18 B XV, fo. 3ʳ.

52 D. Fischlin and M. Fortier (eds), *The True Law of Free Monarchies and Basilikon Doron* (Toronto, 1996), p. 28.

53 Craigie, *Basilicon Doron*, I, p. 22 (1603 edition); Rickard, *Authorship and Authority*, p. 116; Verweij, *Literary Culture of Early Modern Scotland*, p. 75.

54 *CSPScot*, XIII, pt 1, nos 271, 325, 375.

55 Craigie, *Basilicon Doron*, I, pp. 3, 50.
56 'Pedder' = a pedlar or packman – *Dictionaries of the Scots Language* (dsl.ac.uk) – *sub*. 'Peddar'.
57 'Ballop' = the fastenable flap at the front of a man's breeches – *Dictionaries of the Scots Language* (dsl.ac.uk) – *sub*. 'Ballop'.
58 'Resilient in the face of cold and to heat'.
59 Craigie, *Basilicon Doron*, I, pp. 170, 172, 174.
60 Craigie, *Basilicon Doron*, I, pp. 24, 28, 38, 78.
61 Craigie, *Basilicon Doron*, I, pp. 62, 64, 116.
62 Cf. S. Doran, 'Polemic and Prejudice: A Scottish King for an English Throne', in Doran and Kewes (eds), *Doubtful and Dangerous*, pp. 215–35, at pp. 224–8.
63 Craigie, *Basilicon Doron*, I, pp. 30, 34.
64 James VI & I, *An Apologie for the Oath of Allegiance ... Together, with a Premonition of his Majesties to all most mightie Monarches* (1609), STC 14401, p. 45; Craigie, *Basilicon Doron*, I, pp. 38, 48, 50, 78, 80, 140, 142, 172.
65 Craigie, *Basilicon Doron*, I, pp. 6, 30, 32, 34, 36, 38, 40, 44, 48, 50, 52, 54, 64, 66, 68, 122, 130, 142, 144, 150, 158, 172, 184, 206.
66 Craigie, *Basilicon Doron*, I, pp. 128, 130.
67 Craigie, *Basilicon Doron*, I, p. 70; Doran, 'Polemic and Prejudice', pp. 218–19. On James's policy towards the Highlands and Islands, see the text and references in Steven Reid's chapter above, pp. 28–9.
68 *CSPScot*, XIII, pt 1, no. 424; W. Fraser (ed.), *Memoirs of the Maxwells of Pollok* (2 vols, Edinburgh, 1863), II, pp. 41–3.
69 Craigie, *Basilicon Doron*, II, pp. 9–14; *CSPScot*, XIII, pt 1, no. 454. Sempill of Beltries was also, according to Spottiswoode, Melville's source for his extracts from *Basilikon Doron*: John Spottiswoode, *The History of the Church of Scotland*, ed. M. Russell and M. Napier (3 vols, Bannatyne Club, Edinburgh, 1847–51), III, pp. 80–1.
70 TNA, SP 52/66, no. 104.
71 Calderwood, *History*, VI, pp. 220–1; Doran, 'Polemic and Prejudice', pp. 227 and 234–5 n. 79.
72 Craigie, *Basilicon Doron*, I, pp. 74, 76, 78, 80.
73 Cf. Wormald, '*Basilikon Doron* and *The Trew Law*', p. 49.
74 Spottiswoode, *History*, III, p. 81. See also Patrick Anderson's manuscript history, NLS, Adv. MS 35.5.3 (iii), fo. 296ᵛ: 'Incredible it is how many mens heartes and affections he wonne unto him thereby, and what an expectation of him he raysed amongst all men, even to admiration'.
75 Wormald, '*Basilikon Doron* and *The Trew Law*', pp. 51, 52. For the work's reception in England after James's accession there, see J. Doelman, '"A King of Thine Own Heart": The English Reception of James VI and I's *Basilikon Doron*', *The Seventeenth Century* 9 (1994), pp. 1–9.
76 Bowie, *Public Opinion in Early Modern Scotland*, p. 183.
77 McCabe, 'Poetics of Succession', p. 206.
78 S. Doran, *From Tudor to Stuart: The Regime Change from Elizabeth I to James I* (Oxford, 2024), pp. 466–7.
79 E.g. J. Bruce (ed.), *Letters of Queen Elizabeth and King James VI of Scotland* (Camden Society, 1849), pp. 98n–100n: 'I never heard a more deriding scorn ... were I you, they should learn a short lesson .... For your own sake play the king, and let your subjects see you respect yourself'.
80 On poetry and petitioning at the 1603 accession, see R. A. McCabe, 'Panegyric and Its Discontents: The First Stuart Succession', in P. Kewes and A. McRae (eds), *Stuart Succession Literature: Moments and Transformations* (Oxford, 2019) pp. 19–36; M. C. Questier, *Dynastic Politics and the British Reformations* (Oxford, 2019), pp. 271–6. The authors of the puritan Millenary Petition, quoted directly

from *Basilikon Doron* to justify their appeal to the king: 'as your princely pen writeth, the King as a good physician must first know what peccant humours his patient naturally is most subject unto before he can begin his cure' – G. W. Prothero (ed.), *Select Statutes and Other Constitutional Documents Illustrative of the Reigns of Elizabeth and James I* (Oxford, 4th edition, 1913), p. 413; cf. Craigie, *Basilicon Doron*, I, p. 73.

81 A. Courtney, 'Court Politics and the Kingship of James VI & I, c. 1615–c. 1622' (PhD, Cambridge, 2008), ch. 5, esp. pp. 200, 202–3, 209–11, 219–21.

82 Doran, *From Tudor to Stuart*, p. 467; Rickard, *Authorship and Authority*, e.g. pp. 120, 206–7; K. Sharpe, *Image Wars: Promoting Kings and Commonwealths in England 1603–1660* (New Haven, 2010), pp. 18, 35.

83 See, for instance, the 1621 pamphlet *Tom Tell Troath*'s denunciation of James by comparisons with Nero and 'the Grand Signor in his Seraglio', or the French ambassador Tillières's despatches in 1620–2, describing James as governed by 'passions' of 'fear' and 'affection' and grotesquely sating his disordered appetites in drunken devotion to the marquess of Buckingham, like Tiberius on Capri: Courtney, 'Court Politics and Kingship', pp. 210–11, 216.

84 James VI & I, *The Kings Majesties Speach to the Lords and Commons of this Present Parliament at Whitehall, on Wednesday the xxi. of March. Anno Dom. 1609* (1610), STC 14396, sig. B2r.

85 Craigie, *Basilicon Doron*, I, p. 162. See J. Wormald, '"Tis True I Am a Cradle King": The View from the Throne', in Goodare and Lynch (eds), *Reign of James VI*, pp. 241–56: 'James was arguably less obsessed than Elizabeth about [the "*arcana mysterii*" (sic)] and the declared intention of a great deal of his writing was to demystify and explain his kingship' (p. 243); in England James 'came up against the unreal ideal of what the English chose to call harmonious politics' (p. 254).

3

THE JACOBEAN UNION REVISITED, 1603–1607

Andrew Thrush

On 26 March 1603, Scotland's thirty-six-year-old king, James VI, learned that he had inherited the English throne two days earlier from his childless and unmarried distant cousin, Elizabeth I. James immediately assumed that the borders between England and Scotland had dissolved and that a new state called Great Britain now existed. On 3 April he announced to the kirk of Edinburgh that there was now 'no more difference betuixt Londoun and Edinburgh, yea, not so muche, as betwixt Invernesse or Aberdeen and Edinburgh'.[1] By 11 April at the latest he was designing a new coinage that would include not only his new title, 'King of Great Britain', but also a motto, taken from Ezekiel 37:22: 'Faciam eos in gentam unam' (I will make them one people).[2] In mid-May, shortly after arriving in London, James issued a proclamation, commanding his new English subjects to 'repute, hold and esteem both the two realms as presently united, and as one realm and kingdom'.[3]

To James, it was self-evident that his accession to the English throne had automatically united his two principal kingdoms and that God had effected a marriage between himself on the one hand and the island of Great Britain on the other. Like all marriages, he later observed, this union was inviolable, for 'what God hath conjoined then, let no man separate'.[4] Because James held that a union had now been created, he also believed that any laws which undermined that union were now defunct. As he announced to his English subjects by proclamation in October 1604, 'immediately upon our succession divers of the ancient laws of this realm are ipso facto expired'.[5]

James's assumption that his accession to the English throne had immediately created a unitary state known as Great Britain was legally unsound. England and Scotland had not automatically formed one political entity known as Great Britain but continued to exist as separate kingdoms even

DOI: 10.4324/9781003319764-4

though they shared the same king. Nor was James entitled to declare particular English laws null and void. Only parliament had the power to repeal legislation, as the Commons' Speaker, Sir Edward Phelips pointed out when the king opened his first English parliament on 19 March 1604.[6] James, however, like most monarchs, had never received a legal training and failed to appreciate that the Scottish principle of desuetude was unknown in England.[7]

Among those who alerted James to the fact that his accession had not automatically created a new state was the ambitious lawyer Francis Bacon. In the spring of 1603, Bacon expressed alarm that James 'hasteneth to a mixture of both kingdoms and nations, faster perhaps than policy will conveniently bear'.[8] In a treatise written for the king, Bacon observed that what had been achieved so far was an 'imperfect' or dynastic union rather than a merger of the two states. In such a union, each kingdom kept its own laws and institutions (privy council, parliament and Church), an arrangement Bacon likened to adding oil to water, ingredients which remain separate even when mixed. In an incorporating or 'perfect' union, on the other hand, the various components 'cannot be separated and reduced into the same simple bodies again'.[9]

James's desire to create a unitary state owed much to the fact that he wanted the Union to be permanent. That aspiration was threatened because England and Scotland had divergent successions. Should James and his immediate line fail – which was not implausible given the severity of the plague epidemic of 1603 and the fact that none of his children had reached marriageable age – the Scottish throne would fall to James's next male relative, either John Hamilton, first marquess of Hamilton or Ludovic Stuart, second duke of Lennox. England's throne, on the other hand, would descend to an Englishman, either Edward Seymour, Lord Beauchamp, son of the earl of Hertford or George Hastings, fourth earl of Huntingdon. To prevent this from happening, James needed to turn his two kingdoms into one.[10]

Bacon evidently left it to others to impress upon James that the consent of the parliaments of both kingdoms would be required before an incorporating union could be accomplished. By 8 September 1603 at the latest James had been won round, having been reassured by members of the English privy council that a perfect union would be 'an easy affair' to accomplish, or so he later claimed. On that day Scaramelli, the Venetian secretary in England, reported that the English parliament would meet to consider the proposition that England and Scotland be formally united as Great Britain.[11]

Following the opening of this parliament in March 1604, James was initially confident that the Union would be accomplished as easily as the Act recognising his title to the English crown, which was passed just twelve days after the start of the session.[12] However, the English parliament refused to give statutory authority to the creation of a new state called Great Britain. Three years later, when the Union was considered again, it also declined to confer English citizenship on Scottish nationals born before James's accession to the English throne, but confined itself to matters of trade and the abolition of certain hostile laws that had previously governed relations between both kingdoms. Only in the diplomatic sphere was the Union accomplished without difficulty. That is because the king, who necessarily pursued one foreign policy rather than two, required only a single set of diplomats, who were appointed by him rather than parliament. As he chose to accredit only ambassadors of England, these diplomats came to be known abroad, for reasons of convenience, as ambassadors of Great Britain.[13]

The rejection of a statutory Union came as a profound shock to James. Like Bacon, James saw no reason why England and Scotland should remain separate now that they had the same king, since they shared the same island, language, religion and 'similitude of manners'.[14] As he remarked in October 1604, both countries enjoyed 'but one common limit or rather gard of the ocean sea, making the whole a little world within it selfe'.[15] This belief, that a common geography, language, religion and culture implied that the two kingdoms properly formed one political unit, was reinforced by James's reading of Britain's ancient history. Like Sir William Maurice of Clennenau and his fellow Welshmen, the poet William Harbert and the parson George Owen Harry, who claimed that James's accession represented the fulfilment of an ancient prophecy delivered by an angel to Cadwallader (or Cadwallon), the last British king, James believed that his inheritance of the English throne was intended to reunite the realms after long centuries of division.[16] Writing to the Scottish privy council in January 1604, he observed that Scotland and England were now 'joyned togidder under ane head, as they haif bene of lang tyme past'.[17] Nine months later he declared in a proclamation issued to his new English subjects that God had brought about 'the ... reuniting of these two mightie, famous and ancient kingdomes of England and Scotland, under one imperiall crowne'.[18] In point of fact, the two kingdoms had never been united, not even under the Romans.

From the outset, James supposed that he enjoyed widespread support. Some certainly shared his vision of a united Britain. Among the Scots, they included John Russell, who in the spring of 1604 presented to James 'The happie and blissid unioun', and Russell's fellow lawyer Sir Thomas Craig, whose treatise *De Unione Regnorum Britanniae* was published the following year.[19] They also included Dr John Gordon, newly appointed dean of Salisbury, who in a sermon preached before the king in October 1604, echoed James's view that 'the restitution of the auncient name of great Brittannie, by the Kings most excellent Maiestie' had 'come by the very motion, and instigation of Gods holy spirit'.[20] Among the English, the Union was advocated by Francis Bacon and John Thornborough, bishop of Bristol. During the House's opening debate in 1604, at least four members of the Commons, including Sir George More, a veteran of six parliaments, spoke in favour of the Union.[21] However, these were lone voices, for as the law student Humphrey Spurway observed in late

April, the Commons were 'exceedinge much against' the Union.[22] Pauline Croft's assessment that 'those who wanted the Union, apart from the king himself, were a small minority in both countries' is entirely accurate.[23]

In his initial approach to the English parliament, James mistakenly assumed that he was addressing a sympathetic audience which understood the blessings conferred by political mergers. In his opening speech in March 1604, James reminded his listeners that the Wars of the Roses had been ended by the union of the houses of York and Lancaster. He also remarked that England itself owed its existence to the merger of seven Saxon kingdoms.[24] He naturally supposed that the English would welcome an extension to their power which a merger with Scotland would bring. Besides, had not the English themselves long cherished the hope of uniting the two realms in order to close what James described as the Scottish 'back door'? (Whenever England and France had been at war, the French had invariably encouraged their allies the Scots to invade in order to divert and weaken the English.) At a conference between both Houses on 14 April 1604, Lord Chancellor Ellesmere, speaking for the king, reminded the English parliament that the Union was 'no new thing', for under Henry VIII a match had been proposed between the latter's son and heir Prince Edward and Mary Queen of Scots with the aim of creating a single country, 'to witt Brittayne'.[25] Ellesmere might have added that following Henry VIII's death, the objective of uniting the two realms had also been pursued by Edward's uncle, the duke of Somerset, who then ruled England as lord protector. Furthermore, during the early years of Elizabeth's reign, the queen's chief minister, Sir William Cecil, had argued that 'the best worldly felicity Scotland can have is either to continue in a perpetual peace with the kingdom of England, or to be made one monarchy with England, as they both make but one isle divided from the rest of the world.'[26]

James's belief that England stood to gain greater security from union with Scotland was unquestionably correct since it was also shared by the French. In October 1603 the French ambassador, fearful that the Union posed a direct threat to France's strategic interests, proposed to Henri IV that he be allowed to finance, underhand, an anti-Unionist party amongst the Scottish nobility.[27] However, aside from Sir William Cornwallis, few members of the English House of Commons publicly echoed James's view, as Sir Edwin Sandys, one of the leading English opponents of the Union in the Commons, denied that it was necessary any longer to secure England's northern border, France now being a friendly power.[28] Sandys's assertion was astonishingly short-sighted. It was precisely the fear that a foreign power would use Scotland to invade England that led the union of crowns to be replaced with a union of parliaments in 1707.[29]

Since the Union was dear to James's heart, in England's strategic interests and had been vigorously pursued by the English crown a half-century earlier, why then did it founder? Was it doomed to disaster or could failure have been avoided? Were the English the sole obstacle to the Union, as is often supposed, or were the Scots also to blame for its rejection? It is to these important questions that we now turn.

I

The English parliament which assembled in March 1604 met in the immediate aftermath of the Hampton Court Conference. At this conference, James had rejected puritan demands for further reform of the English Church. James had no time for puritans, describing them in his opening speech to parliament as 'a private sect, lurking within the bowels of this nation', whose members were ungovernable, 'being ever discontented with the present government, and impatient to suffer any superiority'.[30] Five weeks later, the French ambassador noted that the Commons were deliberately obstructing the Union because of this speech.[31] This observation, if correct, points to a hitherto unsuspected and important reason for the Union's eventual failure.

There were certainly puritan opponents of the Union in the Commons, among them the London lawyer Nicholas Fuller, who feared that if Scotland ceased to remain a separate kingdom, nonconformists like himself, suffering persecution at the hands of high commission, would have nowhere to flee.[32] However, opponents of the Union also included crypto-Catholics, like the earl of Northumberland's solicitor, Francis Moore. Moreover, the leading opponent of the Union in the Commons, Sir Edwin Sandys, was anything but a puritan. In his *A Relation of the State of Religion*, published in 1599, Sandys expressed admiration for many aspects of Catholic worship and described the Calvinist doctrine of predestination as entirely 'speculative'. Indeed, Sandys's brand of Protestantism made him an Arminian before the fact.[33] In reality, sympathy for further Church reform was no guide to a man's view on the Union. Unlike Fuller, Sir Francis Hastings, one of the leading puritans in the Commons in 1604, favoured the Union, perhaps in the belief that if James were accommodated, he would look more favourably on puritan grievances.[34]

If religious opposition did not account for the Union's failure, neither, perhaps, did the limited nature of the English parliament's powers. On 19 April 1604, the second day of the Commons' Union debate, Sandys observed that the Westminster parliament had no power to unite the two kingdoms because 'England sits here representatively only' and could not legislate for Scotland.[35] This was perfectly correct, of course, but Sandys was making no allowance for the plan outlined five days earlier by Lord Chancellor Ellesmere on behalf of James. Ellesmere had explained that the parliaments of both kingdoms would be required to appoint commissioners who, after reaching an agreement, would report back to their respective parliaments. These would then legislate to implement the commissioners' recommendations.[36] Consequently, when Sandys announced that 'we cannot make laws to bind Britannia', he was not necessarily playing the trump card that he supposed.[37]

Sandys was on firmer ground when he objected that, in seeking to merge his two principal kingdoms, James was attempting something that had never been done before. As Sandys explained, multiple kingdoms, though not unusual in late medieval and early modern Europe, tended to be personal unions, like the Union of Kalmar (1397–1523), which had temporarily joined together the kingdoms of Denmark, Sweden and Norway under a single monarch, rather than mergers. Not even the late fifteenth-century union of Aragon and Castile, which had resulted in most of the Iberian Peninsula being governed by a single monarch, qualified as a merger. 'The king of Spain', observed Sandys, 'hath many kingdoms, but no union in name or laws'.[38] There was in fact only one example in 1604 of an 'incorporating' union, that of Poland and the grand duchy of Lithuania, which had united in 1569 in order to combat the threat posed by Muscovy and the Crimean Tatars. However, most Englishmen were evidently unaware of this union, which had created the largest state in Europe next to Muscovy but which had also not proved wholly successful, as in less than twenty years Lithuania had reasserted its own sovereignty.[39] Not surprisingly, few in the Commons took issue with Sandys's argument that James was acting in an unprecedented fashion.

Taken on its own, the novelty of James's scheme cannot explain the Union's rejection. Other factors were also at play, not least the notorious xenophobia of the English.[40] For many of the latter, the Scots remained foreigners and, although James claimed that the two nations spoke the same language, Scottish accents were regarded as uncouth.[41] Besides, Middle Scots was not the same as English, though the differences between the two were less pronounced than they once had been, while Gaelic, not English remained the language of nearly half of all Scots.[42] Then there was the fact that Scotland was an ancient enemy. Even in peacetime, border raids were a part of everyday life. For the Union to have proceeded, both sides would have needed to embrace one another as friends. However, this was never on the cards, despite such apparently hopeful signs as the marriage in September 1603 of England's lord admiral, Charles Howard, first earl of Nottingham, to the king's cousin, Lady Margaret Stuart.[43]

English hatred of the Scots emerged as soon as the House of Commons began debating the Union in April 1604, fed no doubt by lurid (though not necessarily ill-founded) stories of robberies and murders committed by some of those who had accompanied James south.[44] As England was far wealthier than Scotland, some in the Commons predicted 'a deluge of Scotts' in search of better prospects if the Union went ahead.[45]. On 19 April 1604 Nicholas Fuller observed that a plant taken from barren earth and replanted in fertile soil 'will grow, and overgrow'.[46] During the session of 1606–1607, when the Commons were required to consider whether to naturalise Scots born before James's accession, matters turned particularly nasty. At a conference with the Lords in December 1606, Fuller derided Scottish merchants as 'more like pedlars than merchants', for which he was 'shrewdly chidden'. Two months later, the senior Buckinghamshire knight of the shire Christopher Piggot used 'many words of scandal and obloquy' against the Scottish nation. He might have gone unpunished had not an outraged king intervened.[47] In February 1607, when the Commons debated whether the Scots were entitled to enjoy English citizenship, Sandys declared that the Scots were 'better than aliens but not equal with natural subjects'.[48]

Outside the Commons, anti-Scots prejudice was no less rife. In October 1603 the mayor of Chichester notified the privy council of a drunken cobbler who blamed the Scots for the plague epidemic of that year. Six months later, gangs of 'swaggerers' were reported to be preying on vulnerable homeless Scots in London.[49] In 1604 Ben Jonson earned himself a short spell in prison for a gibe directed at the Scottish inhabitants of the new colony of Virginia: 'I would a hundred thousand of them were there, for we are all one country-men now, you know; and we should find ten times more comfort of them there than we do here'.[50]

James, of course, was well aware of English hatred of the Scots. In mid-April 1604, on the eve of the Commons' opening debate on the Union, he ordered Lord Chief Justice Popham to apprehend the 'damned crew of swaggerers'.[51] However, James underestimated the significance of this hatred and naïvely assumed that the ill-feeling that existed on both sides could be wished away by royal fiat. Immediately on his accession to the English throne, he issued a proclamation in which he instructed his Scottish subjects to acknowledge the English 'as their deirest bretherein and freindis'. He also ordered the inhabitants of both kingdoms 'to obliterate and remove out of thair myndis all and quhatsumever quarrelis ... quhilk hes mentenit discord or distractioun of effectioun amangis thame in tyme past'. In the Scottish Act of Commission of July 1604, James expressed the hope of establishing 'constant love and perfect amytie betwixt both the nations'.[52] He himself did his best to encourage such warm feelings. Shortly before his departure from Edinburgh in April 1603, James advised his eldest son, Prince Henry, to 'looke upon all Englishe men that shall cum to visit you as upon your loving subjectis, not with that ceremonie as towardis straingeris, and yet with such hartlines as at this tyme thay deserve'.[53] Once in England, James promoted Scots to some English conciliar and household offices in the belief that close proximity in his service would foster friendship and respect between the two nations. However, he did not appreciate that the historic enmity could not be eradicated overnight, nor did he foresee that the immediate prospect of a formal union might even stir new animosities.[54] In particular, James's tactic of employing (with few exceptions before 1615) Scots in the offices of his Bedchamber created fresh tensions over the influence and profits Scots enjoyed at court.[55]

Hostility between English and Scots was complicated by the fact that each side supposed that the other was the junior partner and would accommodate its wishes accordingly. This view was particularly pronounced south of the border, where many assumed that Scotland would simply be absorbed into the English state as Wales had been during the 1530s and 1540s. This is hardly surprising, as it was common knowledge that medieval English kings had frequently claimed suzerainty over Scotland. As early as May 1603, the English lawyer Richard Martin, addressing the king on behalf of the sheriffs of London and Middlesex at Stamford Hill, praised James for having 'brought us the addition of another kingdome which warre could never subdue'.[56] During the Commons' opening debate on the Union on 18 April 1604, the Somerset-based squire Sir Maurice Berkeley remarked that union was something to be granted by England to the Scots, since England was 'the more glorious, the more honourable' of the two.[57] James, of course, did not share Berkeley's view of England's innate superiority, but he may have unwittingly helped to reinforce it by announcing shortly after his accession that henceforward he intended to live mainly in England.[58]

To Scots, the idea that Scotland was inferior, and that they should be required to beg the English to take them in, was understandably offensive, even if theirs was the smaller and poorer of the two kingdoms. After all, it was the throne of England that had fallen by inheritance to the king of Scotland, and not the other way round. Now that the distribution of senior English offices was in the gift of their king, the Scots saw no reason why they should not benefit from James's patronage. Following his accession to the English throne, James was accompanied south by many members of the Scottish nobility, including his cousin the duke of Lennox, the marquesses of Hamilton and Huntly, and the earls of Angus, Argyll, Cassilis, Errol, Mar and Moray. Also in attendance was the former ambassador to England, Edward Bruce, Lord Bruce of Kinloss, the Scottish Secretary of State Sir James Elphinstone and the Scottish Lord Treasurer Sir George Home.[59] Many of these Scots expected to be rewarded with high office on their arrival in England. However, only Lennox, Mar, Bruce, Elphinstone and Home were added to the English privy council, and of these five, just two were found posts in the English administration: Bruce, who was made master of the Rolls at the expense of the pluralist lord keeper, Sir Thomas Egerton (who was subsequently compensated by being created Baron Ellesmere and lord chancellor), and Home, who became chancellor of the Exchequer in place of Sir John Fortescue. When James also sought to confer on Lennox the presidency of the English privy council, which office had not been filled under Elizabeth I, and to deprive Secretary of State Sir Robert Cecil of the lucrative mastership of the Court of Wards, he ran into stiff English opposition and was forced to retreat.[60] By early October, most of the Scottish noblemen who had accompanied James to London had returned to Scotland in disgust. Led by George Gordon, first marquess of Huntly, they resolved to petition James for a larger share in England's government, or at the very least equal representation on any future British privy council. Unless their demands were met, they threatened to oppose the Union.[61] James was so alarmed that he sent Lennox to Scotland in February 1604 to break up this combination.[62] Lennox seems to have been only partly successful in this endeavour, for when the Scottish parliament met that spring, the earl of Moray urged its members never to accept the Union. Huntly, too, incurred the king's wrath for his behaviour during the parliament. Moreover, according to the Venetian ambassador, the Scots, angry to learn that they were regarded as inferior, demanded that the English beg to be accepted by them.[63]

An important concomitant of hatred of the Scots was the English fear of a Scottish takeover of key positions in England. It was this apprehension, often written off as mere xenophobia,[64] which caused Archbishop Whitgift and Richard Bancroft, bishop of London, to ensure that there were no vacancies among the royal chaplains and court preachers by the time James reached London in May 1603.[65] It was a fear first given public expression not, as has often been supposed, in the House of Commons but in the Lords, whose speaker, Lord Chancellor Ellesmere, had been forced to surrender the mastership of the Rolls to Scotland's Lord Bruce. According to the Venetian ambassador, on 16 April 1604, two days before the Commons held their initial Union debate, the Lords demanded that no Scot be appointed to any English office for the space of twelve years in order to allow time for the English to win the love and respect of James. They also insisted that none of the four great offices of state – identified by the Venetian ambassador as the lord chancellorship, the lord keepership, the lord chamberlainship and the office of lord high constable – should ever be bestowed on Scots. The Lords' fear of a Scottish takeover was subsequently taken up by the Commons. On 19 April 1604, Fuller demanded that no Scot should be appointed an English magistrate. Four days later Sandys called on James to ensure that only Englishmen held crown offices south of the border.[66]

James was so alarmed by the combined opposition of both Houses that on 29 April 1604 he assured the Commons representatives 'that he had no intention that offices of England should be bestowed on the Scottish'. That November, as the two sets of Union commissioners met, he also told Cecil that in future he intended not to be too hasty in preferring Scots.[67] James was true to his word, for after the appointments of May 1603 few Scots received official positions in London but rather received pensions and cash instead.[68] In addition, James continued to try to allay English fears, reassuring the Westminster parliament in 1607 that his willingness to do favours for the Scots would inevitably diminish the longer he lived in England.[69] However, he did not cease to give the English cause for concern. Quite understandably, James surrounded himself with his fellow Scots, to the dismay of the author of the anonymous 'A Loyall Subiectes Advertisment', who protested that 'your Englishe subiectes [ought] not to be disgraced' as 'the kingdome and people of England have made yow greate'.[70] His generous grants to Scots likewise excited envy. In 1608 James conferred the Order of the Garter on Sir George Home, now earl of Dunbar, in the belief that he was thereby advancing the Union. In reality, this, like other favours done by James for his fellow countrymen, merely irritated some Englishmen still further.[71]

James, of course, found himself in an impossible position. If, as he had told the Scots immediately upon his accession, England and Scotland now made one country, there was no reason for him to exclude his fellow countrymen from senior offices in England. But in trying to accommodate their wishes he had alienated his English subjects and jeopardised the Union. On realising this, he limited Scottish access to English offices. In so doing, he got the worst of both worlds. He upset many of his leading Scottish subjects, who retaliated by vowing to oppose the Union, while at the same time failing to calm English fears.

Concern at the prospect of a Scottish takeover had another, hitherto unnoticed dimension which helps to explain why so few Englishmen proved keen to embrace the Union. Unlike James, many English parliamentarians were not concerned by the two kingdoms' divergent successions. However, they were alarmed by James's solution to this apparent problem, the creation of a unitary state. This would mean that, in the event that James's immediate line failed, the crown would descend to James's next male relative, either Hamilton or Lennox. To many Englishmen, this was not an appealing prospect. As Richard Martin, sitting for Christchurch, observed, it meant that the crown of Britain would fall to 'a Scottish man', to 'no Englishman'. The idea that the crown of a united Britain might remain forever in the hands of a Scot offended English national pride. Not surprisingly, therefore, the Commons subsequently included in their list of objections to the creation of a unitary state the loss of English claims to the crown.[72]

Hostility towards the Scots and the associated fear of a Scottish takeover were not the only reasons why the Union proved to be impossible for James to sell to his English subjects. Another important factor, identified by Conrad Russell, was that most early seventeenth-century Englishmen proved incapable of thinking along federal lines or in terms of divided sovereignty, even though in the late 1540s Protector Somerset had envisaged a loose federation in which the Scots would be allowed to retain their laws and customs.[73] Some sort of federal arrangement, along the lines of the Dutch and Spanish models, would have allowed both kingdoms to retain their own laws and some of their institutions. Indeed, following the Union of 1707, there was no union of laws, only a union of parliaments, it being clearly impossible to merge both legal systems which, as Conrad Russell remarked, had 'different terminologies and concepts'.[74] However, Englishmen, used to thinking in terms of Ireland and Wales, of annexation and conquest, were reluctant to accept that a single kingdom of Great Britain could exist unless England and Scotland were first dissolved and their laws extinguished. To Sir Edwin Sandys, it was axiomatic that there could be no state 'in the plural number', that 'a kingdom is indivisible, and may not contain several kingdoms'.[75] Likewise, Sir Edward

Coke, then attorney-general, later wrote that 'I never read of any union of divided kingdoms', an observation which has fairly been characterised as 'a confession of ignorance'.[76] To such men, a statutory union of the two kingdoms inevitably meant the immediate destruction of English law and the loss of the subjects' liberties, or as Nicholas Fuller bluntly put it, 'No Magna Charta'. That was a frightening prospect, particularly to the lawyer-members in the Commons, who made up more than a fifth of the House's membership[77] and stood to lose their livelihoods. These views did not, of course, go unchallenged. Secretary of State Sir John Herbert, speaking for the king, denied that in taking the name Britain the English parliament would 'take away England'. Sir Roger Aston, an Englishman by birth but James's huntsman for the past twenty-five years, protested, somewhat disingenuously, that all James intended was 'to take upon him the stile of Brittaine', that it was 'not his meaning to exclude England and Scotland; to take away the name, their laws, or liberties'.[78] However, the king's own judges subsequently ruled that all legal processes would be invalidated the moment that the new kingdom of Great Britain came into being.

The fear that England stood to lose by the merger of the two kingdoms is one of the abiding themes of the Union debates, and helps to explain why James was ultimately thwarted in his endeavours. This fear was not confined to members of the Commons. In the Lords' opening debate on the Union, on 16 April 1604, the concern was expressed that some members of the Scottish nobility had demanded that the peerages of both kingdoms should, in effect, be merged, allowing Scots of high rank to take precedence over more junior English noblemen.[79] The English were already finding it uncomfortable that the Scots had a duke (Lennox) whereas they did not, and were disappointed that James had not chosen to redress the balance at his coronation.[80] Royal acceptance of the principle that all peerages, whether English or Scottish, should be ranked simply on the basis of seniority of title, would have added insult to injury. How far the English nobility suspected that the king sympathised with the Scottish demand for a single peerage is unclear. However, a unified peerage was logical if the two kingdoms were to be merged, and James certainly did nothing to allay English concerns. On the contrary, in later years he would go on to confer English titles on Scottish noblemen and permit Englishmen to buy Irish and Scottish viscountcies, allowing their holders to take precedence on local commissions over English barons, to the considerable fury of the latter.[81] In 1607 James provided clear evidence that he intended to unite the two peerages by requiring the Scottish nobility to bring their privileges into line with the more limited rights enjoyed by English peers.[82] The justifiable suspicion that James aimed at a unified peerage helps to explain why, in 1604, members of the Lords quietly encouraged the Commons in their opposition to the Union, furnishing their colleagues in the Lower House with fresh arguments as required.[83]

So far we have considered the role of English opposition to the Union. However, it has not always been appreciated that the Scots may also have played an important part in rejecting James's cherished plans. One reason for this is that Scottish parliamentary sources, unlike their English equivalents, are relatively thin on the ground. For most of the parliaments in these years, we lack detailed accounts of proceedings, nor is there a Scottish equivalent of the English newsletter-writer John Chamberlain to draw upon. Lacking such documentation, one historian mistakenly concluded that the Scots 'do not seem to have thought much about the proposed union', but were 'little more than interested spectators'.[84] Another reason why Scottish opposition to the Union has been overlooked is that the Scots have sometimes been characterised as enthusiastic unionists. There were, of course, enthusiasts for the Union among the Scots, including Dr John Gordon, who argued that, since England had fallen by inheritance to Scotland's king, James would be well within his rights to describe the whole of his expanded realm as Scotland rather than Great Britain.[85] However, the idea that all Scots were zealously in favour of the Union owes much to English propaganda. In the Commons it was said that the Scots were 'so greedy of this Union … that they should receive so much benefit by it, as they cared not for the strictness of any conditions, so that they might attain to the substance'.[86] In fact, as has already been mentioned, several Scottish noblemen, angered by their exclusion from English offices, were actually the first to attack the Union. Nor was Scottish opposition to the Union limited to a few disgruntled aristocrats. In August 1607 the duke of Lennox reported to the king shortly after opening the Scottish parliament that he feared finding just as much opposition to the Union in Edinburgh as at Westminster.[87]

In one key area, that of religion, Scottish opposition was crucial in thwarting James's ambition to create a unitary state. From the outset, James strongly hinted that he wished to merge his two Protestant churches, the Church of England and the Scottish Kirk. In April 1604 James told the Commons that at his death he wished to his legacy to be not only 'one kingdom, entirely governed' and 'one uniformity in laws' but also 'one worship to God'.[88] Six months later, James declared in the proclamation announcing his intention to adopt the style of Great Britain on the coinage and in all future proclamations and treaties, that 'An Unitie of Religion [is] the chiefest band of heartie Union, and the surest knot of lasting Peace'.[89] In December 1604 the Venetian ambassador reported hearing that there were plans afoot to appoint the new archbishop of Canterbury, Richard Bancroft, primate of Great Britain.[90]

For James, the ideal model Church was one drawn up on English rather than Scottish lines. James disliked the fact that in Scotland his claims to royal supremacy, enshrined in the so-called Black Acts of 1584, were contested by radical Presbyterians among the Kirk's ministry, who claimed in 1578 that the 'power ecclesiastical flows immediately from God …, not having a temporal head on earth'. In 1592 the crown's claims to supremacy were watered down by the 'Golden' Act, which gave ecclesiastical officeholders independence in spiritual affairs.[91] James also disliked ministers' antipathy towards episcopacy, which had been all but abolished in Scotland in favour of Presbyterianism. He therefore encouraged the reintroduction of bishops, a policy interpreted even before 1603 as evidence that James wished for union.[92] James's views on the Kirk were most clearly expressed in his 1598 treatise on kingship, *Basilikon Doron*. In this James expressed regret that the Scottish Reformation had been accomplished by a popular rebellion rather than by the monarch. He also accused radical Kirk ministers of trying to frame for themselves 'a democratike forme of gouvernement'. By contrast, many Scots regarded the Kirk as superior to the English Church which, in their eyes, was still tainted with popery.[93]

Not surprisingly, James's preference for an English-style Church was greeted with dismay by the leaders of the Kirk, particularly after the Hampton Court Conference of January 1604, at which James vigorously denounced Presbyterianism. They also grasped the implications of this preference for James's desire to unite his two realms. How could the Union be accomplished without the merger of their Churches, they asked, and how could this be achieved 'unlesse the one give place to the other?'[94] Not surprisingly, many Presbyterian ministers began 'boith fasting and preaching maliciouslie againis the unioun of the kingdoms'.[95] James's desire to impose upon the Scots an English-style Church was most clearly illustrated in August 1607, when Scotland's two archbishops were accorded precedence in the ceremonial procession to open the Scottish parliament, to the dismay of the noblemen present, who reportedly agreed to this arrangement 'but in derision'.[96]

In order to prevent a union of the Churches, the Scottish Parliament took the precaution of excluding the Kirk from the remit of the commissioners sent to London in October 1604 to discuss the Union.[97] This was a serious setback for James, but having previously succeeded in restoring a limited form of episcopacy to Scotland in the teeth of Presbyterian opposition he naturally did not regard it as the end of the matter. According to the Venetian ambassador at least, James asked the Scottish parliament in August 1607 to recognise his 'headship of the Scottish Kirk ... in the form in which it is held in England'. However, this had reportedly been rejected by the Scottish 'Puritans', and so the Venetian concluded that the Union could never take place.[98]

II

The strength of English and Scottish objections to the Union took James by surprise. As he told the Commons in March 1607,

> when I first propounded the Union, I then thought there could have been no more question of it than of your declaration and acknowledgement of

my right unto this crown; and that as two twins they would have grown up together. The error was my mistaking: I knew mine own end, but not others' fears.[99]

In private, James complained that, having committed himself to this project, he found it impossible to withdraw without losing face.[100] As late as December 1608, James harboured hopes of reviving the Union when the English Parliament reassembled.[101]

The eagerness with which James pursued the Union had several unintended consequences for him. One was to be made a hostage to the House of Commons at the start of his first English parliament. In March 1604, shortly before the Parliament assembled, Chancery suppressed the return of the outlawed Sir Francis Goodwin as senior knight of the shire for Buckinghamshire in favour of the privy councillor, Sir John Fortescue. The Commons protested, claiming that they alone enjoyed the right to determine the outcome of disputed elections. Initially, the king supported the lord chancellor, telling the Commons that 'by the law this House ought not to meddle with returns'. However, this prompted the Commons to retaliate. When, on 31 March, Sir William Maurice attempted to begin a debate on the Union in the Commons he was ignored. Not until mid-April, after James conceded the justice of the Commons' demands, did members turn their attention to the Union. A relieved James now supposed that the Commons would show him their gratitude by nodding through the Union. However, this did this not happen, nor did the Commons keep their promise to pass a bill to prevent outlaws from sitting in future. Moreover, on 16 April, shortly after James caved in to the Commons' demands, the Lords voiced their concerns about the Union, which have already been discussed. It can hardly be any coincidence that the speaker of the Upper House was none other than Lord Chancellor Ellesmere, who had just come off worse in his struggle with the Commons thanks to the king. Thoroughly outmanoeuvred and angry, James was left looking foolish and out of his depth.[102] When the judges then agreed with the Commons, that the moment Great Britain came into existence England's common law would be extinguished, his humiliation was complete.

Another result of James's determined pursuit of the Union was that, in 1604 at least, it caused members of his own privy council to work secretly against him, as the French ambassador observed in April 1604.[103] Many members of the council shared the Commons' concern at the legal implications of creating a new state called Great Britain. Chief among them was Robert, Lord Cecil, the king's principal minister in England. Cecil realised that it was unwise to call Great Britain into existence before the laws of both kingdoms had been 'compounded'. In a dispatch to the Scottish Secretary of State Sir James Elphinstone, Cecil described the judges' ruling that English law would disappear if England were to be abolished as 'a very good stop to the work so much desired of his Majesty', a remark that has fairly been construed as 'barely concealed satisfaction'.[104] Six days later, Cecil all but admitted his involvement in the parliamentary opposition to the proposed change of name. In a letter addressed to Lennox he observed that 'they that wish the Union with all their souls protest against the present name both in the higher and lower House'.[105] This hitherto unnoticed letter helps to explain why, two months later, James discussed with Sir George Home whether Cecil could be trusted.[106]

By opposing the proposed change of name, Cecil was trying to save James from the consequences of his actions. He thereby emulated his late father, William Cecil, Lord Burghley, who in 1566, despite his position as Elizabeth I's chief minister, had secretly encouraged parliamentary unrest in order to put pressure on the queen to marry, an exercise in double-dealing that Stephen Alford has described as 'controlled political schizophrenia'.[107] Robert Cecil was not averse to the Union per se, as his letter to Lennox demonstrates. However, he was alarmed at the impatience of James, who ignored his advice, proffered ahead of the 1604 session, to postpone the Union until England and Scotland ceased to view one another through hostile eyes.[108] Since the king also refused to believe that the proposed change of name posed an existential threat to England's common law, Cecil was left with no choice but to work against James underhand.

James's continued pursuit of the Union after 1604 had further ramifications for the relationship between James and Cecil. Although Cecil was elevated in the peerage as earl of Salisbury in 1605, the Union continued to haunt James's chief minister. Over the winter of 1606–7, the earlier plan to get parliament to recognise James as king of Great Britain having now been dropped, Salisbury tried to persuade the Commons to accept the more modest proposals contained within the Instrument of the Union. Drafted by the Union commissioners in the autumn of 1604, this document was described by Salisbury as 'a perfect Union with restrictions'.[109] Salisbury urged members of the Lower House to adopt the commissioners' recommendations and to avoid 'base fear' and 'prejudice'. However, relations between the Commons and the Lords subsequently became fraught following a series of meetings between representatives of both Houses in December 1606. They reportedly ended, 'like the month of March, in storm and tempest'. James was naturally extremely angry that once again his wishes had been flouted. Suspecting that Salisbury was still secretly working against him, he demanded to know why the chief minister's clients in the Commons, among them the lawyer Henry Yelverton, were opposing the Union. Although Salisbury explained 'that I have no such in interest in Mr Yelverton as to think to lead him', James remained dissatisfied and in January 1607 he sent Salisbury a 'first letter of caution'. Though now lost, this letter caused Salisbury considerable anxiety. It also led to a much misunderstood episode: Salisbury's offer to exchange with the king his palatial residence in southern Hertfordshire known as

Theobalds for several royal manors in Hertfordshire, among them Hatfield, with its old episcopal palace.

The Theobalds-Hatfield exchange has often been characterised as a cunning scheme by Salisbury to cheat the king. In actual fact, the difference in the value of the properties exchanged was negligible. Far from attempting to swindle the king, Salisbury was trying to regain James's favour as the king, a keen huntsman, was much enamoured with Theobalds, which boasted an excellent deer park. At the time, of course, Salisbury adopted the pretence that he was glad to be rid of Theobalds, which was expensive to maintain. However, his real motive was political survival, for waiting in the wings to assume the mantle of king's chief minister should he fall from office was his erstwhile ally Henry Howard, earl of Northampton. This tactic proved to be entirely successful. Not only did Salisbury survive as chief minister but James also blamed leading members of the Commons like Sir Edwin Sandys for the failure of the Union. However, having now lost Theobalds, Salisbury was forced to build for himself a new house at Hatfield.

The fact that Hatfield House ultimately owes its existence to the Union is not the only overlooked consequence of James's pursuit of his pet project. Without the Union, the Gunpowder Plot would probably never have occurred, a point that Mark Nicholls alone has noticed.[110] As has already been mentioned, James envisaged from the outset that the Union would be accomplished in several stages. First the parliaments of both kingdoms would appoint separate commissioners to meet in London and discuss the details of the Union before the king. Then, following the commissioners' deliberations, both parliaments would assemble for a second session in order to ratify the commissioners' recommendations. James naturally wanted to present these recommendations to the English Parliament himself, and therefore decided to open the new session in person in November 1605, although by custom only the start of the first session of a parliament required his presence.[111] The only reason for the monarch to attend the beginning of a second or subsequent session of parliament was if the Commons' speaker died between meetings and had to be replaced, as happened twice under Elizabeth I.[112]

James's decision to open the new session in person in order to deliver to Parliament the Instrument of the Union almost cost him his life. It provided the Gunpowder plotters, who felt abandoned by Spain's recent peace with England and decided to take matters into their own hands, with the perfect opportunity to blow up the king, his two young sons and most of the rest of the English political establishment. Their plot was only discovered thanks to Lord Monteagle, who became suspicious after receiving a tip-off from one of the conspirators to stay away from Parliament. James himself quickly realised that his decision to present to Parliament in person the Instrument of the Union had nearly been his undoing. On 9 November 1605, he told Parliament that if it had not beene for delivering of the articles agreed upon by Commissioners of the Unioun, which was thought most convenient to be done in my presence, where both head and members of the parliament were mett together, my presence had not otherwise been requisite here at this time.[113]

What James may not have realised, however, was that the Gunpowder plotters had also planned to exploit ill-feeling towards the Union to justify their actions. In a proclamation prepared ahead of James's intended assassination, they had intended to appeal for support, claiming that by killing the king they had saved the English from union with the Scots. This revelation, which formed part of Guy Fawkes's confession, was political dynamite. It suggested that there were in England many who were prepared to take up arms to prevent union with the Scots. That may not have been true, of course, but as S. R. Gardiner observed, it is hardly surprising that the privy council never exposed the king to embarrassment by making public the offending passage in Fawkes's confession.[114]

Perhaps the most important consequence of James's failed pursuit of the Union was the souring of the king's attitude towards the English parliament. Conrad Russell observed that the rejection of the Union was 'perhaps the most humiliating rebuff suffered by a Stuart king from the House of Commons at any time before the refusal of supply against an invading army in May 1640'.[115] Even allowing for the additional humiliation experienced by James after the Commons' rejection of the Great Contract in 1610, it is hard to disagree with this verdict.[116] It was because he felt the pain of his defeat over the Union so keenly that in November 1608 James told the judges that if he decided to sit in parliament, and preside over its debates, as he was entitled to do, 'hee should bee the better respected'.[117] Like Lord Chancellor Ellesmere who, following the dissolution of the 1604–10 Parliament, included 'the matter of the Union' among the many examples of the Commons' insolent behaviour towards the king, James believed that he had been insulted by the Commons.[118] Perhaps inevitably, James's sense of hurt cast a long shadow. The rejection of the Union, followed a few years later by the Commons' refusal to endorse the Great Contract, eventually persuaded James to do without parliaments. As a result, those who had previously taken their parliaments for granted began to fear, with good reason, that England's representative assembly was in danger of extinction. Although James's experiment in personal rule ultimately failed, this had more to do with the poverty of the crown than with the king's love of the English parliament.[119]

III

Several important conclusions arise from the foregoing brief study, many of them new and some rather unexpected. When James ascended the English throne in 1603, he did so in the mistaken belief that the Union was already an accomplished fact. Once he had been apprised of his mistake, he assumed that a formal merger of his two kingdoms would be easily accomplished by the parliaments of both. He overestimated the strength of his support and failed to consider the profound legal difficulties which faced him, most particularly the implications for the laws of both his kingdoms. He also underestimated the historic enmity between the two nations and the extent of English xenophobia. Instead, he sought to wave away these ancient hostilities with a stroke of his pen and to build bridges between the English and the Scots by allowing the latter to participate in English public life. In the process, he raised Scottish expectations to an unreasonable degree and triggered English fears of a Scottish takeover. Far from lessening the mutual hostility between the two nations, as he had hoped, James inadvertently made matters worse. By attempting to unite the two nations in friendship, he actually drove them further apart.

In a sense, though, James's attempts to reconcile his two sets of subjects hardly mattered when it came to the fate of the Union. Whatever James had done, in the early years of the seventeenth century the Union – even a partial union on federal lines – was almost certainly unattainable. The English, despite having previously hankered after a union, no longer put much stock in the argument that merger with Scotland would afford them greater security because they no longer saw France as the enemy. In that sense it was James's misfortune that it had been England's ally Henri of Navarre who emerged triumphant from the French Wars of Religion rather than his Catholic enemies.

Another reason the Union was unattainable in the circumstances that existed in 1603 was that the English had always assumed that union with Scotland would be accomplished on their terms, that they would absorb the kingdom of Scotland into the English state and remain the dominant party. They had not considered the possibility that the creation of Great Britain would mean that they would be required to share office and wealth with the Scots or that they would be permanently saddled with a Scottish royal family. James might wish to create Great Britain in order to make the Union permanent and so avoid the problem posed by divergent successions, but this objective was not shared by many of his English subjects, for reasons of national pride.

It has always been clear that the English House of Commons was largely responsible for the rejection of the Union. However, the Lower House was by no means alone in its hostility, as the earliest misgivings in the English parliament were actually expressed in the Lords, many of whose members then proceeded to encourage the Commons' opposition. Moreover, the first sign of opposition to the Union came not from the English but from a disgruntled section of the Scottish nobility. How far these unsympathetic noblemen were able to influence wider opinion in Scotland remains unclear. However, the Scots were certainly responsible for ruling out any attempt to unite the Churches of England and Scotland, in the belief, undoubtedly correct, that were such a merger to occur it would be along English rather than Scottish lines. Indeed, James's efforts to 'anglicanise' the Kirk proved increasingly controversial, and stirred formidable opposition, as the reign wore on.[120]

The consequences of James's eager pursuit of the Union were many and varied. From the outset the Union exposed the king to humiliation and helped to sour his attitude towards the English parliament. Eventually James tried to do without parliaments, thereby arousing fears that England's representative assembly faced extinction. The Union also placed a considerable strain on James's relations with his chief minister, Robert Cecil, to whom the king owed a considerable debt of gratitude for helping to ensure that he ascended peacefully to the English throne. Cecil's misgivings about James's plans led him to give underhand support to the Commons in 1604, with the result that James questioned his trustworthiness. Although Cecil was able to allay the king's concerns in the short term, James again grew suspicious when the Commons put up a stiff opposition to his plans to extend English citizenship to his Scottish subjects in 1606. In order to avoid being replaced by Northampton as the king's chief minister, Cecil was forced to placate an angry James. He thereby lost Theobalds, the splendid palace built by his father, causing him to erect a new house at Hatfield, which manor he received by way of exchange from the king. But perhaps the most startling consequence of James's pursuit of the Union lies in the sphere of Catholic treason. The Union provided the Gunpowder plotters with both the opportunity to attack James and a justification for doing so. Had the plot succeeded, it would instantly have put paid to any form of statutory union.

Notes

1 David Calderwood, *History of the Kirk of Scotland* (Wodrow Society, 1845), VI, p. 216.
2 J. Wormald, 'The Union of 1603', in R. A. Mason (ed.), *Scots and Britons: Scottish Political Thought and the Union of 1603* (Cambridge, 1994), p. 37; K. M. Brown, 'The Vanishing Emperor: English Kingship and its Decline, 1603–1707, in *idem*, p. 79.
3 J. F. Larkin and P. L. Hughes (eds), *Stuart Royal Proclamations, Volume I: Royal Proclamations of King James I 1603–1625* (Oxford, 1979), p. 19.
4 *CJ*, I, p. 143.
5 Larkin and Hughes, *Stuart Royal Proclamations*, I, p. 95.
6 *CJ*, I, p. 146.
7 C. Russell, ed. R. Cust and A. Thrush, *James VI and I and his English Parliaments* (Oxford, 2011), p. 32; C. Russell, '1603: the End of English National Sovereignty', in G. Burgess, R. Wymer and J. Lawrence (eds), *The Accession of James I: Historical and Cultural Consequences* (Basingstoke, 2006), p. 11.
8 J. Spedding (ed.), *The Letters and the Life of Francis Bacon, including all his Occasional Works* ... (7 vols, 1861–74), III, p. 77. Bacon's statement caused difficulties for one historian, who argued in spite of it that James did not enter into 'a headlong rush towards union in 1603–4'; B. Galloway, *The Union of England and Scotland, 1603–1608* (Edinburgh, 1986), p. 15.

9 Spedding, *Letters and Life of Francis Bacon*, III, p. 94.
10 C. Russell, 'James VI and Rule over Two Kingdoms: An English View', *Historical Research* 76 (2003), pp. 157–8.
11 *CSPV 1603–1607*, p. 94. However, the severe plague epidemic of that year meant it was not until 31 January 1604 that writs of summons were issued.
12 *LJ*, I, p. 270.
13 Russell, 'James VI and I and Rule over Two Kingdoms', p. 153.
14 *CJ*, I, p. 143; Spedding, *Letters and Life of Francis Bacon*, III, p. 92.
15 Larkin and Hughes, *Stuart Royal Proclamations*, I, p. 95.
16 A. Thrush and J. P. Ferris (eds), *History of Parliament. The House of Commons 1604–29* (6 vols, Cambridge, 2010), V, p. 289; P. Schwyzer, 'The Jacobean Union Controversy and *King Lear*', in Burgess et al., *The Accession of James I*, p. 36; Cadwallader was defeated and killed by Saxon invaders in AD 633.
17 D. Masson (ed.), *The Register of the Privy Council of Scotland, VI: 1599–1604* (Edinburgh, 1884), p. 596 (hereafter *RPCS, 1599–1604*).
18 Larkin and Hughes, *Stuart Royal Proclamations*, I, p. 95.
19 B. P. Levack, 'Law, Sovereignty and the Union', in R. A. Mason (ed.), *Scots and Britons: Scottish Political Thought and the Union of 1603* (Cambridge, 1994), pp. 215, 220.
20 J. Gordon, *EnΩTikon or A Sermon of the Union of Great Brittanie* (1604), p. 28.
21 *CJ*, I, p. 949. The other three were Nathaniel Bacon, Sir John Heigham and Sir Edward Greville.
22 W. C. Trevelyan and Sir Charles Edward Trevelyan, *Trevelyan Papers Part III* (Camden Society, First Series, 105, 1872), p. 67.
23 P. Croft, *King James* (Basingstoke, 2003), p. 54.
24 A similar point was made by Bacon in respect of the Iberian Peninsula, where the various kingdoms were now ruled by a single monarch, the king of Spain.
25 C. R. Kyle (ed.), *Parliaments, Politics and Elections, 1604–1648* (Camden Society, Fifth Series, 17, 2001), p. 67.
26 G. W. T. Omond, *The Early History of the Scottish Union Question* (Edinburgh and London, 1906), p. 28.
27 Galloway, *Union of England and Scotland*, p. 58.
28 W. Cornwallis, *The Miraculous and Happie Union*, sig. D1ᵛ; D. H. Willson (ed.), *The Parliamentary Diary of Robert Bowyer 1606–1607* (Minneapolis, 1931), pp. 259–60.
29 Russell, 'James VI and I and Rule over Two Kingdoms', p. 158.
30 TNA, PRO31/3/37, fo. 112ᵛ; *CJ*, I, 144.
31 TNA, PRO31/3/37, fo. 112ᵛ.
32 Willson, *Parliamentary Diary of Robert Bowyer*, pp. 376–7.
33 Thrush and Ferris, *House of Commons*, V, pp. 390–1, VI, p. 165.
34 Thrush and Ferris, *House of Commons*, IV, p. 576.
35 *CJ*, I, p. 951.
36 Kyle, *Parliaments, Politics and Elections*, p. 67. This method of proceeding had been put before the Scottish privy council three months earlier: *RPCS 1599–1604*, pp. 596–7.
37 *CJ*, I, p. 178.
38 *CJ*, I, p. 186.
39 H.G. Koenigsberger, G. L. Mosse and G. Q. Bowler, *Europe in the Sixteenth Century* (2nd edition, London and New York, 1989), p. 274; Wormald, 'The Union of 1603', p. 31.
40 See, for instance, the remark of the Spanish diplomat the count of Feria in 1558: M. J. Rodríguez-Salgado and S. Adams, 'The Count of Feria's Dispatch to Philip II of 14 November 1558', in *Camden Miscellany XXVIII* (Camden Society, Fourth Series, 29, 1984), pp. 306–7, 334.

41 A. Fraser, *The Gunpowder Plot: Terror and Faith in 1605* (1996), p. 87.
42 W. Ferguson, *Scotland's Relations with England to 1707: A Survey* (Edinburgh, 1977), p. 98; J. Wormald, *Court, Kirk and Community: Scotland 1470–1625* (1981), pp. 60–1.
43 E. Lodge (ed.), *Illustrations of British History, Biography and Manners, in the Reigns of Henry VIII, Edward VI, Mary, Elizabeth and James I*, (3 vols, 2nd edition, 1838), p. 39.
44 For two such reports of Scottish violence, see M. Lee, Jr (ed.), *Dudley Carleton to John Chamberlain, 1603–1624: Jacobean Letters* (New Brunswick, 1972), p. 35; I. H. Jeayes (ed.), *Letters of Philip Gawdy of West Harling, Norfolk, and of London to Various Members of his Family, 1579–1616* (1906), p. 144.
45 *CJ*, I, p. 184.
46 *CJ*, I, p. 177.
47 Thrush and Ferris, *History of Parliament. The House of Commons 1604–1629*, IV, p. 327, V, p. 709.
48 *CJ*, I, 345.
49 Russell, *King James VI and I and his English Parliaments*, p. 14; Fraser, *Gunpowder Plot*, p. 88.
50 Russell, *King James VI and I and his English Parliaments*, p. 87.
51 TNA, SP14/7/29.
52 *CJ*, I, p. 319.
53 H. Ellis (ed.), *Original Letters Illustrative of English History*, First series, III (1824), p. 78. James's letter is also printed, with modernised spelling, in G. P. V. Akrigg (ed.), *Letters of James VI and I* (Berkeley, Los Angeles, London, 1984), p. 211.
54 Wormald, 'Union of 1603', p. 34.
55 N. Cuddy, 'The Revival of the Entourage: the Bedchamber of James I, 1603–1625', in D. Starkey (ed.), *The English Court from the Wars of the Roses to the Civil War* (1987), pp. 173–225.
56 J. Nichols (ed.), *The Progresses Etc. of King James the First* (1828), I, p. *132.
57 Galloway, *Union of England and Scotland*, p. 51; *CJ*, I, p. 949.
58 On taking his leave of the Kirk of Edinburgh in April 1603, James promised to visit Scotland once every three years at least. See Calderwood, *History of the Kirk of Scotland*, VI, p. 216.
59 Anon., *The True Narration of the Entertainment of his Royall Maiestie, from the Time of his Departure from Edenbrough; till his Receiving at London* ... (1603), sig. B4ᵛ; M. S. Giuseppi et al. (eds), *Calendar of the Manuscripts of the Most Honourable the Marquess of Salisbury* ... (24 vols, HMC, 1888–1976), XV, p. 44; McClure, *LJC*, I, p. 193.
60 *CSPV 1603–1607*, pp. 33, 41, 56; Giuseppi, *Calendar of the Manuscripts of* ... *the Marquess of Salisbury*, XV, p. 132; A. J. Loomie (ed.), *Spain and the Jacobean Catholics I: 1603–1612* (Catholic Record Society, 64, 1973), p. 7.
61 Lodge, *Illustrations of British History*, III, p. 54; *CSPV 1603–1607*, p. 106.
62 *CSPV 1603–1607*, p. 106; Longleat, Thynne Papers, VII, fo. 298ʳ.
63 *CSPV 1603–1607*, p. 153; J. Maidment (ed.), *Letters and State Papers during the Reign of King James the Sixth* (Abbotsford Club, Edinburgh, 1838), p. 61. Huntly, though, subsequently denied giving James cause for offence.
64 Bruce Galloway described English concern over offices as 'Commons' propaganda': Galloway, *Union of England and Scotland*, p. 23.
65 P. E. McCullough, *Sermons at Court: Politics and Religion in Elizabethan and Jacobean Preaching* (Cambridge, 1998), pp. 106–7.
66 *CSPV 1603-1607*, p. 148; *CJ*, I, pp. 177, 955. The Venetian ambassador did not state explicitly that he was referring to the Lords, but we can be certain that he was as the Commons did not sit on 16 April.

67 Kyle, *Parliament, Politics and Elections*, p. 97; Akrigg, *Letters of King James VI and I*, p. 236.
68 Galloway, *Union of England and Scotland*, p. 17.
69 *CJ*, I, p. 360.
70 J. D. Mackie, '"A Loyall Subiectes Advertisment" as to the Unpopularity of James I's Government in England, 1603–4', *SHR* 23 (1925), p. 3.
71 *CSPV 1607–1610*, p. 137.
72 *CJ*, I, pp. 187, 958; Galloway, *Union of England and Scotland*, p. 29. For an illuminating discussion of the problem posed by England's and Scotland's divergent successions, and for an explanation as to why the king could not resolve the problem by statutory means, see Russell, '1603: the End of English National Sovereignty', pp. 4–5.
73 M. L. Bush, *The Government Policy of Protector Somerset* (1975), p. 10; Galloway, *Union of England and Scotland*, p. 9.
74 C. Russell, *An Intelligent Person's Guide to Liberalism* (1999), p. 41.
75 Russell, 'James VI and I and Rule over Two Kingdoms', p. 160.
76 Russell, '1603: The End of English National Sovereignty', p. 7.
77 A. Thrush, *The History of Parliament. The House of Commons 1604–1629: An Introductory Survey* (Cambridge, 2010), p. 173.
78 *CJ*, I, pp. 952, 957.
79 *CSPV 1603–1607*, p. 148.
80 *CSPV 1603–1607*, p. 139.
81 A. Thrush (ed.), *History of Parliament. The House of Lords 1604–1629* (3 vols, Cambridge 2021), I, pp. 17–19, 313–14.
82 *CSPV 1607–1610*, p. 36.
83 F. H. Blackburne Daniell et al. (eds), *The Manuscripts of his Grace the Duke of Portland* ... (10 vols, 1891–1919), IX, pp. 12–13; *CSPV 1603–1607*, p. 151.
84 Ferguson, *Scotland's Relations with England*, p. 101. But cf. A. R. MacDonald, 'Consultation and Consent Under James VI', *Historical Journal* 54 (2011), p. 300 ('As early as the first post-union parliament, at Perth in 1604, there was disquiet over the planned incorporating union with England'); K. M. Brown and A. J. Mann, 'Introduction: Parliament and Politics in Scotland, 1567–1707', in K. M. Brown and A. J. Mann (eds), *Parliament and Politics in Scotland, 1567–1707* (Edinburgh, 2005), p. 27 ('on the issue of the union the Scottish parliament was equally unenthusiastic, even if it avoided direct opposition and preferred to allow English MPs to take the lead in wrecking James's project').
85 McCullough, *Sermons at Court*, p. 109.
86 *CJ*, I, p. 361.
87 *CSPV 1607–1610*, p. 27.
88 *CJ*, I, p. 171.
89 Larkin and Hughes, *Stuart Royal Proclamations, I*, p. 95.
90 *CSPV 1603–1607*, p. 201.
91 G. Donaldson, *The Scottish Reformation* (Cambridge, 1960), pp. 203, 212–13, 219, 223.
92 Wormald, *Court, Kirk, and Community*, pp. 128–9; Galloway, *Union of England and Scotland*, pp. 6, 24.
93 R. A. Mason, 'George Buchanan, James VI and the Presbyterians', in Mason, *Scots and Britons*, p. 121; A. R. MacDonald, *The Jacobean Kirk, 1567–1625: Sovereignty, Polity and Liturgy* (Aldershot, Brookfield USA and Sydney, 1998), pp. 88, 104.
94 Galloway, *Union of England and Scotland*, pp. 24–5.
95 Maidment, *Letters and State Papers during the Reign of James the Sixth*, p. 60.

96 Calderwood, *History of the Kirk of Scotland*, VI, p. 669.
97 C. Russell, *The Causes of the English Civil War* (Oxford, 1990), p. 42; MacDonald, *Jacobean Kirk*, p. 104.
98 *CSPV 1607–1610*, p. 36.
99 *CJ*, I, p. 358.
100 *CSPV 1603–1607*, p. 485.
101 McClure, *LJC*, I, p. 273. See also *CSPV 1607–1610*, p. 137.
102 A. Thrush, 'Commons v. Chancery: The 1604 Buckinghamshire Election Dispute Revisited', *Parliamentary History* 26 (2007), pp. 306–8.
103 TNA, PRO31/3/37, fo. 112ᵛ.
104 Russell, 'James VI and I and Rule over Two kingdoms', p. 159.
105 Sir William Fraser, *The Elphinstone Family Book of the Lords Elphinstone, Balmerino and Coupar* (2 vols, Edinburgh, 1897), II, p. 170. For a fuller discussion of this little-known letter, see Thrush, *House of Lords 1604–1629*, II, p. 522.
106 Giuseppi, *Calendar of the Manuscripts of … the Marquess of Salisbury*, XVI, p. 254; Russell, *James VI and I and his English Parliaments*, pp. 15–16.
107 S. Alford, *Burghley: William Cecil at the Court of Elizabeth I* (New Haven and London, 2011), p. 134.
108 S. R. Gardiner, *History of England* (London, New York and Bombay, 1905), I, p. 177.
109 This and the next two paragraphs are based upon my entries on Robert Cecil and Henry Howard in *House of Lords, 1604–1629*, II, pp. 535–7; III, p. 155.
110 M. Nicholls, 'Strategy and Motivation in the Gunpowder Plot', *Historical Journal* 50 (2007), p. 792.
111 In his journal of the 1576 session of the 1572–81 Parliament, the diarist Thomas Cromwell noted of the first day of sitting that the 'the queene came not to the House' because it was a meeting held after a prorogation: T. E. Hartley (ed.), *Proceedings in the Parliaments of Elizabeth I: Volume 1, 1558–1581* (Leicester, 1981), p. 476.
112 Hartley (ed.), *Parliaments of Elizabeth I: Volume 1*, pp. 123–8, 525–6.
113 Calderwood, *History of the Kirk of Scotland*, VI, p. 362.
114 S. R. Gardiner, *What Gunpowder Plot Was* (London, New York and Bombay, 1897), pp. 36, 38. Gardiner also observed that this same information points to the authenticity of Fawkes's confession, as none of the commissioners detailed to interrogate Fawkes would have dared invent such a claim. I am grateful to Steven Clarke for drawing my attention to Fawkes's confession.
115 Russell, *James VI and I and His English Parliaments*, p. 62.
116 A. Thrush, 'The Personal Rule of James I, 1611–1620', in T. Cogswell, R. Cust and P. Lake (eds), *Politics, Religion and Popularity* (Cambridge, 2002), p. 84.
117 Henry E. Huntington Library, California, EL1763.
118 E. R. Foster (ed.), *Proceedings in Parliament, 1610: Volume 1, House of Lords* (New Haven and London, 1966), p. 279.
119 For a detailed exploration of this theme, see Thrush, 'Personal Rule of James I', pp. 84–102; and A. Thrush, 'The French Marriage and the Origins of the 1614 Parliament', in S. Clucas and R. Davies (eds) *The Crisis of 1614 and The Addled Parliament: Literary and Historical Perspectives* (Aldershot and Burlington, 2003), pp. 25–35.
120 MacDonald, 'James VI and I, the Church of Scotland, and British Ecclesiastical Convergence', *Historical Journal* 48 (2005); L. A. M. Stewart, 'The Political Repercussions of the Five Articles of Perth: A Reassessment of James VI and I's Religious Policies in Scotland', *Sixteenth Century* Journal 38 (2007).

4

JAMES VI AND I

A Corrupt Reign or the Reign of Anti-Corruption?

David Chan Smith

Among the more remarkable, but little noticed accomplishments of James VI and I was the generation of an unprecedented archive of early modern administrative corruption in England. The king's widening financial deficit, increased by the expenses of his household and his generous gifts to courtiers, stimulated inquiries into royal administration throughout the reign and led to concerns about malfeasance and misappropriation. Similar inquiries in Scotland had followed on the expansion of central government and the royal household as expenditures outran revenues.[1] His ministers in both countries scrambled to track expenses, discover new sources of income and reduce waste.[2] In England, the papers of Sir Julius Caesar, filled with scribblings about outgoings and incoming revenues, are perhaps the best-known results, but investigations into the navy, the ordnance office, the household, crown lands, timber rights, the Exchequer and the commissions on fees shed even more light on suspected abuses and fraud.

Despite these efforts and several sensational trials of royal officials for peculation, corruption and not anti-corruption has long defined judgements of the reign in England. S. R. Gardiner flatly concluded that 'James's indolence and favouritism had made his court a hotbed of corruption'.[3] Ministerial effort and the gathering of detailed administrative information, unfortunately, did not lead to the fundamental reform of royal finances under James. But the investigations, nonetheless, revealed many practices that contemporaries believed were corrupt, and left historians with a complex body of polemic and data that can inform our understanding of James's kingship and government. This chapter explores how recent perspectives on corruption can direct new approaches to this archive and with them, fruitful examinations of the

DOI: 10.4324/9781003319764-5

tensions over political and legal authority that characterised James's reigns in both England and Scotland.

I James I of England – A Reign of Corruption?

From the earliest accounts of the English reign, there have been no shortage of descriptions of the court as a 'hotbed of corruption' filled with rapacious and oleaginous characters.[4] Corruption oozed from every corner, from the Bedchamber to the council, and leaked in from foreign sources. Spanish gold bought peace yet made the country lazy and unvirtuous.[5] Gifts showered on the earls of Suffolk and Northampton by the king laid the foundations of their mansions.[6] Scottish courtiers retained access through the royal Bedchamber to their 'auld kinge' to beg favour and gifts. Francis Osborne, a court observer, decried this 'beggarly rable attending his Majesty…'.[7] But even Sir Anthony Weldon recognised that while the Scots did well, English courtiers who could also bend the king's ear did better.[8] James was not much help curbing corruption on these accounts – quite the opposite. Although most modern historians have differed from Gardiner on the topic of James's dedication (or lack of it) to work, few have doubted his weakness with money. As Robert Ashton dryly observed: 'from the financial point of view the very presence of James on the throne was emergency enough in itself'.[9] Contemporaries likewise described James's generosity in critical terms. The Venetian ambassador, Antonio Foscarini, explained in 1618 that the king 'takes so much pleasure in giving that it rarely happens that he does not readily grant whatever is asked. Accordingly he has seriously reduced the royal income, loading it with debts, and reduced the treasury from wealth to poverty'.[10] The king was also known for his generosity, even carelessness with money, in Scotland. This was the moral of the story about his tutor George Buchanan, who, displeased with his student's slipshod eagerness to sign petitions, inserted a grant for James's signature that made Buchanan king for a fortnight.[11] Similarly in England, contemporary critics interpreted this excessive gift-giving as a sign of a deeper personal weakness. The king's 'timorous disposition' made him vulnerable to those 'progging for suits' and foreign agents corrupting the court, a weakness compounded by his love of hunting and homosociability.[12]

James's reign over a gift-sprent court incentivised rent-seeking, embezzlement and competition for patronage. This mad and bad spending usefully explains why corruption was so prominent under James following the 'parsimony' and careful governance of Elizabeth.[13] A host of new patents, offices and monopolies transmitted this peculation to the nation at large. Osborne described how the '*nation* grew *feeble*, and over opprest with *Impositions, Monopolies, Aydes, Privy Seales, Concealments, pretermitted Customes etc…* with a multitude of *tricks* more to cheat the English subject'.[14] The consequences were profound and long lasting. Weldon concluded that 'the poore King and State [were] cheated on all hands'.[15] By 'letting loose the golden reignes of discipline, held by his predecessors with so strict a hand; he opened the first gap unto those confusions...' that led to civil war.[16] Osborne was even blunter: the king brought 'the crowne into so great a necessity through a profuse prodigality, [that he] became the originall of his son's fall'.[17] His folly stimulated an environment of corruption; as Gardiner described it, 'his own life was virtuous and upright. But he contrived to surround himself with those who were neither virtuous nor upright'.[18] Gardiner no doubt had in mind the Bedchamber, which was largely populated by Scots.[19] Their access to the royal signature granting pensions and gifts made the Bedchamber an engine of patronage while attracting charges of corruption.[20] Those around the court were keeping track: an accounting of gifts given to Scottish courtiers, for example, was discovered in Sir Edward Coke's papers after the judge's death.[21]

This assessment of James and his rule is the crux of two subsequent interpretations of his English reign. In the older, the corrupt pursuit of lucre and power by courtiers and officials prompted parliament to respond first with complaints about monopolists and other grievances over official misconduct, and then with action. The prime mover was a critical, more assertive House of Commons that attempted to hold abusive and corrupt ministers to account with the revival of impeachment proceedings. Apprehensions about corruption become, in this narrative, a rising and rival source of authority in the early Stuart polity.[22]

The second, narrative revises this interpretation by demonstrating the close linkages between court factions and parliamentarians. Impeachments and trials for corruption were 'almost invariably' partisan actions, managed by leading courtiers and factions who cloaked their power plays under the rhetoric of good government.[23] This 'new political history' has also revealed a destabilising distribution of patronage in the Stuart polity. Early in James's English reign the pattern of governance was Elizabethan, with able ministers advising the king from their perches around the council table. With Salisbury's death, however, corruption began to spread as Jacobean kingship descended into favouritism, culminating in Buckingham's dominance over patronage.[24] The duke's control over the direction of spoils-sharing among the elite produced accusations of corruption by those jealous of his influence, a trend that ultimately weakened the legitimacy of the Jacobean and then Caroline regimes.[25] Wider public apprehensions about the power of the duke and the bad counsel given to James prompted conspiracy theories about Spanish and French corruption of the court and a growing mistrust of royal government that eventually led to violence, spectacularly so in the case of Buckingham's assassination in 1628.[26]

Corruption has long been an interpretative lens to understand Jacobean ideas about rulership, but these narratives have limitations. First, they focus largely on the court and the 'grand' corruption of ministers such as the earl of Suffolk or rampaging patentees hauled before parliament. Yet, royal investigations revealed significant petty corruption that detracted from crown revenues in ways that contemporaries believed were illegitimate or illegal. Second, the study of corruption under James has almost exclusively focused on England. James VI's reign in Scotland has been described as an 'undoubted success', marking the transition from a personal, decentralised government, to a more bureaucratic and centralised state.[27] Yet, Scotland also offers an important comparison to English developments, because James experienced similar financial pressures in that country that were also associated with his court and state building. Third, histories of corruption during the period are almost exclusively about political or official corruption. Yet corruption was broadly understood in the sixteenth and seventeenth centuries, encompassing religious corruption, corruption of the body, and belief in patterns of social corruption and degeneration.[28] Charges of corruption packed a punch because they invoked this complex of meanings about degeneration, decay, disease and sin. This was especially meaningful in English and Scottish societies of the period, which aspired to norms of order and sought religious sanction for worldly authority. Corruption had particularly formidable import because critics represented the abuse of office or legal power as deeply unjust and even irreligious acts.

Finally, a concentration on the political has led some historians to dismiss contemporary accounts of corruption as largely rhetorical, cynical charges in a zugzwang of public shaming meant to corner the accused. Joel Hurstfield notably took up this line of criticism, observing that corruption is 'but a subjective thing' and 'obscures rather than illumines the issues which confront historians'.[29] He rightly noted that historians and other researchers often either vaguely defined corruption or imposed modern norms of administrative behaviour onto the past where values were different.[30] These oversights led to interpretations that much pre-modern officeholding was either very corrupt (by modern standards) or there was little meaningful corruption (because most officeholders normally engaged in 'corrupt' behaviours such as venality).[31] Hurstfield himself defined corruption as the 'subversion' of the state's purpose and duty to provide for the 'welfare of all its members'. This (rather modern and broad) definition enabled Hurstfield to demonstrate corruption's limitations as an analytical category in a world where the intermingling of patronage and public office compromised the state's objectives.[32]

The challenge is, therefore, to understand corruption as those at the time would have interpreted it: that is, to recognise that their ideas of corruption, though different from our own, are analytically valuable. Much of their value lies in their very subjectivity. Different people often see corruption in divergent ways and their attempts to persuade others point to an implicit negotiation over right conduct and moral values. These values, sometimes normative, sometimes heterodox, but always related to beliefs about fairness and integrity, are used to interpret behaviours or conditions in the world. Ideas of political corruption, in particular, ultimately depend on imagining 'what uncorrupted politics might be'.[33] The moral frames that people use to interpret corruption are highly particular to culture, place and time and there is not always consensus within a society about these values. The historiography of late Tudor England has explored, for example, the evolving role of civic republicanism and ideas of political virtue that informed beliefs about the rightful use of power.[34] But political corruption is not only a discursive game: corruption involves behaviours and interests that are felt as real and harmful by those who are aggrieved by them.

The process of persuasion and contestation reveals where values and interests may align or not at a particular moment in a society.[35] Mark Knights's study of Samuel Pepys's defence of his official conduct, for example, explores how the 'clashing definitions of corruption' played out in the 'public sphere' of Restoration England.[36] The study of corruption can also illuminate changing ideas of office and political conduct over time. There was, of course, a very different line between public and private in early modern Britain: modern Weberian bureaucracies uphold the principle that officials are public servants who should exercise their offices disinterestedly. Early modern offices, in contrast, might be the property of individuals, who bought and sold them with the expectation of private enrichment rather than the performance of public duties. Officials took home their records and pocketed fees associated with their positions.[37] This weak separation between public and private also went the other way: the chief financial officers in Scotland were personally responsible for the crown's debts.[38] Yet the early seventeenth century saw an increasing insistence on a distinction between public responsibility and private interest.[39] A culture of public service, in which the officeholder owed a duty beyond the person of the monarch to a more abstract commonwealth, may also have been emerging among those educated in humanist ideas about the public good.[40] Early modern English and Scots could certainly conceive of corruption using a distinction between private interest and public responsibility, a contrast Coke invoked in the impeachment of Sir Giles Mompesson in 1621: 'There is (you have heard) the public good pretended but a private intended'.[41]

Recognising this changing understanding of corruption provides insights into how political institutions and the values that underpin them also transform over time.[42] Tracing these types of changes has, for example, contributed to the emergence of a modernisation thesis in which a sharper, Weberian distinction between public office-holding and private self-interest emerged in the nineteenth century. Continental historians of corruption, especially of Dutch corruption, have focused on the dilemma that caught early modern officeholders in a conflict of values. Officers understood that they had public duties, but also had a responsibility to provide for themselves, families and clients.[43] These patrimonial values might harmonise with public duty even as they also sometimes undercut them. This overlapping and occasionally conflicting system of normative values was eventually resolved in the emergence of a nineteenth-century impersonal bureaucracy that hardened the distinction between public and private. James's reign arguably came at an important point in this slow transition. But to understand this transition, it is first necessary to understand the several ways that James and his contemporaries defined corruption.

II Broadening Early Modern Corruption

Early modern ideas of corruption were sophisticated. Corruption in the sense of defilement or filthiness, *truailliú* in Irish-Gaelic and *truaillidheachd* in Scots-Gaelic, was a frequently lamented phenomenon in early modern Britain. Corruption in early modern England broadly meant decline, decay or the drawing away from an idealised purity, as well as having many more specific meanings.[44] To corrupt was, as Thomas Elyot's dictionary in 1538 defined it, to 'viciate, to destroy, to suborne, to tempte, or procure by gyftes'.[45] Such a ubiquitous phenomenon took many forms. Corruption was a process of decay occurring in nature and in medicine in the corruption of the humours or the air.[46] Commentators, steeped in a religious culture of original sin and the Fall, acknowledged the inevitability of corruption as part of the human condition. John Spottiswoode bewailed, 'for what is it that was ever put in the hands of men to use, that hath not been corrupted?'[47] It was a common word in the confessional disputes of the time, signalling both a threat to the purity of religious belief as well as to the safety of the kingdom.[48] Among early modern Protestants, Peter Lake and Michael Questier have argued, 'popery became a symbol for all sorts of corruption, all sorts of threats to the commonweal'.[49]

Contemporaries summoned up and creatively combined meanings and analogies about corruption from political, religious, medicinal and natural languages. When offering advice about reforming Church corruption, the authors of the Millenary Petition explicitly quoted James that 'the king, as a good physician, must first know what peccant humours his patient naturally is most subject unto, before he can begin his cure'.[50] Unlike modern political approaches to corruption, which have been described as 'de-moralised' and overly technocratic, early moderns strongly held to the moral import of corruption as signalling physical, spiritual and moral deviance, abuse or immorality.[51] They read from Aristotle and Polybius, for example, a process of political decline resulting from the moral corruption of luxury and wealth – a diagnosis that contemporaries sometimes applied to Stuart England. James himself noted that, just as all human bodies suffered disease, in every body politic there were 'naturally enclined corruptions'.[52] These metaphors and beliefs fed into those anti-corruption languages that checked official behaviour and the exercise of power. The springs of these languages of appropriate conduct were numerous. Humanism and civic republicanism have been the most studied.[53] Others drew from traditional complaints about lordly power, beliefs about good counsel, the necessity of honourable service and religious ideas about the sanctity of authority.[54]

Observers applied these ideas about right conduct as lenses to interpret the behaviours of officials.[55] While Elyot explicitly mentioned bribery (the modern offence most associated with political corruption), corruption also encompassed a constellation of misdeeds that included subornation, abuse, oppression, usurpation, exaction and especially extortion.[56] This conceptual field shared a common root: the misuse or abuse of authority and power.[57] Statute and common law had remedies for these misuses, most notably Magna Carta (1215, 1297) and the Statute of Westminster (1275).[58] Likewise, the statutes of 18 Edward II, c. 4 and 20 Edward III, c. 1 sought to curb the partiality of judges, and required them to swear to 'do equal law and execution of right to all ... rich or poor', and not, 'take fee nor robe of any man ... and ... no gift or reward by themselves, nor by other ... of any man that hath to do before them by any way, except meat and drink, and that of small value'.[59]

The distinction between a gift or gratuity (acceptable) and a bribe became an especially contentious issue under James, with bribery seen as a particular vice of the judiciary.[60] Wilfrid Prest's analysis of the legal culture of the period led him to conclude 'that judicial corruption was a fact of life in pre-Civil War England, and that barristers played an integral role as go-betweens in the corrupt relationships of judges with litigants'.[61] Over time, the practice of gift-giving by litigants became unacceptable, marking a change in the norms of belief about corruption. James's reign was part of this inflection point in ideas about corruption in early modern Britain, a debate shaped by legal change and religious discord, as well as economic and financial changes that altered the culture of office-holding and service. Political and legal corruption was not only a breach of trust, but a misuse of divinely sanctioned authority, a misdeed committed, in the conventional phrasing, 'by colour of office'. As law became used for more instrumental ends, charges about private interest masked under public purposes became more acute. Through James's kingship and his efforts at anti-corruption, we can discern these larger structural shifts that were slowly transforming ideas of corruption and eroding trust in royal government.

III Corruption and Reform in England

When James travelled down from Scotland on his way to London in early 1603, he immediately encountered complaints about corruption in England.[62] Among the 'infinite number' of petitions that sought favour and preferment, there were also those that pleaded for reform and pointed to abuses and embezzlement within royal administration.[63] Their evidence suggests a popular belief that the powerful had enriched themselves from the Elizabethan war state to such extent that they 'might pay the queenes debts, because … they gathered enough under hir'.[64] One petition, written by puritans who were preoccupied with temporal corruption, supplies details of some of these complaints as well as proposals for reform. A major issue, for example, was the pluralism of office-holders and doubts about their qualifications, 'by means whereof your highness also is defrauded of your service, and other worthy men of there reward'. Other concerns included the sale of offices, frauds in the royal customs, and the abuses of purveyors of the royal household who used their powers to extort the localities. Royal lands were sold at great discount to the diminution of the revenue, while the fees and ambitions of lawyers led to doubts about their probity and the integrity of legal process. The petitioners also noted abuses in Church offices, including bribery and the purchase of ecclesiastical offices through the intervention 'of ladies of the court for petite bribes of velvet gowns'.[65] Collectors of recusancy fines and their patrons made arrangements with recusants to keep them solvent, if only to mulct them the longer, yet this was a corruption that maintained popery. Similar complaints can be found in other early petitions to the king.[66] These documents underscore how far concerns about official corruption had been alive and well under Elizabeth, despite attempts to represent her as a busy reformer restraining the excesses of her household.[67] Mainstream accounts of the period almost inevitably took up these claims in order to strike a contrast with the reign of James.[68] Yet even under the queen there were complaints about the power of favourites such as Leicester and Essex, and the abuses committed by royal officers, especially William Cecil.[69] The petitions of 1603 reflect these alternative perceptions of the Elizabethan state that James inherited that still await exploration.

Second, the complaints aired in 1603 draw attention to the scope of fraudulent and extortionate practices. The grand corruption of the court and courtiers figured prominently to be sure, but petitioners also inveighed against abuses in the localities. They highlighted the petty corruption of local officers, church courts, local courts, and especially among purveyors. Evidence suggests that their grievances were not wide of the mark. Robert Fletcher, the chief cart-taker among the purveyors who gathered supplies for the royal household, provided something of an exposé about corruption among his subordinates to the earl of Northampton in 1605. He described how he had given his deputies a rousing speech, declaring that they had sworn an oath to serve a 'sacrid king. If wee do keep our hands pure from brybery and corruption, his Majesty will give us more forth of his princely liberality in one ower then we have or can obtain unto by bribery in all our lyves howe long so ever'. Unfortunately, Fletcher soon afterwards came down ill and his underlings did not rely on the promise of princely liberality, instead obtaining warrants and extorting the country 'for their own private gayn ... under pretext of that sleight authoritie ...'.[70]

Finally, these petitions articulate why these practices were thought corrupt. The petitioners were angered by those who used legal authority to impinge on the rights of other subjects, such as officers like purveyors who used their powers to take goods at below market rates, and those who foreclosed opportunities to others by pluralism and inside dealing. They also reveal assumptions that were out of step with the economic realities of the time: that a single office and its revenues were enough to support its officeholder.

How did James respond? Just as in religious affairs, there was a presumption that the king would reform grievances and chart a new course after Elizabeth. Though James's reforming efforts were of a magnitude different from what had come before, their outcome was disappointing. It would be a reign of both corruption and anti-corruption, demonstrating the limitations of royal authority within a political structure requiring many compromises for its political stability and a king particularly sensitive to those arrangements.

IV State Building and Corruption in a European Context

In his pursuit of reform, James faced the broad structural insufficiency of royal finance to keep pace with inflation and the costs of warfare, and the growth of a highly competitive patronage market.[71] These were European-wide problems that transformed governments in France and Spain.[72] Ministers in England and Scotland were likewise 'enterprising' in their search for financial innovations to meet shortfalls, and they introduced new forms of taxation and reward, strategies that were of a piece with those of other monarchies.[73] These measures, in turn, though necessary to finance the state and elicit support from the social elites on which the crown relied, presented new opportunities for the entrepreneurial whose activities raised complaints about corruption and abuse.[74]

James had already negotiated similar changes in Scotland as he sought to assert stronger central government over magnates and the localities there.[75] The expansion of the royal reach demanded administrative expertise and institutional changes, such as the establishment of a permanent exchequer in 1584 and the recruitment of 'meane men' for administration, often with training in law.[76] As would be the case in England, the competition for royal patronage accelerated with the growth in offices and royal resources. Those in the household and the administration contended to obtain gifts, offices and 'proffitable causualties'.[77] While work on patronage and officeholders under James in Scotland 'remains to be done', these rewards and gifts were tools to influence magnates and elites.[78] At the same time, the expense of the royal household and the effect of inflation meant that the ordinary revenue no longer covered expenditures, producing a series of fiscal crises. Attempts to reduce costs while continuing to provide patronage frequently involved struggles over the royal signature and the approval of grants.[79] Similarly, projects meant to increase crown revenues were often politically fraught and administratively difficult. In Scotland these took the form of revocations, the improvement of crown lands, and the expansion of the customs. Jacobean officials would pursue similar reforms in England.[80] The major financial change in Scotland, however, was James's departure south. This move significantly lowered expenses for his household and introduced a period of relative financial stability.[81] The Scottish experience suggests that the sources of complaints about corruption in England were as much to do with general structural shifts facing Renaissance states as James's personal inclinations for an intimate household and rampant gift-giving.[82]

England, a precociously centralised state, also experienced the challenges of inflation, warfare and the costs of elite patronage. Inflation, in particular, eroded the value of royal revenues, so that James 'inherited a financial system which was already close to the point of breakdown'.[83] The revenues of the crown were in the main derived from the royal domain and the customs, and extraordinary supply from parliament where need arose. Yet as Conrad Russell has observed, these traditional sources, saving the customs, did not necessarily float with economic growth to counter rising inflation. Instead, their real value declined over time and attempts to make adjustments often produced political tension.[84] By the eighteenth century, most government revenue was composed of indirect taxes, such as customs and excise, and regular direct taxation voted by the parliament. James's reign lay at the beginning of that point of transition from an old revenue regime to a newer, more flexible structure. James quickly discovered that wholesale reform was difficult and, unlike in France, English ministers did not encourage the widespread creation and sale of offices.[85] They turned instead to expedients, especially the one-time sale of crown lands, and financial experiments such as monopolies, patents and economic projects aimed at retrenchment and revenue growth.[86]

The pressure of inflation on incomes and the availability of royal grants of legal rights and offices encouraged self-dealing among officials and presented opportunities for resourceful courtiers. Inflation, for example, devalued salaries and fees, and thereby motivated officials to find new ways to make money from their positions, or to compete for more offices and patents.[87] The crown was willing to experiment with novel forms of reward to avoid increasing salaries or creating large numbers of new offices.[88] Projectors meanwhile promised the government that their schemes – some wild, some sensible – would raise additional cash. The competition for royal bounty may also have intensified due to demographic growth, resulting in an increase in underlying demand.[89] Richard Hoyle has observed the intensity of this pressure on James, that is, in 'the sheer number of petitions received by the monarch and the pressure on him to make grants of "new offices for the benefit of a private man"'.[90]

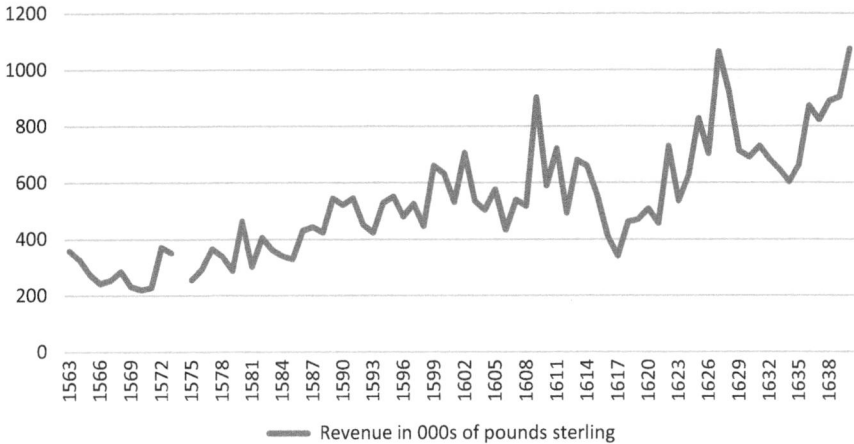

FIGURE 4.1   Revenue of the English crown, 1563–1640.

Source: P. K. O'Brien and P. A. Hunt, *Data prepared on English revenues, 1485–1815* (https://www.esfdb.org/table.aspx?resourceid=12030)

Many of these grants became magnets for charges of corruption.[91] Although both James and Salisbury condemned projectors at one time or another, projects remained a prominent innovation in royal finance and quickly became a by-word for corruption.[92] The burst of regulatory legislation towards the later sixteenth century had shown how law might be used instrumentally to reach social or economic ends.[93] Projectors proposed schemes that sought legal authority or the creation of offices in order to deliver some service to the crown or public, but typically with their own private gain principally in mind. Nor were projectors alone in these pursuits: the growing incorporation of towns, economic societies, and commercial trades benefited insiders at the cost of 'freedom of trade' or the rights of others to engage in their economic livelihoods.[94] These grants often came with public authority: monopolists, for example, had powers to enforce their privileges, sometimes to secure their private profits. Those offended by the enforcement of these grants could in turn bring grievances to parliament about oppressions and extortions, and the wrongful exercise of power. These complaints utilised the language of the public good and commonwealth, making such financial experiments politically inexpedient while stimulating an anti-corruption discourse.[95]

The evidence of Star Chamber suits reveals some of the many cases alleging extortion and oppression that were brought before the courts. While these accusations were sometimes made simply to move the case within the Star Chamber's jurisdiction, Louis Knafla noted the large number of suits for judicial corruption and abuses in his close study of Star Chamber suits in

Kent.[96] These cases touched constables, JPs, county sheriffs and town bailiffs as well as lawyers who were charged with frauds and barratry. Though historians have often seen corruption as a phenomenon of court politics or royal policy, the wider frame of a changing society and its approach to legal rights, patronage and grants suggest a shifting attitude to law, that is, away from law as a moral domain of justice or law that is discovered, to a more instrumental, positivist view of legal resources.

However, it was not always the aggrieved subject who was harmed by the abusive official or patentee. There are different forms of corruption and under James there were many incentives and methods to divert money from the crown that received quiet, popular approbation. Forms of corruption that involved crown revenue, such as the underassessment of subsidies or the misuse of royal resources such as forests, may have suited most and certainly drew fewer complaints.[97] Petty corruption in the localities might be tolerated so long as only the royal revenues were harmed. Many of the gentry were improving landlords themselves and were well aware of the underperformance of the crown estates and the lucrative possibilities of their purchase and exploitation – why encourage the crown to better manage them?[98] Petty corruption also had its own political dynamic. Writing about the situation in Ireland, Sir Robert Jacob, the solicitor general, sought to improve the revenue by restoring the part 'subtracted and purloined by sheriffs, undersheriffs, collectors, clerks and other office'.[99] Remedying these arrangements, which were effectively forms of political compromise, was difficult for two reasons. First, the crown depended on these officials in the localities, including stewards and bailiffs, and they often had little formal remuneration. Second, there was not much incentive for anyone to complain and, therefore, these frauds were harder to discover.

V James the Reformer?

This was James's predicament in England. His personality and experience in Scotland conditioned his response. By the light of modern historiography, James is now acknowledged as a curious, learned man.[100] He was a successful king of Scotland who was particularly canny in his dealings with the serpentine complexities of politics and confessional divisions there.[101] Though his love of the hunt (and the cost of restoring hunting lodges) remains a fact, in England he was nonetheless hard-working and attended to government.[102] His reputed deviousness may well have been a response to the treacherous politics of his day, especially the experiences of his youth in Scotland, and a learned ability to shape his arguments 'as a form of dissimulation'.[103] Even hostile assessments of James rarely described him as personally corrupt. Bishop Goodman opined of James that 'no man living did ever love an honest man more than he did'.[104] Yet no one has been able to exonerate James from the charge of careless or hapless overspending, though this was arguably also the case with many of his predecessors.[105]

James may have given so freely to elicit loyalty and in keeping with his perception of political needs.[106] Royal generosity answered cultural expectations that monarchs should offer rewards in the form of pensions, offices, patents and other emoluments to 'well deserving servants'.[107] James himself advised the use of 'trew liberalitie in rewarding the good', yet he also cautioned about the need to calibrate grants in proportion to 'ranke deserts, and necessitie'.[108] These rewards motivated servants, courtiers and officials and functioned to 'yoke together public service and personal effort in a manner which simultaneously yielded public good and private gain'.[109] James was conscious of the dangers of overspending, warning in Scotland that this would weaken the royal estate.[110] The same caution could be read in the *Book of Bountie*, published in England, which observed that excessive grants would lead the crown to 'lay burdens on Our People'.[111] By assigning royal bounty, James was undertaking the duties of a monarch and he knew the risks attending excessive gift-giving. Why then did he seem to give too much?

James, a foreign king whose succession had been questioned, may have felt vulnerable in England. He cultivated a politics of intimacy and reward that he had used successfully prior to 1603. In Scotland, James had created a close circle of intimates through his Chamber and cultivated personal relationships with leading magnates.[112] James introduced his Scottish model of kingship into the more formal atmosphere of English court life with less success.[113] While in both Scotland and England, this close, privileged circle supported the king personally and politically, it was also expensive, raising pressure to reduce costs or find additional sources of patronage.[114] Yet this generosity was a glue binding the financial self-interest of elites to his rule, and holding together a network of 'trusted servitors'.[115] The king himself alluded to this motive, noting that 'money is like muck, not good, unless it be spread'.[116] Contemporaries similarly observed that this use of patronage among elites was calculated to secure loyalty and to knit together the Anglo-Scottish elite.[117] Bishop Goodman explained that the king's gifts to the Scots 'might be accompanied with prudence, and such political ends; and no doubt but the Scots had formerly very far engaged themselves, and showed great forwardness in defence of his title to this crown'.[118] The flow of money and grants, moreover, was supposedly exchanged among the Scots and the English, and 'the deadly feud between the two nations was utterly forgotten'.[119] What may have been excessive giving also fulfilled the most crucial public purpose of all: securing loyalty to the crown and the stability of the regime. This fountain of patronage, however, may have stimulated ever greater greed in James's courtiers.

As monarch, James sat at the pinnacle of an aggressive and competitive patronage market in England and increasingly in Scotland. Ministers such as Salisbury and Northampton were beset with requests for patronage and sought to build their following by promoting clients in the competition for royal resources.[120] The more so James, who, after all, dispensed the choicest plums: there were 2,500 offices with fees valued at up to 40% of the crown's revenue available for patronage.[121] The desire to enrich or establish a patrimony, or simply to gain status, stimulated an interest among suitors in discovering in royal resources, new as well as old, the means to acquire wealth in imaginative ways.[122] Those who sought preferment or reward were experiencing the same inflationary pressures as the crown and the rising costs to perform as a member of the elite. When a commission set about renovating the steeple of St. Paul's, the story goes, an alderman objected to the building of a new spire. This prompted the quip from another member, 'Mr Alderman, you that are citizens are for the cap: but we that are courtiers, are for the hat and feather'.[123] The competitive expense of Jacobean elite culture was evident in the great prodigy houses of Audley End and Hatfield House. With all these costs to bear, Goodman believed that despite the bounty lavished on leading courtiers and ministers, many were in straitened financial circumstances when they died.[124]

The patronage market was also evolving with the availability of new forms of royal bounty and the sense of the 'increasing importance of money' in the client-patron relationship.[125] James received thousands of petitions over his reign seeking monetary reward as well as many other favours. Hoyle categorised 26% of those petitions handled by the masters of requests between 1603 and 1616 as related to patronage. These ranged from requests for grants of lands, concealments, old debts, offices, monopolies, export licenses and protection from creditors.[126] Shrewd and well-connected individuals watched the market carefully. Household officers, for example, were attentive to the possibilities that their access offered to obtain this patronage, and took to brokering petitions or exploiting grants.[127] The ways in which this market worked, the identities of facilitators and their networks, is still only dimly known. Yet this 'problem of demand' produced a need for institutional controls in Scotland and England.[128] James was not simply overgenerous – he was faced with a crush of suitors and a patronage culture that saw bounty less as a reward for good service than as part of a cash nexus of private interest.

Contemporaries took note of who won these rewards and were quick to complain about the fairness of the distribution of patronage. Again, James's kingcraft is understood against the long-standing view that Elizabeth successfully balanced this distribution among factions. In contrast, James supposedly concentrated his gifts on favourites and intimates who assumed powerful positions as brokers and even monopolists.[129] Influential individuals such as Carr or Buckingham could intervene to derail reform programmes that were inimical to their interests and their control over the flow of reward.[130] The problem of distribution reached a head with George Villiers and his family.[131]

Their grip of the levers of patronage upset norms of counsel and the spoils-sharing among elites, who complained about the influence of private interests, bad counsel and corruption on the king. This produced a 'culture of hostility toward the court' and especially towards Villiers who was accused of corruption at his impeachments in 1626.[132] James may have demonstrated poor judgement by giving too much to one person and his following, yet Villiers was also a capable administrator and occasional reformer who advanced the king's agenda.[133] This agenda often included efforts at reform and the support of anti-corruption during the reign – but was James successful even here?

VI James and Anti-Corruption

James sought to represent himself as a hands-on reformer striking against malfeasance in his governments in Scotland and England.[134] He was foremost a reformer of abuses in legal administration for this was, as he saw it, the root of many corruptions. He complained in his *Trew Law* about the execution of the laws in Scotland, and the hold of the powerful over offices of justice and regalities, citing the condition of the Borders and Highlands in particular.[135] In Edinburgh in 1617, he claimed that he was ready 'to take upon me circuits and to sitt in courts of assize thereby to learne if any might chance to receave any wronges from any of you that have the power and government under me...'.[136] A similar claim to sit in the judgement seat in England was much more controversial and his efforts there, as a law reformer, were more explosive.[137] His intervention in the disputes between the common law courts and Chancery have usually been taken as evidence of his absolutist instincts and contempt for the rule of law rather than an attempt to fix injustices in legal administration.[138] Yet James was attentive to the dutifulness of legal officials, for example, making inquiries into the justices of the peace and their administration of local law.[139] Though he was diplomatic towards the common law judges early in the reign, he held doubts about the probity of the legal profession and modern research has suggested that James's concerns were not entirely misplaced.[140] During his famous clash with Sir Edward Coke, James made clear that he thought the obscurity of the common law – its artificial reason and law French – made it a useful tool for lawyers to enlarge their fees and power.[141]

Early in the reign James responded to calls for reform by issuing proclamations, suspending patents, and attempting to curb the practices of royal purveyors. Acrimony in the parliament of 1604 over the Union and Church matters derailed many of these efforts, but they continued in other ways.[142] James certainly sought to reform corruption within his own household and government, reduce fraud and waste, and grow royal revenue. Though James is often remembered for his claim that the first years of his reign in England were a 'Christmas time', in fact, he was quickly made sensible about his financial predicament.[143] He inherited a debt of £420,000 from Elizabeth (though balanced by monies owing) and his larger household assured him of a structural deficit. The king knew in 1604 that his 'occasions were infinite' as the crown's debts crept upwards, rising above £700,000 later in the reign. By 1605 James could declare to Salisbury that 'it is a horror to me to think upon the height of my place, the greatness of my debts and the smallness of my means'.[144] By 1608, faced with Sir Thomas Lake's discussion of his revenues and debts, James merely 'sighed and that served for answeare'.[145] The most intense phase of reform would begin that year with the death of the treasurer Thomas Sackville, Lord Dorset.

Financial reform had roots back to the 1550s.[146] The desperate financial condition of the crown at that time had led to the production of important records of the office holders (1552) and an increase in customs duties (1558).[147] A decision to limit the sale of offices shifted England from the path followed by France, but left the government to depend on the sale or grant of crown lands to make up shortfalls. Financial troubles plagued the opening years of Elizabeth's reign, leaving Burghley to reshape crown patronage with new forms of reward, including monopolies and import/export concessions in order to reduce the pressure on crown lands.[148] While the traditionalism or innovativeness of Burghley's financial management has been debated, he certainly sought to use crown patronage to bind elites to an insecure regime.[149] Under Dorset (1599–1608), a more thoroughgoing reform was attempted to cut costs and investigate new sources of revenue.

Salisbury, who assumed the office of treasurer after Dorset's death, along with the earl of Northampton and Sir Julius Caesar brought a new energy to the task that culminated in the Great Contract (1610).[150] They catalogued new or lapsed sources of royal revenue and approved projects to search out fraud and peculation in government.[151] For example, proposals had been aired for detailed surveys of crown lands as early as 1599. Many royal estates were simply poorly managed, even by contemporary standards, yielding less than similar private lands and little was known about them in London.[152] There was a strong feeling even under Dorset that stewards were siphoning revenues that were due to the crown. The crown's ignorance of its lands also gave opportunity for their concealment by those in the localities.[153] Surveys, begun under Salisbury, were intended to provide a basis for the revaluation of rents, to recover lost lands, and to investigate the activities of stewards who might be held to account in the Court of Exchequer.[154] Further inquiries targeting stewards and other local officers on the estates in 1610, 1612 and 1620 resulted in their reduction, though they did not return overwhelming evidence of corruption.[155] The significance of these offices and crown leases as forms of patronage and investment made their reform difficult. Improvements to their value from surveys, for example, raised the value of the lands, making leases or sales of crown estates more expensive to those courtiers and individuals who preferred to exploit them under more favourable terms.[156]

Salisbury also oversaw the first of several investigations into peculation in the navy. Northampton led the first in 1608, which was followed by commissions in 1613 and 1618. The problems that the commissioners discovered were suspected even under Elizabeth, although a commission of 1602 – staffed by naval officers – did not achieve significant reform. The 1608 commission was explicitly charged to discover 'abuses, deceits, frauds, corruptions' in the procurement and expenditures of the navy officers. After hearing testimony from over 160 witnesses, the commission prepared a report detailing wide-ranging peculation: theft of supplies and other embezzlements, short-crewing, the misuse of naval ships, among others, amounting to £39,094.[157] The king's response to the report was disappointing: instead of allowing legal process against those accused of corruption, James merely asked them to agree to amend their ways and promise to avoid these practices in the future.

After Salisbury's failure to pass the Great Contract and his death in 1612, others continued his reforming efforts throughout the 1610s, including Lord Ellesmere and Coke. Lionel Cranfield, however, emerged as perhaps the most vigorous of this group, building his career on his expertise in financial management and becoming treasurer in 1621. In these years, investigations proceeded into the household, wardrobe, navy, Exchequer and the Irish administration.[158] The personal involvement of the king in reform was also noticed by observers, especially after 1618, and contemporaries knowingly wrote about their expectation of the extensive abuses that these investigations would uncover: 'his Ma[jes]ty labours verie much to redresse the disorders of the estate …. He is now preparing ane exact examination and censure of the abuses of the Excheker w[hi]ch in all mens opinions ar liklie to proove verie foule'.[159]

New commissions discovered abuses in astonishing detail. While entrenched interests rebuffed another investigation into the navy in 1613, reformers led by Cranfield successfully demonstrated in 1618 how money for naval stores was redirected by purchasing degraded stores, overcharging for ship work, dead pay and the extensive sale of offices.[160] The commissioners particularly censured this traffic in offices and their delegation to deputies, which they believed encouraged peculation and undercut the effectiveness of the navy.[161] Meanwhile, Cranfield and the reformers also scrutinised the Household where annual bills totalled £77,630 by 1617. Expenses for diet under James had risen quickly after his accession by nearly £16,000, leading some to conclude that James was 'infinitely more lavish than Elizabeth'.[162] Burghley had attempted to keep costs at £48,000, yet even this was a reduction of £15,000 from Mary. The sudden rise under James speaks both of opportunism among those obtaining diets at court during the change of the reign and also a rebalancing: Elizabeth, not James, looks like the outlier in expenditures, especially during a time of pressing inflation.[163] Even towards the end of Elizabeth's reign, there was already upward pressure, leading to a commission of 1591 and complaints by the queen herself.[164] Despite new ordinances and a modest reduction in expenses by Dorset, household and building costs continued to rise. Northampton and Salisbury sought to reduce them from 1605 to 1610 and an investigation into the Office of the Works proceeded in 1609. In 1617 a committee was established to investigate the Household led by Cranfield. It examined, in penetrating detail, the actual cost of provisions, the number of diets and the fees of Household officers leading to savings of £21,069.[165] Taken together, these reforming efforts had tangible institutional results, producing a new Household book in 1618 that limited fees and diets, and the establishment on a permanent footing of the naval commission.[166]

James also oversaw trials for corruption of some of his leading ministers. The most spectacular of them were those of the earl of Suffolk, his wife and associates (1618), Francis Bacon (1621), and Cranfield (1624). One of the unusual features of the reign is that many ministers most closely associated with reform, including Cranfield, Salisbury, Bacon, Northampton and Buckingham were themselves identified with or tried for corruption. Lawrence Stone observed that 'the financial ethics of the most resolute of reformers ... differed only in degree from those of the parasites they attacked'.[167] Yet we do not need to assume the cynicism of reformers to understand why their efforts often seemed to provide opportunities for self-enrichment. Anti-corruption has its own incentives aside from altruism. For a king in need of greater revenue, ministers who carried the reforming flag might gain preferment and power. Cranfield, for example, benefitted directly from his work reducing costs in the Wardrobe, receiving £22,354 in his first three years as reward.[168] Anti-corruption was a task as well as a principle, a useful strategy to gain the confidence of a cash-strapped king and for the private profit of the reformers themselves.

VII Conclusion

Anti-corruption and attempts to reform government under James VI and I did produce milestone debates over official conduct, legal authority and began the restructuring of the financial foundation of the monarchy. This latter process had to wait for the controversial measures of Charles I that restored financial balance to the crown and ultimately for the structural reconfiguration of governmental revenues caused by the civil wars and the Restoration settlement.[169] Debates about corruption, and also about the limitations of many of the reforming efforts during James's reign, demonstrate the constraints under which the king operated and the restraints on anti-corruption initiatives and reformers themselves. In fact, many of those arrangements identified as corrupt were often compromises that served some sort of political purpose and were often convenient for those holding lower offices or individuals seeking to avoid or evade payments to the crown. As Weldon claimed, the crown was being cheated on all sides, but to disrupt this peculation was often impolitic.[170]

The toleration of corruption is often politically expedient and even functionally advantageous. The corruption of the system had several functional advantages, most obviously insofar as it provided a supplement to the low salaries of many officers. Reforming parts – reducing costs or excessive fees – did not address the underlying motivations of office holders. To transform this system would require a profound act of administrative imagination such as the Great Contract as well as a willingness to take on entrenched interests. Parliament, which might have been the motor of reform, did pass important anti-corruption legislation, but these measures were often flawed. The Statute of Monopolies (1624) continued to permit the incorporation of whole trades by syndicates, an opening that courtiers were quick to exploit under Charles I.[171]

Anti-corruption is also a dangerous and hard business. John Chamberlain observed the pressure on reformers and the threats that they faced when he commented on Cranfield's participation in the commission to reform the Household: 'he is little beloved in the citie and lesse in the court by reason of this late commission ... wherin he was more forward... and sawcie then any of the rest, but when all is don yt is thought yt will come to nothing, but fall to the ground as such things use to do that are undertaken by unskilfull men ... and against so many and well backt adversaries'.[172] Cranfield's enemies had their revenge at his impeachment.[173] The detection of official corruption is time-consuming and difficult because those involved have a greater knowledge of the administrative apparatus and testify to its norms. Northampton saw little result from his investigation into the navy and Cranfield's investigations required the gathering of painstaking detail down to the number of threads used in naval ropes.

While James ostensibly aligned himself with anti-corruption, was the king actually much of a reformer? Clearly his support was the lynchpin of success for any efforts to reduce waste and fraud. John Cramsie concluded that 'James's commitment could produce results, even in what were usually the safe havens of entrenched interests'.[174] Yet James was often unwilling to disturb these entrenched interests as evinced by the damp squib of the naval commission of 1608. Over his reign, James became more willing to back reformers and took a more active role in their efforts.[175] But rooting out corruption required a willingness to upset political arrangements, and sustained administrative attention, difficult for his ministers and certainly not a skill of the king. Financial matters 'barely interested him', and James found the 'slog of government' tedious, or so it has been argued.[176] His favourites often swayed him, and James was more than prepared to sacrifice anti-corruption drives to political interests. Even a sympathetic study of his early reign concluded that James was the 'greatest barrier to reforms'.[177] The king, politically sensitive, preferred compromise to wholesale transformation. Combatting corruption was difficult, not only due to the influence of incumbents and their superior knowledge of their departments, but because practices that diverted revenue from the crown into private pockets were systemic.

The public awareness of practices that were deemed corrupt, whether officials taking fees that were thought unwarranted or the receipt of gifts by those believed unworthy of rewards, produced a legitimacy problem that further inhibited reform.[178] When Thomas Wentworth addressed parliament in 1610 over the Great Contract, he observed that 'all theise courses would be to no purpose except it would please the king to resume his pencions granted to cortiers out of the exchecquer and to diminish his charge and expences. For (sayes he) to what purpose is it for us to drawe a silver streame out of the contry into the royall cesteme, if it shall dayly runne out thence by private cocks?'[179] The issue was that 'taxpayers did not trust the crown sufficiently', believing that any concessions would be drained away by private interests.[180] Wentworth's solution was that the king might 'live of his owne'.[181] The problem was circular. The more that parliament resisted thoroughgoing financial reform, the more the government resorted to devices that drew complaints about corruption and the greater the resistance that ensued. Confessional suspicion and discord further worsened this problem of trust. The belief that the Spaniards or crypto-Catholics wielded substantial influence over the court floated quietly like a cloud over James's government.

Yet the debate over corruption under Elizabeth and James generated new languages of rights and institutional mechanisms, especially those involving parliament, to control abuses and ensure accountability. The boundaries between legitimate and corrupt behaviour may also have shifted: the distinction between public and private interests seems to have become more acute during the period. Whereas traditional ideas of corruption, bribery and extortion had as their centre the abuse of legal authority, this distinction between public and private was increasingly vital to discussions involving official malfeasance. Future studies might examine how debates over corruption reshaped norms of political behaviour and legal authority during the period, even the very basis upon which authority was exercised. James grappled with forces of change that were perhaps even deeper and more substantial than we have acknowledged.

Notes

1 J. Wormald, *Court, Kirk, and Community: Scotland 1470–1625* (Edinburgh, 2018), pp. 180–1; J. Goodare, *State and Society in Early Modern Scotland* (Oxford, 1999); *idem*, 'Thomas Foulis and the Scottish Fiscal Crisis of the 1590s', in W. M. Ormrod, M. Bonney, and R. Bonney (eds), *Crises, Revolutions and Self-Sustained Growth: Essays in European Fiscal History, 1130–1830* (Stamford, 1999), pp. 170–197.

2 M. Prestwich, *Cranfield: Politics and Profits under the Early Stuarts; the Career of Lionel Cranfield, Earl of Middlesex* (1966); R. Ashton, *The Crown and the Money Market, 1603–40* (Oxford, 1960).

3 *ODNB*, sub 'James VI and I' (article by S. R. Gardiner, print version, Oxford, 1885–1901, vol. 29, p. 177).

4 N. Cuddy, 'The Revival of the Entourage : the Bedchamber of James I, 1603–1625', in D. Starkey (ed.), *The English Court: From the Wars of the Roses to the Civil War* (1987), pp. 173–225.

5 Sir Anthony Weldon, *The Court and Character of King James* (1651), p. 26; Arthur Wilson, *The History of Great Britain being the Life and Reign of King James the First* (1653), p. 28; Francis Osborne, *Historical Memoires on the Reigns of Queen Elizabeth, and King James* (1658), pp. 9–10.

6 Osborne, *Historical Memoires*, p. 10.

7 Osborne, *Historical Memoires*, pp. 3, 53.

8 Weldon, *The Court*, p. 54.

9 Ashton, *The Crown*, p. 186; M. Questier, 'The Reputation of James VI and I Revisited', *Journal of British Studies* 61 (2022), p. 958; T. Cogswell, *James I : The Phoenix King* (2017), p. 33; Prestwich, *Cranfield*, p. 204.

10 *CSPV 1617–1619*, p. 388; similarly, BL, Harleian MS 4648, fo. 428^r; M. Lee, 'James I and the Historians: Not a Bad King after All?', *Albion* 16 (1984), pp. 151–2.

11 I. D. Macfarlane, *Buchanan* (1981), pp. 448–9.

12 Weldon, *The Court*, pp. 26, 51; Peter Heylyn, *Observations on the Historie of the Reign of King Charles* (1656), p. 14; and a similar assessment by the Spanish ambassador: P. Croft, 'Rex Pacificus, Robert Cecil, and the 1604 Peace with Spain', in G. Burgess, R. Wymer, and J. Lawrence (eds), *The Accession of James I* (2006), p. 150; Cogswell, *James I*, p. 7.

13 P. R. Seddon, 'Household Reforms in the Reign of James I', *Bulletin of the Institute of Historical Research* 53 (1980), p. 53.

14 Osborne, *Historical Memoires*, p. 53.

15 Weldon, *The Court*, pp. 55, 173.

16 Heylyn, *Observations*, p. 14.

17 Osborne, *Historical Memoires*, p. 2.

18 S. R. Gardiner, *The First Two Stuarts and the Puritan Revolution, 1603–1660* (New York, 1895), p. 26.

19 Cuddy, 'The Revival', pp. 177, 189–192; D. Newton, *The Making of the Jacobean Regime: James VI and I and the Government of England, 1603–1605* (Woodbridge, 2005), p. 38.

20 Roger Wilbraham, ed. H. S. Scott, *The Journal of Sir Roger Wilbraham* (1902), p. 57; Cuddy, 'The Revival', pp. 187, 199.

21 TNA, C 115/109/8434, likely referring to the survey produced in 1617 in BL Additional MS 58833, fos 21^r–4^r; the amount paid for pensions granted by James was still over £40,000 in 1639; see L. L. Peck, *Court Patronage and Corruption in Early Stuart England* (Boston, 1990), p. 35; Cogswell, *James I*, p. 32 estimates £12,000 annually to Scottish courtiers alone.

22 C. G. Tite, *Impeachment and Parliamentary Judicature in Early Stuart England* (1974); C. Roberts, *The Growth of Responsible Government in Stuart England* (Cambridge, 1966).
23 G. E. Aylmer, *The King's Servants : The Civil Service of Charles I, 1625–42* (1961), p. 179.
24 Questier, 'The Reputation of James VI and I Revisited', p. 952; P. Croft, *King James* (Basingstoke, 2003), pp. 87–99; J. Cramsie, *Kingship and Crown Finance under James VI and I, 1603–1625* (2002), p. 117; Cuddy, 'The Revival', pp. 219–25.
25 T. Cogswell, 'John Felton, Popular Political Culture, and the Assassination of the Duke of Buckingham', *Historical Journal* 49 (2006), p. 366; Peck, *Court Patronage*.
26 Cogswell, 'John Felton', p. 368.
27 Wormald, *Court, Kirk, and Community*, p. 187.
28 M. Knights, 'Religion, Anti-popery and Corruption', in M. J. Braddick and P. Withington (eds), *Popular Culture and Political Agency in Early Modern England and Ireland: Essays in Honour of John Walter* (Woodbridge, 2017), pp. 181–202.
29 J. Hurstfield, 'Political Corruption in Modern England: The Historian's Problem', *History* 52 (1967), pp. 21, 33.
30 Hurstfield, 'Political Corruption', pp. 18, 32.
31 An attempt to avoid this problem through the concept of 'proto-corruption' can be found in J. C. Scott, 'Proto-Corruption in Early Stuart England', in *idem, Comparative Political Corruption* (Englewood Cliffs, NJ, 1972).
32 Hurstfield, 'Political Corruption', pp. 19, 33.
33 B. Buchan and L. Hill, *An Intellectual History of Political Corruption* (Houndmills, Hampshire, 2014), p. 6; M. Philp, 'Defining Political Corruption', *Political Studies* 45 (1997), p. 446.
34 J. G. A. Pocock, *The Machiavellian Moment: Florentine Political Thought and the Atlantic Republican Tradition* (Princeton, NJ, 2003).
35 Buchan and Hill, *An Intellectual History of Political Corruption*, pp. 2, 4–5.
36 M. Knights, 'Samuel Pepys and Corruption', *Parliamentary History* 33 (2014), p. 27.
37 N. Popper, 'An Information State for Elizabethan England', *Journal of Modern History* 90 (2018), pp. 503–35; Cramsie, *Kingship*, p. 54; R. B. Wernham, 'The Public Records in the Sixteenth and Seventeenth Centuries', in L. Fox (ed.), *English Historical Scholarship in the Sixteenth and Seventeenth Centuries* (Oxford, 1956), pp. 11–30.
38 Goodare, *State and Society*, p. 120.
39 L. L. Peck, *Northampton: Patronage and Policy at the Court of James I* (1982), p. 161.
40 J. F. McDiarmid (ed.), *The Monarchical Republic of Early Modern England: Essays in Response to Patrick Collinson* (Aldershot, 2007); Cramsie, *Kingship*, pp. 13–21; P. Collinson, 'The Monarchical Republic of Queen Elizabeth I', *Bulletin of the John Rylands Library* 69 (1987).
41 W. Notestein, F. H. Relf, and H. Simpson (eds), *Commons Debates, 1621* (7 vols, New Haven, 1935), II, p. 193; Edward Coke, ed. J. H. Thomas and J. F. Fraser, *The Reports of Sir Edward Coke* (1826), vol. 11, p. viii.
42 M. Knights, *Trust and Distrust: Corruption in Office in Britain and its Empire, 1600–1850* (New York, 2022).
43 A. D. N. Kerkhoff, D. B. R. Kroeze, F. P. Wagenaar, and M. P. Hoenderboom, *A History of Dutch Corruption and Public Morality (1648–1940)* (Newcastle upon Tyne, 2020); R. Kroeze, A. Vitória, and G. Geltner, 'Debating Corruption and Anticorruption in History', in *idem, Anticorruption in History: From Antiquity*

to the Modern Era (Oxford, 2018), pp. 1–18; J. I. Engels, 'Corruption and Anticorruption in the Era of Modernity and Beyond', in Kroeze, Vitória, and Geltner, *Anticorruption in History*, pp. 167–81; *idem*, 'Corruption as a Political Issue in Modern Societies: France, Great Britain and the United States in the Long 19th Century', *Public Voices* 10 (2016), p. 68.

44 'The perversion of anything from an original state of purity'. Oxford English Dictionary, s.v. 'corruption, n., sense III', April 2023. https://doi.org/10.1093/OED/6807190381; Knights, *Trust and Distrust*, p. 67. For the centrality of moral beliefs about corruption to its definition, see L. S. Underkuffler, *Captured by Evil: The Idea of Corruption in Law* (New Haven, 2013), pp. 54–8 and *passim*; Buchan and Hill, *An Intellectual History of Political Corruption*, pp. 5–6.

45 Thomas Elyot, *The Dictionary of Syr Thomas Eliot Knyght* (1538), fo. 26ᵛ; John Florio, *A Worlde of Wordes, or Most Copious, and Exact Dictionarie in Italian and English* (1598), p. 88.

46 M. Healy, *Fictions of Disease in Early Modern England: Bodies, Plagues and Politics* (New York, 2001).

47 John Spottiswood, *The History of the Church of Scotland* (1655), p. 35.

48 Knights, *Trust and Distrust*, p. 74.

49 P. Lake and M. Questier, 'Puritans, Papists, and the "Public Sphere" in Early Modern England: The Edmund Campion Affair in Context', *Journal of Modern History* 72 (2000), p. 591; Knights, 'Religion, Anti-popery and Corruption'; *idem*, 'Samuel Pepys and Corruption', p. 29.

50 Thomas Fuller, ed. J. Nichols, *The Church History of Britain* (1837), III, p. 194; James VI and I, ed. D. Fischlin and M. Fortier, *The True Law of Free Monarchies; and, Basilikon Doron* (1996), p. 223; James, *A Counterblaste to Tobacco* (1604), sig. A3ᵛ; G. P. V. Akrigg (ed.), *Letters of King James VI and I* (Berkeley, 1984), p. 259.

51 Buchan and Hill, *An Intellectual History of Political Corruption*, p. 3.

52 James, *A Counterblaste to Tobacco*, sig. A3ʳ.

53 Knights, *Trust and Distrust*, pp. 85–9; Cramsie, *Kingship*, pp. 13–21; Peck, *Court Patronage*, pp. 161–207.

54 M. Knights, 'Towards a Social and Cultural History of Keywords and Concepts by the Early Modern Research Group', *History of Political Thought* 31 (2010), pp. 427–48.

55 Buchan and Hill, *An Intellectual History of Political Corruption*, p. 7; M. Génaux, 'Les Mots de la Corruption: La Déviance Publique dans les Dictionnaires d'Ancien Régime', *Histoire, Économie et Société* 21 (2002), pp. 520–1.

56 Knights, *Trust and Distrust*, pp. 93–4; the word was closely associated with the conduct of judges: M. Génaux, 'Social Sciences and the Evolving Concept of Corruption', *Crime, Law and Social Change* 42 (2004), pp. 18–20.

57 The modern offence of misconduct in public office is usually traced to *Rex* v. *Bembridge* (1783), 3 Doug 327, 99 ER 679. See Law Commission, *Misconduct in Public Office* (2020), Appendix, 2.

58 J. Rose, *Maintenance in Medieval England* (New York, NY, 2017); J. Sabapathy, *Officers and Accountability in Medieval England 1170–1300* (Oxford, 2014).

59 Sir Edward Coke, *The Third Part of the Institutes of the Laws of England* (1817), pp. 145–8.

60 Knights, *Trust and Distrust*, p. 94, citing Coke who makes this distinction; W. R. Prest, 'Judicial Corruption in Early Modern England', *Past & Present* 133 (1991), p. 74.

61 W. R. Prest, *The Rise of the Barristers: A Social History of the English Bar, 1590–1640* (Oxford; New York, 1991), p. 311.

62 Cramsie, *Kingship*, p. 73; R. C. Munden, 'James I and the "Growth of Mutual Distrust" : King, Commons and Reform, 1603–1604', in K. Sharpe (ed.), *Faction and Parliament : Essays on Early Stuart History* (Oxford, 1978), pp. 43, 46–9.

63 'Advertisements of a Loyall Subiect' [1603], BL, Additional MS 22601, fo. 12ᵛ.
64 J. Bruce, *Diary of John Manningham of the Middle Temple, and of Bradbourne, Kent, Barrister-at-Law, 1602–1603* (1868), p. 148.
65 TNA, SP 14/1/68, fos 127ʳ–130ʳ, at fo. 128ʳ; N. Tyacke, 'Puritan Politicians and King James VI and I, 1587–1604', in T. Cogswell, R. Cust and P, Lake (eds), *Politics, Religion and Popularity in Early Stuart Britain: Essays in Honour of Conrad Russell* (Cambridge, 2002), pp. 21–44.
66 Munden, 'James I and the "Growth of Mutual Distrust"', pp. 46–7.
67 Francis Osborne, *Historical Memoires on the Reign of Queen Elizabeth* (1658), p. 105.
68 Questier, 'The Reputation of James VI and I Revisited', p. 966; J. E. Neale, 'The Elizabethan Political Scene', in *idem, Essays in Elizabethan History* (1959), pp. 78–9; Osborne, *Historical Memoires*, p. 37. See, e.g., BL, Royal MS 17 C IV ; TNA, SP 12/255/37.
69 S. M. Healy, 'Crown Revenue and the Political Culture of Early Stuart England' (PhD, Birkbeck, 2015), p. 26; Cramsie, *Kingship*, p. 40; D. Morse, 'The Corrupted Court', in D. Morse, *England's Time of Crisis: From Shakespeare to Milton: A Cultural History* (1989), pp. 53–77; Nicholas Sander, *Rise and Growth of the Anglican Schism* (1877), p. 243; A. G. Petti (ed.), *The Letters and Despatches of Richard Verstegan, c.1550–1640* (1959), p. 16.
70 'A Brief and True Discourse of the Kings Majesty's Carttakers' (1605), National Library of Wales, Carreg-lwyd MS I/1694, fos 6ᵛ–7ʳ; Peck, *Northampton*, pp. 148–9.
71 Questier, 'The Reputation of James VI and I Revisited', p. 959; Newton, *Making*, p. 144; Cramsie, *Kingship*, pp. 7–9, 216; P. Hammer, *Elizabeth's Wars: War, Government and Society in Tudor England, 1544–1604* (Basingstoke, 2003), pp. 236–64; D. M. Palliser, *The Age of Elizabeth: England under the later Tudors 1547–1603* (1992), pp. 173–8.
72 Goodare, *State and Society*, p. 103; R. Bonney, 'The Rise of the Fiscal State in France', in B. Yun-Casalilla and P. O'Brien (eds), *The Rise of Fiscal States: A Global History, 1500–1914* (Cambridge, 2012), pp. 93–110; F. Comín Comín and B. Yun-Casalilla, 'Spain: From Composite Monarchy to Nation-State, 1492–1914: An Exceptional Case?', in Yun-Casalilla and O'Brien (eds), *Rise of Fiscal States*, pp. 233–66.
73 Healy, 'Crown Revenue', p. 21; R. W. Hoyle, 'Place and Public Finance', *Transactions of the Royal Historical Society* 7 (1997), p. 203.
74 Peck, *Court Patronage*, pp. 159–60; J. Thirsk, *Economic Policy and Projects: The Development of a Consumer Society in Early Modern England* (Oxford, 1978).
75 J. Goodare, *The Government of Scotland 1560–1625* (Oxford, 2004), pp. 113–27.
76 Goodare, *State and Society*, pp. 121–7; Goodare, *Government of Scotland*, pp. 156–60.
77 Wormald, *Court, Kirk, and Community*, pp. 180–4.
78 Wormald, *Court, Kirk, and Community*, p. 180; Goodare, *State and Society*, pp. 105–6.
79 J. Goodare, 'The Octavians', in M. Kerr-Peterson and S. J. Reid (eds), *James VI and Noble Power in Scotland 1578–1603* (2017), pp. 176–93; Goodare, *State and Society*, pp. 111–12.
80 Goodare, *State and Society*, pp. 113–22.
81 Goodare, *State and Society*, pp. 129–30.
82 C. Russell, 'James and the Problem of Money', in C. Russell, ed. R. Cust, and A. Thrush, *King James VI and I and his English Parliaments* (Oxford, 2011), pp. 154–76.
83 C. Russell, *The Causes of the English Civil War* (Oxford, 1990), p. 166.

84 Russell, *Causes*, pp. 167, 172; M. J. Braddick, *The Nerves of State: Taxation and the Financing of the English State, 1558–1714* (Manchester, 1996).
85 R. Bonney (ed.), *Economic Systems and State Finance: The Origins of the Modern State in Europe 13th to 18th Centuries* (Oxford and New York, 1995).
86 Healy, 'Crown Revenue', p. 22; Cramsie, *Kingship*.
87 Aylmer, *The King's Servants*, p. 183.
88 Cramsie, *Kingship*, pp. 9–10.
89 W. T. MacCaffrey, 'Place and Patronage in Elizabethan Politics', in S. T. Bindoff, J. Hurstfield, and C. H. Williams (eds), *Elizabethan Government and Society : Essays Presented to Sir John Neale* (1961), pp. 108–9; L. L. Peck, 'Court Patronage and Government Policy: the Jacobean Dilemma', in G. F. Lytle and S. Orgel (eds), *Patronage in the Renaissance* (Princeton, NJ, 1981), pp. 21–35; Cramsie, *Kingship*, p. 24; Russell, *Causes*, p. 177; Peck, *Northampton*, p. 25.
90 R. W. Hoyle, 'The Masters of Requests and the Small Change of Jacobean Patronage', *English Historical Review* 126 (2011), p. 545.
91 Aylmer, *The King's Servants*, p. 181.
92 K. Yamamoto, *Taming Capitalism before its Triumph: Distrust, Public Service, and 'Projecting' in Early Modern England* (Oxford, 2018); Cramsie, *Kingship*, p. 175; P. Slack, *The Invention of Improvement: Information and Material Progress in Seventeenth-Century England* (Oxford, 2015).
93 D. Dean, *Law-Making and Society in Late Elizabethan England: The Parliament of England, 1584–1601* (Cambridge, 2002).
94 T. K. Rabb, 'Free Trade and the Gentry in the Parliament of 1604', *Past and Present* 40 (1968), pp. 165–73; Yamamoto, *Taming Capitalism before its Triumph*; C. Brooks, *Law, Politics and Society in Early Modern England* (Cambridge, 2008), pp. 241–71.
95 S. L. Adams, 'The Patronage of the Crown in Elizabethan Politics: The 1590s in Perspective', in J. Guy (ed.), *The Reign of Elizabeth I: Court and Culture in the Last Decade* (Cambridge, 1995), p. 42.
96 L. A. Knafla, *Kent at Law 1602: Star Chamber* (Surrey, 2009), p. xxix.
97 Healy, 'Crown Revenue', p. 21; Russell, *Causes*, p. 170.
98 Healy, 'Crown Revenue', pp. 36, 77.
99 Henry E. Huntington Library, California, MS 15059, fo. 2^v.
100 Questier, 'The Reputation of James VI and I Revisited'; R. A. Houlbrooke, 'James's Reputation, 1625–2005', in *idem* (ed.), *James VI and I: ideas, authority, and government* (Aldershot, 2006), pp. 169–90; Lee, 'James I and the Historians'; J. Wormald, 'James VI and I: Two Kings or One?', *History* 68 (1983), pp. 187–209; M. L. Schwarz, 'James I and the Historians: Toward a Reconsideration', *Journal of British Studies* 13 (1974), pp. 114–34.
101 Wormald, *Court, Kirk, and Community*, p. 178; Cogswell, *James I*, pp. 4, 20; Newton, *Making*, pp. 42, 99; A. Courtney, *James VI, Britannic Prince: King of Scots and Elizabeth's Heir, 1566–1603* (Abingdon, 2024).
102 Cramsie, *Kingship*, p. 7; Newton, *Making*, p. 142; Cogswell, *James I*, p. 35.
103 See A. Courtney above, ch. 2, pp. 47–51; R. M. Smuts, 'Theological Polemics and James I's Diplomacy, 1603–1617', *Journal of Medieval and Early Modern Studies* 50 (2020), p. 517.
104 Goodman, *The Court*, p. 18.
105 Newton, *Making*, p. 144; Cramsie, *Kingship*, p. 40.
106 Healy, 'Crown Revenue', p. 18; Cramsie, *Kingship*.
107 *A Declaration of His Maiesties Royall Pleasure, in what Sort he Thinketh Fit to Enlarge, or Reserue Himselfe in Matter of Bountie*, (1610), p. 3; L. L. Peck, '"For a King not to be Bountiful were a Fault": Perspectives on Court Patronage in Early Stuart England', *Journal of British Studies* 25 (1986), pp. 31–61.
108 James VI and I, ed. N. Rhodes and J. Richards, *King James VI and I: Selected*

Writings (Aldershot, 2003), p. 245. See also the comments of Salisbury in TNA PRO 14/37, fo. 145ᵛ.

109 Cramsie, *Kingship*, p. 22; Adams, 'The Patronage of the Crown', pp. 42–3.

110 James VI and I, *The True Law of Free Monarchies; and, Basilikon Doron*, p. 153.

111 *A Declaration of His Maiesties Royall Pleasure*, p. 3.

112 Wormald, *Court, Kirk, and Community*, p. 179; A. L. Juhala, '"For the King Favours them Very Strangely": The Rise of James VI's Chamber, 1580–1603', in Kerr-Peterson and Reid, *James VI and Noble Power in Scotland 1578–1603*, p. 157.

113 Wormald, 'Two Kings or One?'; Newton, *Making*, pp. 22–5; Cramsie, *Kingship*, p. 25; Cuddy, 'The Revival', pp. 176–7.

114 Juhala, 'For the King', p. 158.

115 Juhala, 'For the King', p. 166.

116 James VI and I, *Regales Aphorismi* (1650), p. 112.

117 Weldon, *The Court*, pp. 171–3. For brief discussion of the development of a British peerage, see J. Morrill, 'Dynasties, Realms, Peoples and State Formation, 1500–1720', in J. Morrill and R. Friedeburg (eds), *Monarchy Transformed : Princes and their Elites in Early Modern Western Europe* (Cambridge, 2017), pp. 23–6.

118 Goodman, *The Court*, p. 21; see also Courtney, *James VI, Britannic Prince*, pp. 202–3 and 230 n. 39.

119 Goodman, *The Court*, p. 204.

120 Peck, *Northampton*, pp. 41–63; Questier, 'The Reputation of James VI and I Revisited', p. 953.

121 Peck, *Northampton*, p. 25; MacCaffrey, 'Place and Patronage in Elizabethan Politics', p. 108; Aylmer, *The King's Servants*, pp. 248–9; Cramsie, *Kingship*, pp. 13–17.

122 Peck, *Court Patronage*, p. 151 notes the importance of additional fees and corruption; Aylmer, *The King's Servants*, p. 292 (Bacon).

123 Lambeth Palace Library, MS 1034, fo. 5ʳ.

124 Goodman, *The Court*, pp. 200–1.

125 Adams, 'The Patronage of the Crown'; Peck, '"For a King Not to Be Bountiful Were a Fault"'.

126 Hoyle, 'The Masters of Requests', p. 565.

127 Hoyle, 'The Masters of Requests',, pp. 576–7; though their influence varied throughout the reign, see A. Courtney, 'Court Politics and the Kingship of James VI & I, c. 1615–c. 1622' (PhD, Cambridge, 2008), pp. 38–50; Cuddy, 'The Revival', pp. 218–19.

128 Hoyle, 'The Masters of Requests', pp. 547, 560, 578.

129 Wormald, *Court, Kirk, and Community*, p. 179; Croft, *King James*, pp. 87–108; Cogswell, *James I*, pp. 52–3; Cuddy, 'The Revival'.

130 Prestwich, *Cranfield*, p. 203.

131 C. Russell, *Parliaments and English Politics, 1621–1629* (1979), pp. 295–7.

132 Questier, 'The Reputation of James VI and I Revisited', p. 956; D. Coast, '"Reformation" or "Ruin"? The Impeachment of the Duke of Buckingham and Early Stuart Politics', *Historical Research* 90 (2017), pp. 719–20; Courtney, 'Court Politics and the Kingship of James VI & I, c. 1615–c. 1622', pp. 186–7, 218–21; Peck, *Court Patronage*.

133 Questier, 'The Reputation of James VI and I Revisited', p. 957; R. Lockyer, *Buckingham: the Life and Political Career of George Villiers, First Duke of Buckingham, 1592–1628* (1981); though doubts about his sincerity as a reformer are discussed in, D. Hebb, 'Profiting from Misfortune: Corruption

and the Admiralty under the Early Stuarts', in Cogswell, Cust and Lake, *Politics, Religion and Popularity*, pp. 103f; G. E. Aylmer, 'Buckingham as an Administrative Reformer?', *English Historical Review* 105 (1990), pp. 355–62.

134 Healy, 'Crown Revenue', p. 263; Cramsie, *Kingship*, p. 74.

135 James VI and I, *The True Law of Free Monarchies; and, Basilikon Doron*, pp. 119, 126.

136 National Library of Scotland, MS 2521, f. 110ᵛ.

137 L. A. Knafla, 'Britain's Solomon: King James and the Law', in M. Fortier and D. Fischlin (eds), *Royal Subjects : Essays on the Writings of James VI and I* (Detroit, MI, 2002), pp. 255–6. But cf. his direct participation in the disputes over the jurisdiction of the Council of the Marches of Wales, the conflict between Chancery and the common law courts, and even his upbraiding of the credulousness of the judges at assize in witchcraft prosecutions: D. C. Smith, *Sir Edward Coke and the Reformation of the Laws* (2014); M. Gaskill, 'Witchcraft and Evidence in Early Modern England', *Past & Present* 198 (2008), pp. 33–70, at p. 43; and the king's comments about the ruinous competition among courts and the need for his intervention, Henry E. Huntington Library, Ellesmere MS 1763.

138 Knafla, 'Britain's Solomon', p. 251.

139 Newton, *Making*, p. 75.

140 Prest, 'Judicial Corruption in Early Modern England'; C. W. Brooks, *Pettyfoggers and Vipers of the Commonwealth: the 'Lower Branch' of the Legal Profession in Early Modern England* (Cambridge, 1986).

141 Akrigg, *Letters of King James VI and I*, p. 243.

142 Munden, 'James I and the "Growth of Mutual Distrust"', p. 68; Healy, 'Crown Revenue', p. 263.

143 Newton, *Making*, p. 35.

144 Akrigg, *Letters of King James VI and I*, p. 261.

145 TNA, SP 14/37/91.

146 Cramsie, *Kingship*, pp. 35–9; Newton, *Making*, p. 119.

147 J. Alsop, 'The Revenue Commission of 1552', *Historical Journal* 22 (1979), pp. 511–33; Braddick, *The Nerves of State*; Adams, 'The Patronage of the Crown', p. 35.

148 Adams, 'The Patronage of the Crown', pp. 39–40.

149 R. W. Hoyle, '"Shearing the Hog": the Reform of the Estates c. 1598–1640', in *idem* (ed.), *The Estates of the English Crown, 1558–1640* (Cambridge, 1992), p. 204; N. Jones, *Governing by Virtue: Lord Burghley and the Management of Elizabethan England* (Oxford, 2015); F. Heal and C. Holmes, 'The Economic Patronage of William Cecil', in P. Croft (ed.), *Patronage, Culture and Power : the Early Cecils* (New Haven, CT and London, 2002), pp. 199–229.

150 Cramsie, *Kingship*, pp. 53–119; N. Cuddy, 'The Real, Attempted "Tudor Revolution in Government": Salisbury's 1610 Great Contract', in G. W. Bernard and S. J. Gunn (eds), *Authority and Consent in Tudor England: Essays Presented to C. S. L. Davies* (Aldershot, 2002), pp. 249–70.

151 L. L. Peck, 'Problems in Jacobean Administration: Was Henry Howard, Earl of Northampton, a Reformer?', *Historical Journal* 19 (1976), pp. 831–58; L. M. Hill, *Bench and Bureaucracy: The Public Career of Sir Julius Caesar, 1580–1636* (Stanford, CA, 1988).

152 D. Thomas, 'The Elizabethan Crown Lands: their Purposes and Problems', in R. W. Hoyle (ed.), *The Estates of the English Crown, 1558–1640* (Cambridge, 1992), p. 67.

153 Thomas, 'The Elizabethan Crown Lands', p. 69.

154 Healy, 'Crown Revenue', p. 264; Hoyle, '"Shearing the Hog"', pp. 207–9, 227; Prestwich, *Cranfield*, p. 226.

155 Thomas, 'The Elizabethan Crown Lands', pp. 71–2; Hoyle, '"Shearing the Hog"', pp. 209–10.
156 Healy, 'Crown Revenue', p. 110; Thomas, 'The Elizabethan Crown Lands', p. 71.
157 Peck, *Northampton*, pp. 152–6.
158 Prestwich, *Cranfield*, p. 228.
159 Cramsie, *Kingship*, p. 150, citing PRO [TNA], SP 14/96/91, fo. 151ʳ (28 Mar. 1618).
160 Prestwich, *Cranfield*, pp. 212–19.
161 'Copy of my third letter to the Lord Marquess Buckingham', 7 November 1618, *The Manuscripts of the Earl Cowper*, vol. 1 (1888), p. 99.
162 Prestwich, *Cranfield*, p. 207.
163 Prestwich, *Cranfield*, p. 210.
164 Prestwich, *Cranfield*, p. 207; TNA, LS 13/280 no. 82.
165 Seddon, 'Household Reforms', p. 47.
166 Seddon, 'Household Reforms', p. 48; Prestwich, *Cranfield*, pp. 215–17.
167 L. Stone, *The Crisis of the Aristocracy, 1558–1641* (Oxford, 1965), p. 494; and cf. Lee, 'James I and the Historians', pp. 159–63.
168 Seddon, 'Household Reforms', p. 52.
169 Healy, 'Crown Revenue', p. 25.
170 Healy, 'Crown Revenue', pp. 158–9.
171 C. Dent, 'Generally Inconvenient: The 1624 Statute of Monopolies as Political Compromise', *Melbourne University Law Review* 33 (2009), p. 438; Thirsk, *Economic Policy and Projects*.
172 McClure, *LJC*, II, pp. 149–50.
173 Seddon, 'Household Reforms', p. 52.
174 Cramsie, *Kingship*, p. 178.
175 Cramsie, *Kingship*, pp. 134, 168–9.
176 Wormald, *Court, Kirk, and Community*, p. 178; Cramsie, *Kingship*, p. 47; D. A. Smith, 'The Error of Young Cyrus: The Bill of Conformity and Jacobean Kingship, 1603–1624', *Law and History Review* 28 (2010), pp. 307–41.
177 Seddon, 'Household Reforms', p. 52.
178 Russell, *Causes*, pp. 175–6.
179 S. R. Gardiner (ed.), *Parliamentary Debates in 1610* (1862), p. 11.
180 Healy, 'Crown Revenue', p. 30.
181 Seddon, 'Household Reforms', p. 54.

5

TOLERATION AND ECUMENISM OR HERETIC-BURNING AND A PAPAL ANTICHRIST?

Another Look at King James VI and I

Anthony Milton

That King James VI and I presented himself to his contemporaries as a man dedicated to the cause of peace is beyond question. The figure of 'Rex Pacificus' was a prominent feature of courtly panegyric under James, which reflected the king's own enthusiastic self-image.[1] That James also pursued a foreign policy that was often directed towards peace treaties and the marriage alliances that would secure them is also very clear. Some critical contemporaries were more than ready to present this as a form of weakness, a personal pusillanimity that reflected either cowardice or a fatal failure to see through the blandishments of foreign ambassadors. One carefully anonymous commentator remarked to the king in 1622 that 'I fear we have too much cause to complain of your Majesty's unlimited peace. The excess whereof hath long since turned virtue into vice and health into sickness'.[2] Some modern historians have been surprisingly apt to repeat these charges.[3] Most recently, though, historians have begun to grasp, not merely that a peace policy was often an appropriate strategy for Britain in these turbulent decades, but also that for James himself it was a policy dictated by sound practical reasoning rather by any simple (or even misplaced) idealism. As Malcolm Smuts has recently noted, peace often made both political and financial sense for James and reflected Britain's 'relatively marginal position in most continental conflicts' during his reign.[4]

In fact, James was quite capable of perceiving peace and reconciliation as dangers to be avoided when they might be construed as being against his interests. He was an outspoken opponent of any prospect of peace between England and Spain in 1602 when he thought this would be 'perrelouse' to his succession to the English throne, and while on the throne his basic foreign policy objective was to prevent a Franco-Spanish rapprochement which

DOI: 10.4324/9781003319764-6

would necessarily threaten British interests. Similarly, if James was temperamentally averse to military conflict, that did not in itself determine his policy (even if he was presumably more than happy at those moments when his personal proclivity and self-image happily coincided with practical politics). In Smuts's words, for James and for other princes at this time 'a preference for peace did not require the renunciation of the use of force under all circumstances' – indeed, limited wars and the threat of military intervention might frequently be necessary.[5]

There was also a religious dimension to James's pacific self-image, as a man keen to avert religious conflict and persecution, who sought to promote peace inspired by an ultimate aim to secure religious unification.[6] Again, his contemporary and modern critics leapt to denigrate this as revealing either hopeless impracticality or a more dangerous vulnerability and untrustworthiness regarding the threat from Catholic Spain.[7] Only in more recent years have scholars grasped that this was more than a mere pipedream. Brown Patterson's exhaustive archival scholarship has helped to unearth a series of initiatives where over many years the king sought in various guises to promote irenical schemes – from a general council of Christendom to include the Church of Rome, via attempts to unite Huguenots and then to secure broader protestant unity, to the international Synod of Dort (to which he sent delegates), and in offering patronage to a series of irenically-minded figures from the apostate archbishop Marc'antonio de Dominis to the Huguenot scholar Isaac Casaubon.[8]

The question remains, however, of whether these were efforts inspired by a straightforward religious disposition that abhorred religious persecution and an ambition towards ecumenism or whether, like James's pacific foreign policy, these were often means to other ends. What I hope to suggest in what follows is that James's apparent tolerationist and ecumenical discourse and initiatives were often predicated on less than irenical ideas, and that they have to be placed next to a whole series of actions and speeches which suggest that he held rather different views of religious toleration and religious unity than are sometimes attributed to him. This is not to suggest that the image of himself as a uniter of Christendom was not sincerely held by James. My intention is not to create a simple juxtaposition between principled rhetoric and cynical practice, but rather to show how James deployed a range of different languages and principles when discussing and responding to religious pluralism, and how the political and personal context could crucially shape how these ideas and factors played out. Moreover, ecumenism and religious toleration as James understood them did not simply correspond to modern assumptions, and to judge him by these standards risks being seriously misled.

Before starting our analysis of James's expressed thoughts and beliefs on religious toleration and ecumenism, however, we must discuss the question of language. James invites historical discussion of his ideas more than any of his contemporary monarchs because (unlike them) he was apparently so eager to express his thoughts, at length and in public. Most famously, of course, he expressed himself in print and made these thoughts available to the widest possible international audience by having many of these works translated into Latin and distributed abroad by his agents. But James also relished giving speeches – in parliament, and in the privy council – but also to discourse semi-publicly at his court, with foreign visitors and ambassadors, men of eminence, minor courtiers and office-holders alike. Many agents, commentators and letter-writers were, therefore, able and eager to report verbatim James's expressed opinions, desires and promises. Such easy loquacity and readiness to perform in public has naturally led historians to read this as evidence of the king's open, big-hearted sincerity – to be either applauded as humane and accessible, or to be derided as naïve, vain and lacking the shrewd reticence and hauteur of more guarded sovereigns. The problem, as contemporaries and later historians have found, is that James was far from consistent in what he said, that fervent assurances were then ignored or contradicted shortly afterwards, and that the broad principles rhetorically invoked then seemed to be disregarded in practice. For those commentators and ambassadors who found themselves misled and wrong-footed, the temptation was to see this as evidence that James was not a serious politician – that he was easily swayed by the last person he spoke to, and that he was lazy, procrastinating or cowardly in not following up assurances of military aid.[9] An alternative reading is that James knew precisely what he was doing – that affable exchanges and professions of friendship and devotion were intended to deceive the recipient about his intentions, and told people what they wanted to hear. If, as a result of their disappointment, people assumed that James was weak-willed and easily swayed rather than calculatingly devious, this meant that they could still believe that the king was persuadable and that it was in their interest to try to win him back.

It makes more sense, then, to see language and rhetoric as James's distinctive political tools – his apparently natural good humour and delight in intellectual argument could be deployed to his potential advantage. And, given James's disinclination towards actual military intervention (and entirely realistic grasp that he did not have the resources to pursue such policies anyway), it was the language of promise, proposal, vision and (when appropriate) displeasure that was the best means at his disposal to secure what he wanted. As Michael Questier notes: 'Not least because James had no incentive to commit himself to military intervention in continental Europe, words here were, as much as they had been in Scotland, his weapons of choice'.[10] We need, then, to think of rhetoric, not as a mere insincere smokescreen but as a conscious instrument of power and diplomacy.

But this means that when we read the king's words and proposals on the subjects of toleration and religious unity, we need to guard against seeing them as simple expressions of his deepest beliefs and motivations, and to beware of lifting stray phrases from their contexts. Each remark needs to be placed in its immediate context to clarify the motivation behind it, and also in the broader context of the king's other expressions and policies to adduce its relative significance.

I Religious Toleration and Persecution

We can begin with James's oft-stated aversion to religious persecution. He expressed this concern so often, and in so many contexts, that it makes sense to take it seriously. Corresponding with Sir Robert Cecil in 1603 he averred that he considered persecution to be 'one of the infallible notes of a false church' and insisted that he could never allow 'in my conscience that the bloode of any man shall be shedde for diversitie of opinions in religion'.[11] The next year, speaking at the opening of his first English parliament, he declared to MPs that 'my minde was ever … free from persecution' and that he had lightened the burden on Catholics wherever possible.[12] The following year he reportedly told the privy council he 'had a naturall aversion' to the shedding of the blood of Catholic nonconformists.[13] In 1607 he warned judges that no priest should be executed 'that would confer, or showed not arrogance and violence, even of them sparingly' and emphasised: 'No torrent of blood'.[14] The 1610 Parliament was told that James held it 'not fit that by blood and cruelty religion should be planted', and he lectured parliament in 1614 that 'I never saw either true or false religion ever bettered by prosecution [*sic*]', and that 'if this [Protestantism] be the true religion, popery will fall' without the need for greater suppression.[15] Similarly, at the opening of the 1621 Parliament, James restated that 'Faith was never well planted with violence'.[16]

It is important, however, to unpack what these words really meant. Almost all of these statements disavowing persecution were made when James was deploring the supposed increase of 'popery' and in almost all cases he was in the same breath specifically urging the more stringent implementation of laws against Catholics.[17] 'Persecution' and the shedding of blood thus defined the self-evidently unacceptable extreme, against which all other forms of discrimination and punishment could be presented as warrantable. James was acutely aware that Jesuits had accused him of persecution,[18] and denials of explicit 'persecution' were partly a form of self-justification and self-definition. In addition, they were (presumably) intended for foreign consumption – thus, in 1614 James was seeking in part to assure parliament of his anti-papal credentials, but by reassuring them that new anti-papal legislation was not necessary he was also keeping his options open in his dealings with foreign princes. It is notable in this respect that the Spanish ambassador observed that in his speech James specifically argued that being considerate towards Catholics would show respect to foreign princes of the same religion – by contrast, this point was not recorded by the English observers (to whom it was not of course really directed anyway).[19] In 1621, restraint of persecution was presented to parliament as simply being a matter of Protestant self-interest. As James explained, rigorous persecution in matters of conscience was 'against his course toward other princes with whom he was a continuall mediator for moderation in like cases of conscience'.[20] Persecution of Catholics would also, of course, scupper plans for a marriage with a Catholic power – and it was the Spanish Match that was foremost in James's mind in 1621 when he sought to pre-empt parliamentary calls for a stricter line on recusancy by saying that compulsion must not be used against consciences.[21]

Perhaps most telling is the context of James's most famous and oft-cited remarks in his letter to Robert Cecil in 1603, where he declared his aversion to persecution and the shedding of blood for religion.[22] This letter was prompted by the fact that James had complained in his previous letter to Cecil that Catholicism was not being suppressed properly in England, and urged more severe execution of the laws given 'the daylie increase that I heare of poperie in Englande'.[23] Cecil in response had tactfully explained the case for tolerating secular priests who had declared their allegiance. The implication that James was more intolerant of Catholicism than Cecil provoked the king to declare his credentials as a model of kingly clemency – clearly it was important for James to feel that he always inhabited the moral high ground in such matters.[24] Nevertheless, he was here objecting to Elizabeth's 1602 proclamation which, while directing the banishment of Jesuits and disloyal secular priests, had nevertheless specifically excluded from the ban those anti-Jesuit secular priests who were prepared formally to acknowledge their duty and allegiance to Elizabeth and submit themselves to her mercy. This was a concession that James would never grant in any of his own proclamations as king of England (and his own more severe response as king of Scotland in the autumn of 1602 drew the admiring and pointed comment of one English commentator that 'he led us the way, and went somwhat beyond us' by requiring an oath from all his nobility and gentry not to harbour Catholic priests).[25] Moreover, the text of Elizabeth's proclamation had claimed that she harboured an instinctive clemency towards all her subjects regardless of their religion, felt a 'naturall disposition' to show mercy wherever possible, and had a 'desire to avoyde all occasions of drawing blood', referring to her own 'milde and merciful connivencie' towards apparently loyal Catholics.[26] James – who had Elizabeth's proclamation in his hands – was therefore quite consciously replicating some of these assertions in his own letter.

II Anti-Toleration

Moreover, even if an aversion to 'persecution' was indeed a sincere personal trait on James's part, he repeatedly emphasised that he was ineluctably opposed to the idea of religious toleration. James's condemnations of religious toleration are numerous and are just as emphatic as his expressions of opposition to religious persecution. James was of course well aware that these were remarks that would play well to his Protestant subjects, especially when they needed reassurance that he was not seeking to offer toleration to Catholics. Such remarks were often, therefore, made to balance stricter policies towards puritans,[27] and were quite deliberately disseminated as widely as possible. Thus, when he declared to his privy council in February 1605 in 'a long and vehement apologie for himself' that if he thought his sons would agree to a toleration of Catholics 'he could wish the kingdom translated to his daughter', James clearly felt that this went down sufficiently well for him to direct that it be declared publicly in the Star Chamber three days later 'by all the lordes in very ample manner' and the day afterwards 'to the lord mayor and aldermen by the recorder'.[28] The king himself then reported this to bishops for more extensive dissemination.[29] But hostility to religious toleration was not confined to the king's public declarations. In the privacy of his copy of the congregationalist Henry Jacob's *Humble Supplication* of 1609, James wrote of Jacob's own appeal for toleration: 'Can the devill devyse a more forcible argument for toleration of poperie?'[30] When James told his 1624 Parliament that he had never intended a toleration of popery ('I never thought nor meant nor ever in word expressed anything that savoured of it'), this doubtless reflected the turn of political events and the demise of the Spanish Match, but it may also have been completely true.[31]

Opposition to formal *toleration* did not, however, mean hostility towards the idea of religious *tolerance* (or as James and his contemporaries would call it, 'connivencie' in not executing laws against nonconformists, either Protestant or Catholic).[32] The distinction between 'toleration' and 'connivencie' was not a careless one. James like his contemporaries knew exactly what 'religious toleration' involved: there were plenty of clear examples of it in Europe at this time, most obviously – and most recently – in France (where the Edict of Nantes had been issued just five years before James succeeded to the English throne) and the petitions that he received from Catholics and puritans for religious toleration explicitly highlighted the examples of France and Poland.[33] However, the implication that James might offer formal religious toleration to Catholics was (as Michael Questier has pointed out) a key element of his foreign and domestic policies. If James never intended to offer such a thing, it was nevertheless tactically important to hint that 'connivance' (which he was happy to own) might indeed lead to 'toleration' (and that the former was a reassuring indication that the latter would follow whenever feasible). If enthusiastic contemporaries made this incorrect assumption, this was not necessarily something to be discouraged (except when – as in the 1624 Parliament – this equivalence was used pejoratively to condemn the 'connivance' being practised).[34]

Private reports that James had made specific assurances in conversation that Catholic religious toleration would be granted are just that – reports (and sometimes deriving from conversations that were presumably not conducted in English). Throughout his life, James showed himself happy to offer 'connivance' to those who did not accept the established religion and publicly declared his readiness to indulge people who kept their alternative religion private.[35] But he seems to have continued carefully to avoid using the 't' word, and this is a reminder that, although James habitually exploited to the full any opportunities for verbal ambiguity, he could also on occasion be very careful in his choice of words.

There was of course a purely practical consideration in the matter of formal Catholic toleration: it was not politically feasible in England, as it would require the approval of parliament, which would obviously not be forthcoming (as the Spaniards themselves fully realised).[36] Moreover, tolerance of individuals without committing to formal toleration more broadly had already made for effective practical politics for James in Scotland before 1603 (in the cases of Huntly, Huntly's Jesuit uncle and several others). It could show Catholics abroad that he was personally well inclined towards his Catholic subjects while still giving scope to godly lesser magistrates and agitating synods to take their own initiatives.[37] There was also a deeper rationale for James's opposition to a formal toleration, and this related to royal authority. A formal toleration would empower individuals to reject with impunity the king's authority in religious affairs. Tolerance of individuals, however, was a matter of mercy and grace on the part of the monarch, which could be discontinued at any moment. Tolerance of this sort thereby reinforced the king's authority over individuals; by contrast, an official toleration would remove the king's ability to provide or withhold favour in this manner. This distinction is perhaps most clearly indicated in the king's speech to parliament in 1610. Here he condemned the 'too great a connivence' that had spared recusants from being presented in the past by judges and bishops. They should all be 'brought under the danger of law' without exception, but (he continued) 'then it is my part to use mercie, as I thinke convenient'. Kings should not 'winke at faults …. But to forgive faults after they are confessed, or tried, is mercie'.[38]

Exchanges of correspondence arguably give us a clearer indication of precisely what James was prepared to say and to envisage when it came to 'connivencie'. Here his exchange with the earl of Northumberland before his English accession is (arguably) revealing. After Northumberland had reported to James in 1603 that Catholics all supported his succession to the English throne but would be happy if he would grant them 'tollerations of there contienses', James very carefully avoided the 't' word in his reply. Instead, he wrote that he would not persecute 'any that wilbe quyet, and give but ane wtward obedience to the law' and would advance 'any of them that will by good service woorthelly deserve it'.[39] Far from promising toleration, this actually implied that it was only by attending Protestant church services that

Catholics could avoid persecution. But this was effectively to require Catholics to conform outwardly to the Protestant Church, and only on that basis would they be allowed privately and discreetly to observe Catholic practices in addition.

More generally, like many advocates of religious toleration throughout history, while the king was not averse to offering tolerance to an allegedly afflicted and passive religious minority, the minority had to keep its side of the implicit bargain by being grateful, passive and declining in numbers. Increasing in numbers, and gaining converts, was specifically not countenanced. As we have noted, James's denunciations of persecution were always accompanied by expressions of alarm at the increase in numbers of Catholics, which James never failed to condemn. In his 1603 letter to Cecil, James disavowed bloodshed but declared that he would 'be sorie that Catholikes shoulde so multiplie as thay micht be able to practise thaire olde principles upon us'.[40] In his March 1604 speech to parliament he declared that he could not permit the increase of Catholic religion without betraying himself and his own conscience.[41] New Catholics were the targets of his particular antipathy. In a speech to Star Chamber in 1616 he dubbed them 'apostates' and 'polypragmaticke papists' and required that they be subjected to 'severe punishment'. He could 'love the person of a papist, being otherwise a good man and honestly bred, never having known any other religion', but 'the person of an apostate papist, I hate'.[42] Partly this hatred could be explained by the fact that, as his proclamation of February 1604 pointed out, this conversion corrupted the individual's duty and allegiance to their monarch.[43] More generally, if tolerance reflected a personal act of clemency by the king, then a refusal outwardly to conform was a betrayal of a personal grant of mercy, and a decision to reject the king's own religion in favour of one that was given mere 'connivance' was an abuse of an act of clemency that was intended for others.

III Conscience

James's hostility towards Catholic converts should also prompt us to scrutinise carefully his remarks about conscience. As we have seen, James regularly invoked his concern not to force people in matters of conscience, and here he was restating the common early modern nostrum that conscience could not be compelled. James had flagged this concern before he came to the English throne. Writing to Elizabeth in June 1591 to express his dismay at the imprisonment of the puritans Thomas Cartwright, John Udall and 'certaine utheris, ministers of the evangele', who had differed from bishops 'in materis tutching thame in conscience', James claimed to owe a duty to such clergy 'as ar afflicted for their conscience', and begged Elizabeth 'maist earnestlie', pleading 'the simplicitie of their conscience in this defence' which 'can not weill be thrallit be compulsion' and warning of the 'grait sclander' caused by their punishment.[44] In March 1604 James told the English Parliament that he abhorred persecution 'or thralling of my subjects in matters of conscience', and in 1621 he again told MPs that 'it was against his nature to be too rigorous in matters of conscience'.[45] Small wonder, then, that a petition for religion presented by the Commons in 1607 pleaded for the restoration of deprived puritan ministers on the grounds that their refusal of ceremonies 'proceedeth only from conscience'.[46]

'Liberty of conscience' was a gloriously unspecific term that was bandied about by the king's advisers. Thus Robert Cecil told the Venetian ambassador in 1605 (in a wide-ranging discussion of the treatment of Catholics that managed not once to mention the word 'toleration') that if papal superiority would be definitively confined to spiritual matters, the king would the next day concede 'liberty of conscience' and permit the exercise of the Catholic religion (*concederà la libertà di conscienza, et permetterà la Religione Cattolica*).[47]

But here we need to remember early modern understandings of 'conscience'. For James, as for most early modern thinkers, the conscience was not a purely independent agent – it needed to be instructed in true belief first.[48] As James declared in *Basilikon Doron*, 'conscience not grounded upon sure knowledge, is either an ignorant fantasie, or an arrogant vanitie'.[49] It followed that a rightly-informed conscience should be treated with restraint and understanding; a poorly-instructed one was deceitful and counterfeit – it could and should be coerced. To have an uninformed conscience, or one that deliberately avoided being correctly informed, was no defence.

James was resolute in detecting an uninformed conscience in the case of 'apostate' Catholics,[50] whom he felt had 'changed their coates' merely 'through curiositie, affection of noveltie, or discontentment in their privat humours'.[51] They had consciously rejected James's authority and embraced Catholicism knowing its current offensive doctrines towards kings. He insisted that they should be severely disciplined, and blamed judges and clergy for not doing this. 'Conscience', then, had its limits.

On the Protestant side there were also faulty consciences, and again this was manifested by the rejection of royal authority in religious matters, despite having the advantage of orthodox Protestant preaching. Here James specifically mentioned puritan separatists who were guilty of 'making the scriptures to be ruled by their conscience, and not their conscience by the Scripture',[52] but he cast the net wider to include Andrew Melville and his Presbyterian colleagues who participated in the forbidden general assembly at Aberdeen.[53]

IV Punishment

These distinctions can help to explain some further extensions of James's thinking when it came to punishment and erroneous belief.

If James stressed his distaste for bloodshed, this did not mean that he was averse to the idea of banishment – indeed, it was often his preferred form of punishment, which he embraced in the cases of Catholic priests and the Melvillian Scottish Presbyterians, and which he recommended (among other penalties) for erring Protestants abroad such as the German-Dutch theologian Conrad Vorstius.[54] Where banishment failed, execution should be expected. James's proclamations against Catholic priests insisted (as Elizabeth's had done) that if the banished priests were to return then they would deserve their execution – 'their blood shall then be upon their own heads'. James told Star Chamber in 1616 that in such cases 'it is a plaine signe nothing will hold them but a halter: such are no martyrs that refuse to suffer for their conscience'.[55] This was not a vague rhetorical flourish on James's part: on the very same day as James's speech the priest Thomas Maxfield was arraigned for escaping from prison, and was executed at Tyburn just ten days later.[56]

Others could face imprisonment – not the decorous restraint enjoyed by the earl of Northumberland with his books and papers but the dank and miserable prisons which could in effect perform the requirements of a death penalty without incurring the need to stain the king's hands with blood. Baptists such as Thomas Helwys who appealed for religious toleration expired in prison.[57]

More severe punishments were held in reserve for the treatment of heresy, and here again we need to revisit James's professed aversion to the spilling of blood. Heresy was the gruesome flipside of the king's desire not to force the rightly-informed conscience, as the heretic's conscience was by definition ill-informed and the heretic was wilful in his deliberate error. If the heretic's conscience would not yield to reason then perpetual imprisonment was the best that could be hoped for. Moreover, when it came to the punishment of heresy, James was more outspoken than most of his contemporaries in his expressed conviction that this should include heretics being burned to death. His views on heresy became an international issue in the case of Conrad Vorstius, whose heterodox writings provoked James to demand that the Dutch States General should expel him from his post at the University of Leiden (and it is a telling reflection on contemporary meanings of the term that James specifically invoked the Dutch commitment to 'liberty of conscience' when insisting that they persecute the heretical Vorstius).[58] Writing to the States General in October 1611, and warning of 'the curse of God' that awaited them if they did not act, James allowed that, if Vorstius 'should denie or equivocate upon those blasphemous poynts of heresie and atheisme, which already he hath broached', this might move the States 'to spare his person, and not cause him to be burned'. But the sentence of burning, James insisted, 'never any heretique better deserved ... wherein we will leave him to your owne Christian wisdome'. Even if he were to prove himself innocent, Vorstius should still be banished. James made it clear that he considered Vorstius 'worthy of the fagot'. This was no quickly-regretted slip of the tongue – the same passage about burning was reproduced in the official edition of James's *Workes* published in 1616.[59]

That this approval of the option of burning heretics was no mere rhetorical flourish is clear when we remember that James would authorise (and indeed reportedly insist upon) the burning of two anti-trinitarian heretics in England just five months after his letter to the States General – indeed this was a consciously integrated display of his defence of religious orthodoxy.[60]

Perhaps more revealing still of the king's views is a conversation that the Scottish delegate Walter Balcanquhall had with James after returning from the Synod of Dort in May 1619. When he was told of the Socinian and Anabaptist errors charged on the Remonstrant ministers Johannes and Petrus Geesteranus at the Synod of Dort, James (according to Balcanquahall) 'did inveigh with great bitternes' against them, and commented that if the States would 'send them over to him, he would bestowe burning on them'.[61] If this was meant as a joke it was in rather bad taste, not least given James's previous track record, and it does not suggest a man who has abandoned his earlier sense that burning people was one weapon in the armoury of the Christian magistrate.

When not urging the burning of people, James was a particularly enthusiastic burner of books. This perhaps reflected the fact that James had treated the press as an extension of royal authority. If his books were a manifestation of sovereign power, then other books that challenged what he wrote were not simply contributions to a print debate but constituted a direct challenge to his authority. While James could commission other authors to defend his printed works, having a book which maintained arguments contrary to his own publicly burnt was the clearest manifestation of royal authority. Orders to burn books gathered steam over the course of James's reign, and embraced works by distinguished thinkers such as the Spanish Jesuit Francisco Suarez and the celebrated German Calvinist divine David Pareus (who had proposed James as the putative leader of a reunited European Protestantism), as well as (of course) Vorstius.[62] There could be few more obvious indications that James's tolerance of the quietly erring conscience did not reflect a liberal indulgence of alternative views.

James's true vision for his subjects was presumably not for a situation where different religions were tacitly permitted, but rather one where all would attend divine service in the Church established under his care (even if they might also privately practise another religion). As we have seen in his response to Northumberland in 1603, James promised an absence of persecution to those who would give outward obedience to the law, which apparently meant church attendance. Bearing this in mind, when James remarked in March 1604 that he would be a friend to Catholics if they would be 'good subjects', we might ponder whether being 'good subjects' similarly meant 'giving outward obedience to the law' in the sense of attending the services of the established Church.[63] When he declared before the privy council in February 1605 that his leniency towards Catholics at his entry to the kingdom had been abused as he had only reduced recusancy fines temporarily because Catholics had not opposed his coming in, James added that he 'gave them a yeare of probation to conforme themselves'. This 'had wrought none effect', so recusancy fines were now to be reimposed more harshly.[64] Similarly, in 1621 James told parliament that compulsion could be used 'to enforce outward obedience to the lawe, [so] that a decorum be kept and noe open profession made of a contrarie religion'.[65] That is, Catholicism might be privately practised, but 'outward obedience to the lawe' (in attending Protestant services) could be compelled without doing any violence to Catholic consciences.

The event that arguably encapsulated James's ambition for the religious lives of his subjects is described by the Venetian ambassador Scaramelli in a letter of 28 May 1603. He reported that 'old Howard [Northampton], who has lately been appointed to the council, and Southampton, who are both Catholics, declare that God has touched their hearts, and that the example of their king has more weight with them than the disputes of theologians. They have become Protestants, and go to church in the train of the king.' This was presumably what James ultimately hoped for and expected from his Catholic subjects – that loyalty to his person would inspire Catholics to attend church and to outwardly profess his religion: the ambassador reported that James had declared that he did not want the recusants to pay money for not attending church, but he wished them all to attend church in the same spirit as he did.[66]

This was, of course, all entirely compatible with a willingness to turn a blind eye to private Catholic devotions, the 'connivance' cited above. We can still find texts published during James's reign that made more unambiguous calls for religious toleration and freedom of speech and worship. They, like James (to whom they dedicated their works), maintained that 'perseqution for difference in religion is a monstrous and cruel beast', but (unlike James) they also in the same breath condemned the burning of heretics and books. Yet these writers were not favoured preachers at James's court, but Baptists who either wisely stayed abroad or perished in James's prisons.[67]

V Ecumenism and Irenicism

King James seems to have regarded himself as having been invested with a unique office as effective defender of the fortunes of European Christendom. This was not just a matter of public rhetoric. So firmly entrenched was the self-image that it could even find its way into maudlin domestic dramas.

Thus he declared to his favourite the earl of Somerset in 1615 that his grief at Somerset's petulance had led him to sin against God by allowing himself to be preoccupied with it to the peril of 'the estate of religion through all Christendom' which 'almost wholly under God lies now upon my shoulders'.[68] The obvious model that beckoned was that of the Emperor Constantine, who exemplified the duty of princes to intervene to prevent disputes in the Church, to regulate true doctrine and secure Christian unity. It is understandable, therefore, that James delighted in invoking the notion of a general council to restore the unity of Christendom. In this, of course, he was not alone. This was an objective to which Christians were obliged to at least pay lip-service, which gave it a certain rhetorical advantage. W. B. Patterson was, however, the first scholar to note just how often in his life James not only spoke of such a thing, but discussed the idea with foreign ambassadors, instructed his own agents to raise the matter, and was happy to debate how such an event might be organised. This would, then, appear to be more than an empty gesture. Most notably, in 1603–1604 James through agents conducted a series of discussions with the pope over the manner in which a general council of the Church might be called to pursue Christian reunion. But Patterson has also traced the king's involvement in persistent discussions of the desirability of Protestant unity, and schemes for drawing up detailed plans of how shared confessions of faith could be devised and religious harmony secured.

Ecumenical and irenical plans and rhetoric require careful unpacking, however. The problem is that historians of ecumenism have a tendency to treat such proposals in a context of ecumenical thought, rather than locating them in the events and other writings, speeches and actions of those like James who promoted them. There is also a danger that ecumenical ideas are treated as a single continuum, whereby every irenical gesture or pursuit of local unity is taken to be one stage in a larger policy working towards the ultimate goal of general Christian unity. However, not only is it far from evident that such actions should be treated as part of a broader project, but such subordinate levels of unity were often based on opposition to other groups – whether it be Lutheran unity directed against Calvinists (and vice versa), or Protestant unity the better to oppose Roman Catholicism. Unity was always aimed against somebody else (after all, even when the unity ostensibly encompassed all Christendom, this was urged against the 'common enemy' – the Turk).

In this context, the unified confessions of faith whose composition and agreement often formed the focus of these apparently ecumenical discussions were often envisaged not as a means of embracing a broader faith community, but rather as a means of better regulating and tightening the boundaries of orthodoxy. Any definition of terms of unity was also an exercise in defining who was excluded from it (that, after all, had been part of the point of the creeds fashioned by the so-called 'ecumenical councils' of the early church – the first of which at Nicaea was presided over by Constantine himself). A determination to make a distinction between 'fundamental' and 'non-fundamental' articles of faith was not, therefore, the shibboleth of a liberal-minded tolerationist, but was a universal aspiration which necessarily involved making a distinction between orthodoxy and heresy. Irenical and ecumenical notions were not necessarily upheld merely by those reacting against the rigid confessionalism of the era; they could be embraced by confessionalism's most zealous advocates. Heresy-hunting could indeed be an integral part of ecumenism.

Ecumenism and irenicism were thus intimately – indeed almost necessarily – bound up with the practice of exclusion. It should not surprise us, then, that the same French Reformed National Synod of Gap in 1604 that promoted a plan for union with the Lutheran churches and sent letters to Dutch, German, English, Scottish and Swiss universities soliciting their assistance in this,[69] simultaneously asked the same universities to join them in a collective censure of the teachings of the German theologian Johannes Piscator on Christ's active and passive obedience, and also for the first time inserted into the French Reformed confession the identification of the Pope as Antichrist.[70] On closer examination, James's apparent ecumenical initiatives often seem to fit these models.

The proposed general council of 1603–1605 was bound up with James's cultivation of amicable relations with the papacy to ensure that they would not inhibit his succession to the English throne. But a broader Christian reconciliation – if it could be achieved – had very specific attractions for James as a ruler. James was frequently preoccupied with how to prevent divisions among his own subjects, egged on from abroad. If a general council could be a means to remove confessional conflict, such a peace would secure an effective *cuius regio eius religio* settlement. If for *politique* writers the ideal of ecumenism also embraced the tolerance of diversity of religious opinion and practice, for James and the fellow Christian princes whom he so often invoked it was a matter of ensuring that their own subjects were religiously united in a manner that meant they could not threaten their rightful sovereign. Removal of 'discords in the Christian faith' would secure the thrones of Christian princes. Similarly, creating a religiously united realm would prevent the intrusion of confessional enemies. As James remarked to the Venetian ambassador in 1617, he hoped 'so to unite all the spirits of England, Scotland, and Ireland that neither the Spaniards nor the French nor anyone else would be able to obtain entrance' (*spera di unire cosi ben tutti li animi dell'Inghilterra, Scotia et Irlanda che ne Spagnoli ne Francesi ne chi si sia vi potrà haver l'addito*).[71] It should be emphasised, then, that this ecumenism was not informed by a broader liberal agenda: rather than securing 'liberty of conscience', it would remove the issues where conscience complicated political allegiance.

There was also a specific 'other' against which Christian unity was here being proposed, and that was the papal deposing power. It is true that James's agent Lord Kinloss told the Venetian ambassador in May 1603 that, if the pope wished to summon a general council, 'which, according to the ancient usage, should be superior to all Churches, all doctrine, all princes, secular and ecclesiastic, none excepted', James would be the first to offer complete obedience to that council's decrees.[72] But just two months later James was protesting to the French ambassador his disdain for the pope's exorbitant pretensions and opining that Henri IV should resist the papacy's claims and forbid the return of the Jesuits. James reportedly stated on this occasion that he would think again if the papacy were to submit to a free and general council of the Church, but this was to make it even more plain that the overthrow of the papacy's temporal claims would be such a council's first objective, after which reunion could follow.[73] This is precisely the point that the Venetian ambassador reported in September of the same year when he observed that the king showed 'a growing desire for the assembly of a free council to discuss the basis of religion and the question of papal authority'.[74]

That the chief rationale of a general council was to curb the pope's secular authority was repeatedly emphasised by James to a variety of audiences. His proclamation of February 1604 declared that Protestant princes could never feel secure given the course and claims of the papal see, and that a general council would help to pluck up the 'roots of dangers and jealousies' which arose as a consequence between princes and their subjects. James was emphatic that the council should 'make it manifest that no ... potentate either hath, or can challenge, power' to dispose of monarchies or 'dispense with subjects' obedience to their natural sovereigns'.[75]

In the years that followed, and with the change of pontiff (in his February 1604 proclamation James had acknowledged that he was 'personally so much beholding to the now bishop of Rome for his kind offices and private temporal carriage towards us in many things'), the anti-papal elements of reunion schemes became even more explicit. After 1605, in a series of confrontations with the papacy, James was even ready to renew the accusation made in his first biblical commentary on Revelation, published in 1588, that the pope was the Antichrist. This charge was made in a curious fashion. The 'Premonition' that prefaced the 1609 edition of James's defence of the Oath of Allegiance devoted more than fifty pages to assembling the case for identifying the pope as Antichrist, but implied (as James also suggested to Catholic ambassadors) that if the pope ceased to maintain his power to meddle in monarchs' temporal jurisdictions then James would no longer charge him with being Antichrist (although most of the evidence assembled for this identification in the preface was not dependent on this specific point at all).[76]

It is important here to stress how dominant anti-papal strains of anti-Catholicism became in James's court. Historians have become accustomed to seeing 'avant-garde conformists' (the precursors of later Laudianism) as an alternative line of development in the Jacobean Church and state, a religious tendency that was more ready to contemplate a pro-Spanish policy and the avoidance of knee-jerk anti-Catholicism. The court prelates Lancelot Andrewes and John Buckeridge are the two figures whom Peter Lake has rightly presented as the key inheritors and advocates of Richard Hooker's avant-garde conformity at James's court.[77] Yet, apart from sermons, their most prominent publications, and their most sustained works of theological and political argument, were very specifically shaped by the king's anti-papal agenda. Both Andrewes and Buckeridge were required to adopt the king's anti-papal rhetoric and arguments in the nearly 2,000 pages of official polemic that they published against Cardinal Bellarmine, dedicated to (and effectively commissioned by) James.[78] Moreover, the arguments of James's 'Premonition' obliged Andrewes and others to defend the king's identification of the pope as Antichrist, and to adopt the associated prophetic view of Church history. Five years after the 'Premonition' was published, Buckeridge was still gesturing towards the king's preferred prophetic Church history by alluding to the unbinding of Satan after 1,000 years' captivity (conventionally identified with the rule of either Pope Gregory VII or Boniface VIII depending on the chronology being deployed).[79] It was anti-papal writings that were the public face of the Jacobean regime, rather than tolerationist or ecumenical works.

VI Protestant Ecumenism

What, then, of James's initiatives in promoting the unity of Protestants? W. B. Patterson has rightly emphasised how James embraced the idea that he was tasked with securing the unity of Protestant princes and protecting the fortunes of continental Protestantism. Here the model of Constantine perhaps seemed more credible – few could doubt that the British king was the leading ruler among the Reformed Protestant Churches.[80] But if this image were to have any ramifications in domestic or foreign policy then we must assume that it was mediated and inflected through other objectives (not least a reluctance to incur any obligation to military intervention). James undoubtedly relished opportunities to play the role of protector and leader of European Protestantism, but this did not mean that the role was dictating policy, or indeed that he did not reserve the right to play other parts, in other productions.

At times, of course, irenical ideal and political pragmatism worked in tandem. Thus, the Cleves-Jülich crisis, the rapprochement of Catholic France and Spain in the aftermath of the assassination of Henri IV, and the proposal for a double Franco-Spanish dynastic treaty, all made the effective unity of Protestant powers vital as a counter-balance, and James sought to promote this in a number of ways. He actively sought to cultivate links to the Evangelical or Protestant Union in Germany, with the negotiations for an alliance culminating in the marriage of his daughter Elizabeth to the new Elector Palatine, Frederick V.[81] His agents were also closely involved in the formal conversion of John Sigismund, the elector of Brandenburg, to Calvinism in 1613. But there were still confessional boundaries to be observed. It is notable that James seems to have specifically forbidden his daughter to practise intercommunion with her husband. The readiness of James's ambassador Sir Stephen Lesieur to participate at the elector of Brandenburg's formal taking of Reformed communion on Christmas Day 1613 (where he was the first person to receive communion, and the only foreign ambassador present) had presumably not been cleared with his monarch beforehand.[82]

In James's moves to secure Protestant unity, we also need to be alert to the diverse objectives and meanings of irenicism that we have already touched upon. Thus, James's intervention in and after 1613 to help resolve the controversy between two Huguenot divines, Pierre du Moulin and Daniel Tilenus over the two identities of Christ was certainly framed in terms of a broader international ecumenical plan, and the temporary resolution of the controversy was capped by the guidelines drawn up by the Synod of Tonneins in 1614 for Protestant unification, which had James's explicit approval.[83] But these were plans that were very consciously drawn up both to pressurise the Huguenot protagonists to reach an agreement and to use the opportunity to draw other Protestant Churches in, at a time when continental Protestant unity was vital in the face of the new Franco-Spanish rapprochement.[84] (French Protestants were also always willing instruments for promoting schemes for continental religious reconciliation given that their desperate need for foreign allies made it vital to knit all the Continent's Protestants together in confessional solidarity.)[85]

These plans were also very clearly about erecting barriers against the spread of heterodoxy. The aim was not a general tolerant peace, but rather a permanent association of Reformed churches which would bind them to act to defend the doctrinal status quo. Thus the Synod of Tonneins specified that if there were any future controversy in one of the subscribing churches, 'nothing can be concluded or decided, or even less innovated, without the consent of all the provinces which have entered into this accord'.[86] Such emphases are hardly a surprise given that James's chosen instrument in this and future bids for Protestant unity was the Huguenot divine Pierre du Moulin. Du Moulin was not just one of the most indefatigable promoters of ecumenical models which attracted King James's support. He was also an accomplished polemicist and avid heresy-hunter, and his schemes were often promoted as the capstone to synods aimed at reaffirming doctrinal orthodoxy and anathematising its opponents.[87]

The Synod of Dort, which met in the Netherlands in 1618–1619 to resolve the controversies between the Remonstrants and their opponents, has also been urged as an example of James's ecumenical schemes.[88] The delegates whom he sent urged peace and moderation, and were tasked by the king with pursuing a broader Protestant reunion scheme proposed by Du Moulin. But the prominence of Du Moulin should alert us to the importance of the broader geopolitical context which necessitated sustaining the unity of the Dutch Republic against Spain. It was readily apparent to James already that this unity was most likely to be achieved by supporting the Prince of Orange in the suppression of the Dutch Remonstrants. That accord was to be secured by reinforcing the boundaries of Protestant orthodoxy, and it is hardly surprising that James was keen to use the opportunity to combine this with the pursuit of Vorstius once more (and also, as we have seen, to recommend the meting out of exemplary punishment to the Geesteranus brothers). With Vorstius, James gave his delegates specific instructions to secure his banishment, and this (rather than any broader Christian reunion) would seem to be the matter that most preoccupied the king as he received reports of the later stages of the synod and the formulation of the canons. When his delegates failed to secure Vorstius's banishment, James instructed his ambassador Sir Dudley Carleton to go in the king's name to the Prince of Orange to demand that Vorstius be exiled immediately. The delegates did still manage to read out in open session the proclamation against Vorstius that had accompanied the public burning of his works at the University of Cambridge several years earlier.[89]

If the Synod of Dort had indeed secured the political victory of the Dutch Contra-Remonstrants, and the collective subscription of all the delegations to the new, more restrictive doctrinal canons with the formal anathematisation of the Remonstrants' heterodoxies, then it is hardly surprising that Du Moulin considered this Synod to be the perfect forum for the promotion of a broader Protestant unity. It is telling that the Huguenot Synod of Alès – with Du Moulin presiding – declared the year after the conclusion of the Synod of Dort that it was 'a powerful remedy to rid the Church of corruption, and to root out heresies'.[90] Once orthodoxy had been properly secured in this way and heresy expelled, moderation and unity could then be pursued, but not before.

It is in this context that we need to read the performances of James's delegates at the synod. When Joseph Hall gave a sermon early in the synod in which he urged delegates to peace, unity and understanding, and the avoidance of unnecessary doctrinal controversies, this was not as conciliatory as it might appear. Hall referred to the king's instructions to the delegates that all present at the synod should adhere to the common faith expressed in the confessions of the Netherlands and other Churches.[91] But at the heart of the Dutch controversy lay the Remonstrant demand that the confession of the Dutch Reformed Church should be amended. This was, then, a very public declaration of support for the Contra-Remonstrants, and Hall's approving auditors understood it as declaring the English to be 'a party against the Remonstrants'.[92] When James's other delegates such as Walter Balcanquahall and Thomas Goad exhorted the synod to peace and to show moderation and gentleness, these were instructions on how the Contra-Remonstrants should conduct themselves in victory; they were not appealing for unity through compromise.[93]

Ecumenism was thus a topic that genuinely interested James. It was a language that he was happy to explore and which he spoke with some fluency, and a project whose plans he was eager to discuss. But James's irenicism was also deeply integrated into the world of everyday politics and the practical and ideological defences of his own position as a Protestant ruler, into the retrenchment of Protestant orthodoxy and the anathematising of its opponents, and into the assault upon ideas of papal temporal power. It was not a mere pipedream, but it was also not an all-consuming policy objective that we can equate with modern ecumenical notions. It was an idea and a language to which James was keen to lay an almost proprietorial claim when events permitted it, and to wield in his own interests when this proved possible. But it was not in itself a political programme in any meaningful sense, and it did not represent a rejection of the dynamics of confessional politics.

VII Conclusion

'Toleration and ecumenism' on the one hand, and book-burning, anathematising theological opponents, heretic-burning and identifying the pope as Antichrist on the other, are not therefore incompatible alternatives for different historians of James VI and I to choose between. Nor are these evidence that James had a schizophrenic or duplicitous mindset. They are different sides of the same coin, and we cannot understand the one without the other.

Notes

1 R. M. Smuts, 'Concepts of Peace and War' in R. Asch, E. Voss and M. Wrede (eds), *Frieden und Krieg in der Frühen Zeuzeit* (Munich, 2001), pp. 216–25.
2 *Tom Tell-Troath: or a Free Discourse Touching the Manners of the Time, Directed to His Majesty* (1622?).
3 For example, T. Cogswell, 'England and the Spanish Match', in R. Cust and A. Hughes (eds), *Conflict in Early Stuart England* (1989), pp. 111–16; idem, *James I: the Phoenix King* (2017), p. ix.
4 R. M. Smuts, *Political Culture, the State, and the Problem of Religious War in Britain and Ireland, 1578–1625* (Oxford, 2023), pp. 544, 637–46.
5 *Correspondence of King James VI of Scotland with Sir Robert Cecil and Others*, ed. J. Bruce (Camden Soc., 1861), p. 31; Smuts, *Political Culture*, p. 544.
6 W. B. Patterson, *King James VI and I and the Reunion of Christendom* (Cambridge, 1997) dubs this a 'complementary goal' to his pursuit of 'international peace' (p. 157).

7 For example, D. H. Willson, *King James VI and I* (1963), pp. 219–21, 272–4.

8 Patterson, *King James and the Reunion of Christendom*.

9 For example, Smuts, *Political Culture*, pp. 545, 552–3.

10 M. Questier, 'The Reputation of James VI and I Revisited', *Journal of British Studies* 61 (2022), pp. 959–61.

11 Bruce, *Correspondence*, p. 37.

12 J. P. Sommerville (ed.), *King James VI and I: Political Writings* (Cambridge, 1994), p. 139.

13 McClure, *LJC*, I, p. 204.

14 J. Spedding et al. (eds), *The Works of Francis Bacon* (14 vols, 1857–74), XI, p. 91.

15 E. R. Foster (ed.), *Proceedings in Parliament 1610* (2 vols, New Haven, 1966), I, p. 51; M. Jansson (ed.), *Proceedings in Parliament: 1614 (House of Commons)* (Philadelphia, 1988), p. 15.

16 W. Notestein et al. (eds), *Commons Debates, 1621* (7 vols, New Haven, 1935), IV, p. 3.

17 Sommerville, *King James VI and I: Political Writings*, pp. 138–41; Bruce, *Correspondence*, pp. 36–8; McClure, *LJC*, I, p. 204; Foster, *1610 Proceedings*, I, pp. 50–1; Jansson, *1614 Proceedings*, pp. 7–8, 14–15, 473. The 1621 Parliament was the one occasion when James did not claim to be worried by the increase of popery (for obvious reasons).

18 Jansson, *1614 Proceedings*, pp. 7, 473.

19 Contrast Jansson, *1614 Proceedings*, p. 8 with Jansson, *1614 Proceedings*, pp. 14–15, 473.

20 McClure, *LJC*, II, p. 345 (and cf. Notestein, *1621 Debates*, IV, pp. 72–3).

21 Notestein, *1621 Debates*, IV, p. 3.

22 For example, R. Lockyer, *James VI and I* (Harlow, 1998), p. 125; *ODNB, sub* 'James VI and I' (article by J. Wormald). Wormald in her account of this correspondence in her *ODNB* life of James I manages to swap the positions adopted by Cecil and James.

23 James was also implicitly seeking to confute accusations that he himself had been outrageously tolerant towards some Scottish Catholic rebels. I am grateful to Michael Questier for this point.

24 Bruce, *Correspondence*, pp. 32–7.

25 McClure, *LJC*, I, p.171.

26 *A Proclamation for Proceeding against Iesuites and Secular Priestes, their Receivers, Relievers, and Maintainers* (1602). Sir Robert Cecil undoubtedly had significant input into both this and James's proclamations on the same subject, so textual similarities may reflect his own work.

27 See for example Questier, *Dynastic Politics*, pp. 288, 293–5, 306–7, 308–11, 317 and *passim*.

28 McClure, *LJC*, I, p. 204 W. Baildon (ed.), *Les Reportes del Cases in Camera Stellata* (1894), p. 189; Questier, *Dynastic Politics*, pp. 294–5.

29 *The Correspondence of Dr. Matthew Hutton* (Surtees Society 17, 1843), p. 172.

30 'King James and the English Puritans: An Unpublished Document', *Blackwood's Magazine* 188, no. 1139 (September 1910), pp. 408–9; J. Morgan, 'Henry Jacob, James I, and Religious Reform, 1603–1609', *Church History* 86 (2017), p. 724.

31 P. Baker (ed.), *Proceedings in Parliament 1624: The House of Commons* (2015–18), *British History Online* http://www.british-history.ac.uk/no-series/proceedings-1624-parl, 19 February.

32 For the distinction between 'toleration' and 'connivencie', see J. F. Larkin and P. L. Hughes (eds), *Stuart Royal Proclamations* (2 vols, Oxford, 1973–83), I, p. 246; Francis Bunny, *Answere to a Popish Libel* (1607); Robert Persons, *A Treatise*

Tending to Mitigation (1607), p. 7; *1624 Proceedings*, 19 February, 24 February, 27 February, 7 April, 29 May. For 'connivencie' towards puritan nonconformity, see Sir Ralph Winwood, ed. E. Sawyer, *Memorials of Affairs of State* (3 vols, 1725), II, p. 15.

33 Henry Jacob, *To the Right High and Mightie Prince, IAMES ... An Humble Supplication for Toleration and Libertie* (1609), pp. 22–3; Gabriel Powel, *A Refutation of an Epistle Apologeticall*, pp. 94, 97; John Colleton, *A Supplication* (1604), p. 9; Anon., *An Epistle, or Apologie of a True, and Charitable Brother of the Reformed Church in favoure of Protestantes, Papistes & Those of the Reformation* (1605), sig. C2ᵛ; Gabriel Powel, *A Consideration of the Papists Reasons* (Oxford, 1604), pp. 24, 29–30. For explicit puritan appeals for 'toleration', see also Josias Nichols, *The Plea of the Innocent* (1602), pp. 17, 29.

34 *1624 Proceedings*, 1 March, 2 March, 7 April, 29 May. Alarm was being expressed here at the report of the bishop of Segovia noting that James was unable to offer 'toleration' without parliamentary approval, but that the 'connivance' which he could proffer instead would amount to the same thing (1 March, 2 March).

35 For example, K. Fincham and P. Lake, 'The Ecclesiastical Policy of King James I', *Journal of British Studies* 24 (1985), pp. 185–6; Lockyer, *James VI and I*, pp. 130–1; Notestein, *1621 Debates*, IV, pp. 3, 74; Bruce, *Correspondence*, pp. 74–6; Sommerville, *King James VI and I: Political Writings*, pp. 200–1, 223.

36 See n. 33.

37 I am grateful to Alex Courtney for this point.

38 Sommerville, *King James VI and I: Political Writings*, p. 200.

39 Bruce, *Correspondence*, pp. 74–6.

40 Bruce, *Correspondence*, pp. 36–7.

41 Sommerville, *King James VI and I: Political Writings*, pp. 139, 141.

42 Sommerville, *King James VI and I: Political Writings* pp. 223–4.

43 Larkin and Hughes, *Proclamations*, I, p. 71.

44 *CSPScot 1589–1593*, p. 528; A. F. Scott Pearson, *Thomas Cartwright and Elizabethan Puritanism* (1925), pp. 463–4.

45 McClure, *LJC*, II, p. 345.

46 Lockyer, *James*, p. 113; *Commons Journals*, I, p. 385.

47 *CSPV 1603–1607*, pp. 227–32. The Catholic appeal for 'liberty of conscience' did not of course extend this principle to Protestant 'heretics' (see N. Davidson '"Fuggir la Libertà della Coscienza": Conscience and the Inquisition in Sixteenth-Century Italy', in H. Braun and E. Vallance (eds), *Contexts of Conscience in Early Modern Europe, 1500–1700* (Basingstoke, 2004)). For the lack of clarity in the usage of the term, it is interesting to note that in 1622 James equated 'liberty of conscience' with a formal toleration when seeking to suppress rumours that this had been granted to Catholics (D. Laing (ed.), *Original Letters relating to the Ecclesiastical Affairs of Scotland* (2 vols, Edinburgh, 1851), II, pp. 700–2). I am grateful to Alex Courtney for this latter reference.

48 See A. Walsham, 'Ordeals of Conscience: Casuistry, Conformity and Confessional Identity in Post-Reformation England', in Vallance and Braun, *Contexts*, pp. 32–3.

49 Sommerville, *King James VI and I: Political Writings*, p. 18.

50 Foster, *1610 Proceedings*, I, p. 51.

51 Sommerville, *King James VI and I: Political Writings*, p. 140.

52 Sommerville, *King James VI and I: Political Writings*, pp. 6–7.

53 Questier, *Dynastic Politics*, pp. 308–9.

54 Questier, *Dynastic Politics*; Winwood, *Memorials*, III, pp. 309–10.

55 Larkin and Hughes, *Proclamations*, I, pp. 71, 249; Sommerville, *King James VI and I: Political Writings*, p. 224.

56 M. Questier, *Catholics and Treason: Martyrology, Memory, and Politics in the Post-Reformation* (Oxford, 2022), p. 434. I am grateful to Michael Questier for this point.

57 *ODNB*, sub 'Helwys, Thomas' (article by S. Wright).

58 Winwood, *Memorials*, III, p. 306.

59 James I, *His Majesties Declaration concerning his Proceedings with the States Generall* (1612), pp. 20, 81; *The Workes of the Most High and Mightie Prince, Iames* (1616), pp. 355–6, 378.

60 D. Como and I. Atherton, 'The Burning of Edward Wightman: Puritanism, Prelacy and the Politics of Heresy in Early Modern England', *English Historical Review* 120 (2005), pp. 1241, 1244, 1248. But note Eric Platt's thorough dismantling of Shriver's argument that the king's intervention was prompted by his being associated with Vorstius by the Jesuit Becanus (E. Platt, *Britain and the Bestandtwisten* (Göttingen, 2015), pp. 43–6).

61 A. Milton (ed.), *The British Delegation and the Synod of Dort* (Woodbridge, 2005), p. 361.

62 McClure, *LJC*, I, p. 488; II, p. 313; C. S. Clegg, *Press Censorship in Jacobean England* (Cambridge, 2001), pp. 76–77, 81–2, 85. The offending passages regarding inferior magistrates from Pareus's commentary on Romans that were directed to be burned in 1622 had ironically been published in his 1612 *Quaestiones* that had been dedicated to James himself and had not raised any eyebrows. The changed political context was the key here (see A. Milton, 'The Church of England and the Palatinate', in P. Collinson and P. Ha (eds), *The Reception of Continental Reformation in Britain* (Oxford, 2010), p. 159).

63 Sommerville, *King James VI and I: Political Writings*, p. 141 (although in 1616 James commented that recusants can be 'peaceable subjects' (p. 223) – but perhaps not 'good' ones?). For his distinction between (Irish recusant) 'half-subjects' and 'good subjects' see *Calendar of the Carew Manuscripts* (6 vols, 1867), V, pp. 290–1.

64 McClure, *LJC*, I, p. 204. Compare James's instructions regarding Huntly in 1606, that proceedings against him should temporarily be stayed for his 'better resolution', but this would cease if he persisted in his errors, and there would be no 'preposterous toleration' (John Spottiswoode, *History of the Church of Scotland* (3 vols, Edinburgh, 1851), III, pp. 187–8). I owe this reference to Alex Courtney.

65 Notestein, *1621 Debates*, IV, p. 3.

66 *CSPV 1603–1607*, p. 42; Questier, *Dynastic Politics*, p. 273. See also the examples of Huntly and Arundel noted in Questier, *Dynastic Politics*, pp. 373–4.

67 Thomas Helwys, *A Shorte Declaration of the Mistery of Iniquity* (1612); Leonard Busher, *Religions Peace: Or a Plea for Liberty of Conscience* (1614); W. K. Jordan, *The Development of Religious Toleration in England* (4 vols, 1932–40), II, pp. 43–52, 274–98; S. Wright, 'Leonard Busher: Life and Ideas', *Baptist Quarterly* 39 (2001); S. Wright, *The Early English Baptists* (Woodbridge, 2006). I plan to discuss Helwys and Busher and their works in more detail elsewhere.

68 G. P. V. Akrigg (ed.), *Letters of King James VI and I* (1992), p. 338. Croft (P. Croft, *King James* (Basingstoke, 2003), p. 174) omits to mention the context of this remark.

69 Patterson, *King James and the Reunion of Christendom*, p. 180.

70 John Quick (ed.), *Synodicon in Gallia Reformata* (2 vols, 1692), I, pp. 227, 238, 266.

71 *CSPV 1615–1617*, p.555 [23 July]; Questier, *Dynastic Politics*, p. 381.

72 *CSPV 1603–1607*, p. 22; Patterson, *King James and the Reunion of Christendom*, p. 37.

73 Questier, *Dynastic Politics*, p. 277.

74 *CSPV 1603–1607*, p. 98.

75 Larkin and Hughes, *Proclamations*, I, p. 73.

76 King James, *An Apologie for the Oath of Allegiance ... together with a Premonition ... to all most Mightie Monarchs, Kings, Free Princes and States of Christendome* (1609), pp. 51–108 (esp. pp. 107–8); A. Milton, *Catholic and Reformed: The Roman and Protestant Churches in English Protestant Thought, 1600–1640* (Cambridge, 1995), p. 108 n. 44; Patterson, *King James and the Reunion of Christendom*, p. 96; Smuts, *Political Culture*, p. 563.

77 P. Lake, 'Lancelot Andrewes, John Buckeridge and Avant-Garde Conformity at the Court of James I', in L. L. Peck (ed.), *The Mental World of the Jacobean Court* (Cambridge, 1991).

78 Lancelot Andrewes, *Tortura Torti* (1609); *idem, Responsio ad Apologiam Cardinalis Bellarmini* (1610); John Buckeridge, *De Potestate Papae in Rebus Temporalibus* (1614).

79 Milton, *Catholic and Reformed*, pp. 109, 294, 296; Buckeridge, *De Potestate*, p. 1114; James, *Apologie*, pp. 106–7.

80 Smuts, *Political Culture*, p. 583.

81 Patterson, *King James and the Reunion of Christendom*, pp. 155–7; Smuts, *Political Culture*, pp. 567–71, 574–5; Questier, *Dynastic Politics*, pp. 324–6, 337–43.

82 Milton, 'Church of England and Palatinate', pp. 154–5.

83 Patterson, *King James and the Reunion of Christendom*, pp. 159–80.

84 Questier, *Dynastic Politics*, p. 338.

85 Here Patterson's remarks on the long-running Huguenot enthusiasm for ecumenical schemes (*King James and the Reunion of Christendom*, pp. 179–80) need to be considered in combination with his earlier comments in the same volume, p. 162.

86 Patterson, *King James and the Reunion of Christendom*, p. 173.

87 *Pace* Patterson's remark that Du Moulin was deeply interested in the cause of Christian unity 'in spite of his activities as a polemicist' (*King James and the Reunion of Christendom*, p. 159), it could be argued that this was *because* of them.

88 Here I differ from Patterson's argument that James dispatched his delegates to Dort as 'a deliberate move to realize his long-term goal of religious reconciliation' and saw the Synod as taking an essential step towards Christian reunion (Patterson, *King James and the Reunion of Christendom*, p. 291). Even if James thought that, having suppressed the Remonstrants and restored political and religious unity in the Dutch Republic, the synod might (as Du Moulin proposed) *also* in the process usefully provide an opportunity to further religious reconciliation (or that it should at least not endanger plans for some future reconciliation with the Lutherans), this does not mean that he envisaged the Synod *principally* as a means to Christian reunion.

89 A. Milton (ed.), *The British Delegation and the Synod of Dort* (Woodbridge, 2005), pp. xlii, 343–7, 360–1, 367–70, 371, 376.

90 Patterson, *King James and the Reunion of Christendom*, p. 194.

91 P. Hall (ed.), *The Works of Joseph Hall* (12 vols, Oxford, 1839), XI, pp. 465–87.

92 *Golden Remains of the Ever Memorable Mr. John Hales* (1673), II, p. 13. See also Bishop Carleton's speech to the States General two weeks previously: Milton, *British Delegation*, pp. 119–22.

93 *Golden Remains*, II, p. 54; *Historisch verhael van 't ghene sich toegedraeghen heft binnen Dordrecht* (no place of publication, 1623), p. 215^r.

6

SETTING DOWN ROOTS

Establishing the Society of Jesus in Jacobean England*

Thomas M. McCoog SJ

In much of the modern-day 'mainstream' scholarly literature there is a kind of received wisdom about aspects of the post-Reformation Catholic community in the later sixteenth and early seventeenth centuries. In particular this is the case with the English members of the Society of Jesus, whose presence in their native country was certainly regarded by many, and not just Protestants, as highly controversial. But a good deal of that modern account is a sometimes-uncritical replication of contemporary opinion. There was another narrative of their place in the English Church and polity, one that has, by and large, been missed – one that was given a new edge by the accession of James VI of Scotland as king of England and Great Britain in 1603. It is, I argue, central to some of the major current debates about the post-Reformation Church and state.

The English Jesuit mission, founded with the arrival of Robert Persons, Edmund Campion and Ralph Emerson in 1580, grew slowly despite the initial high expectations; by the end of Elizabeth I's reign there were fewer than two dozen Jesuits. In addition to England, the mission administered colleges (seminaries) in Rome (1578), Valladolid (1589) and Seville (1592), and established its own college for English boys at St Omers (1593). With the occasional exception of the English College in Rome, no college had an English rector; local Flemish or Spanish provincials governed the institutions to no one's satisfaction.

---

* For the purposes of this chapter, I have revisited and, at times, revised two earlier articles: 'The Establishment of the English Province of the Society of Jesus', *Recusant History* 17 (1984), pp. 121–39; 'The Creation of the First Jesuit Communities in England', *Heythrop Journal* 28 (1987), pp. 40–56.

DOI: 10.4324/9781003319764-7

Roman authorities reorganised the English mission in 1598. But instead of a bishop so desired by many secular clergy and some Jesuits, Rome established an archpresbyterate, an irregular ecclesiastical structure, resisted by the so-called Appellant secular priests.[1] Five weeks later on 6/16 April 1598, the Jesuit superior general Claudio Acquaviva (in office 1581–1615) established an equally novel administration, the prefecture, to bring order into what was quickly becoming an unwieldy, dysfunctional organisation. The superior general nominated a prefect with two assistants (vice-prefects) for Spain and Flanders with their authority vis-à-vis local rectors and provincials defined and regulated. Despite subsequent modifications, the non-English provincials remained dissatisfied with perceived concessions to national sentiment and restriction of their authority.

I A New Dynasty

Concern about the succession to the English throne, a preoccupation that dared not speak its name, increased with Elizabeth's age. The Scottish King James VI intensified his charm offensive in the late 1590s as he advanced his claims to the English throne. As Spain and France dithered in their efforts to find an agreeable Catholic contender, the king of Scotland consolidated support with chameleon-like changes that inflated everyone's expectations by promising all things to all confessions.[2]

Jesuits within England welcomed James's accession and anticipated greater tolerance. All fears, Henry Garnet claimed, had vanished in the expectation of a golden era as long as the pope and Catholic powers did not interfere.[3] Oswald Tesimond clarified the reasons for Catholic optimism: James had promised an unnamed priest that Catholics would 'enjoy complete freedom, keeping their priests and receiving the sacraments in accordance with their own tastes'.[4] John Gerard recalled general Catholic hope occasioned by the accession of James: 'Was it not now time for us to look out and to long that the earth would begin to dry and afford us some quiet habitation upon it'?[5] Jubilant Catholics distributed wine in public squares and allegedly showered the streets with money as they lined the path of the royal progress and bombarded the king with petitions for liberty of conscience and tolerance.[6] Seated safely on the English throne, some argued, James no longer had to fear that his embrace of Catholicism would cause him political difficulties. Now he could act out of conviction. Mirto Frangipani, nuncio in Brussels, informed the cardinal-nephew Pietro Aldobrandini that Catholics in England might have been uncertain whether James would repeal Elizabethan anti-Catholic legislation, but they believed 'that he would turn a blind eye' (*mais pensent qu'il fermera les yeux*) to its enforcement.[7]

After a series of false dawns and frustrated hopes, on 22 February 1604, nearly a year after his accession, James expelled all Jesuits and seminary priests for their open celebration of Catholic sacraments and the Mass, and their reception of the king's subjects into the Roman Church. Thus, any secular or religious priest, even those previously granted a royal pardon, in England after 19 March, and any of them who returned to the kingdom after that date, would suffer the full penalties of the law.[8]

Some expressions of Catholicism had become all too public. Garnet nonetheless remained upbeat. He dismissed the proclamation as mere posturing, more bluff and bluster that would be neither enforced nor implemented.[9] In his parliamentary address on 19 March 1604, however, James warned Catholics that, although he personally disliked persecution, he would become their avowed enemy if they advocated the 'arrogant and ambitious Supremacie of their Head the Pope'.[10] Parliament urged the enforcement of all Elizabethan statutes against Jesuits and seminary priests.[11] As proof that nothing had changed, a secular priest John Sugar and a layman Robert Grissold were hanged, drawn and quartered at Warwick on July 26, and another layman Laurence Bailey was executed in Lancaster in September. Yet many remained convinced of James's good intention despite their execution. Innocenzo del Bufalo, nuncio in Paris, exonerated the king and blamed overzealous magistrates.[12] Meanwhile the pope urged Catholics to patience, obedience and the avoidance of anything that could intensify persecution. Patient forbearance and clear demonstrations of obedience would show the crown the fidelity and loyalty of its Catholic subjects.[13]

Yet Garnet still did not despair. With forty Jesuits in England in 1604, the superior went so far as to imagine that it would be appropriate 'for the Catholic king to found a [Jesuit] college in England, ... a blessed Tower of David ... built in the midst of the heretics'. He anticipated a great harvest once the Treaty of London (1604) was finalised.[14] Hope that Spain would assist faded and died as the Habsburg negotiators abandoned English Catholics with a simple promise that His Catholic Majesty (Philip III) would continue to work for their relief. The construction of a Tower of David would have to wait as Garnet himself admitted a year later.[15] Instead the Gunpowder Plot, discovered on 5 November 1605, devastated the mission.

A proclamation promulgated on 15 January 1606 sought the apprehension of Garnet, Gerard and Tesimond.[16] Garnet and Edward Oldcorne were captured on 27 January, two days after the arrest of Ralph Ashley and Nicholas Owen. Oldcorne and Ashley were executed at Red Hill, Worcester, on 7 April; Owen had died mysteriously in the Tower of London, probably a result of torture, during the night of 1/2 March. Garnet was executed in St Paul's churchyard, London, on 3 May. Thomas Strange, who had returned to England circa 1603 and generally resided with Garnet, was arrested at Kenilworth, Warwickshire, a few days after the plot's discovery, and conveyed to the Tower. Frequently tortured, he remained a prisoner until his exile in 1610. Tesimond was taken as he was reading the posted proclamation, but he shook off his captor in the crowded street and eventually escaped to Calais in the disguise of a pork butcher with a cargo of slaughtered pigs.[17] Gerard's escape to the Continent was much more dignified; in May he left in the retinue of the Flemish ambassador.[18]

In March 1606 Persons warned Acquaviva that heretics and their Appellant clergy allies intended to exploit the plot in their campaign against the Society. Indeed, the accuracy of the descriptions of specific Jesuits in the proclamations raised doubts about the loyalty of all members of the households in which they had been living.[19] On 21 January 1606, Parliament reconvened with a new slate of legislation against Catholic separatism as its priority. After various adjustments and compromises, it passed 'An Act for better discovering and repressing of Popish Recusants' [3 James I, c. 4]. Unlike the Elizabethan anti-Catholic laws, this was intended to flush out church papists and crypto-Catholics by requiring an annual reception of communion with a graduated list of fines and punishments. Enforcement was placed in the hands of justices of the peace. Aware that the fines were not sufficiently burdensome to wealthy Catholics, Parliament allowed the king to refuse the fine in favour of confiscation of two-thirds of the convicted recusant's assets.[20] More controversial and more damaging was the introduction of an oath of allegiance.[21]

II Post-Gunpowder Plot

Garnet had been superior of the mission since 1586, but the mission's governance continued rather seamlessly after his arrest and execution. On 28 June/8 July 1606, Acquaviva appointed Richard Holtby as Garnet's successor, and addressed all Jesuits on the mission. After his eulogy of Garnet, Acquaviva exhorted the Jesuits to zealous steadfastness and perseverance with a reminder that he was spiritually united with them in their sufferings.[22] Robert Jones succeeded Holtby, albeit reluctantly, on 18/28 March 1608, and Michael Walpole followed him in 1615.[23]

Without a novitiate, the mission depended on other provinces for the acceptance of candidates and the formation of novices. Establishment of an English novitiate required an endowment and Roman approval. In the autumn of 1603, Jacques Blaze, bishop of St Omers, edified by the fervour of English Catholics and impressed with the work of Jesuits at the English College, proposed a second foundation to the college's rector Giles Schoondonck. The bishop promised a site and the building, but not an endowment. With Persons's encouragement Schoondonck continued the discussion with the bishop as Persons pursued the matter with Acquaviva.[24] The endowment was provided by Luisa de Carvajal y Mendoza, a Spanish noblewoman much influenced by English Jesuits at Valladolid.[25] Her will granted Persons *carte blanche* to use whatever he needed to erect a novitiate for English Jesuits anywhere in the world.[26] Acquaviva accepted the benefaction on 15/25 January 1605. By June, William Baldwin and Persons had selected Louvain as the most acceptable site.[27]

In 1609–1610, there were approximately fifty-three Jesuits in England and Wales, eighteen at St Omers, and twenty-eight at St John's, the new novitiate in Louvain.[28] As the mission expanded, Acquaviva strengthened its organisation. He appointed Richard Blount, the superior's assistant or *socius* with Richard Holtby, William Wright, Anthony Hoskins and Michael Walpole as Jones's consultors or advisors. Acquaviva established 'spiritual prefects', positions instituted in some provinces by his predecessors to provide spiritual and emotional aid to Jesuits in the vicinity. These 'prefects' assumed many of the responsibilities of the superior and oversaw the spiritual and religious lives of the men under him. In order to keep religious discipline fresh in the minds of the men, the superior general had ordered that each attentively read the common rules of the Society, a summary of its *Constitutions*, and the fourteen points of an instruction issued by Acquaviva on 30 December 1606/ 9 January 1607. Finally, Acquaviva raised the issue of poverty. Each Jesuit on the mission was obliged to provide the superior with an annual reckoning of monies received and spent.[29]

Issued around this time was the intriguing '*Oedipus schedularum*', most likely drafted, as Peter Lake and Michael Questier suggest, to counter a new petition, drawn up by the new archpriest, George Birkhead, and his associates, for an English bishop.[30] As Lake and Questier have made clear, competing ecclesiologies had motivated the Jesuits and their Appellant critics. For the Appellants, Catholicism 'could best be fostered and preserved in England through the conventional, ecclesiastically defined, and controlled conduits of sacramental grace; through the regular ministrations of the secular clergy, organized, if possible, under the authority of bishops, who would bring with them both the much-needed spiritual powers of ordination and confirmation, and the capacity to regulate the affairs both of clergy and of laity'. On the other hand, Jesuits 'formed and sustained by the workings of divine grace, unconstrained by the formal structures of ecclesiastical hierarchy', perhaps inevitably did not argue for the necessity of episcopal governance.[31]

As part of what appeared to be a concerted lobbying campaign, the future Jesuit Thomas Fitzherbert and Sir Oliver Manners presented a report to Pope Paul V on the effective organisation of the bishop-less mission. Instead of the traditional territorial parishes as advocated by the Appellants, the Jesuits organised their 'churches' (*ecclesia*) around a prominent Catholic layperson.[32] Jesuits Robert Jones, John Percy (alias Fisher), Michael Walpole, Thomas Abercrombie, Anthony Hoskins, Richard Blount and William Wright, administered these 'churches' that flourished under the protection of Catholic nobility and gentry, and in so doing confirmed John Bossy's hypothesis that the Society cultivated closer relations with social elites after the separation of the Jesuit and secular clerical missions in 1602.[33] One wonders why only seven Jesuits were mentioned. Was the list compiled to impress? Or did these 'churches' have stability and security that the others lacked? Each of the seven Jesuits was asked whether a bishop was necessary, and each left the final decision to the pope and stressed that candidates not be selected from the factious collaborators with the government but from peaceful clergy working for union within the English mission.[34] The campaign for a bishop continued, but a greater threat to the English mission came from within the Society.

III The Mission under Attack

Despite periodic adjustments, relations between English Jesuits and their host provinces at best remained tenuous. Persons acted quickly to quell any disturbance until his death in 1610.[35] Moreover, Acquaviva continued to protect the mission until his death in 1615.[36] At the opening of the congregation convened to elect his successor on 5 November 1615, ominously the tenth anniversary of the Gunpowder Plot, tension between Spanish and English Jesuits regarding ordinary governance and administration became an issue that concerned the whole Society. '[A]fter mature and careful discussion', the congregation sided with the Spanish: 'it was not desirable to provide for these missions superiors ... who would govern them all, scattered though they be among various provinces of the Society. For this would be a new type of governance in the Society, and it would introduce a distinction of nationalities, contrary to the mutual union of hearts and minds'.[37] The congregation also forbade establishment of colleges, seminaries and novitiates exclusively for one nation. The custom of the Society, the congregation argued, has always favoured mixing persons from different nations 'lest national differences be gradually introduced, to the great harm of the Society'.[38] Accordingly the congregation instructed the superior general to enforce the decree and restore 'the ordinary manner of living in the Society'.[39] Enforcement threatened the very existence of the mission.

England was not represented at the congregation and no one spoke in its defence. Anonymous rejoinders can be found amongst archival documents, but we do not know to whom they were addressed nor whether they were in fact sent.[40] The mission's dismantlement, the apologists argued, unwittingly allied the congregation with the mission's opponents: English government, the Established Church, Protestants, Appellants and other anti-Jesuit Catholics. The goals of the Society's enemies had finally been achieved: Jesuits would be withdrawn from the colleges and the mission.[41] The *apologiae* and defences had no effect: the congregational committee responded that it was simply not expedient for missions to have their own superior.

IV The English Vice-Province

Twice rector of the English College, Rome (1592–1594 and 1597–1598), the new superior general Muzio Vitelleschi (in office 1615–1645) was caught in a dilemma. He could ignore the decree and allow the mission to retain its current organisation, but so doing risked almost certain outrage among the Spanish and Belgian Jesuits, and thus being reprimanded by the congregation of procurators scheduled for November 1619. Or he could implement the decree as instructed by the congregation with possibly dire consequences on the mission in England. In July 1619, he resolved the problem by establishing England as a vice-province and thus no longer subject to the decree. The mission, as Vitelleschi explained to the two Belgian provincials, Carlo Scribani and Jean Heren, was larger than other vice-provinces and indeed some provinces.[42] According to the Annual Letter of 1619–1620, there were 212 members with 100 Jesuits in England and Wales. A specific Jesuit in each mission, most likely the spiritual prefects, was named superior. Others served in Watten, Brussels, St Omers and Louvain. The author of the Annual Letter, either Richard Blount, who had been named superior on 7/17 April 1619, or his *socius* Thomas Talbot, echoed Luisa de Carvajal y Mendoza's scepticism. The prospect of a royal marriage between Charles, Prince of Wales and the Spanish princess María Anna, had not improved conditions for Catholics in England as many had claimed. Catholics in England 'remained undeceived, finding no relaxation of persecution as regards either their property or their families'.[43]

Relations between Spain and England gradually deteriorated after the Treaty of London, a decline accelerated by the assassination of King Henry IV of France in 1610 and popular fears of plots and conspiracies involving Catholics and Jesuits.[44] Indeed, as Calvin F. Senning ably demonstrates, anti-Catholicism even increased because of Protestant successes in Bohemia. James's daughter Elizabeth (later known as the Winter Queen) married Frederick V, the Calvinist Elector Palatine, in 1613.[45] His acceptance of the Bohemian crown in 1619 enthused Protestants in England. Now, according to the Annual Letter, he was 'regarded as one raised up for the destruction of the papists, for the advance of the Gospel, and the conquest of Rome ... with a strong desire to oppress them [Catholics] as opposed to the general interests of the country'.[46] Pursuivants with full authority raided Catholic residences, arrested priests and seized religious goods and vestments. News of the elevation of the Jesuit mission to vice-provincialate status might have chagrined Belgian and Spanish Jesuits, but it also provided Catholics with a glimmer of hope amidst the persecution. Jesuits had led approximately 400 converts from 'the sink of error into the bosom of the Church, a large number, when we take into account either the machinations of the enemy or the sensual allurements of a very worldly age'.[47] Jesuit ministries and works of charity won them the admiration and support of social elites including the French and Spanish ambassadors.[48] At an unknown date in late 1620 or early 1621, Henry Silesdon (*vere* Bedingfeld), appointed procurator by the vice-provincial, travelled to Rome to report on current conditions in England but, more important, the procurator requested that Vitelleschi establish England as a full province within the Society.[49] On 14/24 April 1621, Vitelleschi refused to grant provincial status for England. Asserting that he personally wished to elevate the vice-province, he could not do so because of its instability. There existed a college and houses of formation in the Low Countries, but no endowed, stable residences in England. Moreover, the superior general questioned whether the vice-province would be able to convene the required provincial congregations. Finally, the superior general doubted that the co-rulers of the Spanish Netherlands, Isabella Clara Eugenia and her husband Archduke Albert, would allow Jesuit communities within their territories to be governed by a religious superior stationed in England. But, according to Henry More, SJ, the first province's historian and second provincial, unbeknownst to Vitelleschi, the vice-provincial had already secured their approval before Albert's death on 3/13 July 1621.[50] Until such stability was demonstrated, Vitelleschi could not grant the request.[51] Blount was promoted to vice-provincial on 26 June/6 July 1619.

Administrative changes followed as Blount compiled proof that the vice-province could fulfil the demanded conditions. As we have already seen, Blount divided the mission into smaller geographical units, each with its own superior.[52] He then focused on the convocation of a vice-provincial congregation to elect a representative for the next congregation of procurators generally held every three years and scheduled for November 1622. Vitelleschi allowed Blount to decide whether the congregation would be convened in England or Flanders.[53]

Forty Jesuits gathered in London *in Residencia eiusdem Societatis* (the residence of the same Society) on 14 May 1622 for four days.[54] This residence was most probably located in Hunsdon House at the French embassy in Blackfriars.[55] This was also site of the 'Fatall Vesper' in 1623, a catastrophe to which we shall return later in this chapter. Tanneguy Leveneur de Tillières was the ambassador.[56] Only three Jesuits from the Continent attended; four others were excused. Having been reminded that the procurators of vice-provinces did not have a vote at the congregation of procurators,[57] the assembly elected Henry Silesdon procurator with John Worthington to take his place if necessary. The congregation itself voted against convening a general congregation and turned its attention to its own concerns.

Convinced that the superior general had earlier refused provincial status because of his unfamiliarity with the organisation and works of the vice-province within England, the congregation detailed its institutions and ministries.[58] The vice-province had 240 members, fifty-six of whom were professed of the four vows. In the Spanish Netherlands, the vice-province had a novitiate in Liège, a college in St Omers, a scholasticate in Louvain, and a tertianship in Ghent. The mission had transferred its novices from Louvain to Liège in 1615 into buildings and property purchased in 1614 by John Gerard with funds by provided by Sir William Stanley, Sir George Talbot (later Earl of Shrewsbury) and the Jesuit brother William Browne, brother of Anthony Maria Browne, second Viscount Montagu.[59] Novices would be transferred to Watten in 1624. The scholastics remaining in Louvain were subsidised by Thomas Sackville, son of Thomas Sackville, earl of Dorset.[60] The scholasticate was moved from Louvain to Liège in 1624. Anne Dacre Howard, countess of Arundel and widow of Philip Howard (d. 1595), provided a generous endowment for the tertianship (or the house of third probation) in 1621, a benefaction that returned 1500 *scudi* annually. The tertianship opened in Ghent in 1624 with the expectation it would be transferred to Carlisle after the anticipated Spanish Match.[61]

Within England, the fathers explained, the vice-province did not use particular names out of fear of detection and discovery. Within each mission, there were individual residences and houses, some of which would be classified as houses and colleges elsewhere. These missions, the vice-provincial stressed, did not lack endowments: the ways by which the benefactions could be secured and protected had not yet been worked out. Until that time, the missions had more than sufficient alms for sustenance. Moreover, three houses had already been established in England itself.[62]

The Society in England had suffered financially, assembly contended, because it lacked full provincial status. The mission had already lost two foundations because of rumours that the vice-province was an experiment with no guarantee of permanence.[63] Other endowments had been deferred and might indeed be lost. Similarly, there had been a decline in the amount of collective alms as rumours circulated about the vice-province's demise 'in the next General Congregation, or at least at the death of our Rev. Father General'.[64] Only full provincial status, they argued, would demonstrate that English Jesuits were in the kingdom to stay and were recognised as active members of the Society of Jesus.

Yet, the memorial admitted, the superior general might still have some hesitation and think that provincial status should be again postponed. Vitelleschi might judge that the foundations were too few or not sufficiently secure. To the first, the assembled fathers reminded the superior general, one should not overlook the colleges and houses of formation on the Continent. To the second, the fathers explained, that 'these houses are so firmly established, that it does not think that they could be transferred from the kingdom, even were the benefactors to allow it'.[65]

Two documents, most likely carried to Rome by the procurator, Henry Silesdon, supplemented the petition *Quaenam sit fundationum et domiciliorum in Anglia securitas* that explained how the foundations and houses in

England had been secured against discovery and confiscation.[66] The foundations would be safe even against renewed persecution if the trustees remained loyal and did not betray the Jesuits.[67] Their fidelity was the lynchpin. The author cited the practices of other English clergy and religious to demonstrate this point. The English Benedictine monasteries in Douai, Paris and elsewhere had not transferred out of the kingdom any of the funds given for the support of the Benedictines within England. Indeed, they had so wisely and securely invested that money in some unexplained way that it generated nearly twice as much annually as one would have expected. The secular priests in the College of Arras, which had opened in Paris in 1611, were supported by Sackville's endowment that remained in England: the annual revenue was forwarded to them. The author also cited the example of the Discalced Carmelites in Louvain who had no problem collecting the annual revenue from an endowment in England. Finally, the Society itself already had investments in England. The investments that supported the English Jesuit colleges on the Continent had been transferred out of England; the rest remained within it. The investments that remained within England were still whole, secure, and intact; much that had been taken out had been lost. Experience had, in fact, shown that investments outside England were no more secure than those within the kingdom. Closer examination of the records of the secular clergy revealed that they did not suffer financially at any time during the period of persecution. They continued to receive alms and to collect their pensions and patrimonies. Surely, the author commented, if the secular clergy and other religious orders could secure their foundations, the Society of Jesus could do likewise. Thus, the author concluded, any fear or anxiety that investments within the kingdom ran a greater risk of confiscation and loss was groundless. Such foundations were legally vulnerable, he admitted, because of the statutes against benefactions for 'superstitious uses', but these penal laws could be evaded through a system of trusts as devised by a number of Catholic lawyers to protect endowments and to conceal their purpose.[68] Moreover, he asked rhetorically, would the Society's benefactors, familiar as they were with all aspects of the penal laws, insist that their bequests remain in England if they thought there was any chance that they would be lost or confiscated?

The second half of the document explicated the existence of houses owned and operated by Jesuits within England. Some of these residences had been given over completely to the use of the Society; one had been used by the Society ever since its construction twenty years earlier. Whenever Jesuits stayed in any of these houses, they observed daily routine, the rules and regulations of religious life as laid down in the Society's Institute. If the men did not have to abandon the security of such establishments for their ministries, they could anticipate a long tranquil life. But such monastic life was not compatible with the Society's way of proceeding. Surely it was sufficient that the Society had such refuges at its disposal sanctuaries to which men could resort when necessary and where they could observe religious discipline. In addition, regardless of whether or not there was persecution, Jesuits in the different districts met periodically and for short periods of time lived as a religious community.

Recusant trusts merit further and thorough examination by legal historians who can explore competently the establishment of legal devices of this kind, the role of trustees, and the protection of assets against possible loss.[69] For all practical purposes, the trustee appeared to be the absolute owner. Needless to say, it was incumbent that the person who had set up the trust should demonstrate through legal documents that the trustee was just that. Before the Statute of Frauds (1677) required written declarations as proof, simple, verbal agreement was sufficient for the establishment of the trust. Protection came through the appointment of a number of trustees whose unanimous consent was required for any major decision. There was safety in numbers, especially when the settlor wished to conceal the existence and the nature of the trust. If the settlor wished to confound the issue still further, he would instruct the trustees to alienate the property again to a second trust. To prevent the loss of any estate, real or personal, a number of recusants had already employed trusts. Edward, Lord Vaux (d. 1661) had earlier transferred his estates to friendly and honest trustees. Indeed, Lord Vaux had selected Protestant neighbours in Northamptonshire as trustees, one of whom, William Tate of Delapré Abbey, was notoriously anti-Catholic. In so doing, Vaux made it difficult for the government to prove his ownership and thus less likely that his property would be seized.[70] On the recommendation of Catholic lawyers, English Jesuits now planned to do the same.

The second document was forwarded to the superior general in Rome: *Ratio domiciliorum in Anglia* (An account of the domiciles in England), perhaps at his request for more information.[71] Members of the community residing outside the house were obliged to visit the college for annual retreats, renewal of their vows, and whenever the rector saw fit. Whenever they resided within the college, they would follow the prescribed daily order. And that daily order, the author insisted, would be no different from that followed in Jesuit colleges on the Continent. Moreover, the novitiate in England would be as demanding as that in Flanders. No corners would be cut; nothing would be omitted. Resident Jesuits would teach either Jesuit scholastics or the laymen 'on whom the Catholic religion would largely depend'. The number of students taught would, of course, depend on location and other circumstances, but the author estimated there would be between eight and twelve students in each community. The exposition ended with a detailed analysis and description of each community.

The House of Probation of St Ignatius had an endowment that generated 1,000 *scudi* (£250) annually, a sum sufficient for the support of twenty-five men. The benefactors, referred to in the correspondence as *Ignatius*

Philopatrum (Ignatius lover of the fathers [of the Society]), had not imposed any financial obligations upon the Society.[72] The novitiate building itself could accommodate about half that number; the others would reside and work in the London area, and resort to the novitiate periodically for spiritual conferences, renewal of their vows, spiritual counselling, etc. Within the novitiate, the Jesuits would live a communal life as prescribed in the Society's *Regulae* in comparative security. Unnamed trustees, probably the benefactors themselves, held the endowment in trust and turned the revenues over to the novitiate each year. The building itself was a so-called sanctuary. In this document, sanctuary meant protection: the building was under titled protection and no armed men, with the exception of the king, his councillors and his heralds, could enter it without the express order of the king. Ordinarily such orders were given only in times of rebellion. Even if the building was, for some reason, raided, there were two other residences in the neighbourhood, again both sanctuaries, to which the Jesuits had free and easy access and to which they could flee.[73] Jesuits abandoned their rented rooms and isolated dwellings, and moved into the new novitiate shortly before the feast of St Ignatius, 31 July 1622 with the official opening on the feast itself. Ignatius and Francis Xavier had been canonised on 2/12 March 1622. Daily order was immediately established. Bells signalled the start and finish of the different chores and duties that constituted the novices' daily routine. The Society's *Regulae* and Claudio Acquaviva's *De renovatione spiritus* (About the Renovation of the Spirit) (1583) were read aloud during meals. In their zeal, the novices prayed even more than was required in the Institute; they practised daily mortifications – in fact, they often requested the discipline – and frequently sought personal admonitions from the rector, Richard Banks, who regularly delivered exhortations to the community which were, allegedly, well attended and well received. The novitiate also organised and convened conferences on Christian doctrine for Catholics in the area, and on the Jesuit Institute for members of the Society of Jesus. Within two months of its opening, the vice-provincial made an official visitation, and was delighted with what he had seen.[74] Official documentation does not specify the location of the novitiate, but it seems most likely, as I argued above, that it was situated in the French embassy at Blackfriars.

The second foundation, the College of Blessed Aloysius Gonzaga (who had been beatified in 1605), was endowed by Aloysius *Germanus* (sincere, genuine), the alias chosen by the benefactors. The foundation returned annually 800 *scudi* (£200). The actual building, another so-called sanctuary and properly secured (that is, equipped with priest-holes and other security measures), was located somewhere in Staffordshire. But where? Michael Hodgetts in his study of hiding holes suggests Boscobel situated in Shropshire, but extremely close to the Staffordshire border.[75] Swynnerton, ancestral home of Thomas Fitzherbert, is another possibility. The house itself could accommodate eight to ten Jesuits and was far more adaptable to the demands and the structure of religious life than was the novitiate in London.[76]

The third foundation, the College of St Francis Xavier, was established in Wales. The alias of the benefactors 'motivated by religious zeal and a desire to further the education of Catholic youth' was Francis *Philopatrum*. Their endowment returned 600 *scudi* (£150).[77] The site selected by the vice-provincial was not a sanctuary, but it had nonetheless even better security because of its location in a very isolated part of the country. Moreover, the house had been especially constructed by the Society with sufficient priest-holes and hiding places for forty men. No uninvited person had successfully bypassed the servants and entered the house. Even if someone eventually did, there were more than enough priest-holes to conceal everyone. In case of dire emergency, there were two or three residences in the vicinity to which the priests could flee for safety. Meanwhile the location was most apt for the observance of religious life.[78] Henry Somerset, earl of Worcester was the principal benefactor and the man who hid behind the alias of Francis *Philopatrum*. The property described was Cwm or Combe, a dwelling house in the isolated parish of Llanrothal on the Hereford side of the river Monnow.[79] Part of the Somerset estate, Cwm was divided into an 'Upper' and a 'Lower', each with a walled court in the front and with land valued at £60 *per annum*.

Father General Vitelleschi issued letters patent for the three establishments on 19/29 November 1622. Of the seven Jesuit residences that the Society hoped would soon be converted into colleges, four were so-called sanctuaries and three were appropriately secured. As soon as the arrangements had been made for the foundations, each would be able to support six to eight students who would either live at the school or reside elsewhere. A number of the Jesuits then residing in these houses thought that, once the arrangements had been completed, these houses would be even more fitting for the exercise of religious life than the novitiate in London.[80] Vitelleschi informed Blount on 11/21 January 1623 that he would be the first provincial of the new English province.[81] On 29 January/8 February, Vitelleschi admitted that he had 'come to the conclusion that the title of a regular Province can no longer be denied to it [England], for it has greatly spread the fame of the Society, if not by the number of its houses, at least by the number and gravity of its dangers and labours amongst which it has worked with so much fruit watered by the blood of many martyrs'.[82]

V Context

In a review written more than sixty years ago, the historian-polemicist Hugh Trevor-Roper accused Jesuit historians of practising 'the principle of unequal scholarship: the scrupulous straining at small historical gnats which diverts attention from the silent digestion of large and inconvenient camels'.[83] Despite the wit and the venom, there is more than a nugget of truth in Trevor-Roper's observation. Lest his spectre pursue me through archives and libraries in some Dickensian fashion, I stress the historical context perhaps to an extent that exceeds his demand.

Trevor-Roper could cite the annual letters and the official correspondence supporting the petition for provincial status to illustrate his criticism where, for all practical purposes, the Spanish Match is ignored. The one exception was the previously cited dismissal of claims that religious liberty resulted from the marital negotiations: Catholics in England 'remained undeceived, finding no relaxation of persecution as regards either their property or their families'.[84] But if it had not been for these negotiations, England's path to provincial status – and indeed the influx of other clergy and the nomination of a bishop – would have been more arduous, if not impossible.

The influential Spanish ambassador Diego Sarmiento de Acuña, count of Gondomar returned to England in March 1620 to advance negotiations for the marriage of Prince Charles and the infanta María Anna, and to weaken a Franco-Bohemian faction that urged support for the Elector Palatine and an anti-Catholic, anti-Habsburg alliance.[85] King James, according to Glyn Redworth, welcomed Gondomar 'as a long-lost friend'.[86] Gondomar found a new ally in his campaign in the royal favourite, George Villiers, marquess (and future duke) of Buckingham. By the end of March 1621, as Michael Questier has demonstrated, 'no one could doubt that the passage of any further legislation against Catholic separatists would scupper the marriage negotiations. The Spaniards insisted that an essential precondition for the match was clear proof that the legal penalties for Catholic separatism would be removed'.[87] Both Houses of Parliament passed a new recusant bill on 15 May 1621 but it went no further.[88] Gondomar left England on 16 May.

As negotiations for the Spanish Match progressed, James demonstrated his intentions concerning tolerance to a very suspicious Spain – as illustrated by the comments of Archduchess Isabella to Gondomar whenever he mentioned James's promises of leniency, that these promises had all been made before[89] – by suspending and not repealing the penal laws (repeal required parliamentary approval), as had been predicted by Frangipani in 1603, to the excitement and delight of Catholics and the quasi-apocalyptic anxieties of Protestants.[90] To the shock and anger of many English persons, instead of assisting his son-in-law Frederick who had been chased out of Bohemia in April 1621, James pursued negotiations with the Spanish branch of the Habsburg family for the marriage of his son and heir. Anti-Catholic sermons and propaganda proliferated, as preachers, hacks and playwrights denounced the proposed Spanish Match. Foreign ambassadors in London were astonished by the public resistance.[91] Protests and cries of alarm did not deter James whose 'Directions concerning Preachers', issued on 4 August 1622, decreed 'that no preacher, of what title or denomination soever shall causelesly, and without any invitation from the text, fall into any bitter invective and undecent rayling speeches against the papists or puritans'.[92]

In June 1622, all imprisoned Jesuits and priests in London and elsewhere were freed.[93] In August the king ordered John Williams, bishop of Lincoln and lord keeper of the Great Seal, to send a formal letter to the judges instructing them to suspend the operation of the penal laws, including refusal to swear the oath of allegiance. James's clamping down on anti-Catholic and anti-Jesuit sermons and his suspension of the penal laws left little doubt of the king's intention.[94] In May, before the lord keeper's letter, the Jesuits had gathered at Blackfriars for their vice-provincial congregation. Shortly after the congregation's conclusion, 24–26 May, a series of high-profile theological debates between 'Fisher the Jesuit', who had attended the congregation, and Protestant theologians including Bishop Williams and William Laud, future archbishop of Canterbury, were held in the presence of the king. John Percy (alias Fisher) had reconciled prominent figures to Catholicism, one of whom was Buckingham's mother, Mary Villiers, countess of Buckingham. The disputations were technically for her benefit. Both sides, not surprisingly, claimed victory, but the countess eventually seems to have veered back into a profession of Catholicism.[95]

The vice-province consolidated its endowments during the summer of 1622. The novitiate opened in London on the feast of St Ignatius, 31 July 1622; Jesuits moved into the Cwm in December 1622. Father General Vitelleschi had accepted the three foundations on 19/29 November 1622. In July 1622, the congregation of cardinals, having evaluated the conditions of the Spanish Match, demanded free exercise of Catholicism in the realm. This seemed possible: two months later King James was addressing Pope Gregory XV as 'Most Holy Father'.[96] By the end of 1622, John Digby, earl of Bristol believed that only a few details remained to be settled before the Match would be complete.[97]

From the Protestant perspective, the worst was yet to come. The Jesuits achieved full provincial status on 11/21 January 1623. The former Appellant, William Bishop (d. 1624) was named titular bishop of Chalcedon *in partibus infidelium* on 5/15 March 1623 and was consecrated in Paris on 25 May/4 June. Before his death, he re-organised the Church in Wales and England along traditional lines with the establishment of a chapter (known subsequently as the 'Old Chapter') and other ecclesiastical posts. Catholic clerics started to appear in public. On 29 March/8 April 1623, Vitelleschi acknowledged with approval the provincial's comment that the king now thought more highly of and was better disposed towards the Jesuits.[98]

More alarming (for some) than the public profession of Catholicism was the news that Prince Charles and Buckingham had donned disguises and had set out for Spain in February 1623 to conclude the prolonged negotiations for the marriage, an expedition thoroughly studied by Glyn Redworth.[99] According to the secular priest William Farrar (alias Harewell), the prince's excursion quelled the doubts and apprehensions that had troubled many Jesuits about the marital negotiations: 'the prince his going into Spaine hath turned the winde and filled their sailes full for the other course'.[100]

On 27 June/7 July, Charles met with King Philip IV. To the astonishment of Endymion Porter, the prince announced that 'he had seriously made up his mind to accept the proposals made to him with respect to religion, and also give the securities demanded for their due execution, and that this was the final determination of the king his father'.[101] As rumours swirled, many Protestants feared that Charles would convert to Roman Catholicism to secure his Spanish bride.[102] That did not happen, but James and Charles swore to 'abrogate all existing penal laws within three years, and never to make new ones, as far as lies in our power (*quantum in nobis erit*)'.[103]

On 5 October 1623, after a hazardous voyage, Charles arrived safely in England. Despite the promises, he returned home, in the words of Redworth, 'miraculously transformed into a Protestant champion' to the euphoria and delight of the public.[104] The Spanish marriage was dead in the water. A few days later, Providence registered its disapproval of England's flirtation with Spain with the disaster of the 'doleful evensong', a tragedy that signalled the return of an anti-Catholic backlash.[105] The Blackfriars accident was the first catastrophe suffered by the new English province. Protestant polemicists were not slow to point out that the disaster's date 26 October adjusted to the new calendar became 5 November: the anniversary of the Gunpowder Plot.[106]

Parliament convened on 19 February 1624. By the end of March, James followed its advice to repudiate England's treaties with Spain and to formulate a new foreign policy. Parliament also urged him on 10 April to enforce all penal laws, especially against the Jesuits and seminary priests. In addition, Parliament requested that any future negotiations for the princess's marriage not include any concessions or dispensations to Catholics.[107] Prompted by a parliamentary petition, the king ordered all Jesuits and seminary priests out of the realm by 14 June.[108] Vitelleschi, alarmed by this new enforcement of the penal laws, hoped that the upcoming marriage of Charles and the French princess, Henrietta Maria), to whom Charles turned his attention after the Spanish debacle, would restore the previous peace.[109] The French court was more concerned about the composition of Henrietta Maria's Catholic household than about concessions made to English Catholics. Charles and Henrietta Maria were married in Paris on 1/11 May 1625.[110] Allegedly, Richard Blount wanted a Jesuit named as the queen's confessor and even sought to use the countess of Buckingham to achieve that goal.[111] For whatever reason, no Jesuit was included in the queen's entourage.

VI Conclusion

John Bossy ominously introduces his article 'The English Catholic Community, 1603–1625' with these words: 'The Catholic community has a shadowy existence in the histories of James I'.[112] He attributes this 'shadowy existence' to the general withdrawal of the English Catholic community from the public sphere of political engagement to the private space of seigneurial manor houses, and the loss of interest of Catholic continental powers in the exploitation of recusants as a political force. Bossy's evaluation still rings true, but less loudly. Within the historiography of early modern English Catholicism, significant shadows remain, but one should not equate withdrawal with the lack of historical investigation. More attention has been showered on anti-Catholicism than on the adaptations made by Catholics to the new regime.[113] With the exception of the Gunpowder Plot and the Spanish Match, nothing involving English Catholics has attracted the attention of scholars and of the general public. The glorious age of the heroic martyrs had not passed, but it was waning. No Jacobean bravado matched Edmund Campion's, no escape rivalled John Gerard's for drama. The Catholic equivalents of Sydney Carlton and the Scarlet Pimpernel had died or were in exile. Moreover, there is significantly less archival material. From a narrower Jesuit perspective, the two most significant correspondents had died: Garnet in 1606 and Persons in 1610. Jesuit catalogues and annual letters do become more common during the Jacobean era, but they lack the 'boys' own' excitement of the memoirs of John Gerard and William Weston with their edifying accounts of conversion.[114] With heirs and spares, the Stuart dynasty was secure. Catholics had to make their peace with it.

Regardless of Charles's bride, the Jesuit province continued to prosper. It convened its first congregation at the novitiate in London on 7 February 1625.[115] Subsequent congregations were held in London until 1642. After the Blackfriars disaster, the House of Probation of St Ignatius relocated somewhere in Edmonton where it remained until late 1624/early 1625 when it moved to Camberwell. The community at Cwm prospered as did that in Staffordshire. The number of Jesuits in England and Wales steadily increased: from approximately 112 in 1622 to 152 by 1630. Benefactors endowed the College of the Immaculate Conception, Leicestershire, in 1632, and the College of the Holy Apostles, Suffolk, in 1633.

The Society – and indeed Catholicism in general – had seized the opportunity offered by James's eagerness to demonstrate to suspicious Spaniards that *de facto* tolerance would be granted to English Catholics. With relative immunity English Jesuits consolidated endowments, established religious communities and institutions, and engaged in semi-public ministries. Protestant preachers warned the English public of the dangers posed by Jesuits, dangers that would intensify after the Spanish Match. No one would be safe, they predicted, once the Jesuits were established in England. Protestant fears, albeit exaggerated, were not baseless. John Vicars, a popular chronicler, characterised 1623 as the year 'the Romish Foxes came out of their holes'.[116] But their emergence can be traced back to the first decade of James's reign: the Observant Franciscans (Recollects) returned sometime between 1610 and 1614 and the Discalced Carmelites in 1614. A Capuchin mission to Great Britain and Ireland opened in 1608 and the Dominicans in 1622. The Benedictines had initiated their mission to England in March 1603; by 1621, they numbered fifty-seven in England.[117]

Perhaps as prepublication publicity for this collection, Michael Questier justly urges a revision of the traditional understanding of King James and his reign.[118] King James died on 27 March 1625, an event barely noticed in the official Jesuit correspondence. Informed of the king's death by John Norton (*vere* Knatchbull), Vitelleschi wondered what effect it would have on the province.[119] Perhaps we should rephrase the question. Instead of asking how his death affected English Jesuits, we should ask how his reign affected them. Garnet, Tesimond and Gerard anticipated considerable improvement in the state of Roman Catholics. Regarding James's promises, Tesimond wondered, 'What more could they look for, or desire from the king, than this?'[120] Of course, they desired much more, but the condition of the Society in England had improved considerably as the mission progressed to provincial status financially secure and numerically sound. Construction of a Tower of David had begun.

Furthermore, we might say, what we have here, in the archive of the Society in England, phrased as so much of it is, in the bureaucratic language of day-to-day administrative matters, is an account that appears to be completely at odds with so much of the 'mainstream' narrative of politics and religion in post-Reformation England and the British Isles. In that narrative, members of the Society of Jesus are utterly foreign to contemporary English and British culture and, in addition, are the propagators of the worst aspects of what Protestants tended to call popery – up to and including sedition (an opinion which, as it happens was shared by some contemporary Catholics).

The fact that these Jesuit clergy and their friends in the early seventeenth century could imagine their function in the way that they did speaks volumes for the fluidity of the Jacobean settlement of religion. Indeed, the implications of the journey from mission to province are that the Society's members and their patrons saw a future in which, as did those other Catholic clergymen who thought in terms of a form of episcopacy instituted directly by Rome, the situation of those who identified as Catholics would become much more like the circumstances which prevailed across the majority of Western Europe. By the end of James's reign, many Protestants would, with varying degrees of indignation, have agreed with them.

Notes

1 See T. M. McCoog, SJ, 'Mission or Church, 1570–1640?', in J. E. Kelly and J. McCafferty (eds), *The Oxford History of British and Irish Catholicism, Volume 1* (Oxford, 2023), pp. 107–26.

2 See T. M. McCoog, SJ, 'Harmony Disrupted: Robert Persons, SJ, William Crichton, SJ, and the Question of Queen Elizabeth's Successor, 1581–1603', in *idem, 'And Touching Our Society' Fashioning Jesuit Identity in Elizabethan England* (Toronto, 2013), pp. 283–347; *idem,* 'Converting a King: The Jesuit William Crichton and King James VI and I', *Journal of Jesuit Studies* 7 (2020), pp. 11–33.

3 Garnet to Persons, 16 April 1603, ABSI, *Anglia* III, 32.

4 Oswald Tesimond, ed. Francis Edwards, SJ, *The Gunpowder Plot: The Narrative of Oswald Tesimond alias Greenway* (1973), p. 24.

5 John Gerard, SJ, ed. J. Morris, SJ, *The Condition of Catholics under James I. Father Gerard's Narrative of the Gunpowder Plot* (1871), pp. 20–1, also pp. 22–5.

6 Tesimond, *Gunpowder Plot,* p. 25; Morris, *Condition of Catholics,* pp. 24–5.

7 Frangipani to Aldobrandini, Brussels, 29 April/9 May 1603, in L. Van der Essen and A. Louant (eds), *Correspondance d'Ottavio Mirto Frangipani, Premier Nonce de Flandre (1596–1606)* (3 vols in 4 parts, Rome/Brussels/Paris, 1924–42), III/1, p. 391.

8 J. F. Larkin, CSV, and P. L. Hughes (eds), *Stuart Royal Proclamations* (2 vols, Oxford, 1973–83), I, p. 72.

9 Garnet to [?], 7 March 1604, ARSI, *Angl.* 38/II, fo. 176[r]; Anthony Rivers to Augustino Cornelio [Persons?], London, 4 April 1603 [sic; this should be dated 4 April 1604], AAW, A VII, no. 84; the letter was published in H. Foley, SJ (ed.), *Records of the English Province of the Society of Jesus* (7 vols in 8, Roehampton/ London, 1877–84), I, pp. 60–1.

10 King James VI and I, ed. J. P. Sommerville, *Political Writings* (Cambridge, 1994), p. 140.

11 1 Jac. I, c. iv, in G.W. Prothero (ed.), *Select Statutes and Other Constitutional Documents Illustrative of the Reigns of Elizabeth and James I* (4th edition, Oxford, 1946), pp. 252–3.

12 Del Bufalo to Aldobrandini, Paris, 14/24 August 1604, in B. Barbiche (ed.), *Correspondance du Nonce en France Innocenzo del Bufalo, Evêque de Camerino (1601–1604)* (Rome/Paris, 1964), p. 774.

13 Frangipani to Aldobrandini, Brussels, 10/20 November 1604; Aldobrandini to Frangipani, Rome, 20/30 October 1604, in Van der Essen and Louant, *Correspondance,* III/2, pp. 500–1, 731–2.

14 Garnet to [?], 29 August [1604], Loyola (Spain), Archivo Histórico de Loyola, *Armario. Plúteo 4. Balda 2. Ordenador* 2412.

15 Garnet to Acquaviva, 29 May 1605, ARSI, *Fondo Gesuitico* 651/624.

16 Larkin and Hughes, *Stuart Royal Proclamations,* I, pp. 131–3.

17 P. Caraman, *John Gerard: The Autobiography of an Elizabethan* (1951), p. 205, n. 2.

18 Caraman, *John Gerard,* pp. 204–10, 258.

19 Persons to Acquaviva, 18 March 1606, ABSI, *Coll. P* II, 428.

20 Catholics, technically, therefore faced financial ruin. Either they paid a monthly fine, or compounded for the value of two-thirds of their estates. Compounding became the crown's preferred option. Within a few months Richard Blount was bemoaning imminent financial devastation for principal Catholic families: Blount to Persons, November 1606, ABSI, *Coll. M,* 99.

21 Prothero, *Select Statutes*, p. 259. See also J. J. LaRocca, SJ, 'English Catholics and the Recusancy Laws 1558–1625: A Study in Religion and Politics' (PhD, Rutgers, 1971), pp. 235–41.

22 Acquaviva to English Jesuits, Rome, 28 June/8 July 1606, ARSI, *Angl.* 1/I, fos 3ᵛ–4ʳ.

23 T. M. McCoog, SJ and L. Lúkacs, SJ (eds), *Monumenta Angliae* (3 vols, Rome, 1992–2000), I, p. lxxxvii.

24 Persons to Schoondonck, Rome, 25 September/5 October 1603, ABSI, 42/12/6, fos 1405ʳ–6ʳ. See also A. J. Loomie, SJ (ed.), *Spain and the Jacobean Catholics* (2 vols, 1973, 1978), 1, pp. 17–20.

25 Kathryn Marshalek highlights Luisa de Carvajal y Mendoza's opposition to the proposed 'Spanish Match' in June 1612 as a 'misguided project' despite endorsement by crypto-Catholic schismatics and Spanish courtiers. See her 'Luisa de Carvajal in Anglo-Spanish Contexts, 1605–14', *Renaissance Quarterly* 75 (2022), pp. 882–916, at pp. 907–8. Was her opposition to the marriage the result of Jesuit influence? Or was she out-of-step with Jesuits in England? Perhaps future research on English Jesuit attitudes to the proposal will answer this question.

26 G. Redworth, *The She-Apostle: The Extraordinary Life and Death of Luisa de Carvajal* (Oxford, 2011), p. 92.

27 Acquaviva to Baldwin, Rome, 8/18 June 1605, ARSI, *Fl. Belg.* 1/II, p. 952; same to same, Rome, 31 August/10 September 1605, ARSI, *Fl. Belg.* 1/II, p. 963; same to same, Rome, 14/24 December 1605, ARSI, *Fl. Belg.* 1/II, p. 975; ARSI, *Angl.* 38/II, fo. 117ᵛ; ARSI, *Hist. Soc.* 134, fo. 50ᵛ.

28 McCoog, *Monumenta Angliae*, 1, pp. 188–90, 195–7, 198–202.

29 Instructions to Robert Jones, Rome, 18/28 March 1609, ARSI, *Angl.* 1/I, fo. 9ᵛ; Annual Letter of 1615, ARSI, *Angl.* 31/I, pp. 633–34 (translated in Foley, *Records*, 7/2, p. 1077).

30 P. Lake and M. Questier, *All Hail to the Archpriest: Confessional Conflict, Toleration, and the Politics of Publicity in Post-Reformation England* (Oxford, 2019), p. 287.

31 Lake and Questier, *All Hail to the Archpriest*, p. 25. See also McCoog, 'Mission or Church', pp. 124–5.

32 For a fascinating comparison between these manorial 'churches' and Dutch *schuilkerken*, see Benjamin J. Kaplan, *Reformation and the Practice of Toleration: Dutch Religious History in the Early Modern Era* (Leiden, 2019), pp. 164–203.

33 'The English Catholic Community, 1603–1625', in A. G. R. Smith (ed.), *The Reign of James VI and I* (1973), pp. 91–105, at p. 98.

34 ARSI, *Angl.* 36/II, fos 268ʳ, 317ʳ.

35 See for example my 'Fostering Harmony and Respect. English Jesuits in Seville, 1592–1605', in McCoog, *'And Touching Our Society'*, pp. 261–81.

36 See T. M. McCoog, SJ, 'New Situations; New Structures? Claudio Acquaviva and the Jesuit Mission to England', in P. A. Fabre and F. Rurale (eds) *Claudio Acquaviva's Generalate (1581–1615) and the Emergence of Modern Catholicism* (Chestnut Hill, 2017), pp. 145–64.

37 J. W. Padberg, SJ, M. D. O'Keefe, SJ, and J. L. McCarthy, SJ (eds), *For Matters of Greater Moment: The First Thirty Jesuit General Congregations* (St Louis, 1994), p. 256.

38 Padberg et al., *For Matters of Greater Moment*, p. 257. See also T. M. McCoog, SJ, 'Resisting National Sentiment: Friction between Irish and English Jesuits in the Old Society', *Journal of Jesuit Studies* 6 (2019), pp. 598–626.

39 Padberg et al., *For Matters of Greater Moment*, p. 257.

40 E.g. ARSI, *Angl.* 32/II, fos 1ʳ–2ᵛ.

41 ARSI, *Angl.* 32/II, fos 3ʳ–8ᵛ, 479ʳ–485ᵛ.

42 Vitelleschi to Heren, Rome, 17/27 April 1619, ARSI, *Gal. Belg.* 1/I–II, pp. 495–6. The Belgian province was divided into the Flandro-Belgian and Gallo-Belgian provinces in 1612.

43 'Annual Letters of the Vice-Province of England', in Foley, *Records*, V, p. 987.

44 See, for example, A. Bellany, *The Politics of Court Scandal in Early Modern England* (Cambridge, 2002), pp. 181–211.

45 See C. F. Senning, *Spain, Rumor, and Anti-Catholicism in Mid-Jacobean England* (New York, 2019).

46 'Annual Letters of the Vice-Province of England', in Foley, *Records*, V, p. 987.

47 'Annual Letters of the Vice-Province of England', in Foley, *Records*, V, p. 988.

48 'Annual Letters of the Vice-Province of England', in Foley, *Records*, V, p. 989.

49 ARSI, *Angl.* 32/II, fos 129ʳ–30ᵛ, 133ʳ⁻ᵛ.

50 Henry More, SJ, 'The Erection of the Vice-Province of England into a Province [Being a Translation of Book X Sections 1, 3, 6 of his *Historia*]', *Letters and Notices* 18 (1885–6), pp. 407–12, at p. 409.

51 The responses are dated 14/24 April and 24 and 26 April/4 May, ARSI, *Angl.* 32/I, fos 127ʳ–8ᵛ, 135ʳ–6ʳ. See also Vitelleschi to Blount, Rome, 7/17 April 1621 and 11/21 April 1621, ARSI, *Angl.* 1/I, fos 135ʳ–6ʳ.

52 More, 'Erection of the Vice-Province', pp. 407–8.

53 Vitelleschi to Blount, Rome, 16/26 March 1622, ARSI, *Angl.* 1/I, fos 154ᵛ–5ʳ.

54 ARSI, *Congr.* 57, fos 44ʳ–9ᵛ, 52ʳ–4ᵛ.

55 [Joseph Agius, SJ], 'Memorable Sites in London', *Letters and Notices* 52 (1937), pp. 292–303, at p. 292.

56 More, 'Erection of the Vice-Province', p. 409.

57 See Vitelleschi to Blount, Rome, 16/26 March 1622, ARSI, *Angl.* 1/I, fos 154ᵛ–5ʳ.

58 ARSI, *Angl.* 32/I, fos 102ʳ–4ʳ (translated as 'The Erection of the Vice-Province of England into a Province', *Letters and Notices* 18 [1885–6], pp. 344–51).

59 M. J. Walsh, *Heythrop College 1614–2014* (2014), p. 13; Foley, *Records*, VII/1, pp. xlvii–viii.

60 Sackville's generosity was not restricted to Jesuits; he also subsidized a writer's college for English secular clergy in Paris. See M. C. Questier (ed.), *Newsletters from the Archpresbyterate of George Birkhead* (Camden 5ᵗʰ series, 12, Cambridge, 1998), pp. 10, 84–9.

61 ARSI, *Hist. Soc.* 134, fo. 9ʳ; Vitelleschi to Richard Banks, Rome, 2/12 August 1623, ARSI *Angl.* 1/I, fo. 178ᵛ; same to Blount, Rome, 2/12 August 1623, ARSI *Angl.* 1/I, fos 179ʳ–80ʳ, 182ᵛ; Foley, *Records*, VII/1, pp. liii–iv.

62 More, 'Erection of the Vice-Province', pp. 345–7.

63 Was the foundation proposed by Jacques Blaze, Bishop of St Omers, in 1603 one of these? Another may have been a foundation offered to the Society in 1612 and accepted by Acquaviva. This unnamed benefactor, four years later, exonerated the Society of Jesus from the charge of having neglected to fulfil his intentions. The benefactor may have been Sir Thomas Leedes. See ABSI, *Anglia*, IV, pp. 46, 47. On Leedes, see M. C. Questier, *Catholicism and Community in Early Modern England: Politics, Aristocratic Patronage and Religion, c.1550–1640* (Cambridge, 2006), pp. 56–8. One may wonder if there is any connection between this unfulfilled endowment and the college of the secular clergy that opened in Paris in 1611.

64 More, 'Erection of the Vice-Province', p. 348.

65 More, 'Erection of the Vice-Province', p. 350.

66 ARSI, *Angl.* 32/I, fos 109ʳ–110ᵛ.

67 At least once, a Jesuit betrayed the Society and tried to secure the assets of a college. See T. M. McCoog, SJ, 'Apostasy and Knavery in Restoration England: The Checkered Career of John Travers, SJ', *Catholic Historical Review* 78 (1992), pp. 395–412.

68 According to the Chantries Act of 1547 (1 Edward VI, c. 14) and its subsequent development in the Act against Jesuits and Seminary Priests of 1585 (27 Elizabeth I, c. 2), any grant, gift or legacy of either real or personal estates, assigned to superstitious 'popish' uses, was forbidden and discovery would result in their forfeiture to the crown.

69 See J. E. Myers, 'Catholics, Property, and the Experience of the Penal Laws in Eighteenth-Century England: Evidence from the Vincent Eyre Manuscripts', *British Catholic History* 36 (2022), pp. 66–84, and S. M. Cogan, *Catholic Social Networks in Early Modern England. Kinship, Gender, and Coexistence* (Amsterdam, 2021), pp. 229–40, as examples of this practice.

70 G. Anstruther, *Vaux of Harrowden: A Recusant Family* (Newport, Monmouthshire, 1953), pp. 395–6, 402, 419.

71 ARSI, *Angl.* 32/I, fos 114^r–15^v.

72 Vitelleschi lamented the difficulty in writing letters for benefactors who did not wish their identities to be known: Vitelleschi to Blount, Rome, 10/20 August 1622, ARSI, *Angl.* 1/I, fos 161^v–2^r.

73 ARSI, *Angl.* 32/I, fos 96^{r-v}, 114^{r-v}.

74 Edward Alacambe (*vere* Astlow) to Father General, 17/27 October 1622; Blount to same, 4/14 September 1622, ARSI, *Angl.* 32/I, fo. 144^{r-v}.

75 M. Hodgetts, *Secret Hiding Places* (Dublin, 1989), pp. 187, 198–9.

76 ARSI, *Angl.* 32/I, fos 96^r, 109^r–110^v, 114^r–15^r; ARSI, *Hist. Soc.* 134, fo. 91^r.

77 ARSI, *Hist. Soc.* 134, fo. 91^r; ARSI, *Angl.* 32/I, fos 96^r, 109^r–10^v, 115^r.

78 ARSI, *Angl.* 32/I, fo. 115^r.

79 Building on my research, Hannah Thomas has investigated Jesuit activity in Wales. See her 'Missioners on the margins? The territorial headquarters of the Welsh College of St Francis Xavier at the Cwm, c. 1600–1679', *Recusant History* 32 (2014), pp. 175–96; 'The Society of Jesus in Wales, c. 1600–1679: Rediscovering the Cwm Jesuit Library at Hereford Cathedral', *Journal of Jesuit Studies* 1 (2014), pp. 572–88; idem, '"Books which are necessary for them": reconstructing a Jesuit missionary library in seventeenth-century Wales and the English borderlands, c. 1600–1679', in T. Bela, C. Calma and J. Rzegocka (eds), *Publishing Subversive Texts in Elizabethan England and the Polish-Lithuanian Commonwealth* (Leiden, 2016), pp. 110–28; idem, 'Catholics in Wales', in R. E. Scully, SJ, and A. Ellis (eds), *A Companion to Catholicism and Recusancy in Britain and Ireland* (Leiden, 2022), pp. 339–67. We await her monograph.

80 ARSI, *Angl.* 32/I, fo. 115^r.

81 Vitelleschi to Blount, 11/21 January 1623, ARSI, *Angl.* 1/I, fos 167^v–8^r. See also ARSI *Angl.* 32/I, fos 125^r–6^v; ARSI, *Congr.* 57, fos 49^r–50^v, 55^r–60^r.

82 More, 'Erection of the Vice-Province', pp. 351–2.

83 H. Trevor-Roper, 'Twice Martyred: The English Jesuits and Their Historians', in *idem, Historical Essays* (1957), pp. 113–18, at p. 117.

84 'Annual Letters of the Vice-Province of England', in Foley, *Records*, V, p. 987. Richard Blount claimed: 'Matters go worse than ordinary and yet the expectation is worse, more being promised than is actually put in execution' (Blount to [?], [late December 1618], ABSI, *Anglia*, IV, 55 as cited in M. Questier, *Catholics and Treason: Martyrology, Memory, and Politics in the Post-Reformation* (Oxford, 2022), p. 445).

85 James preferred a negotiated settlement of the Bohemian crisis by diplomacy and marital alliances, and not by a confessional war. See S. Adams, 'Spain or the Netherlands? The Dilemmas of Early Stuart Foreign Policy', in H. Tomlinson (ed.), *Before the English Civil War: Essays on Early Stuart Politics and Government* (1983), pp. 79–101, 196–200.

86 G. Redworth, *The Prince and the Infanta: The Cultural Politics of the Spanish Match* (New Haven, 2003), p. 27.

87 M. Questier, *Dynastic Politics and the British Reformations, 1558–1630* (Oxford, 2019), p. 399.

88 Questier, *Catholics and Treason*, p. 455.

89 Redworth, *Prince and the Infanta*, p. 44.

90 Redworth, *Prince and the Infanta*, p. 2. Also see V. Caldari and S. J. Wolfson (eds), *Stuart Marriage Diplomacy: Dynastic Politics in their European Context, 1604–1630* (Woodbridge, 2018).

91 P. Lake, 'Anti-Popery: The Structure of a Prejudice', in R. Cust and A. Hughes (eds), *Conflict in Early Stuart England* (1989), pp. 181–210, at p. 187. Also see T. Cogswell, 'England and the Spanish Match', in Cust and Hughes, *Conflict in Early Stuart England*, pp. 107–34, at p. 111.

92 *King James his Letter and Directions to the Lord Archbishop of Canterbury concerning Preaching and Preachers* (1642), p. 4. See also T. Cogswell, *The Blessed Revolution: English Politics and the Coming of War, 1621–1624* (Cambridge, 1989), p. 32; M. Questier (ed.), *Stuart Dynastic Policy and Religious Politics, 1621–1625* (Camden 5th series, 34, Cambridge, 2009), p. 34; S. Altman, *Witnessing to the Faith: Absolutism and the Conscience in John Donne's England* (Manchester, 2023), pp. 23–6.

93 Questier, *Stuart Dynastic Policy*, p. 31.

94 Questier, *Dynastic Politics and the British Reformations*, p. 409; *idem*, *Stuart Dynastic Policy*, p. 32; Cogswell, 'England and the Spanish Match', pp. 118–19.

95 See T. H. Wadkins, 'King James I Meets John Percy, SJ (12 May, 1622): An Unpublished Manuscript from the Religious Controversies Surrounding the Countess of Buckingham's Conversion', *Recusant History* 19 (1988), pp. 146–54; *idem*, 'The Percy-"Fisher" Controversies and the Ecclesiastical Politics of Jacobean Anti-Catholicism, 1622–1625', *Church History* 57 (1988), pp. 153–69.

96 W. B. Patterson, *King James VI and I and the Reunion of Christendom* (Cambridge, 1997), p. 313.

97 Patterson, *King James and the Reunion of Christendom*, pp. 319–20; Cogswell, 'England and the Spanish Match', p. 125.

98 Vitelleschi to Blount, Rome, 29 March/8 April 1623, ARSI, *Angl.* 1/I, fo. 169ᵛ.

99 On various cultural aspects of this trip, see A. Samson (ed.), *The Spanish Match: Prince Charles's Journey to Madrid, 1623* (Aldershot, 2006). See also J. Elliott, 'A Troubled Relationship: Spain and Great Britain, 1604–1655', in J. Brown and J. Elliott (eds), *The Sale of the Century: Artistic Relations between Spain and Great Britain, 1604–1655* (New Haven, 2002), pp. 17–41, at pp. 23–7.

100 Farrar to John Bennett, [London?], 12/22 March, 1623, in Questier, *Stuart Dynastic Policy*, p. 215.

101 As cited in Redworth, *Prince and the Infanta*, p. 123.

102 Robert Cross challenges Redworth's claim that Spain insisted on the prince's conversion to Catholicism as a precondition for the marriage. See R. Cross, 'Pretense and Perception in the Spanish Match, or History in a Fake Beard', *Journal of Interdisciplinary History* 37 (2007), pp. 563–83.

103 Redworth, *Prince and the Infanta*, p. 182. See Questier, *Stuart Dynastic Policy*, p. 51.

104 Redworth, *Prince and the Infanta*, p. 138; Patterson, *King James and the Reunion of Christendom*, p. 345. See B. C. Pursell, 'The End of the Spanish Match', *Historical Journal* 45 (2002), pp. 699–726 for an interpretation of Charles's *volte-face*.

105 Cogswell, 'England and the Spanish Match', p. 127.

106 Foley, *Records*, I, pp. 76–98; Questier, *Stuart Dynastic Policy*, pp. 64–5; A. Walsham, '"The Fatall Vesper": Providentialism and Anti-Popery in Late Jacobean London', *Past and Present* 144 (1994), pp. 36–87.

107 Patterson, *King James and the Reunion of Christendom*, pp. 345–9.

108 Larkin and Hughes, *Stuart Royal Proclamations*, 1, pp. 591–3.

109 Vitelleschi to Silesdon, Rome, 1/11 January 1625, ARSI, *Angl.* 1/II, fo. 212ʳ.

110 On the marriage and the negotiations, see M.-C. Canova-Green and S. J. Wolfson (eds), *The Wedding of Charles I and Henrietta Maria, 1625: Celebrations and Controversy* (Turnhout, 2020).

111 Questier, *Stuart Dynastic Policy*, p. 114.

112 Bossy, 'English Catholic Community', p. 91.

113 See, e.g., A. Milton, 'A Qualified Intolerance: The Limits and Ambiguities of Early Stuart Anti-Catholicism', in A. F. Marotti (ed.), *Catholicism and Anti-Catholicism in Early Modern English Texts* (Basingstoke, 1999), pp. 85–115; A. Milton, *Catholic and Reformed: The Roman and Protestant Churches in English Protestant Thought, 1600–1640* (Cambridge, 1995), pp. 31–92; and Lake, 'Anti-Popery'.

114 P. Caraman (ed.), *William Weston: The Autobiography of an Elizabethan* (1955).

115 ARSI, *Congr.* 59, fos 111ʳ–21ᵛ.

116 As cited in Cogswell, *Blessed Revolution*, p. 38.

117 T. M. McCoog, SJ, 'The Jesuits and Other Male Religious Orders in Britain and Ireland', in Scully and Ellis, *Companion*, pp. 85–124, at pp. 97–101.

118 M. C. Questier, 'The Reputation of James VI and I Revisited', *Journal of British Studies* 61 (2022), pp. 949–69.

119 Vitelleschi to Norton, Rome, 14/24 May 1625, ARSI, *Angl.* 1/II, fo. 218ᵛ.

120 Tesimond, *Gunpowder Plot*, p. 24.

7

REX PACIFICUS AND THE SHORT PEACE, 1598–1625*

Noah Millstone

James VI and I died with Britain on the brink of war, but his funeral did little to endorse the coming conflict. The Biblical motto *beati pacifici* (blessed are the peacemakers), which James had embraced over the final decade of his life, was prominently displayed on a funeral standard. In his sermon, the late king's chaplain and favourite John Williams elaborated a parallel between his departed patron and the biblical King Solomon ('in all his actions saving his vices', joked John Chamberlain). Solomon was twice crowned, 'so was King James'. Solomon's childhood 'was rough ... so was that of King James'. Solomon was learned, a writer, a patron of the Church, an 'improver of his home commodities'; so was King James. The culmination of the comparison was peace: in the days of Solomon,

> every man liv'd in peace under his vine and his fig tree ... and so they did in the blessed days of King James. And yet towards his end, King Solomon had secret enemies, Razan, Hadad, and Jeroboam, and prepared for a war upon his going to his grave ... so had, and so did King James. Lastly, before any hostile act ... King Solomon died in peace ... and so you know did King James.

'Surely', Williams concluded, 'actions of peace (whatever debauched people say to the contrary) set out a prince in more orient colours than those of war, and great combustions'.[1]

* I am grateful for the advice and assistance of Waseem Ahmed, Alastair Bellany, Chris Kyle and the editors.

DOI: 10.4324/9781003319764-8

Of all James Stuart's many personas, perhaps the most durable has been the *rex pacificus* – the peacemaking king. It has also been the most controversial. James's very public embrace of peace as a motif of his kingship raised questions that continue to divide scholars. Was James's interest in peace opportunistic, ideological or a reflection of his timorous personality? How far, exactly, did his commitment to peace extend – that is, what was he willing to give up for the sake of peace?

Contemporaries were exercised by all these questions, but at the heart of their concern lay a more fundamental controversy over the value of peace itself, or at least, of the particular, nervous peace that prevailed across Europe in the early seventeenth century. Between 1598 and 1609, a series of treaties – Vervins (1598), Lyon (1600), London (1604), Zsitvatorok (1606) and Antwerp (1609) – brought at least temporary settlements to the late sixteenth-century wars of religion. The survival of this European peace depended on concerted efforts to prevent regional crises from escalating into trans-regional war. It was thus highly contested, fragile and ultimately short-lived, collapsing in 1619–1620 with revolt of Bohemia and the beginnings of the Thirty Years' War.[2]

Over the last fifteen years, there have been serious and detailed efforts to re-evaluate James's approach to the European situation, in important unpublished PhDs by Robert Cross and Cynthia Fry and recent books by Michael Questier and Malcolm Smuts.[3] This chapter builds on their revisions by seeking to understand James's position as *rex pacificus* against the European background of the 'Short Peace'. James certainly played an important role in the construction and maintenance of European peace, but his choices – however personal or strategic they may have been – unfolded in a wider context. Proposals for peace found wary if receptive audiences not only in London but also in Brussels, Madrid, Prague, Paris and the Hague. Rather than simply drawing on European sources to enrich our understanding of James's conduct – to see what the Dutch were saying about him, and the Flemish, and the Spanish, and the French, etc. – I argue that the dilemmas of Jacobean foreign policy were relatively common across other contemporary states and can, to an extent, be understood as a product of the novel international situation, which pushed governments in unfamiliar directions. The Short Peace provides essential context for understanding James's conduct and identifying what, if anything, was distinctive about his approach to Europe.

The shift to peace posed serious problems for European governments. For decades, many had portrayed themselves as the protagonists of religious or even apocalyptic conflicts against irreconcilable enemies; conflicts whose only acceptable outcome was total victory. Peace meant giving up these ambitions. But it also meant finding a new legitimating language, emphasising the fruits of peace instead of the iron logic of religious war. James's embrace of peace as a motif of his kingship was partly a response to this problem and resembled similar contemporary changes in the legitimating discourses of other dynastic states.

Across Europe, the shift to a relatively deconfessionalised and conciliatory foreign policy generated opposition. While scholars like Cross and Smuts persuasively argue that the view of James as weak and corrupt is mistaken, these characterisations are not merely nineteenth-century inventions. Rather, they were contemporary characterisations and often seductively persuasive ones. But the fact that these characterisations were contemporary does not mean that we should adopt them uncritically; rather, we must historicise them and understand the practices and forces that made them persuasive: a para-Tacitean practice of explaining political decision-making in terms of character, disposition and inclinations, and a general critique of the early seventeenth-century peace as an enervating, effeminate age poisoned by corruption and confessional complacency. Understanding James in European context will thus help explain the descriptions of his personality that have, in turn, shaped views of his kingship for 400 years.

What follows has four main parts. The first identifies four principal meanings of 'peace' in early Stuart political discourse: absence of rebellion, peace between England and Scotland, the peace of the Church and, most controversially, peace with foreign neighbours. The second part explores the early seventeenth-century turn to peace, paying particular attention to the early modern understanding of what motivated it and to the practices that maintained it. Parts three and four reconstruct the discursive and representational strategies that the Jacobean government and its supporters pursued to legitimate the peace, and the critique of peace launched by malcontents.

I Four Kinds of Peace

In the Bible, peace was everywhere: in the interpersonal sense of friendly relations between neighbours, in the apostolic sense of unity within the ecclesia, or the psalmic sense of quietness and repose. In his 1620 sermon on the Jacobean motto *beati pacifici*, the royal chaplain John Denison recognised a fourfold division: the peace of reconciliation between God and man; the peace of consolation, an internal peace with one's own conscience; the peace of association, a 'civil peace ... between man and man'; and the peace of eternal salvation. 'The Hebrews', Denison explained, 'under the name of Peace, do comprehend all prosperity and felicity whatsoever'; 'the word', observed John Stradling, was thus 'full of ambiguity'.[4]

In early Stuart political discourse, the term 'peace' was not quite so flexible, but it was used in at least four different ways. All were comparative, contrasting some state of quiet with some other state of unrest, discord or conflict. The first and earliest usage referred to the absence of civil conflict within the kingdom. This is the sense invoked in the many panegyrics to Queen Elizabeth that praised her peaceful reign. In a formal speech in London, the recorder Richard Martin claimed that Elizabeth maintained a 'long and blessed peace of five and forty years'. A Cambridge poet wrote:

Peace did her reign begin, peace it maintain'd,
Peace gave her leave in peace hence to depart;
Peace she hath left behind; which no way stain'd
With bloody war, rejoyceth England's heart.
Though we a King of Peace have in her stead
Yet let us mourn – the Queen of Peace is dead.[5]

This theme recurred over and over again in succession literature.

There is something paradoxical, or even unmoored from reality, about these remarks. In 1603, England had been at war with Spain for nearly twenty years. Compared to most surrounding polities, however – Ireland, Scotland, the Low Countries, France – Elizabethan England's domestic politics had been relatively quiescent, troubled only by two abortive rebellions and a handful of unsuccessful assassination plots. Roman Catholics, of course, disagreed with this characterisation, but they were not the ones writing the panegyrics.

This meaning of peace, 'no civil discord nor domestic strife', as a figure of Peace put it in a Chester entertainment of 1610, was particularly salient at the moment of James's accession.[6] Contemporary observers had believed that Elizabeth's death would inaugurate a contest over the English throne, involving a number of different foreign and domestic claimants. Many worried that this contest would only be settled by force. James's surprisingly smooth accession highlighted the absence of the expected civil conflict, and peace therefore became a principal theme of how people both described and remembered the moment. 'When he was first proclaimed', the preacher Thomas Adams argued two decades later, 'what heard we but peace?'[7]

Second, Jacobean cultural production used 'peace' as a way to discuss the union of Scotland and England. Here the personal union of the crowns was more than enough, since it eliminated, or appeared to eliminate, the possibility of war between the two kingdoms. These conflicts had been quite frequent during the early and mid-Tudor periods. Although there had been no Anglo-Scottish war since 1559/1560, the possibility of a hostile Scotland, allied with England's enemies, was ever-present, driving extensive English meddling in Scotland's internal politics, not least the long-term imprisonment and eventual execution of the Scottish queen. The personal union would not quell all violence – border raids would continue – but it did have some practical consequences, including defortification of the border and the pursuit of a joint

Stuart foreign policy.[8] Orators, poets and iconographers celebrated the personal union as a route to peace. Several of the devices planned for James's entry into London in March 1604 alluded to this. Most strikingly, Thomas Dekker had planned to stage an encounter between armoured figures of St George and St Andrew, the knightly patron saints of England and Scotland; instead of fighting, the pair would have embraced and walked arm in arm.[9]

Thirdly, 'peace' was used to describe a state of the Church, particularly meaning a Church not seriously riven by internal disputes. W. B. Patterson has drawn attention to early seventeenth-century eirenicist movements, which sought to bridge confessional divisions between Lutheran and Reformed Protestants or even between Protestants and Catholics. Although he gestured at such possibilities from time to time, in reality James appears to have had little interest in reconciliation movements. For James, the important peace of the Church was domestic. Differences of opinion certainly existed in the Church of England and grew in salience throughout the reign. But Peter Lake and Kenneth Fincham have described a Jacobean approach to managing these disagreements that consistently distinguished between those willing to compromise with government demands, who were encouraged, and those unwilling, who were, from time to time, purged.[10]

This practice, of maintaining peace within the Church by careful management of internal theological polemic, may explain James's adoption of the biblical slogan *beati pacifici*. This motto was widely used only after 1616, particularly after its inclusion on the frontispiece of James's collected works published in that year. In the preface to that collection, James Montagu stressed James's efforts to maintain ecclesiastical quiet. The contemporary point of contrast, at least for the theologically aware, would have been the Reformed Church of the Netherlands, where the controversy between Arminian 'Remonstrants' and Gomarist 'Counter-Remonstrants' over the theology of grace had reached a fever pitch, filling pamphlets and threatening schism and civil war. The 1616 Church of England was, by contrast, a model of internal peace, containing traditional Reformed bishops, occasionally conforming puritans, and avant-garde conformists with clear Arminian tendencies.

This approach was necessary, James thought, because internal divisions within Protestantism left a dangerous opening for papalist criticism. In other words, the context of the Jacobean approach to the English Church was a larger polemical war against Roman Catholicism. Lambeth Palace Library owns a copy of a radical puritan *Humble Supplication for Toleration and Liberty* (1609), with the king's own heavy and hostile annotations. James's contradictions and sneering jokes repeatedly demonstrate that one of his major objections to Protestant nonconformity was that it presented Roman Catholicism with a disunited front. 'Your factious behaviour giveth indeed an excellent relish and advantage to the papists', he wrote at one point; 'the Protestant party', he wrote in another, 'cannot but languish indeed when as her bowels are so gnaw[ed] by her own viperous and ungracious brood, so as, having a strong foreign adversary on the one side, she is on the other part never at rest within her own doors'.[11]

For James and his supporters, those who stirred controversies within the Church were *peace-breakers*. Denison's sermon on *Beati Pacifici*, preached before the king and published in 1620, was ironically framed as an aggressive attack on such men. For if peace-makers are blessed, Denison explained, 'the peace-breaker must needs be cursed; if the one be *filius Dei*, the other must needs be *filius Diaboli*'. Chief among the peace-breakers was the Devil, closely followed by the popes and the Jesuits, 'men sent forth to cast about the wildfire of broyles in kingdoms and commonwealths'. But the Church of England had peace-breakers of its own. 'We are encumbered', Denison told his auditory, 'with certain contentious brethren, who strive as earnestly about matter of ceremony and circumstance, as Saint Jude exhorteth us to do for the faith'.[12] There were other peace-breakers, particularly 'lawyers' who manufacture 'suits and controversies', but Denison repeatedly returned to the 'puritans', and those who 'arrogate to themselves the names of brethren, the people of God, and the like'.[13] 'What are these', he asked, 'but the devil's bellows, and his seedsmen?'[14] By contrast, Denison hoped that his sermon would drive readers 'to a serious consideration and correspondent thankfulness for these blessed days of peace and grace which we enjoy, under the government of the most wise, learned, and religious king that ever this nation had'.[15]

The irony of Denison's rhetorical violence in defence of peace was not fully lost on the preacher. 'I have been taxed, by some', he explained, with 'too much tartness ... against those who dissent from our Church in her ceremonies and government, and for ranking them with peace-breakers'.[16] Some of those who disagreed about ceremonies were themselves of a 'peaceable disposition', and deserved quiet; 'but when I observe some others', Denison wrote, 'either by their books, sermons, or conferences, to be proud, factious, and contentious; blame me not for taxing them as enemies to our peace'.[17] For Denison, contention about 'ceremonies' was distracting English Protestant divines from the real fight, the 'just and weighty quarrel' with Roman Catholicism.[18]

The fourth usage of 'peace' was to describe the absence of foreign war. As with the others, this sense grew prominent at particular moments: during and immediately after the Anglo-Spanish treaty of 1604; during the Dutch truce negotiations of 1607–1609; and, as war engulfed Europe, from 1619 until the end of James's life. This form of peace was undoubtedly the most controversial.

II Peace as Interest and Disposition

The geopolitical landscape of the early seventeenth century was deliriously complex. It was constituted by a familiar competition for status, security, reputation and power, and particularly by the twin poles of dynasty and religion. But the roster of actors was immense. In addition to the monarchies of Spain, France, Britain, Denmark, Sweden, Poland and the Imperial throne, there were a handful of practically acephalous urban republics; a horde of minor dukes and princelings, some of quite substantial power; more or less durable alliances, such as the Swiss and the Grisons; and the emergent United Provinces of the Netherlands, whose evolving political structures not even the Dutch quite understood. The larger states were themselves internally fractured as aristocratic clans competed for influence and office and religious minorities worked to protect their privileges or acquire new ones. Athwart political boundaries lay transnational religious affinities: communities of exiles; religious orders such as the Jesuits operating across the European theatre, though not always in concert; and Reformed Protestants trying to convert ties of friendship and education into lines of military and financial support. Alliances and networks, therefore, developed not only between states but also between states and groups of non- or sub-state actors, including local factions, confessional networks and noble malcontents.

Simply learning the names of all these people, the location of each place, each state's relative strengths and weaknesses, and their formal ties of allegiance, was difficult. Understanding what each group was doing, and predicting what they were likely to do next, was nearly impossible. Under pressure, alliances might strengthen or dissolve; an ambitious prince might suddenly convert and seek new allies, or just as suddenly die, leaving his projects to unravel. Religion was important, certainly, but as a guide to conduct, unreliable: the immaculately Catholic duke of Savoy, for example, spent years petitioning for admission to the so-called 'Protestant Union' of Auhausen.[19]

States tried to understand and influence this constantly shifting system through the practices of intelligence and diplomacy. European states expanded both significantly during the war years of the 1590s. From 1598, these practices expanded again, as former combatants began to establish important resident embassies with one another. The unfolding peace was structured by treaties, ironed out by teams of diplomats working for weeks or sometimes years to find suitable terms. Negotiations for what became the Treaty of Antwerp (1609), which suspended the war between Spain and the United Provinces of the Netherlands, began in late 1606 and included representatives from France, Britain and a host of other interested states.

A recent cultural turn in diplomatic history has emphasised the ambassador's role as a cultural mediator, but the core practice of diplomacy, that is to say, negotiation, remains something of a mystery. Ambassadors received instructions, wrote dispatches, had face-to-face meetings with sovereigns, ministers, minor officials, courtiers and ambassadors from other states, advanced proposals and made concessions. Whatever the importance of gift-giving and ceremony, early seventeenth-century diplomats regarded negotiation as the 'substance' of their task. Studies of the 'micropolitics' of negotiation in later seventeenth-century and early eighteenth-century Europe are suggestive but further research is needed if we are to understand how the early seventeenth-century peace was constructed and maintained.[20]

As King of Scots, James had engaged regularly with foreign powers: proposing confessional alliances, marrying into the Oldenburg dynasty of Denmark-Norway and rallying support for his claim to the English throne.[21] After 1603, James established a joint diplomatic service, retaining existing English embassies in France and the Netherlands and installing new permanent, residential embassies or agencies in Venice, Turin, Brussels, Madrid and the Empire, as well as sending numerous extraordinary missions. He regularly inserted British representatives into peace negotiations, including the Treaty of Antwerp (1609), and the first (1610) and second (1614–1615) Cleves-Jülich crises. British diplomats also tried to interpose in brewing internal conflicts in the Empire between the league of Auhausen and the Emperor Matthias (1612), and in France between the regency government and the rebellious princes of the blood (1616).

James's interventions were generally aimed at securing better conditions for his local allies. British agents sometimes tried to enflame antagonisms and consolidate opposition in a way that might conceivably result in war: in Venice, against the papacy; in the Empire, among Protestant estates against the Emperor; and, in France, among rebel princes against the regency government of Marie de Médicis. But there is only one relatively minor example of James actively providing material support to a belligerent in a new war – a secret financial contribution to the duke of Savoy during the war of the Montferrat Succession.[22] For the most part, James's diplomats were directed to seek peaceful solutions to the problems they dealt with.

In all this, British diplomats were not unique. Both Spain and France maintained networks of European ambassadors; and both networks, for the most part, were mobilised to tamp down or contain regional conflicts rather than expand them. This was not a cast-iron rule, but in the first two decades of the seventeenth century it was the prevailing tendency, to a degree that often left Europe's martial spirits disgusted. There were local reasons for all this. The Habsburg regime in Spain had grown convinced that peace was the only way to rebuild its shattered finances, and became extremely cautious and circumspect about intervening in conflicts in the Rhineland and Italy. After Vervins, Henri IV generally preferred vigorous sabre-rattling to open conflict; following his assassination (1610), the regency led by his wife pursued a policy of peace to insulate Louis XIII, during his minority, from foreign entanglements.

Britain's expanded diplomatic presence was partly a matter of status competition. There were only a half dozen or so sovereign kings in Europe and James believed his position gave him licence to interpose in local disputes even in far-off regions. Sometimes these ambitions sound grandiose: Sir Robert Cotton's *Answer to Certain Military Men regarding Foreign War* (1609) imagined James acting as 'Arbiter of Europe', arguing that as France and Spain were equally balanced, even 'a little weight' could sway the outcome of any conflict.[23] Indeed, British intervention was often so light as to be barely noticeable. But interventions in the Empire and Italy remained minor precisely because Britain had both so little to offer and so little to lose. For states closer to the Atlantic, Britain's role was potentially much larger. If James's views were never decisive even for his close neighbours, his positions were certainly relevant. Relations with the Dutch worsened considerably during James's reign, but the Stuart ambassador continued sitting on the Dutch Council of State, the 'cautionary towns' of Flushing and Brill remained in British hands until 1616, and the Dutch continued to employ significant numbers of English and Scottish regiments in their armies. In France, James had close relations with both the ultra-Catholic Guise family, as a member of the House of Lorraine, and with the Protestant minority, whose rights and privileges his envoys regularly defended.[24] Spain was particularly interested in maintaining British friendship and in accommodating James's demands. Spanish politicians had become convinced that the English war had been the most senseless of their many conflicts, and their strategy for rebuilding power in northwestern Europe rested on their new alliance with Britain.[25]

European diplomats and statesmen understood this immensely complex situation using a cognitive toolkit they called 'reason of state'. 'Statist' or 'politic' observers tried to see behind the veils of secrecy and misdirection created by prudent actors to work out what was 'really' going on. Although this sometimes presents as a sort of Realpolitik, it was in fact an early modern intellectual apparatus with its own prejudices, predilections and blind spots. As I have argued elsewhere, 'politic' statesmen asked certain kinds of questions and expected certain kinds of answers: uncovering the secret intentions of wise princes, analysing faction and using interest as a way to calculate how states might act.[26] This approach to the political flourished in many different parts of early modern culture, but it was particularly prevalent in diplomatic reports, which were in some ways its natural home.

One major category of politic thinking that has not received sustained attention is *disposition*. For politic observers, understanding the preferences, tendencies and indeed the whole subject position of individual actors was one of their most important tasks. The notion of individualised subject position and personality was regularly elaborated in instructions. In 1572, the educator Johannes Sturm became the English agent at Strasbourg; in 1577, the Secretary of State Sir Francis Walsingham wrote to Sturm to explain his duties more precisely. Sturm needed to

> write more at length and more fully respecting the state of the times and the dispositions of men ... the times in which we live are abounding in dangers, and the dispositions of the men with whom we have to contend, are not without their infinite recesses and deep concealments: which nevertheless betray themselves I know not how, and are laid open for our good, in proportion as they are more diligently observed, and as we consider the new alliances which they are making every day.[27]

Walsingham's terminology – directing Sturm to report on the *mores* and *ingenium* of particular men – suggest something about the origins of this interest.[28] In republican and early imperial Roman literature, *mores* referred to something like moral character, hopefully shaped by proper education. *Ingenium* was a complementary expression, meaning something like 'disposition'. It was regularly used by Tacitus to connect people's actions to their character. Galba was 'savage in character' [*ingenio trucem*; *Historiae* 1.21]. Drusus's decision to punish his mutinous soldiers reflected an *ingenium* inclined to harsher courses. And when Tiberius reached the pinnacle of power, he dropped the pretence of moral rectitude and revealed his true *ingenium*. There are dozens of similar uses in Tacitus's works alone.[29] When Walsingham asked for a report on the *ingenia* of the princes of Germany, he was asking what sort of people they were, and what inclinations they had.

These sorts of instructions recur regularly. In 1606, the French statesman Nicolas de Neufville, seigneur de Villeroy, instructed Antoine de la Boderie to work out how English politicians were 'disposed' and how they 'inclined'.[30] In April 1607, the French agents in the United Provinces, Pierre Jeannin and Paul Choart de Buzenval, were told to 'take pains to discover, as quickly and certainly as they can, the inclinations and dispositions, both of the Estates in general, as well as of particular people, who are powerful there'. They were also to make similar inquiries about the dispositions of the Habsburg negotiators.[31]

Even more detailed injunctions appeared in advice on politic observation. Thomas Palmer's 1606 *Essay* on politic travel outlined a series of 'accidental' secrets, difficult to discover but nevertheless 'mete materials to divine of future things'. These included a character portrait of the prince: his wisdom or discretion; his relationship to his advisors; his choice of servants; and 'what spirit he is of, how studious to war and peace'. By these, Palmer explained, 'the inclination of the PRINCE and his ability and weakness may be concluded'.[32] A set of 'most notable and excellent instructions for travellers', organised into branching diagrams, advised readers to observe how a prince 'doth carry himself ... wherein may be observed':

1 His Court
2 His wisdom
3 His inclination to

   1 Peace.
   2 War.

4 How he is beloved or feared of his

   1 People.
   2 Neighbours.

5 His designments enterprises, &c.
6 His disposition, studies, and exercises of

   1 Body.
   2 Mind.

7 His Favourites.
8 The confidence or distrust he hath in his people.[33]

The *Politicke Survey of a Kingdom* (c. 1606–1611) instructed observers to 'take notice of the qualities ... of a prince's mind', including his 'aptitude and natural disposition': his 'wisdom', particularly to be seen in the choice of servants; his 'fortitude' as 'judged by his actions, his justice, in rewarding the good and punishing the evil'; his 'trust or his suspicious nature and distrust'; the 'ability of his wit and the nature of his thoughts and affections', and so on. Of particular importance was the attitude towards conflict, of which the *Politicke Survey* identified three possibilities: warlike, 'always striving to add to their estate' by conquest; 'moderate, never inclining to war but in cases where the diminution of the state was threatened, such a one was Queen Elizabeth and such is now King James'; and 'thirdly quiet and base, embracing peace with all dishonour and loss, such were Richard II and Henry VI kings of England'.[34]

This sort of thinking underlay the descriptions that European diplomats regularly produced of James's personality. Within days of his accession, the Venetian ambassador in Paris told his employers that James was 'said to be personally timid and averse from war'.[35] There are numerous similar descriptions. None of them are mere personality sketches. Indeed, early seventeenth-century observers had a frustratingly limited interest in recording details of each others' personalities, even compared with people later in the century. Rather, these observations represent a form of intelligence-gathering, primed to fit into politic analysis and statist thinking. If James was a certain sort of person, perhaps that would help predict how he would be likely to act.

At the same time that diplomats were trying to work out a prince's dispositions, however, prudent princes were trying to conceal them. One way to do this was through cultivating a stoic imperturbability. Some princes practised keeping their faces or bodies almost entirely immobile when speaking to outsiders; the French diplomat François Bertaut described the Spanish King Philip IV as presenting like a 'statue'. This physical comportment produced a sort of blank expression that was meant to be difficult to read. One can, perhaps, see a similar self-presentation in the elaborately serene face of Charles I in the many Van Dyck portraits of that unhappy prince.[36]

Despite the efforts of his tutor George Buchanan to mould him into a 'rex stoicus', fearing nothing and desiring nothing, James's approach was very different.[37] Rather than cultivating silence, the king liked to talk, sometimes at length, and sometimes in an apparently unguarded way. But this does not mean his speech revealed his true self; rather, James was adept at presenting himself differently to different audiences. Diplomats often left meetings with James convinced he was sympathetic to their employer's position, or at least pliable. These impressions seldom lasted, and the ambassadors – like so many of James's subjects – often found they had been fed with words rather than deeds. 'It is very difficult to give a certain judgment in an affair that depends on a person fashioned like this king' concluded a French envoy, 'who is artificial and disguised above all the rest of the world'.[38]

Describing a prince's 'disposition' or personality was not a spontaneous impulse; rather, it was an early modern analytic technique closely aligned to reason of state, with its own structures and norms. And the reports were further shaped by James's own deliberate misdirection. The portraits of James VI and I drawn by such men are instructive, but they have to be read with both these points in mind.

III Peace and Legitimacy

Whatever James's personal inclinations, the fact remains that, after 1604, England and Ireland did find themselves at peace after decades of war. This had a number of domestic implications, but perhaps the most visible was the need to reconfigure one of the Elizabethan government's principal legitimating motifs. Defending England against an implacable foreign, papist enemy had been central to the monarchy's self-presentation and to justifying the increasingly onerous demands it placed on the country. How could the king explain the importance of his kingship without an enemy to confront? Versions of this problem affected polities across Europe, and cultural products – paintings, ballets, books – extolling and explaining the benefits of peace accordingly appeared across the Continent.

Admittedly, James was not allergic to military gestures. In Scotland, James had personally led military expeditions aimed at suppressing rebellious subjects.[39] On his voyage south from Edinburgh in 1603, he paused in Berwick to review the fortifications and fire a cannon. A 1616 engraving by Francis

Delaram posed an armed king on horseback before a navy; an anonymous reproduction in 1621 added armour. Coins often depicted James in armour, and the obverse of his Great Seal depicted him both mounted and armed, in full gallop.[40] Perhaps the most belligerent representation James's subjects regularly encountered was on the silver half-crown: the obverse has a mounted, armoured James, bearing a sword, while the reverse quotes Psalm 68: '*exurgat deus dissipentur inimici* [let God arise and his enemies be scattered]'.[41]

But this is a small minority of the representations produced during James's lifetime. James's association with peace began almost immediately after his accession to the English throne, and was particularly central to monarchical culture in 1603–1604. The representations of James's kingship shifted over time, and these shifts were not unidirectional, but the image of the king as *pacificus* remained one of the most visible and distinctive motifs of Jacobean cultural production throughout his life (and, indeed, after his death).[42]

At his accession, James was greeted as a king of peace and plenty: by Henry Petowe, in his account of James's July 1603 coronation; and in Sir John Moore's oration to the king at Winchester in September of the same year. Most of these initial depictions invoked peace in the first or second senses described above, referring to absence of civil strife or the union between England and Scotland. However, it was rapidly evident that James intended to end England's war with Spain. James seems to have issued some sort of 'public edict' very shortly after his accession in late March 1603, which clarified that the new king was 'in good amity and friendship with all the princes of Christendom' and expected the war to end. In May, James declared all privateering commissions void; a proclamation dated 23 June allowed English privateers to keep Spanish ships captured before 24 April, after which even ships at sea ought to have heard of the 'discontinuance' of what was already described as the 'late war'. In Brussels, Archduke Albert likewise ordered a ceasefire and a general release of prisoners, and extended Scottish commercial privileges to English and Irish merchants.[43] Formal negotiations for the peace begin in May 1604. But the direction of travel was clear enough for peace to be central to the designs of an elaborate royal entertainment staged in the City of London on 15 March 1604. The entertainment, structured like a *joyeuse entrée*, consisted of several temporary structures designed by the architect Stephen Harrison and placed throughout the City. Each was sponsored by a different London constituency; each was adorned with Latin mottoes and allegorical drawings; and each served as a frame for a little playlet.

All the elements were meant to celebrate the Stuart monarchy, and peace was a major theme. In his Latin oration, William Hubbocke called James '*pacis cultor, et a pace excultus* [a promoter of peace, promoted by peace]'. A gate on Gracechurch Street, sponsored by London's Italian community, featured an allegorical figure of peace holding an olive branch, and quoted

Virgil's direction to the Romans, that they would '*pacique imponere morem* [establish the conduct of peace]'. Figures of, or references to, peace could likewise be found at Cheapside, at Charing Cross (where allegorical figures of peace and plenty sat under a bower), and even at the Royal Exchange, whose sponsors, the Dutch, were extremely edgy about the implications of an Anglo-Spanish alliance.[44]

The most elaborate invocation of peace, however, was the final device, composed by Ben Jonson. The immense structure was designed as a Temple of Janus, with a multi-faced head and a helpful label for those who could read Latin but not recognise the pagan god on sight, 'sacred to Four-Faced Janus [*Jano quadrifonti sacrum*]'. Within was an allegorical figure of Peace, accompanied by Plutus or wealth, and attended by her handmaidens Quiet, Liberty, Safety and Felicity, each treading underfoot the grovelling figures of Mars, Tumult, Servitude, Danger and Unhappiness. The peace-themed mottoes, alluding to Virgil and Silvius Italicus, included remarks such as 'one peace is better than innumerable triumphs'. At the end of the playlet, the gate was ceremonially shut, literally performing the Roman custom at the end of a war.[45]

It is not at all clear what the king, much less the crowd of Londoners, made of the show. Thomas Dekker was clearly disappointed that the king did not halt long enough for the playlets he wrote to be fully performed, while Gilbert Dugdale – who published a report of the entertainment – confessed he could not get close enough to appreciate the detail of the structures or hear many of the speeches.[46] This was a perennial issue for learned Renaissance entertainments: the main effect was magnificence, effort and expense, rather than any particular message. For those who were responsible for the messaging, however, the theme they chose to echo back to the king was peace.

Four days later, in his first remarks to the English Parliament, James described 'the blessings which God hath in my person bestowed upon you all'; the first of these was 'outward peace: that is, peace abroad with all foreign neighbours'. Where James had 'found the state embarked in a great and tedious war ... only by my arrival here, and by the peace in my person, is now amity kept'. The king promised that he would never 'interrupt your public peace' unless the safety or 'honour of the kingdom' were at stake; 'in which case, a secure and honourable war must be preferred to an unsecure and dishonourable peace'. But, given the many 'blessings of peace', flourishing towns, wealthy merchants and increase of trade, James hoped such a day would never come.[47]

A 1604 medal commemorating the peace with Spain echoed the peace-and-plenty motif. On the reverse, facing a figure of *religio*, an allegorical figure of peace held a palm frond and a cornucopia.[48] The motto, 'henceforth, peace, plenty and glorious religion [*hinc pax copia claraq[ue] religio*]' is not a specific classical or biblical tag, but may gesture at a 1599 papal medal.[49]

(Even here, though, the iconography is ambiguous. Some versions of the medal feature a Nicholas Hilliard miniature portrait of James in a fancy hat and shirt. A later version, however, replaced this with a portrait of James in armour, wearing a laurel wreath – a symbol of victory.[50])

Figures of, and references to, peace continued to appear in orations, masques and entertainments for the rest of the reign. In September 1606 at Hampton Court, John King labelled James 'our Solomon or *Pacificus* ... who hath turned swords into sithes, and spears into mattockes, and set peace within the borders of his owne kingdomes and of nations about us'.[51] Allegorical figures of peace appear in the entertainments produced for the king of Denmark in 1606 and for Prince Henry at Chester in 1610. Jonson's *Masque of Hymen*, produced for a court marriage in 1605/1606, features a character describing James as 'the Priest of Peace'.[52] James could not later recall exactly how all this fell out. 'I know not by what fortune, the dicton of *pacificus* was added to my title, at my coming in England ... but I am not ashamed of this addition; for King Solomon was a figure of Christ in that, that he was a king of peace'.[53]

Modern historians usually associate James with the biblical motto *beati pacifici* – blessed are the peacemakers, from Matthew 5. 9 – but it is difficult to determine when James selected this as a motto. As far as I can tell, it never appeared on coins, whose mottos usually referred to the union of England and Scotland (e.g., '*faciam eos in gentem unam* [I will make them one people]' early in the reign; '*quae deus coniunxit nemo separabit* [what God conjoined no man will separate]' later.[54]) The phrase *beati pacifici* does not appear very often in English printed texts, perhaps because it was not the universally preferred Latin rendering of Matthew 5.9. *Beati pacifici* was used by the Vulgate, and by Erasmus, but Theodore Beza's translation ran instead '*beati, qui sunt pacifici*'.[55] The motto was present on an engraving by Simon van de Passe that scholars have assigned to the first decade of James's reign,[56] and was deployed occasionally thereafter, particularly by Van de Passe himself in a 1616 engraving and various medals and by Daniel Mytens in the well-known 1621 portrait.[57] Van de Passe's 1616 engraving received special endorsement because it was used as the basis for the portrait accompanying the publication of James's collected *Workes* in 1616. The facing frontispiece likewise featured allegorical figures of religion and peace, the latter holding a cornucopia. In his preface, the dean of the chapel royal James Montagu extolled the peace and James's role in it:

> Never hath there been so universal a peace in Christendom since the time of our Saviour Christ, as in these his days: And I dare say, as much, if not more, by the procurement of his Majesty, than by any other earthly means in this world. A peace (to let foreign parts pass) so entertained at home; that in his Majesty's three kingdoms, apt enough by constitution, and not

unaccustomed by practice, to be at variance, there hath been no civil dissension at all. With peace God hath given us plenty: So that, if peace and plenty have not made us too wanton, I know not what we want.[58]

IV Peace Contested

Not everyone was happy with the early seventeenth-century peace. Throughout the reign, critics argued that peace was dangerous. Peace meant deserting Britain's allies or co-religionists and allowing its enemies to prosper. It sapped Britain's martial vitality, introducing a crippling, effeminate weakness into British society. Courtly advocates of peace were not merely misguided, but corrupt, either secret Catholics, Spanish agents or both. In the view of these critics, the 'natural' state of British foreign policy was at the head of a European alliance of largely Protestant countries, aimed at the destruction of Catholic and especially Spanish power. Any deviation from this represented a foreign incursion into British political life.

As Alexandra Gajda has shown, the roots of this discourse lay in the English debate about how to respond to the 1598 Franco-Spanish Peace of Vervins. Numerous figures within or close to the Elizabethan government, including Sir Walter Raleigh and the earl of Essex, worried that the English government would end the war with Spain prematurely, on disadvantageous terms, abandoning the kingdom's allies in the Netherlands. The negotiation of the Treaty of London (1604) raised similar issues.[59]

Between 1604 and 1618, the anti-peace or 'patriot' discourse continued to simmer in jeremiads against courtly luxury, crypto-Catholic courtiers, and appeasement. Militant Protestants regularly called for James to act as a godly prince by leading some sort of anti-Catholic crusade, which some envisioned as a military alliance that would culminate in the capture of Rome.[60] A significant proportion of observers, even within the Jacobean regime, appeared to sincerely hope that the tense confrontations of the 1610s would erupt into open war. But the power of the critique was limited because there was no actual conflict in which Britain could participate. Being a militarist in 1613 was difficult because, even if James had been willing to fight, there was no war for Britain to fight in.

This critique of peace had proponents within the very heart of the government. 'The true strengths of our kingdom do daily decay', wrote Archbishop George Abbot in distress; 'the minds of our people are distracted at home, and the adversary insulteth over us, and scorneth us abroad, besides the secret machinations which they practise upon us ... we are enchanted', he concluded, 'by the false, fraudulent, and siren-like songs of Spain'.[61] One of the frames through which historians have analysed Jacobean foreign policy has been via factional conflict within the government, particularly between a

'Spanish faction', advocating closer relations with Spain, largely suspicious of confessionally motivated entanglement and perhaps crypto-Catholic themselves; and a 'Protestant Cause faction', who sought a more muscular posture in defence of European Protestantism, usually in alliance with France and against Spain.[62] This framing can be misleading, but it does correctly point to significant disagreement within the Jacobean government, from diplomatic secretaries to privy councillors, about how Britain ought to engage with Europe. This disagreement became more intense in the late 1610s and early 1620s, as confessionally tinged war again broke out in the Low Countries, France and especially the Empire, but in general, we should see many of the positions and policies adopted by James's government as contested within that government as well as within the wider political society.

The disagreement and factionalism that prevailed in Britain was mirrored in other countries. Spanish historians have identified a group of councillors and officials associated with a policy of 'quietness', including the royal favourite Lerma and Juan Fernández de Velasco, duke of Frías and constable of Castile. Lerma's policies were opposed by a more 'hardline' group associated partly with veterans of Philip II's administration, such as Juan de Idiáquez and the conde of Miranda, as well as with senior viceroys and diplomats including Baltasar de Zúñiga; the duke of Osuna, viceroy in Naples; the marquis of Villafranca, viceroy in Milan; the marquis of Bedmar, ambassador in Venice; and the conde of Oñate in Vienna. J. H. Elliott even suggests that something about the position of early modern diplomats – watching helplessly as their position was degraded by the concessions and errors of their employers – might push such men to favour confrontation. In the late 1610s, Villafranca came to believe that all the house of Austria's enemies – the Venetians, the Dutch, the Bohemian and Hungarian rebels, the English, the Ottomans – were engaged in a general conspiracy to destroy Habsburg power.[63] This slightly paranoid interpretation was eerily similar to the suspicions that haunted British diplomats such as Sir Dudley Carleton and Isaac Wake.[64] And alongside this high political confrontation, Lerma was the target of an incessant campaign of court libel, complaining about his dominance and depicting him as corrupt. In the wake of the truce with the Dutch, an ambassador explained, 'they in a sort call him traitor, saying that so dishonourable prohibitions of peace (whereof they hold him a principal contriver) cannot proceed out of other entrails, than those of a traitor and a coward'.[65]

The political culture of the United Provinces was very different, but it too experienced a serious debate about the value of the peace. These debates occurred both in the closed-door meetings of the 'regents', the provincial noblemen and urban oligarchs that ran Dutch affairs, and among a wider public through rumour and printed pamphleteering. Between 1606 and 1609, opposition to, or at least scepticism about, peace negotiations with Spain emerged from mercantile communities in Amsterdam and Zealand,

and coalesced around the military leader Maurice of Nassau. The controversy over the truce negotiations helped produce the republic's culture of print pamphleteering, or at least greatly expanded it, tripling the output of topical printed pamphlets. The debate on the truce thus represented a 'decisive period' in Dutch pamphleteering, with public debate continuing at a high volume even after the immediate crisis had passed. The debate resumed as the Twelve Years' Truce inched towards expiration: different 'high' political factions opposed continuing the truce, or favoured it, or even hoped to convert it into a formal, open-ended peace. To some extent, the debate about war and peace polarised along the same lines as the Remonstrant/Counter-Remonstrant division: critics of the Holland statesman Johan van Olden-barnevelt accused him of favouring the Remonstrants precisely *because* they were crypto-Catholics, and therefore both his pro-Remonstrant and pro-peace positions were coherent parts of his overarching plan to betray the Republic to Catholic powers.[66]

The aristocratic revolt (1614–1616) led by the prince of Condé against France's regency government, was also partly framed as a critique of Marie de Médicis's policy of détente with Spain. Condé's printed manifesto ran through a litany of domestic complaints, including corruption and the exclusion of important nobles – particularly himself – from important decisions. But it also harped repeatedly and specifically on divergences between Marie's foreign policy and those pursued by her late husband Henri IV. It pointed to inaction in the face of threats to Navarre and the war in Montferrat, a general abandonment of France's allies in northern Italy, and the 'rushed' double marriage with the Habsburgs. As a result of court corruption, weakness and partiality, Condé concluded, France had lost its position as 'arbiter of Christendom … holding the balance between the two great factions of Europe', which had been 'acquired so gloriously by the late king'.[67] There is little sign that Condé really 'believed' any of the things he said about the regency government, and the manifesto should probably be read as a laundry list of plausible complaints that Condé hoped would lend his nakedly self-serving revolt a patina of legitimacy. But this at least suggests that the direction of French foreign policy was a serious area of concern among France's political elite, as indeed it continued to be in the 1620s and 1630s.

The Short Peace did not last. After several successful attempts to contain regional conflicts, the Bohemian Revolt of 1618–1620 shattered the delicate combination of cross-confessional cooperation and restraint that had prevented pan-European war. A number of things had changed: the 1606 peace with the Ottomans lessened the need for cooperation within the Holy Roman Empire, after which confessional fractures there became much more salient. The increasing economic impact of Dutch encroachment on the Spanish and Portuguese empires, particularly in the Indian Ocean, made both the Spaniards and the Dutch less invested in maintaining peace in Europe.

More broadly, a generational change in political leadership displaced many of the figures who had built the peace in the first place. Within two years, Marie de Médicis was exiled from the French court (1617); the duke of Lerma lost power in Spain (1618); Cardinal Melchior Klesl was arrested in Vienna (1618); and Johan van Oldenbarnevelt was arrested and executed in the Netherlands (1618–1619). Most of these displacements at least partly reflected disagreements about how to conduct foreign policy. These shifts were exacerbated by the deaths of Emperor Matthias (1619), Philip III of Spain (1621), and Archduke Albert of the southern Low Countries (1621), all of whom had long experience negotiating with confessional and geopolitical opponents. In the first decade of the seventeenth century, political leadership almost everywhere had been pushing for peace. By 1621, they were itching for war. The result was disaster: the resumption of religious conflict in France, the end of the Twelve Years' Truce, and the eruption of war in Germany.

James was, in some ways, the last survivor of the peacemaking generation, and he struggled to adjust to the new world. The final years of his reign were rocked by political convulsions about how Britain ought to respond to the unfolding European polycrisis. The problems were, as always, both dynastic and confessional. James's Calvinist son-in-law, the Elector Friedrich V, had accepted the crown of Bohemia from the rebel estates against James's advice (though with the encouragement of the Stuart ambassador). The destruction of the Bohemian army at White Mountain in 1620 was followed shortly thereafter by the invasion of Friedrich's hereditary lands by two armies. One was sponsored by Friedrich's Catholic cousin, Maximilian, duke of Bavaria, who had been promised Friedrich's electoral title by the new emperor. The other was the Spanish Army of Flanders, which poured across the border from the southern Low Countries. Here was the Protestant-Catholic conflict James had long feared, with his daughter and grandchildren caught in the middle. 'I did not think I should have lived to have seen a mutation from so general a peace, which hath been in our time', wrote the Stuart ambassador in the Hague, 'to so general a war and so bloody a one as that into which by degrees we are falling'.[68]

James spent years chasing a diplomatic solution. An embassy to the emperor offered little hope: Ferdinand's concerns lay in the Empire, and in his relationship with Bavaria; Britain simply had nothing that he wanted. The only hope for a diplomatic solution lay with Spain. Spain had influence with the emperor, both because Spanish military support was an important prop for Ferdinand's power and because of their shared dynastic interest. Spanish troops occupied the most important parts of Friedrich's lands, including (after 1622) his seat at Heidelberg. And Spain did have a significant interest in maintaining good relations with Britain, particularly as it edged back towards war with the Dutch. Spain, James hoped, had both the means and the motive to arrange for Friedrich's restoration, putting the genie of confessional war back in the bottle. The deal would be sealed with a marriage alliance between James's son Charles and the Spanish princess María Anna.

This was classic Short Peace-era statesmanship, but without willing partners its success was limited, to say the least. The Spanish government was happy to maintain Britain's friendship, and was probably willing to go through with the marriage alliance, but the new king and his new advisors had no interest in a politics of quietness and containment: they wanted victory. And with Catholic troops on the march against Protestants in France, Bohemia, Germany, and the Netherlands, British domestic politics exploded. The 1621 English Parliament dissolved in acrimony, amid demands for military action on the Continent. Despite government orders to keep silent on 'matters of state', preachers across England attacked the Spanish alliance, while Scottish crowds burned and pillaged Dunkirk ships that took refuge in their harbours.

The number of manuscript and printed pamphlets produced by the controversy was relatively small compared to the debates in the Netherlands or France, but several were widely circulated and became very influential. *Haec-Vir* (1620) blamed the kingdom's men for abandoning the vocation of war, allowing their 'arms to rust', and trading martial virtue for 'softness, dullness, and effeminate niceness'.[69] A vignette Samuel Ward created for his *Woe to Drunkards* (1622) visually represented recent moral decay, contrasting a Bible, a muscly leg in a stirrup, and mailed glove holding a lance ('thus of old') with a pack of cards, a fashionably attired male leg and a hand that managed to hold both a pipe and a cup of wine ('thus now').[70]

The most prominent anti-peace pamphleteer was the puritan minister Thomas Scott. Scott's breakout *Vox Populi* (1620) purported to represent a debate between Gondomar, Spain's ambassador to Britain, and members of the Spanish Council of State. The pamphlet argued that Spain aimed at universal monarchy and the extirpation of Protestantism; that everything Spain did were attempts to advance that project; and that, more particularly, the Stuart-Habsburg marriage treaty and the larger policy of peace with Britain were all part of a secret Spanish plan to take over the world.

Spain had pursued this agenda secretly, by recruiting what Scott termed a 'Spanish faction' active in other countries. This network of sympathisers represented an 'invisible kingdom, and an unknown number of subjects in all dominions'. Scott gave Spain's group of secret traitors a handful of particular faces. An allusion to an 'honourable earl and admirable engine (a sure servant to us and the Catholic cause whilst he lived)', whose main service was engineering mistrust between King James and the 1614 House of Commons, was the late Henry Howard, earl of Northampton. The other agent Scott mentioned was the Dutch statesman Oldenbarnevelt, described as 'our most experienced petitioner and sure friend', who aimed to dissolve the alliance between England and the Netherlands, to weaken both and pave the way for reconquest.[71]

Scott's pamphlet has rightly been read as a critique of England, and its details about Spanish high politics are quite sketchy. But elements even of this were, nevertheless, real and perceptive.[72] Although printed in 1620, the pamphlet was set in 1618, and Scott evoked the jealousy aroused by Lerma's dominance, depicting the favourite's power as 'wax[ing] heavy towards declension'.[73] More importantly, *Vox Populi* depicted Spanish policy-makers as *divided* on the right approach to Britain. The point of the supposed meeting was to satisfy the papal nuncio, as 'if the mystery were not unfolded and the ground of those counsels discovered', the 'overtures of peace and amity with the English ... might engender suspicion and jealousy betwixt the pope' and the king of Spain.[74] When Gondomar mentioned the English marriage treaty, the archbishop of Toledo indignantly protested that no such treaty should be made, both on religious and fiscal grounds, forcing others to defend the policy as in the long-term interests of Catholicism and Spain.[75] When Gondomar claimed that English Catholics would side with a Spanish invasion force, another councillor argued that English Catholics might in fact side with 'their own king (though a heretic) [rather] than with his Catholic Majesty a stranger'.[76] In other words, Scott imagined – correctly, in fact – that there were many figures within Spanish politics who saw peace with Britain as *insufficiently pro-Catholic*, just as many people in Britain saw it as insufficiently pro-Protestant. The task of the meeting, within Scott's frame, was to reassure those people that the peace was, after all, a Catholic plot.

The peace was valuable to Spain because it had bred weakness in Britain: 'their bodies by long disuse of arms were disabled and their minds effeminated by peace and luxury'.[77] 'The commons generally are so effeminate and cowardly', Gondomar noted later, that

> at their musters (which are seldom and slight, only for the benefit of their muster-master) of a thousand soldiers, scarce one hundred dare discharge a musket, and of that hundred, scarce one can use it like a solider. And for their arms, they are so ill provided, that one corslet serveth many men, when such as show their arms upon one day in one place, lend them to their friends in other places to show when they have use.... Thus stands the state of that poor miserable country, which had never more people and fewer men.[78]

This weakness was exacerbated by the new East India trade, which the Spanish were happy to permit because it was a mere trade in luxuries, 'carrying out gold and silver, bringing home spice, silks, feathers, and the like toys', leading to an 'insensible wasting in the common stock of coin and bullion'. This waste of treasure was also a waste of sailors, 'not one of ten returning.

Which I am glad to hear', Gondomar noted, 'for they are the men we stand in fear of'.[79]

King James had allowed all this to happen because of his idiosyncratic commitment to peace. 'The king of England', Gondomar explained, 'who otherwise is one of the most accomplished princes that ever raign'd, extremely hunts after peace, and so affects the true name of a peacemaker, as that for it he will do or suffer anything'. He was also in bad financial straits; through the Spanish marriage treaty, James 'hop[ed] … (though vainly) to settle peace, and fill the exchequer'.[80] In Scott's eyes, James's personal commitment to peace was a vulnerability that Spain could exploit. If Spain did 'resolve upon an invasion', the time was 'never' so 'fit as at this present, security of this marriage and the disuse of arms having cast them into a dead sleep, a strong and wakening faction being ever amongst them ready to assist us, and they being unprovided of ships and arms, or hearts to fight, an universal discontentment filling all men'.[81]

These themes recurred throughout Scott's output: Scott's *Belgick Pismire* (1622), for example, mourned the decline of 'exercises, especially shooting, running, wrestling, and the like strenuous and manly sports' that had rendered Englishmen strong, active, healthful, 'honourably esteemed of our friends' and 'terrible to our enemies'. When these were abandoned, 'I know not upon what peaceable and politique pretences … our bodies are generally weakened; our manners corrupted; our healths impaired, and our estates wasted in drunkenness, gluttony, lechery and pride'.[82] But the fullest indictment of peace, indeed of the entire era of the Short Peace, was advanced in Scott's *Belgick Soldier* (1624). 'Peace', Scott wrote, 'or if you will dissembling contracts of peace' – that is, the treaties – had 'proved like a standing pool' to Europe, 'affording nothing … but mud, stench, vermin, toads, locusts, and increase of foul contagion'.[83] In each part of Europe, peace had led invariably to corruption, weakness, and the secret extension of Habsburg power. In the Empire, the 'outward lenative courses, laying aside all forcible arms and imperious overruling the princes', had hidden a creeping aggrandisement of the house of Austria. These courses included alliances with Poland and Saxony; the presence of Spanish troops in the east; and the decay of civic virtue in the imperial cities, 'afraid of nothing but the corruptions of peace, and the excess of a dissolute life'.[84] Just as 'a cozening peace' had led to the treacherous death of Jan Hus at the Council of Constance, so had the Bohemians erred in disarming after the peace with the Ottomans. 'No sooner were these poor Hussites disarmed, but fire and faggots were prepared, and the passionate Protestants roared outright, that ever they desisted from war, to be betrayed unto a dissembling peace'.[85]

In France, Henri IV's early reign, spent in war, had been a monument to his 'greatness', 'but when peace was contracted, his honour was distracted, his country defiled, his towns vitiated, his faith violated'.[86] Without the bracing threat of foreign war, France had been troubled by a series of discontented grandees and treacherous royal favourites: various members of the house of Lorraine, the duc de Biron, the marquis d'Ancre, and the duc de Luynes, all 'instruments of Spain, to keep France busy at home ... and divert the several kings from looking toward Navarre, Milan, Naples, the succouring of the Switzers, Grisons, and those territories'.[87] The whole range of French religious opinion was discontented by Henri's turn to peace: 'the Protestants hung their heads for his lukewarmness, the papists gnashed their teeth for his policies, the neuters feared him, the atheists abhorred him, his wife dissembled, and an Italian upstart contrived his destruction'.[88] Paradoxically, Louis XIII's open war against the Huguenots was preferable, as it at least led to 'increase of religion, and firm opposition against unprincely cruelty'.[89]

Elizabethan England had likewise been made great by war, 'but what hath the peace done?' Scott asked. 'It hath made us drunk with ease and carelessness, forget our God, be uncharitable to our neighbours, neglect our calling, sleep in security, accustom ourselves to foolish exercises, and by studying every man for his private [interest], the whole kingdom is confounded with poverty and wretchedness'. Peace had diverted men to adventure to the Indies, which was not merely wasteful but positively immiserating, since it resulted in the loss of treasure in exchange for mere luxury commodities.[90] 'Hath it not proved our sickness, and wrought upon our corrupt bodies like a fever, not only obnoxious in itself, but bringing on apace other diseases. And have we not taken a liberty to sin, because no punishment followed suddenly ... the country is weighed, and found lighter by 14 millions in 15 years; we are haunted with beggars, undone in our trades, pestered in the prisons, the Commonwealth overrun with poverty, the people cry out of misery, and fear and terrors make us all amazed'. 'Young men', Scott claimed, 'are grown so proud' that they 'consume themselves with comparative expenses to their superiors; filling their houses with children, and the Commonwealth with bankrupts; so that there is no preventing of these mischiefs but war'.[91]

In Scott's view, confessional division – what he called 'contrariety of religion' – made a secure peace impossible.[92] Similar arguments had been advanced for decades about the importance of uniform religion for maintaining civil peace *within* a state, but, in Scott's view, religious division equally compromised peace between states. 'Show me in any part of Christendom', Scott reasoned, 'where any person professing the Reformed religion hath been spared, were he friend, neighbour, or kinsman, if that side had strength enough to reach his throat ... and this will continue as long as Antichrist reigns'.[93] Scott's preferred solution was, curiously, an 'equal toleration of religion through all Christendom', albeit with only 'one religion ... professed, and publicly preached in one place, though others might there live safely and freely without impeachment of their consciences, persons, or goods'. In this vision of Europe, each state would choose one version of Christianity for public worship. Internally, each would allow religious minorities to live in private unmolested; externally, each would respect the public religions endorsed by their neighbours. 'I verily believe', Scott wrote, 'that this, or something like it, is that which his Majesty aims at, if he could effect it as well in Italy, France, and Spain, as he would upon those or better terms, willingly grant it in England. Otherwise he sees it would be prejudicial and disadvantageous to the truth, to permit a toleration only in England, except he could likewise establish it universally'.[94] In the meantime, it was better to have 'a safe war … rather than an unsafe peace, which, bringing in corruption, would soon open a door to the conqueror'.[95] Instead of preferring religious uniformity and endorsing toleration only reluctantly and temporarily in the name of civil peace, as other advocates of toleration tended to do, Scott imagined a hopeful, Jacobean future of religious pluralism while demanding religious war now.

In response to these criticisms, regime publicists mounted a sustained defence of the peace. Their efforts were led by James himself. 'I have reigned about eighteen years among you', James told the English Parliament in 1621; 'if it be a fault in me, that ye have been at peace all this time, I pray you pardon it: for I took for an honour unto me, that you should live quietly under the vines and fig trees'.[96] When the Parliament failed after the Commons petitioned for a breach with Spain, demanding what James characterised as 'a public war of religion through all the world at once', James criticised the MPs for their interference in foreign affairs. His intervention is usually read as an absolutist assertion – as though the Parliament had interfered in matters that belonged only to him by right and power – but James also emphasised that they simply lacked the experience and competence to understand the international situation. 'Who can have wisdom to judges things of that nature', James asked, 'but such as are daily acquainted with the particulars of treaties, and of the variable or fixed connection of affairs of state, together with the knowledge of the secret ways, ends, and intentions of princes in their several negotiations; otherwise, a small mistaking in matters of this nature, may produce more effects than can be imagined'.[97] Denison, a royal chaplain, agreed. The criticisms levelled by Scott and other militarists were appallingly naïve: *dulce bellum inexpertis*. 'Surely no man knows thoroughly the benefit of peace', Denison explained, 'but he that hath seen the doleful face of war'. Anyone who had witnessed the terrible vistas Denison conjured – injury, sexual assault, destruction and death – could not but 'acknowledge, that the name of peace is precious.... But alas', Denison observed, we sit under our vines, and under our fig trees, yea, and we enjoy abundant blessings in peace, yet we are not so happy as to see our happiness; yea, we are grown, through our plenty of peace, to disesteem it, as the Indians do their fragrant woods in fires, who by much use are weary of them, and as the Israelites did Manna, who by reason of their plenty did loath it.[98]

The push to launch a war against Spain accelerated in 1624, driven by Prince Charles and James's favourite, the duke of Buckingham. The pair had become frustrated with Spanish promises during a trip to Madrid; visions of glory danced in their heads.[99] Addressing the 1624 Parliament's advice to break off the treaties, James told them that while he had been 'all the days of my life a peaceable king, and have had the honour in my titles, and impresses to be styled *Rex Pacificus*', he grudgingly accepted that things might have gone too far for negotiation.[100] But the wily king remained cautious, and continued to delay. In early 1625, he finally authorised an English expeditionary force; by March, James was dead.

V Conclusion

The first generation of early Stuart historians were not particularly kind to King James VI and I. The *Court and Character of King James*, widely attributed to the former courtier Sir Anthony Weldon, depicted the peace with Spain, 'so disadvantageous for England, that it and all Christendom have since both seen and felt the lamentable effect', as an artefact of Jacobean court corruption, 'bought' with 'an infinite mass of treasure, prodigally cast about the English court'.[101] James himself was 'wholly addicted to peace' and 'spent much treasure, in sending stately ambassadors to treat his enemies (which he esteemed friends)'; had he 'spent half the money in swords he did in words, for which he was but scorned', he could have preserved the Palatinate and 'saved much Christian blood since shed'.[102] William Sanderson agreed: Doncaster's mission to the emperor in 1619–1620 was a 'wild goose chase', and in fact had been 'purposely so designed by the king; only to spend time, and to amuse men's expectations (who were wild after a war)' than to actually seal 'a treaty concerning the lost Palatine'.[103] Even those who depicted the peace itself as honourable were sceptical about its moral effects. King James had a 'peaceable mind' and 'nothing now but bravery and feasting, the parents of debauchery and riot, flourished among us', wrote Arthur Wilson. 'Peace is a great blessing, if it bring not a curse with it; but war is more happy in its effects'.[104]

According to a brief animal prophecy published by William Lilly in 1645, in the line of English monarchs since Henry VIII, King James was styled *vulpes*, the fox.[105] The *Court and Character of King James* put this characterisation under James's frontispiece portrait as an ironic counterpoint to the motto *Beati Pacifici*; the facing title page added for good measure a remark usually attributed to Louis XI of France, the politic hero of Philippe de Commynes's influential politic history: '*qui nescit dissimulare nescit regnare* [he who does not know how to dissimulate does not know how to rule]'[106], which the author of the *Court and Character* offered as an alternative motto for the king.[107] For the author, these two *sententiae* – *qui nescit dissimulare nescit regnare* and *beati pacifici* – were ultimately in conflict; for James's 'love to the latter, made him to be beaten with his own weapon in the other, by all princes and states that had to do with him'.[108] James was constantly 'abused, and would be abused, by over much credulity', not only in the treaty of the Spanish Match but also 'in all other negotiations'.[109]

In 1648, the painter, projector and quondam Stuart diplomat Sir Balthazar Gerbier offered a unique interpretation of these events to the exiled Queen Henrietta Maria and the young Prince Charles. In Gerbier's version, James had never been fooled by Spanish promises; rather, the king understood well enough that the Spanish alliance was unlikely to secure the return of the Palatine lands. But James simultaneously entertained strong doubts about Britain's capacity to wage a land war in the Rhineland against the Army of Flanders and its allies. 'In fine', Gerbier wrote, James

> resolv[ed] to suffer in his reputation, in the opinion of the world, as one abused, and by the subtlety of the Spanish minister persuaded to the said treaty, rather than to make it appear (as in a war it must have done) that the whole force of his three kingdoms and all his allies could not have constrained the emperor, the king of Spain, and the duke of Bavaria to restore the Palatinate.

In Gerbier's telling, James had deliberately 'cho[sen] rather to suffer an eclipse of his personal reputation for wisdom' rather than 'to bring into such hazard the reputation and force of those kingdoms he governed, in a war whereof he could reasonably promise himself no good event'.[110]

Although they pointed in different directions, these early modern accounts all saw James's approach to Europe as problematic, as something that required explanation. And their preferred way of explaining James's conduct was to try to work out what was going through his mind. Was James ruled by his natural timidity and dispositional preferences? Or did he have a 'realistic' approach, shaped by a sober appreciation of the strengths and weaknesses of his position?

Most historians have continued to approach Jacobean foreign policy in quite similar terms, unconsciously reproducing tropes of early modern analysis. But we are not restricted to early modern categories; we can pose the question in different ways. One way to do this is to notice how similar James's experience was to those of his contemporary princes. James created a network of diplomats that constantly posed as mediators in regional conflicts: so did France and Spain. Apologists for James's kingship glorified peace and the fruits of peace: in an age of treaties, so did government propagandists across the Continent. Critics denounced the Jacobean peace as weak, effeminate, a sign of court corruption and a betrayal of true religion: similar or even identical attacks were made against Lerma, Marie de Médicis and Oldenbarnevelt.

James's conduct was nevertheless distinct in a few basic ways. Many of James's contemporaries felt compelled to begin their reigns with military adventures as a way to secure their reputations as soldiers. Philip III's advisers insisted such a course was mandatory, and Philip accordingly spent several years attempting to achieve a notable success in Ireland or North Africa. After Louis XIII seized control of the French government in 1617, one of his first acts was to attack enclaves of French Protestants, triggering nearly a decade of civil war. Even Archduke Albert, who genuinely favoured a peace with the United Provinces, believed it was essential to begin his reign over the southern Low Countries with victory on the battlefield.[111] And of course James's heir, Charles I, launched a war against Spain almost immediately after James's death.

As a young king of Scotland, James had perhaps been under similar pressure, and had personally led troops against Scottish rebels. But at his accession to the English throne, James made no similar gesture: he prepared no new assault on Spain, not even a new army to suppress the Irish rebels. This may have been partly because he was already an adult, and already a king – Philip III, Louis XIII and Charles I all succeeded as young men with something to prove, though Albert had in fact been even older when he received the sovereignty over the southern Low Countries. James was thus unusually well-positioned to pursue peace. But here, I think, we can also see the effects of inclination, temperament or even ideology. James did not particularly want to fight, but more importantly he did not regard military adventurism as essential to kingship in the way that many of his contemporaries did. 'Every king is not a peace-maker', reflected Thomas Adams; 'ours, like a second Augustus, hath shut the rusty door of Janus's Temple; so making peace, as if he were made of peace'.[112]

Gestures at religious peace were often, and perhaps inherently, aggressive; in a similar vein, the Stuart king's politics of peace was also a politics of power. James insisted that he alone had the authority and perspective to shape his kingdoms' relations with other polities. The emergence of something like a mass anti-peace politics renewed James's suspicion of popularity and popular institutions, and triggered attempts to suppress 'lavish speech' and critical preaching. James's relations with the English Parliament, always vexed, reached a nadir in December 1621 thanks to a dispute about whether the House of Commons might use their traditional privilege of free speech to debate foreign and dynastic policy. The interlocking problems of finance, mass politics, Parliament and foreign policy would cloud the rest of his reign – and, indeed, shape the reigns of his successors.

The world changed, but James did not. This may have been a result of his disposition, or a calculation of interest, but it also may have been something like habit. The old methods had once been new, and had managed to keep Europe from tearing itself apart for twenty years; perhaps James had simply become accustomed to work this way, and hoped it would be enough to avoid disaster. It wasn't.

Notes

1 J. Doelman, *King James I and the Religious Culture of England* (2000), ch. 5; BL, Lansdowne MS 885, fo. 117^r; John Williams, *Great Britains Salomon* (1625) [STC 25723], pp. 38–9, 56–8; TNA, SP 16/2/80 [Chamberlain to Carleton, 21 May 1625].
2 B. J. García García, *La Pax Hispanica: Política exterior del Duque de Lerma* (1996); P. C. Allen, *Philip III and the Pax Hispanica, 1598–1621: the Failure of Grand Strategy* (2000); R. G. Asch, *Vor dem großen Krieg. Europa im Zeitalter der Spanischen Friedensordnung 1598–1618* (2020); N. Millstone (ed.), *Europe Between the Wars: The Short Peace, 1598–1618* (forthcoming).
3 The traditional framing derived from S. Adams, 'The Protestant Cause: Religious Alliance with the West European Calvinist Communities as a Political Issue in England, 1585–1630' (DPhil, Oxford, 1973); R. Cross, 'To Counterbalance the World: England, Spain, & Peace in the Early 17th Century' (PhD, Princeton, 2012); C. Fry, 'Diplomacy & Deception: King James VI of Scotland's Foreign Relations with Europe (c. 1584–1603)' (PhD, St Andrews, 2014); M. Questier, *Dynastic Politics and the British Reformations, 1558–1630* (Oxford, 2019); R. Malcolm Smuts, *Political Culture, the State, & the Problem of Religious War in Britain & Ireland, 1578–1625* (Oxford, 2023).
4 John Denison, *Beati Pacifici: the Blessednes of Peace-Makers* (1620) [STC 6583], pp. 5–9; John Stradling, *Beati Pacifici* (1623) [STC 23352], p. 1 Doelman, *James and Religious Culture*, pp. 86, 96–7.
5 John Nichols (ed.), *The Progresses, Processions, and Magnificent Festivities, of King James the First* (2 vols, 1828), I, pp. *129, 10; see also pp. 121–3, etc.
6 Nichols, *Progresses*, II, p. 301.
7 Questier, *Dynastic Politics*, chs 4–5; Smuts, *Political Culture*, ch. 9; P. Kewes and A. McRae (eds), *Stuart Succession Literature: Moments and Transformations* (2018); Thomas Adams, *Eirenopolis* (1622) [STC 112], p125; Doelman, *James and Religious Culture*, p. 87.
8 Smuts, *Political Culture*.
9 Nichols, *Progresses*, I, p. 340.
10 W. B. Patterson, *James VI and I and the Reunion of Christendom* (Cambridge, 1997); K. Fincham and P. Lake, 'The Ecclesiastical Policy of King James I', *Journal of British Studies* 24 (1985), pp. 169–207.
11 Lambeth Palace Library, 1609.42, 28, 30.
12 Denison, *Beati Pacifici*, pp. 34–5, 40, 42.
13 Denison, *Beati Pacifici*, pp. 44–5, 85.
14 Denison, *Beati Pacifici*, p. 35.
15 Denison, *Beati Pacifici*, sig. A2^{r-v}.
16 Denison, *Beati Pacifici*, sig. A4^r.
17 Denison, *Beati Pacifici*, sig. A4^{r-v}.

18 Denison, *Beati Pacifici*, sig. A5^r.

19 BL, Additional MS 18639, fo. 118^v [Isaac Wake to James, 17/27 Nov. 1615]; Smuts, *Political Culture*, pp. 602–3.

20 T. A. Sowerby and J. Hennings (eds), *Practices of Diplomacy in the Early Modern World c. 1410–1800* (2017); L. Bély, *Espions et Ambassadeurs au Temps de Louis XIV* (1990); D. Croxton, *Peacemaking in Early Modern Europe: Cardinal Mazarin and the Congress of Westphalia* (1999); M. R. Thorp and A. J. Slavin (eds), *Politics, Religion and Diplomacy in Early Modern Europe* (1994).

21 H. G. Stafford, *James VI of Scotland and the Throne of England* (1940), pp. 124–34, 150–3, 227, 244–5; Fry, 'Diplomacy and Deception', *passim*; A. Courtney, *James VI, Britannic Prince: King of Scots and Elizabeth's Heir, 1566–1603* (Abingdon, 2024), ch. 8.

22 Smuts, *Political Culture*, pp. 601–2.

23 BL, Cotton MS Cleopatra F VI, fos 37^v–8^r; N. Millstone, 'Sir Robert Cotton, Manuscript Pamphleteering, and the Making of Jacobean Kingship during the Short Peace, ca. 1609–1613', *Journal of British Studies* 62 (2023), p. 145.

24 BL, Stowe MS 171, fo. 205^r [James to the duc de Guise, May 1610] and *passim*; Smuts, *Political Culture*, pp. 571–81.

25 García, *Pax Hispanica*, pp. 48, 84–7.

26 N. Millstone, 'Seeing Like a Statesman in Early Stuart England', *Past and Present* 223 (2014), pp. 77–127.

27 H. Robinson (ed.), *The Zurich letters: Comprising the Correspondence of Several English Bishops and Others, with Some of the Helvetian Reformers, during the Early Part of the Reign of Queen Elizabeth* (2 vols, Cambridge, 1842–5), II, p. 286 [Walsingham to Sturm, 23 April 1577].

28 Robinson, *Zurich Letters*, II, appendix, p. 176.

29 S. G. Daitz, 'Tacitus' Technique of Character Portrayal', *American Journal of Philology* 81 (1960), pp. 30–52; C. Gill, 'The Question of Character-Development: Plutarch and Tacitus', *Classical Quarterly* 33 (1983), pp. 469–87.

30 Antoine le Fèvre de La Boderie, *Ambassades de Monsieur de la Boderie en Angleterre…* (5 vols, Paris, 1750), I, p. 34 [Villeroy to Boderie, 6/16 May 1606].

31 Bibliothèque Nationale de France, MS fr 7078, fos 449^r, 460^v–1^r.

32 Thomas Palmer, *An Essay of the Meanes how to Make our Travailes, into Forraine Countries, the more Profitable and Honourable* (1606) [STC 19156], pp. 123–5.

33 *Profitable Instructions* (1633) [STC 6789], pp. 14–15.

34 Bodleian Library, Oxford, MS Rawlinson C 878, fos 15^r–17^v.

35 *CSPV 1603–1607*, pp. 12–16 [Cavalli to the doge and senate, 10/20 April 1603].

36 J. H. Elliott, 'The Court of the Spanish Habsburgs: a peculiar institution?', in P. Mack and M. Jacob (eds), *Politics and Culture in Early Modern Europe: Essays in Honour of H. G. Koenigsberger* (Cambridge, 1987), p. 13.

37 A. Pollnitz, *Princely Education in Early Modern Britain* (2015), pp. 288–9.

38 James had been like this since adolescence: Courtney, *James VI, Britannic Prince*, p. 54; Bibliothèque Nationale de France, MS fr 15989, fo. 61^r [Tanneguy Leveneur de Tillières, to Louis-Philogène Bruslart de Sillery, marquis de Puisieulx, 22 April/2 May 1621]; Smuts, *Political Culture*, pp. 545–6, 552.

39 S. Murdoch, 'James VI and the Formation of a Scottish-British Military Identity', in A. Mackillop and S. Murdoch (eds), *Fighting for Identity: Scottish military experience c.1550–1900* (2002), pp. 5–11; Courtney, *James VI, Britannic Prince*, pp. 73, 111–13, 138, 142, 145–8, 152–3.

40 Nichols, *Progresses*, I, pp. 64–7; K. Sharpe, *Image Wars: Promoting Kings and Commonwealths in England, 1603–1660* (2010), pp. 74–90; BM E.5109; or the Spur Ryal, BM 1854, 0621.77.

41 BM, E.718; 1854,0621.59.

42 Sharpe, *Image Wars*, p. 14; Doelman, *James and Religious Culture*, p. 73.
43 Nichols, *Progresses*, I, pp. 237, 240, 275, 272, 277; *By the King. Although we have Made it Knowen* … (1603) [STC 8321]; TNA, SP 14/1/111 [draft declaration, May 1603]; Joseph Cuvelier, 'Les Préliminaires du Traité de Londres (29 Août 1604)', *Revue Belge de Philologie et d'Histoire* 2 (1923), pp. 289–90; Smuts, *Political Culture*, pp. 547–8. A quick end of the Anglo-Spanish war was likewise expected in Paris as early as 10/20 April 1603: *CSPV 1603–1607*, p. 7 [Marin Cavalli in Paris to the doge and senate, 10/20 April 1603].
44 Nichols, *Progresses*, I, pp. *331, 345, 356, 361–3, 349.
45 Nichols, *Progresses*, I, pp. 373–4, 389–95.
46 Nichols, *Progresses*, I, pp. 415–19.
47 James VI and I, ed. J. P. Sommerville, *Political Works* (Cambridge, 1995), pp. 133–4.
48 L. Syson and C. Barclay, 'A Medal Die Rediscovered, a New Work by Nicholas Hilliard', *The Medal* 22 (1993), pp. 3–11.
49 The medal, struck in 1599, probably to commemorate the recovery of Ferrara, features on the reverse a cross, an olive branch and a palm frond, and the motto 'Hinc Pax Hinc Victoria'. Filippo Bonanni, *Numismata Pontificum Romanorum* (Rome, 1699), 2: 496–7; BM, G3, PMAE6.178; A. Modesti, *Corpus Numismatum Omnium Romanorum Pontificum (C.N.O.R.P.). Volume IV da Sisto V (1585–1590) a Paolo V (1605–1621)* (Rome, 2006), p. 625, n. 977.
50 Cf. BM, M.7009 and M.7011. The second is usually dated as later because the first version described James as the king of England and Scotland, whereas he preferred to be described as the king of Great Britain, as this medal does.
51 John King, *The Fourth Sermon Preached at Hampton Court on Tuesday the last day of Sept. 1606* (Oxford, 1606) [STC 14974], p. 46; Fincham and Lake, 'Ecclesiastical Policy', p. 169.
52 Nicholls, *Progresses*, II, pp. 73, 294, 301, 4.
53 James, *A Meditation upon the Lords Prayer* (1619) [STC 14384], p. 93; Doelman, *James and Religious Culture*, p. 85.
54 Cf. BM, E.5109 (1603–5) to BM E.5110 [post 1609], E.756 [1621–23], E.726 [nd].
55 *Novum Testamentum*, trans. Erasmus (Basel, 1519), Secundum Matthaeum, p. 7; *Biblia Sacra*, trans. Tremelius, Junius and Beza (Hannover, 1712), sig. Bbb3^r.
56 Sharpe, *Image Wars*, p. 72.
57 Sharpe, *Image Wars*, pp. 64, 72. It appears on a series of Van de Passe medals of 1616 [BM, 1872,0401.1]; BM, M.7053.
58 James VI and I, *Workes* (1616) [STC 14344], sig. e1^v.
59 A. Gajda, 'Debating War and Peace in late Elizabethan England', *Historical Journal* 52 (2009), pp. 851–78; *eadem*, 'War, Peace and Commerce and the Treaty of London', *Historical Research* 96 (2023), pp. 459–72.
60 Millstone, 'Sir Robert Cotton'; [Thomas Craig], *Les Trophees du Roi Iacques I* (1609), sig. a4^r, fos 9^r, 21^v, etc; Doelman, *James and Religious Culture*, pp. 80–1.
61 BL, Additional MS 72242, fo. 33^r [Abbot to Trumbull, 31 August 1614].
62 Abbot referred to a 'Spanish faction' in a letter to Trumbull: BL, Additional MS 72242, fo. 43^v [Abbot to Trumbull, 15 May 1615]; Adams, 'Protestant Cause', pp. 243, 249, 254, etc.
63 A. E. Roel, 'Política Francesca de Felipe III: Las Tensiones con Enrique IV', *Hispanica* 31 (1971), pp. 305–6; J. H. Elliott, *The Count-Duke of Olivares: The Statesman in an Age of Decline* (1986), pp. 55–6; García, *Pax Hispanica*, pp. 20–1.
64 Smuts, *Political Culture*, p. 633.
65 Hatfield House, Cecil Papers, 125/39 [Cornwallis to Salisbury, 5 March 1607/8];

P. Williams, *The Great Favourite: The Duke of Lerma and the Court and Government of Philip III of Spain, 1598–1621* (2006), pp. 150–1; and more generally, B. J. García García, 'La Sátira Política a la Privanza del Duque de Lerma', in F. J. Guillamón Álvarez and J. J. Ruiz Ibáñez (eds), *Lo Conflictivo y lo Consensual en Castilla: Sociedad y Poder Político 1521–1721* (2001), pp. 261–95.

66 C. E. Harline, *Pamphlets, Printing, and Political Culture in the Early Dutch Republic* (1987), pp. 3–8; M. Stensland, 'Peace or No Peace? The Role of Pamphleteering in Public Debate in the Run-up to the Twelve-Year Truce' in F. Deen, D. Onneking and M. Reinders (eds), *Pamphlets and Politics in the Dutch Republic* (2010), pp. 227–52; A. Pettegree and A. der Weduwen, *The Bookshop of the World: Making and Trading Books in the Dutch Golden Age* (2019), pp. 45–67; J. den Tex, *Oldenbarnevelt* (2 vols, 1973), II, chs 9–10.

67 Henri de Bourbon, prince of Condé, *Double de la Lettre Escritte Suivant le Vray Original a la Reyne Regente* (1614), pp. 5–6.

68 BL, Additional MS 72273, fo. 85ᵛ [Carleton to Trumbull, 10 October 1622].

69 J. A. Gianoutsos, *The Rule of Manhood: Tyranny, Gender, and Classical Republicanism in England, 1603–1660* (Cambridge, 2020), p. 117; citing *Haec-Vir* (1620), sig. C2ʳ.

70 Samuel Ward, *Woe to Drunkards* (1622) [STC 25055], title page.

71 Thomas Scott, *Vox Populi* (1620) [STC 22098], sigs A4ᵛ, B3ʳ, C1ʳ.

72 Questier calls some of the details about England 'uncannily accurate': *Catholics and Treason: Martyrology, Memory, and Politics in the Post-Reformation* (Oxford, 2022), p. 452. Errors in Spanish high politics included naming the duke of Villahermosa as president of the council of Aragon, and a factional enemy of the duke of Lerma, while in fact the dukedom of Villahermosa was in abeyance in 1618 (Scott, *Vox Populi*, sig. A2ᵛ), and the duke of Medina de Rioseco as being president of the council of war, when he was in fact only nineteen years old (Scott, *Vox Populi*, sig. B2ʳ⁻ᵛ).

73 Scott, *Vox Populi*, sig A2ᵛ–3ʳ.

74 Scott, *Vox Populi*, sig. A2ʳ.

75 Scott, *Vox Populi*, sig. B1ᵛ.

76 Scott, *Vox Populi*, sig. B2ᵛ.

77 Scott, *Vox Populi*, sig. B2ᵛ.

78 Scott, *Vox Populi*, sig. C1ᵛ.

79 Scott, *Vox Populi*, sig. B4ʳ.

80 Scott, *Vox Populi*, sig. B1ᵛ.

81 Scott, *Vox Populi*, sig. C1ᵛ.

82 Thomas Scott, *The Belgick Pismire* (1622) [STC 22069], p. 13.

83 Thomas Scott, *The Belgick Souldier ... Or, Warre was a Blessing* (1624) [STC 22072], p. 14.

84 Scott, *Belgick Souldier*, pp. 19, 20.

85 Scott, *Belgick Souldier*, p. 22.

86 Scott, *Belgick Souldier*, p. 28.

87 Scott, *Belgick Souldier*, p. 27.

88 Scott, *Belgick Souldier*, p. 28.

89 Scott, *Belgick Souldier*, p. 28.

90 Scott, *Belgick Souldier*, p. 39.

91 Scott, *Belgick Souldier*, p. 41.

92 Scott, *Belgick Pismire*, p. 56.

93 Scott, *Belgick Pismire*, p. 57.

94 Scott, *Belgick Pismire*, p. 92.

95 Scott, *Belgick Pismire*, p. 51.

96 TNA, SP 14/119/47 [Speech of James I, 30 January 1621]; Doelman, *James and Religious Culture*, p. 91.

97 James, *His Maiesties Declaration* (1621) [STC 9241], pp. 33–6.
98 Denison, *Beati Pacifici*, pp. 12–14. See also the rhyme of Robert Aylett: 'Some loathing peace, wish war, because unknown, / To them peace is like manna, common grown': *Peace and her Foure Garders* (1622) [STC 1002], sig. A2ʳ; Doelman, *James and Religious Culture*, p. 93.
99 The classic account is T. Cogswell, *The Blessed Revolution: English Politics and the Coming of War, 1621–1624* (Cambridge, 1989).
100 Parliamentary Archives, HL/PO/JO/10/1/19, 119r [James's speech, 5 March 1624]. Over sixty handwritten copies of this speech survive.
101 [Sir Anthony Weldon], *The Court and Character of King James* (1650) [Wing W1273], pp. 25–7.
102 *Court and Character*, pp. 83–4.
103 William Sanderson, *Aulicus Coquinariae* (1651) [Wing S645], pp. 69–70.
104 Arthur Wilson, *The History of Great Britain* (1653) [Wing W2888], p. 91. See also pp. 28, 167, 172, 239 etc.
105 The whole reads: 'Mars, Puer, Alecto, Virgo, Vulpes, Leo, Nullus': William Lilly, *A Collection of Ancient and Moderne Prophesies* (1645) [Wing L2217], p. 1.
106 *Court and Character*, frontispiece and title page.
107 *Court and Character*, p. '130' [recte 103].
108 *Court and Character* p. '130' [recte 103].
109 *Court and Character*, pp. 168–9.
110 BL, Additional MS 4181, fo. 17ʳ⁻ᵛ.
111 García, *Pax Hispanica*, pp. 38, 50; L. Duerloo, *Dynasty and Piety: Archduke Albert (1598–1621) and Habsburg Political Culture in an Age of Religious Wars* (2012), pp. 104–118, 123–142.
112 Adams, *Eirenopolis*, p. 124.

8

INCONSISTENCY RE-ESTABLISHED

James I and Government Policy in Ireland

David Heffernan

In the late spring of 1615, a letter from King James I arrived at Dublin for his viceroy in Ireland, Sir Arthur Chichester. The monarch was not happy. He had recently perused a report of a survey which Josias Bodley, the director-general of fortifications and buildings in Ireland, had carried out of the Ulster Plantation, encompassing the six counties of west Ulster in the north of Ireland: Armagh, Cavan, Donegal, Fermanagh, Londonderry and Tyrone.[1] Having closely read this, James had been disappointed to learn that a majority of the British undertakers to whom estates had been granted there in the summer of 1610 had failed to perform the articles of plantation by which they had been expected to abide. These had called for each grantee to build a manor house and bawn or fortification on their estate, one which would become the focal point of a nucleated settlement of English, Welsh and Scottish tenants which he would bring over to Ulster to replace the Irish that were to be removed onto separate designated precincts. Bodley's report revealed that most undertakers remained utterly negligent. Some were behaving as though they had simply forgotten that the lands they had received had been given in return for promises that they would actually further James's great act of British social engineering in Ireland. What was especially galling, the king remarked, was that he could have been at a much greater profit had he dispensed of the lands in Ulster, some three and a half million statute acres of them, in a different manner. Instead he had elected to commence the plantation as a means of civilising Ulster and securing it against future acts of violence. He therefore ordered Chichester to redouble his efforts to force the undertakers to live up to their commitments and commanded him to send Bodley back to Ulster in 1616 to report on what progress could be made in

DOI: 10.4324/9781003319764-9

the year that followed.[2] At the foot of his letter, in an unusually large script, James stated,

> My Lord, in this service I expect that zeal and uprightness that you will spare no flesh, English or Scottish; for no private man's worth is able to counterbalance the perpetual safety of a kingdom, which this plantation being well accomplished will procure.[3]

James's letter provides an insight into the approach of the first of the Stuart monarchs towards Ireland. Here we have him clearly displaying his zeal for the Ulster project, in the inception of which he was a major driving force.[4] By creating a new British society, one in which Protestant English and 'inland' Scottish settlers would live side by side civilising the wayward Irish, Ulster would become the embodiment of the union of crowns, the plantation the societal personification of James's reign. The survey Bodley had undertaken in 1614 on which James was reflecting was the third such crown survey to have already been carried out on the plantation, just four years after the initial grants were made. Previous surveys had been made in 1611 and 1613 and further ones would follow in 1616, 1618 and 1622, each generally of greater sophistication and detail than the previous.[5] There is also no denying that James had cost himself much money by dispensing of the vast lands in question in 1610 in the way which he did. But at the same time, the letter he sent to Chichester in March 1615 was one of James's rather sporadic engagements with Ireland. As vocal and energetic as he was about the Ulster project on this occasion, he could just as easily spend protracted periods of time engaged in a fairly *laissez-faire* approach to his Irish kingdom, particularly so in the first years of his reign. Similarly, the last seven or eight years of his life saw Ireland largely degenerate into a source of ill-gotten revenue and factional wrangling. The following explores James's approach towards Ireland during his reign, with a particular focus on the Ulster Plantation.

I Elizabethan Inconsistency

Any assessment of James's handling of Irish policy needs to bear in mind what preceded it. There is absolutely no doubting that the reign of Queen Elizabeth saw events unfurl in Ireland that had an enormous bearing on the history of the island. When the daughter of Henry VIII and Anne Boleyn came to the throne in 1558, the English crown's hold over Ireland was tenuous in places and non-existent in others. Only in the Dublin-centred Pale in the province of Leinster was the crown's rule firm. Over a quarter of a century though, going back to the tumultuous 1530s through to 1558, a more forward policy had been gradually adopted, leading to the inception of regional wars, plantations and efforts to extend effective government control into new regions through administrative aggression backed up by regional garrisons.[6] Nevertheless, that process was slow and throughout her reign Elizabeth faced major wars in Ireland every few years.[7] By the time James came to throne the largest conflict of all, the Nine Years' War (c. 1593–1603), was coming to an end after Elizabeth had finally accepted that Ireland needed an expensive solution and had sanctioned the recruitment of an enormous army that at one stage was nearing 20,000 men, at least officially. The leader of that revolt, Hugh O'Neill, second earl of Tyrone, was all but defeated in Ulster by the beginning of 1603. When he finally surrendered to the viceroy that had overseen the crucial final three years of the war, Charles Blount, Lord Mountjoy, after famine had wracked the north of Ireland and cannibalism was allegedly being engaged in, Elizabeth was already dead, though Tyrone did not know it when he made his surrender to Mountjoy.[8]

On the face of it, this creates the impression that a coherent, violent and energetic policy had been engaged in by Elizabeth's government in Ireland for the better part of half a century, one which resulted in the complete conquest of the country by 1603. But this is actually not the case. In reality Elizabethan policy had been enormously inconsistent. When it came to policies surrounding colonisation and plantation, decision-making had oscillated between a limited system of military garrisons and loosely planned colonies, followed later by efforts at cheap 'semi-private' plantation before the realisation in the 1580s that a more systematic state-run plantation of Munster should be organised.[9] Similar to-ing and fro-ing had characterised a great many other things, the primary imperative from Elizabeth's perspective always being to not spend much money in Ireland. This saw plans that were hatched one year abandoned not long after, once costs began to escalate. Alternatively, changes in who was directing policy from London, specifically whether William Cecil, Lord Burghley, or Sir Francis Walsingham had gained the ascendancy over Irish policy at court, could lead to major shifts from year to year. There was not an energetic, coherent policy followed across the forty-five years of Elizabeth's reign. Instead an inconsistent approach prevailed, one based on short-term expediency and ad hoc reactions to the crises Ireland threw up almost every few months.[10] And contemporaries knew this. We find some of Elizabeth's privy councillors such as Walsingham and Nicholas Bacon in the 1570s and 1580s specifically advising her on the merits of adopting a coherent policy programme and then sticking with it over many years.[11] This advice was not listened to. The question then that arose when James came to the throne in 1603, at least from an Irish perspective, was whether or not he would prove any more consistent in his approach than Elizabeth had been.

II Quiet Beginnings

One thing which might have shaped James's reign in Ireland to have a consistent approach early on was the advice he received from the political community across the Irish Sea in the first years of his reign. There certainly was no shortage of individuals in Dublin, Cork, Waterford, or the very many garrisons and fortified towns throughout the country, with concerted opinions on how the country might be governed. At the height of the Nine Years' War a huge volume of treatises and policy papers had been drawn up by senior and middling government officials, military captains, clerics and minor bureaucrats across Ireland venturing proposals on how to win the war and on how the country should then be reshaped once it was over. Some of these texts are well-known today, most conspicuously Edmund Spenser's *A View of the Present State of Ireland* and Richard Beacon's *Solon His Follie*. Well over 200 such treatises and policy papers are extant for the last decade of Elizabeth's reign and there is no doubt that many people in Ireland were eager to share their opinions concerning Irish policy.[12] Surely then, James would be inundated with papers of a similar kind, ones trying to shape how the new monarch would settle the country as the war was coming to an end in tandem with the commencement of a new reign.

This was not the case. There was a peculiar lack of political lobbying from Ireland in the first years of the reign. It was not non-existent. A number of individuals of a clerical or religious bent, such as the pluralist bishop of Cork, Cloyne and Ross, William Lyon, and the president of the provincial council of Munster, Henry Brouncker, composed some treatises between 1603 and 1607 arguing that now was the time to finally try and make progress in spreading the Protestant Reformation in Ireland.[13] In 1604, another old Munster hand, the chief justice of the province, William Saxey, penned one of the only substantial reflections on a wide range of policy matters produced during these years. 'A Discovery of the Decayed State of the Kingdom of Ireland, and of Means to Repower the Same' began with a dramatic metaphor in which Saxey likened James's third kingdom to a house that was on fire or a ship that had sprung a leak, with the legist bringing word so that the situation might be redressed before the house or ship of Ireland burned to the ground or sank to the seabed. One of the most detailed discussions of religious, military, judicial and civil policies written in the mid-1600s followed. Yet James was curiously absent from Saxey's considerations. He addressed his treatise to Robert Cecil, then Viscount Cranbourne and soon to be earl of Salisbury.[14]

Saxey's paper was joined in 1604 by a lengthy treatise written by the respected Old English lawyer and official, Richard Hadsor.[15] But generally these are the exceptions that prove the rule. Lyon, Brouncker, Saxey and

Hadsor were joined by only a handful of other writers, notably the prominent jurist, John Davies, who became a prolific composer of policy papers on Ireland over the first decade of James's reign.[16] However, for the most part, there was a severe decline in the number of individuals offering counsel to the monarch from Ireland in the first years of James's reign, with some, most notably John Harington, a godson of Queen Elizabeth and a noted satirist at court, perhaps making pronouncements of dubious sincerity.[17] One writer, Captain John Dowdall, even felt it was appropriate to resubmit a policy paper he had written at the height of the Nine Years' War to James in 1604, despite the war being over and many of its proposals and deductions now being irrelevant.[18] It all points towards a surprising lack of interest in offering advice to the new monarch once he came south to London in 1603. There are only around two dozen such policy papers extant for the period between 1603 and the flight of the Ulster earls in the autumn of 1607, a somewhat inconsequential number when compared with the level of counsel Elizabeth received in the final decade of her reign.

The policies which James sanctioned in Ireland during these years, for he cannot be said to have played an overly interventionist role down to 1607, reflected this lack of counsel. An initial caretaker government for the absentee Mountjoy and then Chichester from 1605 onwards did not begin to do anything drastically different from what been underway in Ireland prior to the Nine Years' War. Realising that sweeping executions and land confiscations would not be practical at the end of the conflict, thousands of Irish swordsmen and their lords were pardoned by the king and things basically picked up where they had left off in 1593.[19] There was the semblance of activity. Many knighthoods were handed out, for instance, early in the reign, much as they were in England.[20] Government creep and intervention by regional administrators in Ulster, Connacht, Munster and the more wayward parts of Leinster continued, backed again by the rampant use of martial law commissions, though this time with very little chance of any resistance. The approach here was to continue treating Ireland as a security threat that could be cost-effectively contained through martial law and coercion.[21]

James seemed to have had little objection to this essentially Elizabethan approach. There were some alterations in other respects, ones which had the mark of a new reign. Between 1603 and 1607 a small cadre of Scotsmen, some of whom were close to James for many years, were promoted to positions of importance in Ireland. One was James Fullerton, an educator and intelligencer who had been involved in the foundation of Trinity College, Dublin in the early 1590s and who had subsequently become an agent of the Scottish crown in Ireland. He was promoted to senior government positions in the new reign and was also rewarded with lands and other perquisites.[22] In Antrim in the north-eastern corner of Ireland, James quickly acknowledged Sir Randall MacDonnell in possession of the large tracts of land which his ancestors had held there for centuries. Two further Scotsmen, Hugh Montgomery and James Hamilton, began to acquire large tracts of land throughout east Ulster from Irish landholders there whose economic fortunes had been devastated by the war.[23] Still, while the advancement of figures like Fullerton, Hamilton and Montgomery was clearly important, there was no grand project promoted by the new king in Ireland during the first years of his reign, despite the time being ripe to attempt one as the war came to an end in 1603. James did not even try to reshape the central administration in Dublin in any way or follow up on the investigations which had been underway into men like the archbishop of Dublin, Adam Loftus, or the future earl of Cork, Richard Boyle, both of whom were suspected in the 1590s of stealing vast sums of crown money. Post-1603 they were allowed to quietly settle back into Irish colonial society with wealth, the origins of which could not be easily explained.[24]

As we will see very shortly, from the autumn of 1607 onwards, developments in Ulster created a scenario in which James's interest was drawn to Ireland and for a period of seven or eight years between 1608 and the mid-1610s his gaze was considerably focused on a project there. But as animated as James would be by the Ulster Plantation, his Irish sight was often quite myopic. Many issues which might have warranted his attentions, and crown resources to deal with them, were simply ignored, not least the manner in which the south coast of Munster became a haven of international piracy during James's reign.[25] This was reflected in the fact that the number of treatises and policy papers being sent to England from Ireland remained limited on matters other than discussion of the Ulster Plantation and possible plantations to be initiated elsewhere in Ireland. We might also attribute the very fact that Arthur Chichester remained in office as viceroy of Ireland for over a decade from his appointment in 1605 until his eventual replacement by Oliver St John in 1616 to James's lack of intervention in Irish policy. This was an unusually long term for a viceroy to serve, one that was not matched by a governor in a single term in Ireland under Elizabeth.[26]

III The Royal View of Ireland

This lack of engagement with Ireland by James in his first years begs a question: just how much did he actually know about the country? The answer is quite a bit, at least by the standards of late medieval and early modern rulers of England. It is important to remember in assessing this that the north of Ireland, the province of Ulster, was closely connected geographically, politically and economically to the Outer Hebrides and south-western Scotland. As the ennoblement of Randall MacDonnell attests, that clan had longstanding connections to east Ulster and numerous other groups such as the MacLeods did as well.[27] Therefore, Scottish monarchs and lords like James were much more aware of the nuances of Ulster's politics than was, for instance, a monarch like Elizabeth I of the politics of Connacht, the western province of Ireland, when she came to the throne in 1558. Moreover, James had developed extensive diplomatic connections in Ireland during the Nine Years' War as he sought to remain abreast of developments in the country. Equally, agents such as Fullerton kept him informed of what was occurring on the ground in Dublin in the years prior to the succession.

In a sense James was more informed about Ireland when he first became king of the country in 1603 than was someone like Henry VIII, a monarch who was profoundly ignorant of Ireland even many years after he had become lord thereof.[28] For instance, when writing to Chichester in the summer of 1611 about his decision to send over the former wartime governor of Munster, Sir George Carew, as a commissioner to undertake a range of duties in Ireland, James was able to reflect on how Carew's commission paralleled that which had been granted to the Elizabethan vice-chamberlain and privy councillor, Sir Francis Knollys, when he was dispatched to Ireland by Elizabeth I in 1566. Included in Knollys's duties had been a mission to Ulster to observe affairs there amongst the Irish and the Scots and to report back to London thereon. Of course, James might well have simply been briefed on this by his ministers. Yet there is also the possibility that he was himself aware of the sojourn of Knollys in Ireland a half a century earlier, as the vice-chamberlain was a figure who had acted as guardian over his mother, Mary, Queen of Scots, in the north of England in the late 1560s, had maintained a correspondence with several figures in Scotland as James was growing up, and whose son, William, the king had created first Baron Knollys in 1603.[29] As explored further below, James also played an active role in establishing Carew's commission in 1611.[30]

Not all of James's views of Ireland and its people though were positive. It is a well-established fact that the king was deeply critical of Gaelic culture, so many elements of which were still found in parts of the Scottish Highlands and the Western Isles. He had made this clear in his *Basilikon Doron*, written in 1598–1599. Here James remarked that one of the great duties of any King of Scotland was to reform the 'alluterly barbares' Scots of the Highlands and Outer Hebrides by 'planting Colonies among them of answerable In-lands subjects, that within short time may reforme and civilize the best inclined among them; rooting out or transporting the barbarous and stubborne sort, and planting civilitie in their roomes'.[31]

These views had already found practical expression in Scottish policy. In October 1598 the Fife Adventurers, a consortium of twelve Scottish gentlemen, including the likes of Ludovic Stuart, second duke of Lennox; Patrick Leslie, a younger son of the earl of Rothes; Sir James Anstruther; and George and David Home, had set off from Leith and the ports of Fife with over 500 soldiers and additional retainers to take over the Isle of Lewis from the MacLeods, whose legal title thereto had been challenged by the crown the previous year. This was the first of three attempts between 1598 and 1609 by the Fife Adventurers to enforce the legal title James had given to them over the MacLeod lordship and in the process to reduce one of the unreformed groups of Scottish lords whose Gaelic cultural mores James so reviled.[32] Similarly, the Statutes of Iona, passed in 1609, sought to reform the Western Isles and root out the elements of Gaelic culture found there. Amongst other things, the Statutes required the lords of the Gaelic parts of the country to send their sons to Lowland Scotland to be educated there and effectively prohibited the retention of Gaelic bards by the Scottish lords in the Highlands and the Outer Hebrides, even though the presence of such Gaelic figures at the royal court in Scotland was not in itself unheard of during James's reign.[33] The Fife initiative broadly failed, but Ulster would soon offer a means for the king to achieve success against Gaelic culture elsewhere.[34] Indeed there was even some overlap in the personnel involved in both enterprises. In Ulster, James's goal, as iterated in a speech given before the Blessed Parliament in March 1610 just as the plans for the plantation were being finalised, was to cleanse the problems brought about by the barbarism of the Gaelic Irish and the backward religious landscape of the country.[35]

IV The Great British Project

James's approach towards Ireland might perhaps be described as distracted during the first years of his reign. He had greater issues which concerned him in England, most notably the establishment of peace with Spain and the creation of a new hybrid 'British' court presided over in London by a Scottish king and featuring many Scottish magnates and courtiers who had come south with the monarch. The fallouts from the Bye, Main and Gunpowder Plots also drained his attentions.[36] Like virtually all of the Tudor monarchs before him, what finally focused James's attentions on Ireland in a concerted way was an emergency. In September 1607 the earls of Tyrone and Tyrconnell, Hugh O'Neill and Rory O'Donnell, along with many other Ulster lords and landholders, left the north of Ireland without permission, bound for the Continent. They would eventually find their way to Rome, igniting fears along the way of a new war if they managed to acquire Papal or Spanish aid for their cause.[37] These latter concerns would ultimately not materialise into tangible problems, yet the sudden departure of the earls from the north of Ireland immediately opened up the question of what would be done with their vast estates in west Ulster. Collectively those who had taken flight from Ireland had controlled a vast proportion of the land from Lough Neagh and the River Bann westwards to the Atlantic Ocean on the west coast of what was then known as Tyrconnell, the modern-day county of Donegal.

Even before James would have received news of the flight of the earls in England, there were officials in Ireland putting pen to paper to propose a wide range of schema for how to dispense of the land. Nearly all agreed that a plantation of one kind or another should be undertaken. There were no dissenting voices suggesting that the king should instead find more biddable members of the O'Neills and O'Donnells to elevate as new earls that would take the place of the departed Tyrone and Tyrconnell. Oliver St John, a senior member of the Irish council and the master of the ordnance in Ireland, proposed that James should keep the lands in question in his own hands and rent out estates to the Irish of Ulster on punitively high rents.[38] Others such as the Old English legal official, Richard Hadsor, and the anglicised army captain, Francis Shane, echoed St John's proposals in asserting that this should be a mixed plantation, primarily consisting of English servitors and Irish tenants. Shane explicitly noted that the Irish should be provided with lands in return for the high rents which they would pay.[39] James Perrot suggested that towns, replete with military governors and garrisons, would be the best means to pacify Ulster in the aftermath of the flight.[40] A number of personal petitions for lands in west Ulster also began to emerge in 1608. For instance, in the early winter of 1608 the Staffordshire gentleman, Sir William Whorwood, petitioned for an estate of between 1,000 and 2,000 acres in Ulster.[41]

A striking element of this is that James was seemingly not directly involved in the petitions and proposals at all at this early date. All the policy proposals about the plantation and explorative requests for land were directed to Salisbury or in the exceptional case of Whorwood to Sir Julius Caesar, a senior Jacobean official with a particular interest in Irish policy. And yet there is the distinct sense that individuals knew that James needed to be appealed to even when not being petitioned directly. For instance, in November 1607, another senior government official, Edward Brabazon, had sent his own proposal concerning Ulster to Salisbury. Here he called for a division of the available lands, with the 'inland Scottish nation' settling the north of the province and English colonists taking the southern regions around Armagh, Cavan and Fermanagh. The use of the term 'inland Scottish' was significant. As we have seen, this was the exact phrase which James had used nearly a decade earlier in the *Basilikon Doron* when describing the need to civilise the Gaelic Scots of the Outer Hebrides. This term 'inland' Scots had been completely absent from the diction of English policy commentators in Ireland as recently as the 1590s. Clearly in introducing it now into their treatises and policy papers, even if they were addressed to Salisbury, individuals such as Brabazon were appealing to the monarchical prejudices of the king by couching their proposals in terms he favoured.[42]

This was also the case with the most important document received early on in the planning process for the Ulster Plantation, following the receipt of which we clearly begin to see James's active involvement in the whole affair. A 'Project for the Plantation of Tyrone' was composed in Ireland in December 1608, well over a year after the flight of the northern earls. The paper was drawn up by a number of very senior Irish officials, amongst whom the attorney general of Ireland, Sir John Davies, the chief justice of king's bench, Sir James Ley, and James's stalwart eyes and ears in Ireland for the last two decades, Sir James Fullerton, were prominent. Chichester's name was conspicuously absent.[43] Their proposal was for the lands of Tyrone, which at that time included both the large modern-day county of Tyrone and the barony of Loughinsholin, to be distributed amongst a mix of English and Scottish grantees, servitors who had provided years of service to the government in Ireland and prominent Irishmen in the region. Institutions such as the Church of Ireland were also to be provided for, and lands would be set aside for the development of corporate towns and a free-school. Throughout Davies, Ley and their allies appealed to James's sensibilities, repeatedly using the term 'inland' Scottish when describing the kind of men from the king's home country who they believed should receive lands in Ulster.[44]

As soon as the 'Project' was received in London the king suddenly became a more active participant in the planning process. Davies and Ley travelled over to court and presented the paper there during the Christmas season of 1608. When they did it met with unalloyed approval.[45] On 17 January 1609 the privy council wrote to Chichester noting that the king had lately attended two meetings of the council concerning the plantation and had so liked the proposal outlined in the 'Project' that it was resolved to apply the same scheme to all six of the escheated counties, not just Tyrone.[46] James's ministers proceeded quickly thereafter. By the end of January the 'Project' had been adapted into a book which was published in London as *A Collection of Such Orders and Conditions, as are to be Observed by the Undertakers, upon the Distribution and Plantation of the Escheated Lands in Ulster*. The finalised text was quickly circulating around the Stuart dominions.[47] A cursory comparison of the 'Project' and the *Orders and Conditions* reveals that the published document was based to a very great extent on the text Davies and Ley had brought over just weeks earlier. After more than a year of proposals and false starts, with these mostly being directed to Salisbury, once a scheme arrived before James that he liked, he not only sanctioned it but ordered his ministers to move quickly to implement it and to apply it beyond Tyrone to all of west Ulster.

As the planning process continued with relative speed through the rest of 1609 and 1610 James continued to play an active role in it. For instance, in the spring, summer and early autumn of 1609, responsibility for soliciting applications for estates in Scotland was devolved to the government in Edinburgh and dozens of individuals petitioned for them.[48] Then there was a sudden *volte-face*. We have markedly little documentation with which to gauge how it occurred, but at some stage in the autumn or early winter of 1609, James decided to largely divest the government in Edinburgh of its role in matters and, instead, he began approaching some of the senior-most

Scottish nobles to convince them to take up some of the largest estates in Ulster in the precincts or baronies earmarked for Scottish undertakers. These included the duke of Lennox, who as we have seen had already been involved in the expedition to Lewis back in 1598; his brother, Esmé, Lord d'Aubigny; Andrew Stewart, Lord Ochiltree; James Hamilton, earl of Abercorn; and Michael Balfour, Lord Burley.[49] Further down the social ladder there is clear evidence that James had personally intervened to ensure that several Cunninghams had acquired estates together in the precinct of Portlough in Donegal.[50] He also patronised Patrick Crawford's receipt of a proportion of lands in the servitors' precinct of Kilmacrenan and Doe in western Donegal.[51]

The same level of micro-managing of the selection of the English undertakers by the king is hard to identify. When it came to these, Chichester, who was unhappy with the overall plantation scheme, had to be pacified to some extent and several precincts that were set aside for Englishmen were actually given over to government servitors in Ireland, a group the viceroy was disappointed had not been given a greater share elsewhere in the plantation. Hence were the baronies of Omagh and Clogher in Tyrone and Lifford in Donegal largely bestowed on people who had either served in government positions in Dublin or in the army during the Nine Years' War.[52] However, when it came to some of the other baronies the king must have been influential. For instance, we find Thomas Cornwall, a gentleman of the privy chamber of James's son and heir at that time, Prince Henry, and subsequently a member of Prince Charles's household, receiving an estate in Lifford too. Numerous other individuals who received estates in the English precincts would seem to have done so based largely on court connections.[53] This tendency continued for years to come. As late as 1616, when the Worshipful Company of Clothworkers were actively appraising over half a dozen petitions by individuals who wanted to lease their estate in Londonderry from them, they were coerced into giving consideration to a late petition made by Alexander Stewart, perhaps the same individual who later became earl of Galloway. The company had been informed that the king favoured Stewart's application. Ultimately he did not end up taking their lands, but just weeks later the company leased the estate to Sir Robert McClelland, another Scot with connections to the king who had emerged as a surprise late candidate to acquire the tenancy without going through the same formal process that other applications had.[54] Clearly, when it came to the selection of those who would receive estates in Ulster in 1609 and 1610 and for many years thereafter, James was showing a degree of interest in Irish affairs that had not been there in the first half a decade of his rule from London.

The same level of interest was visible with the Londonderry Plantation. In the late spring of 1609, not long after the *Orders and Conditions* had been published in London and Edinburgh, Sir Thomas Phillips, a longstanding English servitor in Ulster who had acquired his own landed interest around

Coleraine, appeared in London with proposals for the economic and logistical might of the City of London to become involved in the Ulster enterprise. Before long, plans were in the firmament for the corporation and the capital's fifty-five livery companies to be co-opted into colonising the county of Coleraine and the barony of Loughinsholin. Whether James was directly responsible for much of the scheme or not remains open to debate. Nearly twenty years later Phillips would claim that the king broadly devised it, but Phillips's motives in making this assertion at that time were certainly open to scrutiny.[55] In Coleraine and Loughinsholin the City and companies would be charged with developing the towns of Derry and Coleraine as major trading centres in the north of Ireland replete with hundreds of houses, along with the fisheries of the River Bann and Lough Foyle. The lands granted to them would be formed into the new entity of the county of Londonderry. By January 1610 'Articles of Agreement' were in place and the City's mercantile community were being taxed with an initial subsidy of £20,000 to finance the Londonderry Plantation, a sum which would more than triple in the years ahead.[56]

Throughout the negotiations in 1609, the heavy taxing of the City's merchants and tradesmen through 1610, 1611 and 1612, and then the intermittent levying of subsidies for years thereafter, it was clear that James was eager to promote the Londonderry Plantation. A perusal of the voluminous court-minutes extant for many of the most prominent livery companies involved, such as the Goldsmiths, Clothworkers, Vintners and Skinners, reveals that successive lord mayors of London and other civic officials were constantly being bidden by the king to promote the scheme and to further it as quickly as possible once it was entered into in January 1610. James's enthusiasm and pressure was needed. These same court-minutes reveal dozens of merchants and tradesmen across the City who were bitterly opposed to being forced to become involved in 'the Irish business'. Many ended up being sent to the debtors' prisons, the Wood Street Compter and the Poultry Compter, for periods until they agreed to pay over the few shillings or pounds that had been levied on them.[57] It is doubtful that this level of pressure could have been applied on the Londoners to become involved had the king not been so personally invested in the project.

Once the plantation was actually in progress and letters patent were issued to dozens of grantees or their agents in Ireland in the summer and autumn of 1610, James was an enthusiastic overseer of his great British project. There is a level of engagement with it from London that was not discernible in the king on any other Irish issue up to that time. Thus, in mid-April 1611 he was intervening on behalf of some of the Scottish undertakers in the county of Fermanagh for them to be favoured in the disputes that had arisen with the Irish across the six counties as a result of the plantation being based on deficient surveys.[58] Just over a week later he wrote to Chichester with an extensive memorandum on religious reforms that were to be enacted throughout the plantation lands in response to a report he had received from the bishop of Raphoe, Andrew Knox, whose diocese covered much of Donegal.[59] Further correspondence with the viceroy, on the provision of pensions to Irishmen who were disillusioned with their land grants and on measures to be taken to garrison government forts in west Ulster, followed in May.[60] In June, James was overseeing the dispatch of George Carew to Ireland on his commission, which included a remit to visit Ulster and report on the progress of the plantation a year after its inception.[61]

And so it went on. In late July, James wrote to Chichester out of concern at reports he had received that the Scottish undertakers were being hindered in their efforts in Donegal by a servitor, Paul Gore, and the MacSweeneys who formed several of the most prominent Irish septs in the county.[62] In the spring of 1612, we see a period in which the king was writing to Chichester on an almost weekly basis regarding various elements of the plantation, while these letters also attest to his meeting with petitioners at court on the same issues or additional correspondence with other individuals in Ireland.[63] The pattern is clear. James was enthused by the Ulster project and was committing time to it. This was evident too in the regular surveys into the plantation and its progress which he ordered and which we have already heard of. These were commissioned in 1611, 1613, 1614, 1616, 1618 and 1622, with the City of London also undertaking its own surveys of Londonderry in 1613 and 1616 under pressure from the king.[64] An additional muster of Ulster's military capacities was also carried out by George Alleyne in 1618 in conjunction with a more conventional survey of the plantation's progress by Nicholas Pynnar.[65]

This could not last forever, especially so given the manner in which the plantation project failed to live up to the expectations James had of it. Ambitious targets had been set whereby each undertaker was to build a castle or manor house surrounded by a bawn or defensive wall within three years. Nucleated settlements that would grow into villages and then towns were to develop around these, and the Irish were to be removed from the estates of the undertakers within three years and replaced with British settlers from England, Scotland or Wales. This proved impractical almost everywhere. The men who were granted estates in west Ulster, some owing to the personal interventions of the king, often did not have either the necessary wealth to realise these lofty objectives or else were uninterested and had accepted their estates simply with a view to acquiring them and then selling them on for a quick profit. Within a year Chichester was writing to London seeking for the rules of plantation to be altered; the Irish needed to be kept on the estates of the English and Scottish undertakers for longer in order to provide labour and the building deadlines needed to be extended to at least four years. Extra allowances were duly made. Nevertheless, the revised deadlines were also missed, and by the late 1610s, there were discussions about altering the rules of plantation to allow the English and Scottish undertakers to retain Irish tenants on one-quarter of their lands. None of this was aided by the fact that the land surveys carried out in 1608, 1609 and 1610 were wholly deficient and had drastically underestimated the amount of land involved, leading to estates as large as 10,000 or so acres being incorrectly adjudged to be 1,500 acres and the like.[66]

As all of this occurred, James grew more resentful of how the plantation was being overseen. Then his attention waned. We have seen at the outset that he wrote angrily to Chichester in the spring of 1615 about the findings of Bodley's survey the previous year.[67] There is a similar level of creeping disillusionment in other royal correspondence concerning Ulster in the mid-1610s. Then the extant correspondence from James to officials in Ireland on the Ulster Plantation simply drops off. Between the summer of 1616 and early 1620, James's correspondence with Chichester's successor in the vice-regal office, Oliver St John, was very minimal. When there was a renewed burst of royal correspondence on the Ulster enterprise in 1620, much of it was concerned with the military preparation of the province in light of the changed international situation following the outbreak of the Thirty Years' War in central Europe.[68] Elsewhere we find a brief half-hearted letter from James to St John on 7 June 1620 in which he ordered the viceroy to put the articles of plantation into effect, almost as though he had suddenly remembered after a long *lacuna* that they had not been implemented.[69] It was not that the plantation had failed. In the long run it transformed the demography and society of Ulster in ways which still resonate profoundly four centuries later. However, it had not been implemented in anything near the manner which was envisaged back in the halcyon planning days of 1609 and 1610 when James had so enthusiastically pursued it.

The king was also culpable himself in all of this. For example, in the mid-1610s he was writing favourably to the administration in Dublin concerning a virtual fiefdom that the family of George Tuchet, Lord Audley, had received of the entire precinct of Omagh in Tyrone back in 1610. By then, though, it should have been apparent to all at court, based on the very surveys that James had commissioned, that Audley and his extended family members had been very negligent in their efforts in Omagh. They had built a number of fine castles here, yet on the matter of peopling the proportions with British tenants and removing the Irish, they had done absolutely nothing.[70] Still, far from chastising Audley, James ordered Chichester to ensure that he was given more land again by treating him favourably in the matter of land conceal-ments in Ulster.[71] Questions arise here about how early modern governments and monarchs were informed, or in this case misinformed, about distant parts of their realms, but there is no doubt that James was acting against his own designs for Ulster when he favoured petitioners like Audley. This is just one distinct example of how the monarch's ambitions for his great Ulster project ran aground as the 1610s went on, not just based on the overly ambitious nature of the enterprise, but also on how he intervened himself on many occasions to act against the scheme.

V Buckingham, Middlesex and Ireland

That James's interest in and engagement with the Ulster Plantation declined from 1616 onwards was owing to several interrelated developments. First, Chichester's long spell as Irish viceroy came to an end at this time and the extensive correspondence which James had engaged in with him was not replicated with his successors, St John, and Henry Cary, first Viscount Falkland.[72] Secondly, St John was a client of George Villiers, James's famous favourite who was soon to be elevated to become the duke of Buckingham.[73] The year 1616 thus represents the point at which the Villiers takeover of Irish officialdom began. As Victor Treadwell explored so comprehensively in his immense study of *Buckingham and Ireland*, the duke and his followers managed to acquire control over nearly every element of Irish policy and government.[74] As he did so, James's own management of Irish affairs declined. Everything from the filling of senior offices in Dublin to the management of the customs system and the rewarding of provincial officials was increasingly controlled by the Villiers affinity. Where James played a major role was in sanctioning the dramatic escalation in the sale of honours and noble titles in Ireland in the late 1610s and into the 1620s.[75] It was a policy of expediency based on the manner in which the king had brought the crown's wider finances across the three kingdoms into a problematic state through low taxation, profligate spending at court and the rewarding of favourites and officials, all overshadowed by the inflation crisis which governments across Europe were universally facing at the time.[76]

This diminished interest of the king in Ireland and Irish affairs from 1616 onwards is again paralleled by a decline in the number of policy papers being produced in Ireland. There was a marked decline in those that were being produced in the second half of the 1610s after the flush of policy papers that appeared from late 1607 onwards attendant on the plantation in Ulster. Those that were sent to England from 1616 through to 1620 generally concerned proposals regarding a number of smaller plantations which were now being undertaken in regions such as Wexford, Longford, Leitrim and other parts of the Irish midlands that had not previously experienced state-organised plantation under the Tudors.[77] A notable feature of these latter enterprises was the manner in which they were overseen by Buckingham's clients in Ireland such as the Parsons brothers, William and Lawrence.[78] There is nothing approaching the same level of engagement by the king with the planning and implementation of these initiatives as there had been for Ulster between 1608 and 1615.

While the period between 1616 and the early 1620s was unquestionably a fallow one in terms of James's interest in Irish affairs, there is also absolutely no denying that the latter part of the reign witnessed an attempted overhaul of the Irish establishment that spoke of a royal concern for the kingdom that had hitherto only been elicited by the Ulster Plantation. In 1622 the widest-ranging Commission for Irish Affairs yet seen in early modern Ireland was commenced. In all twenty-one commissioners, being a mix of officials, legists and MPs from England and numerous key administrators and government servants in Ireland, ones who crucially were considered to be somewhat politically neutral, were appointed to investigate a truly broad spectrum of policy matters in Ireland.[79] Assessment of everything from the finances of the government there and the state of the Protestant Church of Ireland to the progress of the plantations that had been established going all the way back to the mid-Tudor period were included in the remit of the commission. The political context was clear. Lionel Cranfield, just then ennobled as the earl of Middlesex, had managed to acquire a position of considerable influence over the government in England, not owing to his relationship with the king, but purely on the basis that he might be able to remedy the crown finances which seemed to have soured so badly since Buckingham's ascendancy had commenced.[80] It would lead to the production of an enormous series of reports on a huge range of matters in Ireland.[81]

Here is not the place to chart how the commission functioned or what its voluminous findings were. It is relevant only to highlight that James's dedication to it was half-hearted. He sanctioned it in the political chaos that ensued from investigations into corruption and financial malfeasance by the English Parliament in 1621. When it unearthed many, many issues in almost every sphere of official life and government policy in Ireland, the king could not but sanction it to continue its work and draw up extensive plans for the reform of the country. But then when political shifts in England led to the impeachment of Middlesex and the scuppering of his reform agenda, the findings of the 1622 commission were shelved in 1624 and Buckingham's ascendancy over Irish policy was assured for another four years. The most surprising thing about James's approach to the 1622 commission was that he did so little with so much information.[82]

VI Conclusion

Much else might be said of James's approach towards Ireland. There were developments in the kingdom during his reign that would have major implications for Ireland for decades to come. One such was the Irish Parliament of 1613 to 1615, the first sitting of which included an infamous dispute over the rival candidacies of Sir John Davies and Sir John Everard for the speakership.[83] In so comprehensively alienating the Old English community from the government in its actions in 1613 and the years that followed, the crown ensured that when a new revolt broke out in Ireland in 1641, it, unlike the Nine Years' War a half a century earlier, would be strongly supported by the Old English.[84] The reign also set the tone for that of King Charles I in Ireland. The sale of honours and noble titles continued apace following James's death in 1625; Buckingham and his affinity exercised great control over Ireland until his assassination in 1628; the Protestantisation of the country was pursued in the same often lack-lustre manner; and there was no change of viceroy or general direction as a result of the turnover of monarch.[85] While we must be wary of generalisations, a certain level of inconsistency in the formulation of Irish policy continued for several years into the next reign. James had failed to create a more coherent or consistent approach to policy formation in the country.

In a speech which he made before the court of Star Chamber in the summer of 1616, James reflected on the nature of kingship. 'A king', he stated 'hath two offices', first 'to direct things to be done' and then 'to take an accompt how they are fulfilled; for what is it the better for me to direct as an angel, if I take not accompt of your doings'.[86] He was surely correct in this, but did he actually put this precept of his own into practice when it came to Ireland? It would appear not, or at best that he did so selectively and in a sporadic man-ner. No early modern monarch could ignore a dominion like Ireland, yet at the same time there were periods in which James's government was simply func-tional, not energetic or innovative. Then there are questions about who was doing the directing at times. Salisbury exerted exceptional control over the governance of Ireland during the first decade of the reign. Chichester was an extremely powerful viceroy. Finally, an unwieldy amount of influence over Irish affairs was exerted by Buckingham from the late 1610s onwards. Perhaps all of this was reflected in the decision by so few officials and interested parties in Ireland to write to James offering policy ideas for the country. Beyond pro-posals for plantation there was a marked decline in the number of treatises being produced on early Stuart Ireland from those that had done so in Elizabethan times. Instead, a sort of *laissez-faire* approach to Ireland prevailed during James's reign. Only in the instance of the Ulster Plantation was the king hugely animated. And that too had its limitations. As the king's disappoint-ment with it grew in the 1610s, his focus wandered from it. In short, James's reign saw the policy inconsistencies of the Elizabethan era continued.

Notes

1 The best general introduction to the Ulster Plantation remains P. S. Robinson, *The Plantation of Ulster: British Settlement in an Irish Landscape, 1600–1670* (Belfast, 1984). On its place within British colonial activity in early modern Ireland, see N. Canny, *Making Ireland British, 1580–1650* (Oxford, 2001).

2 W. P. Pakenham-Walsh, 'Captain Sir Josias Bodley: Director-General of Fortifications in Ireland, 1612–1617', *The Royal Engineers Journal* 8 (1908), pp. 253–64.

3 The king to Chichester, 25 March 1615, Bodleian Library, Oxford, Carte MS 30, nos 64–5, calendared in *CSPI, 1615–1625*, no. 49, pp. 25–6.

4 A. Stewart, *The Cradle King: A Life of James VI and I* (2003); P. Croft, *King James* (Basingstoke, 2003); R. Lockyer, *James VI and I* (Harlow, 1998); J. Wormald, 'James VI and I: Two Kings or One?', *History* 67 (1983), pp. 187–209.

5 On the background of these surveys, see the introduction to D. Heffernan (ed.), 'Three Surveys of the Londonderry Plantation, 1613–16', *Analecta Hibernica* 50 (2019), pp. 1–61.

6 There is a growing body of literature on this. For a good introduction, see D. Edwards, 'The Escalation of Violence in Sixteenth-Century Ireland', in D. Edwards, P. Lenihan and C. Tait (eds), *Age of Atrocity: Violence and Political Conflict in Early Modern Ireland* (Dublin, 2007), pp. 34–78.

7 C. Lennon, *Sixteenth-Century Ireland: The Incomplete Conquest* (Dublin, 1994).

8 J. O'Neill, *The Nine Years War, 1593–1603: Tyrone, Mountjoy and the Military Revolution* (Dublin, 2016) is now the definitive study of the war. On the political background and causes of it, see H. Morgan, *Tyrone's Rebellion: The Outbreak of the Nine Years War in Tudor Ireland* (Suffolk, 1993).

9 M. MacCarthy-Morrogh, *The Munster Plantation: English Migration to Southern Ireland, 1583–1641* (Oxford, 1986).

10 N. Canny, *The Elizabethan Conquest of Ireland: A Pattern Established, 1565–76* (Hassocks, 1976); C. Brady, *The Chief Governors: The Rise and Fall of Reform Government in Tudor Ireland, 1536–1588* (Cambridge, 1994); D. Heffernan, *Debating Tudor Policy in Sixteenth-Century Ireland: 'Reform' Treatises and Political Discourse* (Manchester, 2018).

11 D. Heffernan, 'Debating Irish Policy at the Court of Elizabeth I, *c.* 1558–1580', in D. Edwards and B. Kane (eds), *Ireland and the Renaissance Court: Political Culture from the Cúirteanna to Whitehall, 1450–1640* (Manchester, 2024), pp. 105–22.

12 D. Heffernan, 'Political Discourse and the Nine Years' War in Late Elizabethan Ireland, *c.* 1593–1603', *Historical Research* 94 (2021), pp. 282–302.

13 Lyon to Chichester, March 1607, TNA, SP 63/221/35(a) (*CSPI, 1606–1608*, no. 179, pp. 131–3); Henry Brouncker, 'Concerning Reformation of Religion in Ireland', 1606, TNA, SP 63/219/102(a) (*CSPI, 1603–1606*, no. 834, pp. 543–5). On the Protestant Reformation in Ireland during this era, see A. Ford, *The Protestant Reformation in Ireland, 1590–1641* (Dublin, 1997).

14 William Saxey, 'A Discovery of the Decayed State of the Kingdom of Ireland, and of Means to Repower the Same', *c.* December 1604, TNA, SP 63/216/59 (*CSPI, 1603–1606*, no. 397, pp. 217–28).

15 J. McLaughlin (ed.), 'Select Documents XLVII: Richard Hadsor's 'Discourse' on the Irish State, 1604', *Irish Historical Studies* 30 (1997), pp. 337–53.

16 Davies's papers are numerous. See a sample of published ones in H. Morley (ed.), *Ireland under Elizabeth and James I* (1890).

17 John Harington, 'A Short View of Ireland Written in *Anno* 1605', *Anecdota Bodleiana* 1 (Oxford, 1879).

18 D. Heffernan, 'John Dowdall's "The Natures and Dispositions of the Irish Nation" (1599), Royal Ms. 18 A LVI', *Electronic British Library Journal* (forthcoming, 2025).

19 J. McCavitt, *The Flight of the Earls* (Dublin, 2002).

20 W. A. Shaw, *The Knights of England: Volume 2* (1906), *passim.*

21 D. Edwards, 'Legacy of Defeat: The Reduction of Gaelic Ireland after Kinsale', in H. Morgan (ed.), *The Battle of Kinsale* (Wicklow, 2004); *idem*, 'The Plight of the Earls: Tyrone and Tyrconnell's "Grievances" and Crown Coercion in Ulster,

1603–7', in M.-A. Lyons and T. O'Connor (eds), *The Ulster Earls and Baroque Europe* (Dublin, 2010), pp. 53–76.

22 D. Edwards, 'Securing the Jacobean Succession: The Secret Career of James Fullerton of Trinity College, Dublin', in S. Duffy (ed.), *The World of the Galloglass: Kings, Warlords and Warriors in Ireland and Scotland, 1200–1600* (Dublin, 2007).

23 M. Perceval-Maxwell, *The Scottish Migration to Ulster in the Reign of James I* (1973), ch. 2.

24 T. O. Ranger, 'Richard Boyle and the Making of an Irish Fortune, 1588–1614', *Irish Historical Studies* 10 (1957), pp. 257–97.

25 C. Kelliher, *The Alliance of Pirates: Ireland and Atlantic Piracy in the Seventeenth Century* (Cork, 2020).

26 Both Sir Henry Sidney (1566–71, 1575–8) and Sir William Fitzwilliam (1571–5, 1588–94) served for nearly as long as Chichester did as Irish viceroy, but their periods in office were not contiguous.

27 See, for instance, C. Brady, 'East Ulster, the MacDonalds and the Provincial Strategies of Hugh O'Neill, Earl of Tyrone, 1585–1603', in W. P. Kelly and J. R. Young (eds), *Scotland and the Ulster Plantation* (Dublin, 2009), pp. 41–61.

28 C. Maginn and S. Ellis, *The Tudor Discovery of Ireland* (Dublin, 2015).

29 The king to Chichester, 24 June 1611, Philadelphia Papers, vol. 1, p. 479 (*CSPI, 1611–1614*, no. 152, pp. 73–4); *ODNB, sub* Knollys, Sir Francis (article by W. T. MacCaffrey).

30 See below, pp. 211–12.

31 C. H. McIlwain (ed.), *The Political Works of James I* (Boston, 1918), p. 22. On James's attitude towards his Irish and peripheral Scottish subjects, see M. Lee, *Great Britain's Solomon: James VI and I in his Three Kingdoms* (Chicago, 1990), pp. 196–232.

32 A. MacCoinnich, *Plantation and Civility in the North Atlantic World: The Case of the Northern Hebrides, 1570–1639* (Leiden, 2015), pp. 91–175.

33 A. Cathcart, 'The Statutes of Iona: The Archipelagic Context', *Journal of British Studies* 49 (2010), pp. 4–27; A. Courtney, *James VI, Britannic Prince: King of Scots and Elizabeth's Heir, 1566–1603* (Abingdon, 2024), p. 49.

34 J. Wormald, 'The British Crown, the Earls and the Plantation of Ulster', in É. Ó Ciardha and M. Ó Siochrú (eds), *The Plantation of Ulster: Ideology and Practice* (Manchester, 2012), pp. 18–32, esp. p. 22 contrasts the Scottish initiatives with the Ulster one.

35 McIlwain, *Political Works*, pp. 319–20.

36 M. Questier, *Dynastic Politics and the British Reformations, 1558–1630* (Oxford, 2019), ch. 5.

37 McCavitt, *Flight of the Earls*.

38 St John to Salisbury, 9 Oct. 1607, TNA, SP 63/222/155 (*CSPI, 1606–1608*, no. 402, pp. 303–4); J. Barry, 'St John, Oliver', in J. McGuire and J. Quinn (eds), *Dictionary of Irish Biography* (9 vols, Cambridge, 2009) (*DIB* hereafter).

39 Hadsor to Salisbury, 23 Sept. 1607, TNA, SP 63/222/141 (*CSPI, 1606–1608*, no. 267, p. 281); Shane to Salisbury, 30 Nov. 1607, TNA, SP 63/222/181 (*CSPI, 1606–1608*, no. 470, pp. 339–43).

40 Perrot to Salisbury, *c.* Oct. 1607, in R. A. Roberts, M. S. Giuseppi, G. Dyfnallt Owen, et al. (eds), *Calendar of the Manuscripts of the most Honourable the Marquess of Salisbury …* (24 vols, 1883–1976), XIX, p. 451.

41 Whorwood to Caesar, 27 Nov. 1608, BL, Lansdowne MS 159, fo. 149^r.

42 Brabazon to Salisbury, *c.* Nov. 1607, TNA, SP 63/222/204(a) (*CSPI, 1606–1608*, no. 506, p. 384); R. Armstrong, 'Brabazon, Edward', in *DIB*.

43 On Davies and Ley, see H. S. Pawlisch, *Sir John Davies and the Conquest of Ireland: A Study in Legal Imperialism* (Cambridge, 1985); *ODNB*, *sub* Ley, James, first earl of Marlborough (article by W. Prest).

44 Davies, et al., 'Project for the Plantation of Tyrone', 20 Dec. 1608, TNA, SP 63/225/280, fos 256ʳ–60ʳ.

45 The Venetian ambassador wrote to the doge and senate on 2 January 1609 to report that the king had resolved on a new plantation for Ireland. This was almost certainly in response to the 'Project': see Marc Antonio Correr, Venetian ambassador in England, to the doge and senate, 2 Jan. 1609, in *CSPV, 1607–1610*, no. 400, pp. 209–10.

46 Privy council to Chichester, 17 Jan. 1609, Philadelphia Papers, vol. 3, p. 365 (*CSPI, 1608–1610*, no. 230, p. 129). Chichester also attested to the influence of the 'Project' in the shaping of the *Orders and Conditions* when he received his own copy of the printed book in early March. See Chichester to the privy council, 10 March 1609, TNA, SP 63/226/44 (*CSPI, 1608–1610*, no. 292, pp. 157–61).

47 *A Collection of Such Orders and Conditions, as are to be observed by the Undertakers, upon the distribution and Plantation of the Escheated Lands in Ulster* (1609); Correr to the doge and senate, 20 Feb. 1609, in *CSPV, 1607–1610*, no. 444, pp. 234–5; Correr to the doge and senate, 27 Feb. 1609, in the same volume, no. 449, pp. 237–8.

48 D. Masson (ed.), *The Register of the Privy Council of Scotland* (14 vols, Edinburgh, 1877–98), VIII, pp. 792–4.

49 For brief biographies specifically relating to the roles of these lords in the Ulster Plantation, see Perceval-Maxwell, *Scottish Migration*, Appendix B.

50 The king to Chichester, 20 April 1612, Philadelphia Papers, vol. 2, p. 13 (*CSPI, 1611–1614*, no. 465, pp. 262–3).

51 The king to Chichester, 8 May 1610, Philadelphia Papers, vol. 1, p. 399 (*CSPI, 1608–1610*, no. 749, p. 444); G. Hill, *An Historical Account of the Plantation in Ulster at the Commencement of the Seventeenth Century, 1608–1610* (Belfast, 1877), p. 323. On the fortunes of these figures in Donegal, see R. J. Hunter, 'Plantation in Donegal', in W. Nolan, L. Ronayne and M. Dunlevy (eds), *Donegal: History and Society* (Dublin, 1995), pp. 283–324.

52 D. Heffernan, 'The Selection of the English Undertakers in the Ulster Plantation, 1609–10', *Irish Historical Studies* 48 (2024), pp. 1–24.

53 C. G. Foljambe, *The House of Cornewall* (Hereford, 1908), pp. 217–18; Robert Hunter's notes on the Ulster Plantation grantees, The Public Records Office of Northern Ireland, D 4446|A|1|112.

54 Volume of extracts of the Clothworkers Company court-minutes containing the records relating to the company's Londonderry estate, *c.* 1609–76, Clothworkers Hall, CL/G/Irish/B/2/9, pp. 59–61.

55 T. W. Moody, *The Londonderry Plantation, 1609–41: The City of London and the Plantation in Ulster* (Belfast, 1939), pp. 62–7.

56 Moody, *Londonderry Plantation*, pp. 62–98.

57 See, for example, Skinners Company Court Minutes, 1551–1617, Guildhall Library MS 30,708/1, fo. 127ʳ; Clothworkers Hall, CL/G/Irish/B/2/9, pp. 8–9.

58 The king to Chichester, 17 April 1611, Philadelphia Papers, vol. 1, p. 461 (*CSPI, 1611–1614*, no. 65, p. 30).

59 The king to Chichester, 26 April 1611, Philadelphia Papers, vol. 1, p. 462(a) (*CSPI, 1611–1614*, no. 68, pp. 31–2).

60 The king to Chichester, 3 May 1611, Philadelphia Papers, vol. 1, p. 465 (*CSPI, 1611–1614*, no. 80, p. 44); the king to Chichester, 7 May 1611, *CSPI, 1611–1614*, no. 90, p. 48.

61 The king's instructions to Carew, 24 June 1611, Philadelphia Papers, vol. 1, p. 482 (*CSPI, 1611–1614*, no. 150, p. 73); V. L. Rutledge, 'The Commission of Sir George Carew in 1611: A Review of the Exchequer and the Judiciary in Ireland' (PhD, McGill University, 1986).

62 The king to Chichester, 27 July 1611, Philadelphia Papers, vol. 1, p. 490 (*CSPI, 1611–1614*, no. 200, p. 87).

63 See letters dated 1, 11 and 19 March and 20, 21 and 29 April 1612, all from the king to Chichester, Philadelphia Papers, vol. 1, pp. 539, 547, 551; vol. 2, pp. 13, 15, 17 (*CSPI, 1611–1614*, nos. 443, 450, 452, 465, 467, 469, pp. 251–2, 254–8, 262–5).

64 Heffernan, 'Three Surveys'; the king to the archbishop of Dublin and Sir John Denham, Lords Justices, 28 May 1616, *CSPI, 1615–1625*, no. 238, pp. 120–1 on James's role in the Londoners' survey of 1616.

65 R. J. Hunter, *The Ulster Plantation in the Counties of Armagh and Cavan, 1608–41* (Belfast, 2012), pp. 117–19.

66 For an interesting overview of the successes and failures of the plantation in light of these rules of plantation, see R. Gillespie, 'Success and Failure in the Ulster Plantation', in Ó Ciardha and Ó Siochrú (eds), *The Plantation of Ulster*, pp. 98–118.

67 See above, pp. 200–1.

68 The king to the lord deputy and chancellor of Ireland, 29 Oct. 1620, TNA, SP 63/235/32 (*CSPI, 1615–1625*, no. 702, p. 300).

69 The king to St John, 7 June 1620, *CSPI, 1615–1625*, no. 640, p. 287.

70 The king to the lord deputy, 17 Oct. 1615, Bodleian Library, Carte MS 30, nos 67–8 (*CSPI, 1615–1625*, no. 173, p. 92); R. Loeber and T. Reeves-Smyth, 'Lord Audley's Grandiose Building Schemes in the Ulster Plantation', in B. MacCuarta (ed.), *Reshaping Ireland, 1550–1700: Colonization and its Consequences: Essays Presented to Nicholas Canny* (Dublin, 2011), pp. 82–100. For a damning account of the failures in Omagh nearly a decade after the inception of the plantation, see the relevant sections from Pynnar's survey, 1618–19 in Hill, *Historical Account*, pp. 535–8.

71 The king to Chichester, 17 Oct. 1615, Philadelphia Papers, vol. 2, p. 346 (*CSPI, 1615–1625*, no. 174, pp. 92–3).

72 S. Kelsey, 'Cary, Henry, first Viscount Falkland', in *DIB*.

73 V. L. Rutledge, 'Court-Castle Faction and the Irish Viceroyalty: The Appointment of Oliver St John as Lord Deputy of Ireland in 1616', *Irish Historical Studies* 26 (1989), pp. 233–49.

74 V. Treadwell, *Buckingham and Ireland, 1616–1628: A Study in Anglo-Irish Politics* (Dublin, 1998), esp. pp. 47–70.

75 C. R. Mayes, 'The Early Stuarts and the Irish Peerage', *English Historical Review* 73 (1958), pp. 227–51; J. Ohlmeyer, *Making Ireland English: The Irish Aristocracy in the Seventeenth Century* (Yale, 2012), pp. 27–50.

76 See chapter nine on 'James and the Problem of Money' in C. Russell, ed. R. Cust and A. Thrush, *King James VI/I and his English Parliaments* (Oxford, 2011), pp. 154–76.

77 See, e.g., George Calvert, 'A Project for the Division and Plantation of the Several Small Territories in the County of Wexford', 1616; Oliver St John, 'A Project sent by Oliver St John, kt., Deputy of Ireland, concerning the Plantation of the County of Longford to the Lords of the Council in England', 1618; Oliver St John, 'The Lord Deputy's Second Advice concerning the Plantation of Longford and O'Carroll Country', 1618, all calendared extensively in J. S. Brewer et al. (eds), *Calendar of the Carew Manuscripts preserved at Lambeth Palace, 1515–1624* (6 vols, 1867–73), V, nos 164, 198, 205.

78 B. MacCuarta, 'The Plantation of Leitrim, 1620–41', *Irish Historical Studies* 32 (2001), pp. 297–320.

79 V. Treadwell (ed.), *The Irish Commission of 1622: An Investigation of the Irish Administration, 1615–22, and its Consequences, 1623–24* (Dublin, 2006), pp. xxvii–lii.

80 M. Prestwich, *Cranfield: Politics and Profits under the Early Stuarts* (Oxford, 1966); R. H. Tawney, *Business and Politics under James I: Lionel Cranfield as Merchant and Minister* (Cambridge, 1958).

81 Treadwell, *Irish Commission of 1622, passim.*

82 Treadwell, *Buckingham and Ireland*, pp. 148–248.

83 Two excellent studies of the Stuart Irish parliaments, including the 1613–15 sitting, have recently appeared: C. A. Dennehy, *The Irish Parliament, 1613–89: The Evolution of a Colonial Institution* (Manchester, 2019); B. McGrath, *The Operations of the Irish House of Commons, 1613–48* (Dublin, 2023).

84 A. Clarke, *The Old English in Ireland, 1625–41* (1966). On the 1641 rebellion, see Canny, *Making Ireland British*, ch. 8.

85 Treadwell, *Buckingham and Ireland*, pp. 249–309.

86 McIlwain, *Political Works*, p. 338.

9

PLAY IT AGAIN, SOLOMON

The Burning of Edward Elton's Books and the Religious Policy of James I at the End of His Reign

Peter Lake

In February 1625 Richard Montague wrote to John Cosin. Amongst a plethora of other news and hectic preparations for the publication of his *Appello Caesarem* Montague remarked that 'by the next return I shall hear by you what a goodly fire our sabbatarian heretics made at the cross'. Montague was referring to the burning, at Paul's Cross on 13 February 1625, of two volumes – one, *God's Holy Mind*, a catechetically organised exposition of the Ten Commandments (and a pendant *Plain and easy exposition of the Lord's Prayer)*[1] by Edward Elton, the recently deceased minister of Bermondsey in Southwark, and the other 'a little book of Mr Denison's'.[2] In all some 800 copies were burnt in what Daniel Featley called 'the greatest holocaust that hath been offered in this kind in our memory'.[3] According to a newsletter to Joseph Mede of 18 February, both volumes had been burned 'for containing schismatical doctrine of the Lord's day and administration of the sacrament'. The whole affair must have made quite a spectacle.

Daniel Featley recalled that 'the wits of the city' devised a 'conceited pageant', complete with 'an emblem and motto'. This consisted of an image of St Paul's Cross with 'a number of men, partly running away, that they might not see such a spectacle, partly weeping and wiping their eyes to see a book so full (as they conceived) of heavenly zeal and holy fire sacrificed in earthly and unhallowed flames'. To one side stood the author throwing his books on the fire and on the other stood a 'popish shaveling' looking on in triumph. All of which made it clear just what Featley thought had been at stake, without him actually having to say so.[4]

According to another newsletter to Mede (written at the end of January), Thomas Gataker, a leading London preacher, had been consigned 'to the Fleet' for writing a letter of approbation printed at the front of Elton's tome.[5]

DOI: 10.4324/9781003319764-10

Gataker himself confirmed this in memoirs of 1654, where he reminisced that, having been imprisoned in the Fleet, he had been freed through the good offices of that godly courtier the earl of Manchester and his brother Sir Charles Montague, only to be placed under house arrest again and further suspended from his ministry 'by his majesty's special command'.[6] Stephen Denison, the author of the little treatise burnt with Elton's book at the Cross, was also suspended from his lectureship at St Katherine Cree for 'maintaining that [which was] in Mr Elton's posthumous book about the lawfulness of private communions'. According to Gataker, however, these London ministers were small fry, caught up in a court manoeuvre aimed at 'others far greater than myself, even the archbishop himself'. In fact the immediate target appears to have been not so much Archbishop Abbot as his chaplain, Daniel Featley, who had licensed most of the rest of Elton's and indeed of Denison's oeuvres and, indeed, the other book at the centre of the affair (if not of the flames) William Crompton's *Saint Austins Summes*.[7]

The affair culminated in two days of back and forth between the king and Crompton, involving, on the one hand, Featley (and behind him, presumably, Abbot and other godly courtiers such as Manchester) and, on the other, a group of 'Arminians', centred on Richard Neile and William Laud and their clients and protégés, John Cosin and Richard Montague. In the middle, stood James I, as ever both the manipulator and the manipulated, tweaking and twisting the claims and counter-claims of his courtiers and advisors to suit his own agenda. In short, the whole scene has much to tell us about the politico-theological atmosphere at court and in the capital at the very close of James's reign, as all the major ecclesiastical players at court sought either to curb and contain, or to exacerbate and exploit, the energies and passions unleashed by the fuss over the Spanish match, the incipient war with Spain and the polemical activities of Richard Montague.[8]

I What Was Wrong with Edward Elton's Books?

At the Cross, Elton stood accused of maintaining that the private reception or administration of the sacrament was 'absolutely unlawful' even in the case of extreme sickness; that 'the Church hath no power to ordain' holy days and that 'God's people are not bound to observe the same once ordained by the Church'; that church music was unlawful; that it was also unlawful for Protestants to marry Catholics; that no man should wear foreign apparel; for affirming, with the anabaptists, 'that the speech of our Saviour to Nicodemus "unless a man be born again of water and the Holy Ghost he cannot enter into the kingdom of God" is not to be understood of infants but of men of years'; for maintaining that Christ did not mean to restrict us to the words of the Lord's Prayer and that it was 'extreme idleness' to be so restricted.

But the most substantial nexus of errors with which Elton was charged were his 'many judaical opinions about the observation of the Lord's day'; such as that 'in the time of harvest the fruit of the ground is rather to rot then be taken in …; that no man may drink of wine or stout drink upon that day unless he hath it already at hand in the house …; that there may be no lawful recreation allowed or used at any time of that day and that neither children nor servants are in any wise to obey their fathers and masters, commanding them to carry home a piece of work, as a suit of apparel or pair of shoes but to refuse it, though it were their utter undoing'.[9]

These accusations can be closely followed in copies of Elton's book/s that survived the flames. In essence, though somewhat exaggerated, they nearly all had some basis in Elton's works. Elton was indeed a strict Sabbatarian, holding that 'neither custom nor authority of man or angel can give liberty for such works to be done on the sabbath as are not warranted by the word of God; the law of God is immutable and therefore none can dispense with it'.[10] Sabbath observance ranked very high on Elton's list of religious observances and priorities; the 'keeping' of 'the rest of the commandments', depending, as it did, 'on the keeping of this'.[11] Religious duties performed on the sabbath were subject to a special blessing in that they were performed on the sabbath.[12] Similarly, Elton maintained that if they were told to work on the sabbath by their masters or parents, subordinates should simply 'not to do the thing, being evil and a sin in itself, but rather patiently to undergo any punishment his master shall lay on him'.[13]

On holy days the evidence is more equivocal. Certainly, Elton had an intensely circumscribed sense of the role of human ordinances and ecclesiastical traditions in divine worship.[14] It was, he claimed, 'idolatry' to add to, or detract from, the essential worship of God. Human intent to honour God must be grounded in the word of God. We were not 'to worship God by carnal rites and ceremonies and human devises but in such things as are agreeable to the will of God revealed in his word'.[15] The Church, therefore, had no business making things left indifferent by God parts of necessary divine worship. And yet the Church did have a residual right, indeed a duty, to prescribe rules of time, place, convenience and order to regulate the conduct of outward worship. This position left Elton plenty of room to adumbrate what had become the stock moderate puritan defence of outward conformity,[16] and certainly allowed the Church to ordain days other than the sabbath for divine worship. Thus, at one point Elton argued that 'in all ages' it had been 'a liberty' of the Church 'to set apart one or more of the six days either to public fasting or to solemn rejoicing for some benefit received'. However, it was crucial that 'the appointment and observation of them be held a thing indifferent', 'not placing the worship of God in them nor greater holiness in those days, but that they may be appointed only for the assembly of God's people for the exercise of the word and prayer'.[17] This placed such days in a decidedly subordinate relationship to the sabbath. Moreover, the Church did not have power to 'set apart days for holy meetings and to dedicate and consecrate those days to the honour of saints and angels'.[18] Thus, while Elton was not quite guilty as charged, he was certainly seeking to set the sabbath apart from all other holy days, driving a wedge between them through his rigid distinction between divine ordinances, essential to spiritual worship, and indifferent human ceremonies and traditions, attendant upon that worship.

This did not mean that he held that God's people were not obliged to observe such days, but merely that their obligation to do so came from a decidedly lower authority than did their obligation to observe the sabbath, since 'God alone can make and give laws truly and properly binding the consciences of men.... Princes and magistrates must be obeyed so far as they command in the Lord and for the Lord, but God must be obeyed simply and absolutely and perpetually, in all his commandments, without exception'.[19] There was no question where that left the Book of Sports. James I had long associated extreme sabbatarianism with puritan bibliolatry and disobedience. Opinions like that explain why.

It was, of course, that same distinction between direct divine command and intermediate human authority that underlay Elton's equally severe definition of idolatry and his concomitant claim that true Christians should have no contact at all with idolators, let alone marry them.[20] The same attitudes underpinned his rejection of church music. Here was a human ordinance antithetical to divine worship, because 'they commonly carry away our hearts from heavenly meditations and do rather fill them with carnal pleasure than with spiritual joy and delight'.[21]

The accusation concerning Elton's attitude to foreign apparel was similarly accurate and similarly based on the uncompromising scripturalism and moralism that contemporaries quite rightly took to be typical of the godly. 'The Lord hath threatened to visit such as wear strange apparel', Elton thundered, citing Zephaniah 1. 8; a prohibition that occurred in the midst of dire warnings against certain sorts of provocative stage plays, mixed dancing and 'riotous, lascivious, garish, disguised and new-fangled attire'.[22] Just as with the sabbath, we can see in these passages Elton's puritan legalist scripturalism and moral rigorism cutting against the grain of common social practice – what James and others took to be the dictates of social propriety, subordination and order. More particularly, while Elton's strictures had a general social and cultural relevance, particularly in London, a centre of conspicuous consumption, commercialised leisure and of frequent contact with papists, they had a particular relevance for the court, with its obsession with fancy 'foreign' dress, relatively elaborate external worship, habitual easy contact with idolators and recent plans for a marriage alliance with Spain.

On the sacraments, too, the accusations levelled against Elton were more or less accurate. Both of his deviant opinions – on private communion for the sick and on baptism – occurred first during his discussion of whether the sacraments were absolutely necessary for salvation. This Elton was very concerned to deny; since 'the wind bloweth where it listeth (that is) God gives grace and vouchsafes favour to whom, when and where it pleaseth him'.[23] Taking on a crucial text, oft quoted to defend the absolute necessity of baptism to salvation – John 3. 5 'verily, verily I say unto thee, except a man be born of water and of the spirit he cannot enter the kingdom of God' – Elton responded by claiming firstly that 'that place is not to be understood of infants, but rather of men of years', and secondly that 'it is not necessary that the word (water) should signify material water, no more than the word (fire) Math 27. 12 should signify material fire'.[24]

The final accusation – about Elton's attitude to the Lord's Prayer – seems, if anything, the least substantiable of all. Having maintained that 'we are not to refuse this form of prayer nor the using of the very words of the Lord's Prayer', Elton also insisted that 'we are not to confine ourselves only to the words of the Lord's Prayer and to use no other words'. 'It were extreme idleness and superstition to use the words of the Lord's Prayer alone, and none other'.[25] Having first conceded that since 'repetitions in prayer are not simply forbidden and altogether unlawful, holy men have used them', he went on to equate 'such repetitions as are idle and vain' as with the practices of 'the heathen' and 'the papists'.[26]

For Elton the chief use of the Lord's Prayer was to serve as a 'pattern and direction' for our own prayers. That left room for a variety of forms of prayer – from the silent mental petitions to be used in the street and other public places, to avoid the otherwise inescapable appearance of pharisaical display and spiritual pride, to other more formal modes of more or less set prayer for both private and public worship.

Elton did not make much of the doctrine of absolute predestination in his commentary on the Decalogue, which was designed to extract out of the commandments an elaborated guide to godly living, rather than an introspective, assurance- and predestination-centred pietism. His commentary on the Lord's Prayer was, however, suffused with predestinarian references and assertions. Opening with a denial that we should pray for 'all the men in the world, for Christ prayed not for the world', Elton insisted that we should rather pray 'for all God's elect and for the whole Church of God and for men of all sorts and degrees, places and conditions'.[27] And so the word 'us' in the petition 'forgive us our trespasses' was glossed as meaning 'both ourselves and others yet being on earth of God's election, whether already called or yet un-called'.[28] The notion that 'a child of God cannot finally fail or fall from grace' was accepted as axiomatic.[29] The related doctrines of assurance and sanctification were affirmed, and the subjective experiences that went with them prayed for. 'Arminianism' featured prominently in a list of 'erroneous and false doctrines and superstitions' which also included 'paganism, turkism, judaism, papism ... and Anabaptism'.[30]

The petition 'lead us not into temptation' prompted a lengthy disquisition on the relationship between divine omnipotence and the existence of sin and evil, with Elton going out of his way to explain that 'God's permitting of Satan to tempt a man to sin is not a bare permission, God only looking on and only suffering Satan to tempt him, but it is a powerful working permission'. This naturally raised the issue of how, then, God could avoid being seen as the author of sin, a question to which, both here, and in his discussion of the petition 'thy will be done', Elton devoted pages of convoluted prose.[31] 'If God permit sin, he doth it willingly or against his will: if willingly, then it is not by bare permission, by a powerful working permission. If against his will, then is he not omnipotent to let and hinder anything he willeth not, and that is blasphemy to think'.[32] God then directly willed sin but not 'sin simply considered in itself, as it is sin and against his commandment, but only willeth the event and coming to pass of sin'. This he did 'not by effecting it, but by withholding his grace from his creature, and not hindering it when he might ... and so only by consequent God willeth the event of sin, he not hindering it' but 'willingly permits it to be done, for a good end (namely) the glory of his name in the execution of his justice, or the manifestation of his mercy'.[33] This was a bog-standard, if uncompromising, expression of contemporary Calvinist orthodoxy, but unlike Elton's other 'puritan' opinions this attracted no hostile comment, still less condemnation, in the royal anathematisation of his works.

On the one hand, we could see the allegations against Elton as yet another emanation of a traditional Jacobean, order- and obedience-centred critique of puritanism. James had long equated extreme sabbatarianism with puritan subversion and Elton's equally extreme views on idolatry, marriage with papists and the mores of court and capital were also redolent of the popularity and truculence that James had always associated with the godly since his days in Scotland. Here was the quintessence of puritanism as James (and Ben Jonson) understood it, and, on the logic that since he was so obviously a 'puritan' Elton must also be a nonconformist, it is unsurprising that, despite his voluble protestations in print to the contrary, Elton should have been outed as a notorious and persistent nonconformist; an accusation that Featley had been able to refute by asking innocently how was it, then, that his diocesan – one Lancelot Andrewes – had felt able to leave him in unmolested possession of his living for all these years?[34]

But, on the other hand, we might see these charges as a product of the newly insurgent Arminian attempt, led by Richard Montague, but supported by the Durham House set gathered around Bishop Richard Neile, and increasingly William Laud, to redescribe central features of the moderate puritan or reformed take on the position of the Church of England as, in fact, a (puritan) conspiracy to take that Church over from within; an attempt that had now to be rejected once and for all, if, that is, the national Church were to revert to the state of pristine, apostolic, purity, intended by its founders, and on that basis, now, at last, be able effectively to refute the charges habitually lodged against it by the papists. Or, better yet, perhaps we should see the move against Elton and the others as an attempt to convert that first form of anti-puritanism into the second.

II The Political and Polemical Context

In order to pursue that line of inquiry, it is necessary to place the burning of Edward Elton's books in the specific political and polemical contexts provided by the last years and months of James's reign. These had, of course, been framed in fundamental ways by the Palatine crisis and the ensuing fuss over the Spanish Match, the reaction against which did much to revivify and sharpen James's anti-puritanism. For here were moderate puritans – men such as Samuel Ward of Ipswich, Andrew Willet, even Thomas Scott, the author of the notorious tract *Vox Populi*, who at least presented himself as a moderate – all of whom seemed to have been successfully integrated into the Jacobean Church, coming out in the pulpit, and even in print, to criticise James's most prized policy initiative, in the process trampling all over some of the flowers of the royal prerogative as James understood them.[35] Here, then, was confirmation that all the dark warnings about the real nature of the populist puritan threat issued from the very outset of the reign by the likes of Lancelot Andrewes had been right all along.[36] In short, the perfect opportunity for *avant garde* conformists and Arminians such as Richard Montague to seize the initiative and convert the king's traditional, indeed conventional, but hitherto also remarkably flexible, anti-puritanism, into a wholesale reaction against the English reformed tradition, now rebranded as puritanism.

That move was itself a product of another set of controversies set off by the response to the Spanish Match, and the renewed activities of English Catholics, exploiting the opportunities afforded them by the regime's need to avoid the least suspicion of 'persecution' if a papal dispensation for the marriage with the infanta were to be obtained. In the course of those developments, the royal favourite, Buckingham's mother converted to Catholicism.[37] This was a propaganda disaster for the court, since it represented precisely the sort of papist advance towards the centres of power that, it was widely feared, the match would produce. As Katie Marshalek has explained, this prompted a series of attempts to win the countess back to the Protestant fold, through a series of debates involving the Jesuit who had converted her, John Percy, and various Protestant divines. These debates took place first in person, in the presence of the countess, and in one of them James himself played a very prominent role.

Manuscript accounts and then printed pamphlets were produced recounting what happened to a wider public. Centrally involved in these exchanges on the Protestant side were William Laud, then bishop of St Davids and Francis White, a lecturer at St Paul's.

These disputations, centred on the countess of Buckingham and the court, spawned others in the city of London, one of which, at the house of Sir Humphrey Lynd, concerned the spiritual fate of his kinsman, Edward Buggs. Initially planned as a rematch of the debate between White and Percy, it was White's second, none other than Daniel Featley, who came to play the central role on the Protestant side. Whereas Laud and White had taken a more moderate tack in disputing the visibility of the Church, with Laud admitting, when the countess asked him point-blank whether she could be saved within the Church of Rome, that indeed she could, Featley took an altogether harder line; not tracing the visibility of the Church of England solely through the error strewn and corrupted, yet still true, Church of Rome, but rather, in the Foxeian mode, through the groups of so-called heretics, but in fact true believers, who had kept the true Church alive even at the height of Antichrist's reign over the Church.

These debates about the visibility of the Church, and the struggles over the countess of Buckingham's soul that produced them, developed into a contest between Lambeth Palace and Durham House, the issue being whether the hard line pushed by Archbishop Abbot and his chaplain Featley against popery, or the more moderate one being advanced by Laud, White and ultimately Richard Montague, was the more effective way to combat the papist threat.

The ensuing competition was not explicit. The two sides did not directly engage one another, but rather conducted their dispute through the very different ways in which they sought to counter the popish threat, with their success in some sense turning on whether and by whom the countess was restored to the fold.

In the course of these exchanges, James was brought into close and sustained contact, and even collaboration, with the Durham House group. Wanting the Spanish Match to go forward, but also wanting to preserve his own Protestant credentials, James was in the market for a style of anti-popery that gave ground to the papists – admitting, not grudgingly, that Rome was indeed a true Church – while also providing the basis for the rejection of 'popery', as James defined it. And so confronted with the blast of anti-popery coming out of Lambeth – which included an unlicensed tract by Featley, which was an account of his first debate with the Jesuit, Percy (better known by his alias of 'Fisher'), and, remarkably, a tract by Archbishop Abbot himself which, licensed by Featley, appeared anonymously, but displayed Abbot's arms,[38] Durham House responded, in collaboration with James himself. Not only did Bishop Neile instruct Featley not to debate a second time with Fisher, over the soul of Mr Buggs, but November 1623 found James, Laud, White and Lancelot Andrewes, the ideological *eminence grise* of the Durham House group, in a series of meetings about the publication of White's response to Percy's manuscript tract on the nine points put to him by James himself in the course of their earlier debate in 1622. Later, in January 1624, Laud recorded meeting first Buckingham and then James to discuss his account of the debate with Fisher, in the course of which meeting James apparently expressed incredulity that the archbishop of Canterbury should have written such a book, and encouraged Laud to publish his. In December James commanded it to be printed, although Laud demurred, successfully requesting that it appear under the name of a third party, his chaplain Richard Baylie.

It was into these fraught exchanges that Richard Montague launched his notorious tract, a *New Gagg for an Old Goose*. Finished in December 1623, it was ready for print by January 1624 and published in March. Montague's book is best seen as an attempt to bring the anti-puritanism provoked in court circles by the 'puritan' reaction against the Spanish Match into direct contact with the on-going dispute between Durham House and Lambeth Palace over the best way to counter the Catholic threat. Montague's book, which has been conventionally viewed as an Arminian attack on a now puritanised Calvinism, was actually framed by the conceit that various nameless female members of his flock in his Essex parish had fallen victim to the wiles of certain Catholic priests. He had tried to arrange a debate with these unnamed 'popish rangers', but they had refused, sending him instead John Heigham's *Gagg of the Reformed Gospel*, to which his book was a response. Montague had thus conjured a situation, in rural Essex, exactly parallel to the circumstances surrounding the countess of Buckingham, at court, in the process providing himself with a perfect laboratory in which to demonstrate the superiority of his own approach to such matters.

The premise of his book was that the Church of England needed clearly to repudiate many of the opinions and positions attributed to her both by the papists and by some of her own misguided, 'puritan' defenders, if the real points at issue between the two Churches were ever to emerge and the debate with the papists ever definitively to be won. This was a strategy that allowed Montague to vindicate his own doctrinal *bona fides* as an enemy of popery while, at the same time, attacking what he took to be the extreme predestinarian, anti-sacramental, anti-sacerdotal, rabidly anti-popish, de-sacralising, and even sacrilegious, Protestantism, or in Montague lexicon, 'puritanism', espoused by all too many of the Church of England's most fervent Protestant defenders. This allowed Montague to appear to be attacking the papists while also attacking a version of puritanism expanded to include not merely conforming puritans like Edward Elton or Stephen Denison but even the likes of Daniel Featley. Hence the attempt to associate Featley with what were presented as the flagrantly puritan opinions of Edward Elton, amongst which were not (yet) numbered his predestinarian beliefs.

With Montague's book the hitherto *sotto voce* contest between Lambeth Palace and Durham House over how best to best the papists came out into the open, in the process morphing into a direct confrontation between English Protestants about (amongst other things) predestination and puritanism. All in all, Montague's was a nervelessly audacious intervention, quite at odds with the extreme caution being displayed, in precisely the same circumstances, by William Laud.

III Richard Montague and William Crompton, Compared and Contrasted

Featley found himself in hot water in December 1624 and January 1625 not only for licensing Elton's book but also another tract, this one by William Crompton, called *Saint Austins Summes*.[39] This purported to be, and, by some canons of orthodoxy was, a fairly standard piece of anti-Catholic polemic, ostensibly a mere extension of an earlier squib by Alexander Cooke called *Saint Austins Religion*. There Cooke had sought to refute a number of popish claims with sole recourse to the works and authority of St Augustine. Crompton extended Cooke's short thirty-page tract by adding a further seventy-two questions at issue with the Church of Rome, which he then handled in exactly the same way. The work presented itself as a response to a piece of Catholic polemic by John Brereley and fitted within a long-standing genre of Protestant writing which used patristic sources to disprove Catholic claims of Protestant novelty and error.

But in fact, on closer inspection, a plausible case can be made that Crompton's book was intended as a tactfully indirect, but doctrinally explicit, reply to Montague, which, without actually naming him, in fact took up many of the central points raised in *A New Gagg* and resolved them in senses very different from those reached by Montague – and all on the unimpeachably patristic authority of St Augustine, and in the course of defending the national Church against popery.

Montague's book had been published in March 1624, while Crompton's was entered in the Stationers' Register in August and had a dedicatory epistle dated 13 October. The book may even have been in some sense a collective product, with Featley and Cooke in effect helping if not to write, then at least heavily to edit, the volume, using Crompton's first drafts.[40]

In order to make these claims stick we need to examine quite closely the different positions adopted by Crompton and Montague on a series of crucial topics central both to the previous debates about the visibility of the Church, and the emergent more exclusively predestinarian controversies about Montague's notorious book.

i Crompton States His Credentials; the Church Fathers and the Question of Conformity

To begin with Crompton's whole approach, using the authority of St Augustine to refute the claims of the papists was not only a stock English Protestant move, it was also perfectly designed to refute one of Montague's central claims that that there existed in the Church of England 'some Protestants especially of preciser cut', afflicted with all too cavalier an attitude to the Fathers. 'I like not that the ancient fathers should be philipped off like schoolboys with snips'.[41]

On the subject of ceremonial conformity, Crompton quoted St Augustine's claim that so long as ecclesiastical traditions were not 'repugnant to the written word' they should be accepted. Ambrose had urged on Augustine the observation of 'the custom of that Church' in which one was living, as the only way to avoid both taking and giving offence. Advice good enough for Augustine was certainly quite good enough for Crompton. 'I have', he told the reader, 'ever loved peace and conformity to the true Church in matters of indifferency',[42] and 'thus I had rather yield something from my own supposed knowledge then rend myself from the Church where I live, only because I see them as some harmless ceremonies, neither burdensome nor superstitious'.[43]

In such passages, Crompton was announcing himself to his readers as a moderate puritan defender of a certain gloss on the Church of England's position, but certainly not as the desacralising vandal, the vulgar, sacrilegious 'peddler', of Montague's imaginings.

ii On the Sacraments

On the sacraments, Montague countered the popish claim that English Protestants did not believe that baptism was necessary for salvation by insisting that their Church maintained and justified the contrary 'against schismatic humours, not papists, but puritans near at home'. This rendered it quite clear that the Church of England held that 'it is impossible ordinarily for a man to be saved that is not baptised. Upon which persuasion of that necessity of water and the Holy Ghost we, following the use and warrant of antiquity, have tolerated, practised and defended the private baptism at home by lay people'.[44]

Montague went on to excoriate all those who tried to limit the necessity of baptism for salvation through recourse to the doctrine of predestination, what he termed 'that supposed decree of God touching absolute necessity of salvation'.[45]

Both men agreed, then, that baptism was only *ordinarily* necessary to salvation. However, while Montague chose to close his discussion with the observation that 'ordinary way unto life eternal, there is none but by baptism of water and Holy Ghost',[46] Crompton orientated his treatment of the same question very differently. 'The sacrament itself', he conceded, 'avails much in admitting and receiving young infants into the outward assembly of the elect, but not to confer grace … to the conversion of the heart. Baptism may be where saving grace never was, and saving grace maybe where outward baptism never was, because not the defect, but the contempt, of a sacrament … doth condemn men'.[47] Crompton then moved to his inevitable conclusion: 'for if a man may be saved … to whom this corporal baptism is wanting then this corporal baptism is not absolutely necessary to salvation'.[48] It was a point he was only too happy to discuss, in marked contrast to Montague, in direct relation to the decree of election. 'It is the common tenet', he wrote, 'of our English divines that those children whom God in his eternal counsel hath elected, dying without the outward act of baptism, are saved'.[49]

There was, however, a form of baptism that *was* essential to salvation, and that was '*baptismus flaminis*, which is a fit preparation of the heart for the receiving of saving grace and this is simply necessary to salvation, without which none can be saved'. But this was not necessarily tied to the outward ceremony of baptism, but vouchsafed to the elect (baptised or not) and denied to the reprobate (baptised or not).[50] Crompton was explaining the same point actively rather than passively when he claimed that 'without faith and repentance the outward act of the Church doth little avail'.[51] It was, therefore, with this *baptismus flaminis* 'that elected saints of ripe years are baptised really and actively: elected infants are baptised with it only really and habitually'. Thus, while outward baptism was 'necessary to salvation by reason of the commandment and of the ordinary outward means to salvation', the spiritual baptism 'was necessary by a simple and absolute necessity'.[52]

We can see precisely the same sorts of difference of approach and emphasis in Crompton's and Montague's discussion of the real presence. Montague organised his discussion around the question of whether Protestants held that 'the bread of the supper is but a figure of the body of Christ'.[53] Citing the words of the official catechism – ('and I would no other were tolerated') – Montague had great fun denying the charge.

Sir, we acknowledge right willingly and profess that in the blessed sacrament (as you call it of the altar) the body and blood of our Saviour Christ is really participated and communicated and by means of that real participation life from him and in him is conveyed unto our souls. This we believe and profess in knowing that he is able to effect it who hath spoken it by that mighty working whereby he is able to do whatsoever he hath said. We are not solicitous for the manner how he worketh it, not daring to pry into the secret counsels of the most high. We have learned that 'revealed things are for us, secret things are for God'.[54]

On this basis, following Hooker, Montague was able to take a magnifi-
cently distanced view of the many disputes about the nature of the real presence that had riven the Church. 'Therefore, we wonder why the world should
be so much amazed at or distracted with those inexplicable labyrinths of
consubstantiation and transubstantiation which only serve to set the world in
division, nothing to piety nor yet information'.[55] It was enough for faithful
Christians

> ingenuously to profess that by this sacrament Christ giveth us his very
> body and blood and really and truly performs in us his promise in feeding
> our souls into eternal life. As for the manner how, ... this inexplicable, that
> unutterable, it is faith only that can give resolution. Trans or con we skill
> not of .... Life begun in baptism by the laver of regeneration is confirmed
> and sustained in the holy supper by his body and blood. How? I cannot
> explicate .... When Christ gave it, he said 'this is my body'. It was never
> denied to be his body; ... it is affirmed still to be his body.[56]

Crompton, however, came at this issue from a very different direction. Quite
unlike Montague, he was obsessed with overthrowing popish claims that the
sacraments worked *ex opere operato*. Accordingly, he continually harped on a
distinction between the outward elements and inward workings of the spirit, a
distinction that had virtually no place in Montague's exposition. 'Grace comes',
he stressed, 'by operation of the spirit and not by power in the elements'.
'Conferring of grace is attributed to the word and not to the elements upon
which the word works'.[57] There was no causal link to be established between
the outward elements and the inward grace: 'There is no proportion between it
and grace, as there ought to be between cause and the effect, for grace is a
supernatural form, which no element doth contain, for then of necessity it
should ever produce supernatural acts, which you [the papists] deny'.[58]

Such claims inevitably had an effect on Crompton's rendition of the doctrine of the real presence. Just like Montague, he was anxious to deny the
papists' claim that English Protestants reduced the sacrament to a mere sign,
maintaining that the Church of England holds 'that Christ is really present
after consecration two ways: first in respect of the sacramental signs which
offer and exhibit that which they signify: secondly in respect of the commu-
nicant's faith'.[59] However, in marked contrast to Montague, he did not then
move to God's omnipotence as the best way to get out of discussing the whys
and wherefores of how all this worked. On the contrary, he derided this as a
popish manoeuvre typical of the likes of Bellarmine.[60]

All of Crompton's emphasis went on spiritual effects of divine grace 'in the
worthy receiver'; on the presence as it was real to 'the communicants faith'.
And this led him to discuss the sacraments directly in terms of the doctrine of
predestination and of the basic dichotomy between the elect and the

reprobate, in ways that were anathema to Montague. 'Wicked men and such as be void of a lively faith, although they do carnally press their teeth (as Austin says) the sacrament of the body and blood of Christ, yet in no wise are they partakers of Christ .... Wicked reprobates do all dissent from Christ, therefore, they eat not his real body but the sacrament of his body: the visible elements which are common to good and bad, when as life and salvation (which necessarily follows the participation of the body and blood of Christ) is proper only to good men, as St Austin speaketh, and therefore he makes a distinction between the visible and invisible matter of the sacrament ... the one being proper to all, the other proper to the elect only'.[61]

Crompton's consistent division between inner spiritual realities and outward forms and elements, his refusal to present either sacrament as simply necessary for salvation, and his gloss on the doctrine of the real presence were all in stark contrast to Montague's position. The two men might not have had mutually exclusive sacramental theologies, but the basic orientations, the fundamental polemical and pietistic thrusts, of their stated positions were very different. Here the role of the doctrine of predestination stood out. It was precisely in such different choices about polemical orientation and doctrinal priority, and the relative emphases placed on one *topos*, doctrine or argument rather than another, that the differences between the two men's positions showed most clearly.

iii Antichrist, and the Inerrancy and Invisibility of the Church

As one might expect both Montague and Crompton spent a good deal of time on the issues of visibility and inerrancy that had dominated the earlier debates with the Jesuit Fisher. Montague chose to respond to what he pictured as the two basic popish claims – that Protestants held that the Church could both err *and* be invisible. He flatly denied both assertions. On visibility, he declared that 'the church hath ever been visible since there was a church', adding that 'in England especially how can this fellow impute invisibility to us who claim and prove a succession and therefore needs a visibility from the time of the apostles'.[62] This seemed to imply that the English Church, defined as a visible institutional Church, had always, even at the height of popery, been a true Church, part of that Catholic Church that could never disappear or err. When Montague chose to speak of invisibility he turned from the visible to the invisible Church and thus to the notion of the elect. It was only in the sense that both the 'Church triumphant and the saints militant', that is, God's elect both in heaven and in this life, were 'known only to God alone' that the Church could be said to be invisible. 'Otherwise than so', he grandly told his papist adversary, 'we do not speak of invisibility'.[63]

On the question of whether the Church could err, Montague admitted that while it was clear that individual visible Churches could err, even to destruction, the Catholic Church, taken in the right sense, could not. Everyone, of course, would agree with that; the real question was what one might mean by the Catholic Church. 'The Catholic includeth two things', Montague explained, 'universality of time and place, or universality of place only. In the former acceptation take the Church, that *coetus evocatus* which hath been heretofore and which is now, make it up. The apostles, their disciples and all their successors are included and so the Catholic hath not, did not, cannot err, either in fact or faith, fundamental or less fundamental'.[64] This was to define the Church as all the true believers who had throughout its history remained faithful to the doctrinal deposit of the apostles.

But the Catholic Church could also be defined 'according unto universality of place'. In that mode, 'the Church of Christ is twofold, *diffusive* or *representive*'. The Church *diffusive* was comprised of 'every part and member and every place' but the Church *representive* was constituted by 'a general council for the whole, or all particulars that make up the whole'. This meant, Montague maintained, that 'the Catholic Church at this day cannot err in all her parts, nor in *faciendis*, matter of fact, nor *credendis*, points of belief, dangerously. The Church representative, true and lawful, never yet erred in fundamentals and therefore I see no cause but to vouch she cannot err in fundamentals'.[65] And so, if the appropriate distinctions were made, the Church, taken in the right senses as both *collective* and *representive*, 'in the largest extent, could not err at all'. That is to say 'not err in points of faith'. For 'faith is fundamental or accessory. There none is; here error may occur'.[66]

Of course, this did not mean that the Church, even thus defined, could not, or had not erred. There had always been disagreements and errors, even amongst the apostles, and certainly amongst the Fathers. Citing Ephesians 2. 20, he wrote,

> we read that they [the Fathers] were built upon the foundation of the apostles and the prophets. What then? Could they not err? Dare you say so? They could, for they have, and are shaken off from that foundation, but so long as they stood fast, they erred not, holding one faith, one Lord, one baptism Ephes. 4. 5, which if you and we do at this day, by your own argument, (avoid it if you can) we err not.

As for the admonition to unity in 'one heart, one soul of the believers', contained in Acts 4:32, that was 'in reference of love one to another, not in unity of doctrine all with one another'. For, Montague observed, 'there were differences in that union, for example, *inter* Paul and Barnabas, and might be disproportion in their doctrine, as dissimilitude in the habitude and condition of those sheep in one sheep fold, under one shepherd, and yet all hear the shepherd's voice, John 10, 16'.[67]

The making of such distinctions was crucial to Montague's overall both anti-papal and anti-puritan projects, which turned on the distinction between points fundamental, where error was fatal, and points accessory, where disagreement, and therefore error, were both to be expected and entirely allowable. For 'error may be where blame is none'.[68] His aim was to out certain doctrines, mistakenly taken to be fundamental by many of his contemporaries, both Catholic and Protestant, as merely accessory or disputable. As we shall see, amongst such beliefs were the nature of the real presence, the fine details of predestination, the identity of the pope as Antichrist, the precise relations between free will and divine grace in effecting conversion and salvation, about all of which final or complete knowledge was impossible. Discussion and disagreement about such topics were appropriate in the schools, amongst scholars, but they had no place in the popular pulpit, before the people. Failure to observe such distinctions and limits could only have disastrous consequences; consequences from which Montague was currently trying to rescue the English Church.

Thus, even in the midst of conducting a virulently anti-Catholic polemic, Montague was able to make remarkable appeals for Christian, rather than for merely Protestant unity. He did this by excluding from the pale of potential irenicism and agreement to differ those extremist elements on both sides of the confessional divide – crudely, puritans and Jesuits – who insisted on making things inherently debatable and peripheral, essential. Amongst English Protestants, that meant outing a range of divines, the likes of Featley included, as 'puritan'. And so, what was presented as a work of anti-papal polemic, became also a virulent attack on puritans, to whom Montague could refer in the most slighting of terms as 'the puritan faction' or 'factionists'; taken up with 'giddy conceits', such people were, he exclaimed, 'none of ours; no more than the Donatists, Meletians or Novatians were anciently the Catholic church, or their fooleries to be imputed to the Church'. 'Were the innovating humour predominant in them', Montague claimed, such people would 'prescribe a form of religion to Jesus Christ' himself, were he to come again.[69]

Montague's position on the issues of inerrancy and visibility was composed of largely consensual elements; the claims that throughout its history the Church had contained professors of the one true faith; that the first five general councils had not erred, and so that the Catholic Church (properly understood) had not, and could not err; that there was a crucial distinction to be drawn between fundamental doctrines, necessary to salvation, and accessory matters; the notion that the invisible Church was a term properly belonging to God's elect; even the claim that the Church of England enjoyed an institutional continuity stretching from an ancient past before popery came to these shores, through the height of popish error, to the present. To all of these propositions nearly every educated English Protestant would have assented, as Anthony Milton has shown.[70]

It was how Montague combined those elements, and the conclusions that he drew from that combination, that set off alarm bells, as he seemed to embrace the Roman Catholic Church as a member of the Catholic Church, though one in error, with altogether too much enthusiasm, even as he repudiated the English reformed tradition in many of its essential elements, and seemed to suggest that, if attention were placed on the central, fundamental beliefs and practices, the Churches of Rome and of England were far closer together than many people on both sides of the confessional divide were prepared to admit.[71]

Crompton approached these same issues from an altogether different direction. He opened, in marked contrast to Montague, by seizing on Catholic claims to inerrancy, equating them with the Brownist view that 'the Church of Christ should be absolutely pure of sin and error'.[72] This, he maintained, was patently absurd. The Church militant would always be subject to faults and errors. However, with Montague, Crompton was careful to distinguish between the different senses in which the term Church militant could be taken. It was 'either particular and visible' – like the Church of England – 'which by woeful experience we find to have been subject to error and hath suffered shipwreck, leaving the star which should have directed her to her haven of happiness'.[73] That seemed effectively to split off the institutional visibility and continuity of particular Churches from the issue of inerrancy. In explaining how the Church could be said not to err, Crompton then turned from particular visible Churches to 'the universal and invisible Church, which', he conceded while 'during her militancy' she could 'partially err in her members' – for in this life even members of the elect were subject to sin and error – 'yet totally and in fundamental points she cannot'.[74] There would, in short, always be members of the elect in the world, who would keep the fundamentals of true belief alive.

This, of course, raised the question of visibility. Such people might always be there, but in what senses would they, the Church, always be visible? In marked contrast to Montague, Crompton, started his discussion of this issue with the doctrine of election. Since 'God's elect Church shall never be seduced from him, there must be a visible Church, even in the height of the reign of Antichrist, though not so conspicuous to the world as at other times, neither is this contradicted by any Protestant that ever I read'.[75]

For Crompton, then, but not for Montague, the doctrine of election became the central underpinning that ensured that, however bad things got, however much Antichrist raged and error seemed to prevail, a Church of true believers must continue to exist. This enabled him to affect the same insouciance on the question of visibility that he attributed to St Augustine, who, while he maintained that 'the Catholic Church must continue to the end of the world', had never contended that the Church 'shall ever be alike visible'.[76] On Crompton's view, then, the extent of the true Church's visibility might vary widely, according, first to the circumstances of the Church itself and, second, to the situation and spiritual condition of the people looking for it. Here he cited Augustine on the two-fold state of the Church: 'first, of prosperity, and then she flourished, being as manifest to the world as a city upon a hill, which cannot be hid during that state', and second, in 'the state of persecution and then she may be obscured with multitude of scandals'.[77] While the Church was 'ever visible in her own nature', she could be said to be 'invisible, that is hindered from our sight', first, if we lacked the eye of faith with which to discern her; second, if we lacked 'the will ... to see her'; and third, 'for want of light', 'when the clouds of persecution have caused a gross darkness to over-spread the world ... then the Church though visible *in potentia* shall not actually appear in the world'.[78]

Crompton, in short, was far more comfortable than Montague with the notion of relative invisibility, and was prepared to have direct recourse to the doctrine of election and the notion of the invisible Church of the elect when handling issues of Church visibility and inerrancy and, in marked contrast to Montague, placed no emphasis on the institutional continuity and visible succession of particular national Churches. For his part, Montague would have no truck with the notion of even a relative invisibility of the true Church and sought simply to contradict popish charges on this score, rather than, with Crompton, to finesse and circumvent them.

These differences showed most clearly in their divergent treatments of Antichrist. For Montague, with his insistence on visible succession, a vision of the Church dominated for large portions of its history by the reign of Antichrist had little attraction, and so, if he did not quite deny that the pope was Antichrist, he at least maintained that 'whether the pope be Antichrist, the Church resolveth not .... Nor can or ought the several fancies of private men to be imputed to the authorised and approved doctrines of the Church: a fault more than ordinary with you papists to charge the Church of England with every private opinion that any man holdeth in our Church, though he be singular and alone'.[79] His own view was that while the popes or the papacy 'were *an* Anti-Christ, carrying themselves as they do in the Church', 'for the state Antichristian, the Turk and the pope together may seem to make it, and, for the person, some one notorious varlet above the rest'.[80]

Crompton, on the other hand, was certain that the pope was Antichrist and that that claim represented the doctrinal opinion of the Church of England, which 'is set down by the pen of our dread sovereign', James I himself.[81] Antichrist was 'not one person but a succession of persons'[82] who, 'pretending the name of Christ, shall be willing to have himself esteemed a Christian. Antichrist is Christ's pretended servant and therefore no open adversary', which certainly ruled out both the Turk and the claim that

Antichrist was one person whose reign had yet to begin – Montague's 'one notorious varlet above the rest'.[83]

iv Predestination

As one might have expected from their treatments of the sacraments and of Church visibility, the theology of grace provided perhaps the clearest example of the differences between the two men. As ever, the divergence between their approaches showed most clearly in the propositions against which they chose to organise their accounts. Typically, Montague chose to deny what he presented as the papist claim that all Protestants believed that 'God by his will and inevitable decree hath ordained from all eternity who shall be damned and who saved'.[84] Rather than take a hard doctrinal line himself, as ever, Montague chose to emphasise (accurately enough, of course) that this was a doctrine at issue on both sides of the confessional divide. Wherever one looked one found

> in the point of election for life and reprobation unto death Protestants and papists are many ways at odds, in opposition and each divided at home amongst themselves. Not for the thing, which all resolve, but for the manner in which they differ: agreeing in the main that 'it is so', disagreeing on the by, how it cometh so? As if God meant to reserve no secrets unto himself, but impart them to all men, as if it were not enough to save some and cast others off, but he must give account of doing so.

To cross-question God on this subject represented the highest presumption, a wading into 'the hidden secrets of the Almighty' precisely at the point where the 'grand apostle stood at gaze with "O the depth" and in consideration cried out how unsearchable are his ways'.[85]

Invoking the same passage, Edward Elton had held Paul's ejaculation to be perfectly compatible with frankly absolute doctrines of election and reprobation. The same was not true of Montague. He characterised the view that Peter and Judas had been elected and reprobated by a God 'as absolute to decree, as omnipotent to effect', 'without respect of anything but his own will, insomuch that Peter could not perish, though he would, nor Judas be saved, do what he could', as 'the private fancy of some men'. It was certainly not the opinion of all Protestants, since 'the Lutherans in dismay do detest and abhorr it'. Moreover, 'the Church of England hath not taught it, doth not believe it, hath opposed it', 'not presuming to determine of when, how, wherefore or whom: secrets reserved to God alone'.[86] Having established as much, Montague then limited himself to the observation that it was 'God's will that all men are to be saved and to come to the knowledge of the truth', and therefore 'that he was not willing that any should perish but all should come unto repentance'.[87]

But if all were offered salvation, it necessarily followed that it was not God's fault or choice if all men did not accept the offer.

> God foresaw it in Adam and in Judas, but prescience inferreth not predestination. For not because foreseen, therefore effected, but because effected therefore foreseen. The treason of Judas, the fall of Adam, God foresaw and suffered, this is certain: God was author of neither positively. That good which they had they had from God. This woe and unhappiness came from themselves.[88]

Having, by these means, rejected the doctrine of absolute election, Montague was able summarily to dismiss the related doctrine of assurance. Reacting to the papists' claim that Protestants held that 'everyone ought infallibly to assure himself of his salvation and to hold that he is of the number of the predestinate',[89] Montague pointed out that 'this opinion is an inference upon that former of necessary election unto life and therefore those Protestants, who make not the former an article of their creed, build upon no such infallibility unto themselves, nor prescribe it to be believed of others'.[90]

Crompton dealt with the same issues very differently, organising his case around the question of whether St Augustine had, in effect, made God the author of sin. This was one of the most common allegations made against the absolute predestinarian position by both papists and Arminians, and it raised immediately the doctrine, not so much of election, as of reprobation, a doctrinal nettle which Crompton proved himself altogether happy to grasp.

> That God did reprobate some to damnation Bellarmine confesseth it to be St Austin's opinion. Reprobation according to St Austin's learning (saith Bellarmine) is nothing else but God's predestinating to destruction. One company of men are predestined to reign eternally with God, another to undergoing eternal punishment with the devil. And did not God then reprobate some to damnation? ... How could Christ say you are not of my sheep unless he had seen that they were predestinated to everlasting damnation? And did not God then reprobate some to damnation? The son of perdition was predestined to perdition, saith St Austin.[91]

This, however, did not mean that God was the author of sin. In explaining how, Crompton left his sole reliance on Augustine and had recourse to the scholastic subtleties of Thomas Aquinas. 'God', Crompton proclaimed,

> is the author of reprobation and consequently of damnation, this is plain, by the definition given by Aquinas .... It is an act of God's providence, permitting some to fall into sin and bringing the punishment of damnation upon them for sin and in it we may consider two acts. The first negative; *nolo misereri*, having a purpose to pass by some without any other known

cause to us than his will. The second is affirmative, *volo punire*; proceeding from the justice of God, not without some intuitive respect both to actual and original sin; so that reprobation is not the cause of the fault (that proceedeth from the corrupted will of man, left to itself) but is rather, indeed, the cause of the punishment due the fault'.[92]

It was only after a display of elaborately scholastical reasoning, involving a range of showily technical Latin terms, that Crompton resorted to the language of mystery and doctrinal tact that Montague habitually used to avoid all such discussion. 'Now to ask a reason why God chooses this man and passes by that is forbidden by St Austin. Judge not, if thou wouldst not judge falsely; it pleases God to punish men so, yet not unjustly because secretly'.[93] Montague had made that move far earlier in the chain of his argument both in order to shift the topic of predestination into the terrain of the unknowable and peripheral, and to open it up to his own Arminian views.

We can observe precisely the same sort of differences of approach in the two men's accounts of free will. For Montague this was again 'a question of obscurity which better might have been over passed in silence, [again] fitting rather schools than popular ears'.[94] As he told his popish interlocutor, 'the concurrence of grace assisting with free will, the correspondence of free will with prescience, providence and predestination is much debated in your schools. Intricate disputes are hereupon inferred, questions almost inextricable'. There was a similar variety of opinion on the Protestant side, but, as with predestination, all were agreed on the essentials. 'Man in a state of corruption had free will', 'in matters moral', 'in actions natural and civil' and 'in actions of piety, such as belong unto his salvation. But *quatenus* and *quale* is the question as much amongst yourselves as with us', Montague told the papists.[95]

However, having located the intricacies of this issue under the sign of the dubious, the debatable and the inessential, as with predestination, Montague proceeded to insinuate his own view of the matter into the public domain, in effect equating it with

> the doctrine of the Church of England. Prevented by grace and assisted therewith, he [fallen man] then putteth to his hand to procure augmentation of that grace and continuance unto the end. No man cometh to God but he is drawn. Drawn, he runneth or walketh as his assistance is, and from his own agility and disposition, to the end. This is enough, and the wisdom of the Church hath not ventured far to put a tie of obedience upon men's belief in points of inextricable obscurity almost, of the concordance in working of grace and predestination with free will.[96]

Crompton took a very different view of the matter. To begin with he located the question of free will amongst 'the weightiest topics wherein you [the papists] dissent from the Church of England'.[97] Here, he told the papists, that St Austin teaches that 'man after his fall hath no freedom of will to do good, without the grace of God preventing him and working it in him'.[98] 'Man may turn from good to evil by free will and from evil to good by God's help, not by the freedom of our own will'. 'Grace is not obtained by free will, but our will is truly freed by grace'.[99] 'Man's will in the act of conversion doth co-operate with God's grace, not of itself, but as it is enabled thereunto by the preventing and working grace of God'.[100]

With the issue no longer peripheral, but central, to the debate between Rome and the Church of England, Crompton's whole emphasis was placed on the total depravity of man's will after the fall. Both men might agree on the necessity for prevenient grace, but there their agreement ended.[101]

The doctrine of perseverance – the issue of whether, as Crompton put it, 'true justifying faith, once had, may be lost'[102] – found the pair in open opposition. For Montague, this raised 'points for the maior part' 'fitter for schools than popular discourses, and may be held or not held without heresy either way'.[103] Certainly, the proposition that 'faith once held cannot be lost' was not one which the Church of England had endorsed. On the contrary, there were a variety of viable opinions available on the subject, of which Montague described the view that true faith could be lost both 'totally and finally' as 'indeed the assertion of antiquity and your school'.[104] While formally reserving his own opinion on the subject – 'I determine nothing in this question positively which the Church of England leaveth at liberty unto us' – Montague heavily implied that he himself agreed with antiquity, 'the Protestants of Germany' and the 'Church of Rome', holding that true faith could indeed be lost totally and finally.[105] The opposite opinion he described slightingly 'as a stoical paradox, grounded upon the fatal necessity and concatenation of causes'.[106] As for the 'learnedest in the Church of England they assent unto antiquity in their tenet'.[107] Montague himself went on to produce long passages arguing that just as the faith of reprobates like Simon Magus and Judas had indeed been a true faith, which they had subsequently lost, so the true faith of saints such as David, Solomon or Peter had indeed been totally lost when they fell into sin. Such 'faith' 'totally lost, may eternally be lost, and also not be lost eternally, though totally, for a time, because God again will restore them to grace and, except he would do so, they could not rise to grace but, because his will is not put into practice by his power, he necessitates no man so irreversibly unto life nor death. Those that have lapsed totally may also perish fatally'.[108] So long as 'men in the Church have means in Christ, it is possible' – but, he added, not 'necessary' – for them 'to be renewed by repentance'.[109] In other words, for all his protestations that this was a matter that could safely be left 'to the private opinions of men',[110] there was little doubt where Montague stood on the question of perseverance.

Crompton, of course, took precisely the opposite view. 'That he which once hath received a lively faith and is thereby justified before God can never finally fall away is the tenet of our English divines', and of St Augustine, he proclaimed.[111] Here he adduced two frankly predestinarian arguments:

first that no man can be essentially and effectually justified before God but he that was before predestinated to everlasting life …. Secondly, that no man that is predestinated can fall away finally from the faith …. The number of the elect is so certain that neither one can be added to them, nor one taken away from them, and therefore none of them can finally lose justifying faith.[112]

Thus, while there is 'such a help of perseverance given to the saints that, by this gift, they cannot chose but persevere', the same was not true of the reprobate.[113] 'Some of the sons of perdition, having not received the gift of perseverance, do begin to live in the faith which works by love and a while to live faithfully and justly, and afterwards fall away'. This was to have a 'temporary faith, which may make the sons of perdition seem just for a while, and yet, being unable to endure to the end, do fall away from their seeming justice'.[114]

All of which surely suggests that Crompton's book was indeed a response to *A New Gagg*. (At the very least, almost no clued-up contemporary could have avoided reading it as such.) But if Crompton's book was a reply to Montague's, it was a notably moderate one. It proceeded not through direct assault or refutation, but rather by occupying the same polemical territory; addressing many of the same issues, using the same sorts of argument as Montague had, it sought to use Augustine to move many of the doctrinal positions from which Montague wanted to free the Church of England back into line with what he termed, variously, 'the opinion of the Church of England',[115] 'the doctrine of the Church of England',[116] 'the practice of the Church of England',[117] or 'the common tenet of our English divines',[118] or just simply the 'divines of the Church of England',[119] of whom he mentioned a range, stretching from Hooker and his admirer William Covell to the moderate puritans William Fulke and Andrew Willett. In short, while Montague at least affected to adhere strictly to what the English Church could be said formally to have professed in her foundation documents, which he listed at one point as 'the communion book, the book of articles, the book of consecrating bishops and ordering priests and deacons',[120] Crompton had a far looser set of criteria for determining what the Church of England held. From Montague's perspective this was dangerously close to entrusting the definition of the national Church's position to mere 'private men' and common assumption; precisely, in fact, what he claimed to be reacting, so strenuously, against.

IV Hampton Court Revisited? Great Britain's Solomon Concludes the Crompton Affair

Crompton's book was dedicated to the king's favourite, the duke of Buckingham. In the dedicatory epistle, Crompton recalled the duke's sterling services in the cause of true religion during his trip with Prince Charles to Madrid in pursuit of the Spanish Match. 'It was your constant resolution ... seconded by practice in a foreign nation, where it was most dangerous, that, as you ever had been, so you would continue to be, a defender and professor of the truly ancient Catholic faith, which first gave encouragement to a solitary country muse to present itself to the view of your grace'.[121] Having started with flattery, however, Crompton ended with exhortation.

> Now you can honour God in nothing more than in labouring to defend and countenance the true religion, especially in these dangerous and back-sliding days, and who knows whether he hath not called you to this honour for such a time as this? To invite and entreat your superiors, to instruct and direct your equals, to compel and constrain your inferiors to come and taste of this banquet ... to believe and maintain the truly ancient Catholic faith taught twelve hundred years ago by St Austin, and now maintained by the Church of England?[122]

This, of course, was precisely how Buckingham wanted himself represented in 1624 – as the Protestant champion returned from Madrid who, having stood in the gap against the papists, and seen through the wiles of the Spaniards, was now (with Prince Charles) doing his all to convince a doubting king to defend true religion in a war against Spain. Here, in short, was the language, and indeed the programme, of Professor Cogswell's patriot coalition.[123] It was a rhetoric and agenda fatally threatened by the divisions and passions being unleashed by Montague's book – which, of course, was precisely why Montague and his friends were hoping to get a favourable hearing from James, whose political and diplomatic aims and priorities were decidedly not those of his son and favourite. Given the associations between Crompton's book and the Montague affair, Crompton's calling on Buckingham to rally to the Protestant cause meant more than just seeing off the papists, who had so recently converted his mother, it also meant coming out definitively against the Arminianism of Montague and his ilk.

Not only that, Crompton also petitioned that 'your name and patronage might procure it a freer entrance to his majesty to whose presence (if it be not pressed to death in the way) it hath vowed to come'.[124] The book, then, was designed for James. Moreover, the book did indeed gain access to the royal presence, albeit ironically enough not through Buckingham's patronage but through the activities of Montague's allies at court, anxious to tar both Crompton and Featley with the brush of puritanism. In short, when James sat down to determine what to do about Elton, Crompton and Featley, there was a great deal at stake.

Fortunately, we know a good deal about James's reaction to the affair from three rather different sources. The first is Featley's own printed account, his *Cygnea Cantio* of 1629; the second, a much later manuscript life of Crompton, which reproduces much of Featley's account, adding anecdotal material gathered verbally from Crompton's son and further manuscripts in the son's possession;[125] and the third, certain crucial passages in Laud's diary.[126] Of these, two are retrospective, in Featley's case self-interestedly so, which leaves Laud's diary as the only genuinely primary source generated at the time of the events. However, taken together, they enable us to put together a remarkably clear picture of just what happened.

According to Featley, James interviewed him on two consecutive days; on the first he was cross-questioned over the licensing of Elton's book, and on the second, both Crompton and Featley talked to the king about the defects of *Saint Austins Summes*. Both exchanges seem to have taken place in the presence of Richard Neile and William Laud, but significantly not of Featley's patron, Archbishop Abbot. The manuscript life of Crompton is quite clear in identifying both men as the moving forces behind the affair. 'Two potent prelates, viz. Dr Neile ... bishop of Durham and Dr Laud, bishop of Bath and Wells, complained of Mr Crompton to the king as of a dangerous young man who, if he were not a heretic, yet certainly was a schismatic, no friend to the Church of England, but disaffected to her government'.[127] Neile had possession of Featley's manuscript explanation of his conduct, and Laud was asked first by Buckingham and then by the king to go through Crompton's account of his views 'to correct them as they might pass in the doctrine of the Church of England'. The aggrieved printer involved, Robert Mylbourne, who was 'three score and ten pounds' to the bad after the seizure of nearly 900 of his books and his subsequent imprisonment, was quite definite in fingering Neile's protégé and Montague's intimate, John Cosin, as the man behind the destruction of Elton's book.[128]

Over the conveniently dead Edward Elton, Featley had been able to plead relative ignorance – he had been reading the manuscript with a view to licensing it for the press but had only reached page 52 when news had reached him of Elton's death, whereupon he stopped reading. 'Whilst the author lived', he explained, 'I might and did alter, with his consent, what we thought fit, but after his decease, I left off intermeddling in such a work wherein I could not suffer all things to pass as they were in that copy *bona conscientia*, nor yet change or amend anything *bona fide*'. Thereafter, without Featley's knowledge or permission, the book had found its way into print.[129]

With Crompton's book, however, Featley could not slough the charges off so easily, and his reply to James was that, since the book had come dedicated to Buckingham, he had decided, rather than turning it down flat, to edit and amend it for the press. In other words, he told the king, if you do not like it now, you should have seen it before I started correcting it. To prove the point, the original manuscript copy was produced and Featley showed the king the sections that he had purged. These involved assertions of the essential parity of the clergy, holding that 'the distinction of bishops and presbyters' was not '*de jure divino or apostolico*' but '*de ecclesiastico* only'; that – shades of Elton's book and the Spanish Match – marriage between parties of a different religion was unlawful; and, finally, that the innocent party in a marriage ended for adultery should be able to remarry.[130]

Confronted with Featley's account of his own doings and the range of material in Crompton' s book, in both its purged and unpurged states, what did James do? To which aspects of the book did he take particular objection, and what fate did he visit on poor Crompton? Both accounts agree that, perhaps predictably, James pounced first on the issue of Church government, expatiating on one of his favourite ecclesiastical themes, the *iure divino* status of bishops, and converting, as he thought, Crompton to his view of the matter. The other two censured sections were quickly dismissed as simply wrong, and then James turned his attention to four main issues: Crompton's treatment of the sign of the cross; the role of women in baptising infants in emergencies; whether and in what sense Christ could be said ever to have been ignorant; and whether St Augustine had indeed denied salvation to children that died unbaptised.

On the first point, Crompton, even in the printed version of the book, had ascribed the origins of the ceremony to the heretic Valentinus, acting 160 years after Christ. This claim was part of a longer disquisition in which Crompton made his distaste for the ceremony quite clear. Since its original use had been against 'pagans who used to make it a derision against Christians', 'being now freed from the company of infidels, it is not necessary to continue the practice of it for that end'. As a sign or token of 'man's militancy against the enemies of his soul it might and ought (especially in that infancy of the Church, there being less need in this maturity) to be lawfully used, but to make it a part of baptism, as though baptism were not perfect without it, was then, and is now, unlawful'.[131] This was as close to overtly nonconformist criticism of the national Church as Crompton came and it is surely not going too far to see in this passage a lightly coded message through which he hoped to signal to the alert reader his identity as a man of godly principle, rather than some knee-jerk conformist on the make.

When he had first seen that passage, Featley explained, he had tried to tone it down, firstly by adding the words '(as some report)' before the claim about Valentinus's role in the creation of the ceremony and then by inserting a longer passage at the end of the discussion that was in fact omitted from the printed version. This, however, did not satisfy James who delivered a vindication of the sign's purity and antiquity, based on a re-reading of the passage from Irenaeus cited by Crompton. On baptism by women, James, at least on Featley's account, rather astonishingly rewrote history, denying that he had changed the prayer book on that subject at Hampton Court, since women had never been allowed to baptise in the Church of England. On the issue of Christ's ignorance, that provoked a detailed discussion between James, Featley and Crompton of the relevant scriptural passages and modern authorities, with James discoursing at length on the relative value of modern reformed and patristic authorities in the conduct of theological argument. Finally, on the issue of Augustine's attitude to infant baptism, James dismissed Crompton's attempt to get Augustine off this particular hook. It was an error, and there was an end of it. Again, this allowed James a long excursus on the proper use of the Fathers and a detailed debate on the issue with Featley.[132]

We also know from the manuscript life of Crompton, citing a manuscript until recently in the possession of Crompton's son, that he was also asked to comment on a series of other subsidiary questions, which related in part to his own book and in part to issues raised in Elton's. Clearly the enquiry 'whether there are degrees of angels by creation' referred to Crompton's assertion of their essential equality, in nature if not always in function, and was related to Crompton's similar views on ministerial parity. The interrogatories about whether 'the sacraments do confer grace *ex opera operato*'; 'whether baptism be necessary to salvation'; 'whether Melchisedeck's offering was a sacrifice'; 'whether it was lawful to have images *ad usum historicum*'; and 'whether it was lawful to prescribe days of fasting' all had echoes in the case assembled against Elton. Clearly something like an image of puritan deviance and heterodoxy had been extrapolated out of Elton's texts, and Crompton was being required to locate his views in relation to it.[133]

It is worth noting here the deafening silence on the subject of predestination. For Crompton was told to reply in writing to these queries, extracted from his book, none of which concerned predestination, despite that doctrine's prominence therein. Those questions were probably the origin of the manuscripts that Laud was asked to vet by Buckingham and the king. In short, these exchanges give us precious evidence about James's views on puritanism, predestination and the relations between them in the months immediately before his death.

Judging from a crucial entry in Laud's diary, the question of predestination was now being posed in a peculiarly pointed form at court. The entry reads: 'Thursday I delivered these papers back to Mr Crompton. The same day at York House I gave my Lord of Buckingham my answer what I thought of those papers. The same day I delivered my L. my little tract about doctrinal puritanism in some ten heads, which his grace had spoken to me that I would draw for him, that he might be acquainted with them'.[134] Now while the text of the 'little tract' is lost, we have some sense of its contents from Peter Heylyn's account, in his biography of Laud. 'These doctrinal heads being ten in number', wrote Heylyn, 'related to the indispensable morality of the Lord's day sabbath, the indiscrimination of bishops and presbyters, the power of sovereign princes in ecclesiastical matters, the doctrine of confession and sacerdotal absolution and the five points so much disputed about predestination and the concomitants thereof'.[135]

In short, we have here a condensed version of Montague's picture of the private men who had sought to hijack the position of the English Church, explicitly organised under the heading of puritanism. The list of issues encompassed, on Laud's view, by the term doctrinal puritanism bears, of course, a striking resemblance to the issues thrown up by the furore over Elton's and Crompton's books, now given an explicitly predestinarian twist by the addition of the five points from the Synod of Dort. In line with the polemical tactics pursued in public by Montague, Laud's tract was even more explicit and aggressive since, in effect, it equated with puritanism the five points of Dort, which since they had been approved by the official English delegation, sent by James himself to that synod, had until very recently counted as something like royal policy.

Laud's (and Montague's) was a definition of puritanism that would have encompassed not only Elton and Crompton, not to mention Gataker and Denison, but also the likes of Daniel Featley, and even his patron Archbishop Abbot. On his own view, that of his boss Archbishop Abbot, and, in certain moods, even of James himself, in his role as the licenser as mediator, Featley was, or had been, part of the answer to the problem of puritanism; someone who eased the integration of moderate puritans like Elton and Crompton into the Jacobean Church, by purging their works of their obnoxious puritan excrescences, and then allowing them to join the mainstream of English reformed divinity. But for Laud or Montague or Cosin, all this made him, and his ilk, major facilitators, if not members, of the fifth column of doctrinal puritans busy undermining the national Church from within. On this view, then, the likes of Featley were a very big part of the puritan problem. Thus, we find Montague complaining to Cosin that Lambeth Palace was riddled with 'Dr Featley and his puritans. It will never be well 'til the king rid him out of that house'.[136]

While Montague stuck his neck out in public and in print, typically Laud pursued these tactics only in private, in a document prepared for Buckingham's eyes only, that has not survived. In using Buckingham here as an intermediary to the king, Laud was doing, in manuscript, the equivalent of what Crompton had been trying to do via print.

All of which raises the question of what precisely Buckingham's role was in all this. On the one hand, there was a sense in which Crompton was the duke's client or would-be client. Not only was his book dedicated to the duke, but in the manuscript life of Crompton Buckingham is pictured sedulously protecting the unfortunate clergyman. As soon as he had arrived in London, Crompton 'made his application to the duke, [and] acquainted him with the true state of his controversy'. Buckingham responded by taking Crompton under his wing, instructing him under no circumstances 'to go unto the king till his [the duke's] return from hunting'; a ploy disrupted when Neile and Laud told him that 'being in town, willing or unwilling, he must attend'.[137] Nevertheless, as we shall see, the duke continued to put in a good word for Crompton, and yet it was at Buckingham's request that Laud first got involved in the affair, and at the duke's behest that he wrote 'doctrinal puritanism'. These contradictions can best be explained, if not altogether resolved, by placing these events within what was a crucial juncture in the duke's career. Having, with Prince Charles, after their return from Madrid, moved heaven and earth to construct a 'patriot coalition' behind the policy of war with Spain, Buckingham had naturally both attracted and benefited from the support of hot Protestant and puritan proponents of war like Elton and Crompton. The presence, in both their books, of pointed asides about the danger of marriage to idolators spoke eloquently to their place within that very recent religio-political conjuncture, when the duke's political project had been coterminous with that of the rabidly anti-popish godly. Yet James's agenda had never been that of his son and favourite. While, as Professor Cogswell has shown, the political circumstances of 1623/1624 had allowed a coach and horses to be driven through the royal declaration of 1622, which had forbidden public discussion of predestination, royal marriage and relations with the Church of Rome, there is no reason to suppose that James himself approved of the results. James still wanted to avert war, and, if anything, after the frustrations and short-term defeats of the 1624 Parliament, had even less reason to be reconciled to the godly agenda and style of the likes of Elton and Crompton than he had before. He also had every reason to want to disrupt the always tenuous coherence and unity of the patriot coalition assembled so hastily by Charles and Buckingham.[138]

It is this situation that helps to explain the ambiguous role played in these events by Buckingham. In his continuing pursuit of a forward policy against Spain, he desperately needed the support of the godly. His newfound status as Protestant hero demanded that he be seen to succour the likes of William Crompton in their time of trouble. And yet, at precisely the same time, he was presumably coming under heavy pressure from James to give over his popular wooing of a puritan constituency, the seditiousness of whose views the assault on Elton and Crompton was designed to prove. Into this situation came William Laud: at once, perhaps, the king's man and (as his diary reveals him) a freelancing suitor for the duke's patronage and trust. Laud and the other denizens of Durham house were already well known to the duke; after all, it was to them, rather than the likes of Abbot and Featley, that he and the king had turned to reconvert his mother from her recently acquired Catholicism. In his comments on Crompton's answers, and more explicitly in 'doctrinal puritanism', Laud offered the duke guidance through the thickets of theological controversy in and through which the puritan threat both concealed and revealed its insidiously subversive presence. In short, what was at stake here was a struggle, not just for the king's ear, but also for the duke's. Buckingham responded to these contrary pressures by privately listening to Laud, and speaking up for Crompton before the king. In other words, he refused to decide, and deferred to James.[139]

As for James, the anonymous account later included in the life of Crompton shows him using his interviews with Crompton and Featley to reprise his act as a Solomonic judge, presiding over an exchange of views, alternately agreeing, admonishing and instructing, in effect conducting a royal theology seminar. 'Sometimes the king would vary the question and frown upon Mr Crompton, which did not a little gratify and please his adversaries. At other times his majesty would speak kindly to him, favour him and take his part, which did much amaze and trouble them'.[140] Here was James (again) demonstrating his own learning and acuity, while also drawing the limits of acceptable theological speech and religious opinion. This was the Royal Supremacy in action, personified in the theological facility and political sagacity of the prince, with James's control over proceedings, and indeed over the wider balance of forces in his Church, being reflected back to him in the changing faces and shifting emotions of the participants, as they watched him pick his way through the issues at hand, distributing plaudits and brick-bats, encouragement and admonition, as he went. In the to and fro of theological argument, with all the attention centred on him, James was in his element, but he was also making a political and religious point. It was, in a way, a repeat performance of the Hampton Court Conference, albeit on a far more intimate stage.

By the end, Featley was allowed (successfully) to beg the royal pardon and to kiss the royal hand.[141] As for Crompton, at Buckingham's prompting, the king allowed that he saw much promise in the young man: 'for I see that he hath more ability to encounter an enemy in defence of a very father then some men of greater name in the Church'. At the conclusion of the interview, James gave Crompton forty pieces in gold and sent him packing with the words 'Mr Crompton go home unto your studies, follow them hard and I will take care of your preferment'.[142]

This was to revert to the classic Jacobean method of dealing with puritanism: first ensure outward conformity (which Crompton and Elton, not to mention Gataker and Denison, had always offered, albeit, on rather downbeat terms), then, insist on certain restraints and self-censorings of opinion, certain ritual genuflections before symbolically charged issues (like the *iure divino* status of episcopacy or the sign of the cross) and, finally, round the whole thing off with an offer of reward and preferment in return for good behaviour. Here was the policy of incorporation and inclusion of which Featley had been so enthusiastic and effective an agent, alive and well just weeks before James's death.[143] It was also the sort of indulgence towards the bacillus of moderate puritanism that appalled the likes of Neile, Laud and Montague.

To get a true sense of the significance of this seemingly rather downbeat outcome, we should consider the things that James had not done. Most notably he did not embrace Laud's notion of doctrinal puritanism, or take the opportunity offered to him by Crompton's (and Montague's) books to grasp the nettles of predestination, or of the Antichristian nature of popery or the pope. Quite remarkably given the nature of the central texts and the controversies aroused by Montague's alleged Arminianism, predestination played no role either in James's condemnation of Elton's books, or his cross-questioning of Crompton.[144]

As for the sanctions at his disposal, rather than quietly restoring them to their ministries, James could have come down like a ton of bricks on Crompton, Denison and Gataker. He could have admonished, or disgraced and even sacked Featley. He could even have connected the dots between Featley and Abbot and disgraced, sidelined or even suspended the archbishop. After all, he had done that before, and Charles was to do it again after 1629. He could have roundly condemned Crompton and all his works, and warmly embraced or endorsed the new anti-Calvinist anti-puritanism being pushed, in public and in print, by Montague, and, in private and in manuscript, by Laud. Or he could have done the opposite and embraced the moderate, *sotto voce*, condemnation of Montague contained in Crompton's tract, and thus nipped the Arminian threat in the bud. But he did none of those things, but rather returned to a version of the status quo ante. Featley himself commented on what he termed 'the sweet close which his majesty set … to the late harsh sounding business about the publishing of two treatises',[145] and sought to exploit that outcome by writing and publishing his own account of the affair. According to the printer Mylbourne, James himself approved this tract for print and, it was 'licensed on January 15 and order was given for the present printing thereof'.[146] Remarkably, then, James was quite happy to have his Solomonic performance celebrated in the press, by the very party these proceedings had been intended to ruin.

Yet James was not just reprising the greatest hits of Jacobean consensus, of the Calvinist/reformed hegemony that had previously made it effectively impossible for sentiments like Montague's to get into print.[147] For now, in the face of the fuss stirred up by the *New Gagg*, James was self-consciously expanding the range of the thinkable, sayable and the printable in the most spectacular way, not only by allowing Montague to print his second, even more uncompromising version of his position, in his *Appello Caesarem*, but to do so, as the title implies, in a tract, dedicated to the king, which appealed to James himself in effect to protect and vindicate him from his legion of (puritan) critics. Without doing anything like endorsing their views, James was keeping the Arminian, hyper anti-puritan card very much in play.

While all this certainly represents a significant shift of position on James's part, it seems very unlikely that it was a product of a theological change of mind. No one with an ounce of Arminian principle in them could have viewed Elton's and Crompton's heavily predestinarian texts with the complaisance, indeed total unconcern, displayed by James, who was, it seems, playing politics, not embracing the full-scale Arminian or Laudian agenda being proffered to him in Montague's books, or Laud's 'little treatise'.

How significant this seeming change of royal front would have turned out to be, would have been a function of what happened next. But what happened next was James's death, an event which prevents us from seeing how James would have simultaneously manipulated and contained the forces and passions that he had put in play by seeming to patronise Montague. Certainly, the outcome of the Elton/Crompton affair implies that James had not come down off the fence yet, but rather, by opening up the field of possibilities, he was putting the spotlight back on himself as the ultimate arbiter of events; in the process leaving the various suitors for his favour, and the soul of the national Church, on tenterhooks. It is perhaps not going too far to see this as part of the process, described by Katie Marshalek in the next chapter, whereby James sought to seize the policy initiative back from his son and favourite and thus avoid the worst consequences of the patriot coalition.

Crompton's covert, but doctrinally explicit, response to Montague was only one of a range of possible responses. Some – Matthew Sutcliffe, George Carleton, Daniel Featley amongst them, conformists to a man – would come down hard, using the language, not merely of Arminian but of popish and Pelagian, error, and even heresy, to condemn Montague's views. Others, however, less 'puritan', better connected, or more subtle than such (men like Joseph Hall or Robert Sanderson, or indeed John Cotton), would use precisely the same royal rhetoric of moderation and unity as that invoked by Montague to gloss Montague's book into relative insignificance.[148] Back that sort of solution and all might yet return to something like what had passed for normal for much of James's reign. Perhaps that is what James would have done. But given the complexities of the political/diplomatic/religious situation in the mid-1620s, it is all but impossible to say. (This was an option that remained open to Charles, and one that he sedulously refused to take.)

Certainly, the Elton/Crompton affair reveals, as Katie Marshalek argues in the next chapter, that months, indeed weeks, before his death James remained very much in control of affairs. Not only had he not ceded the making of policy to his son and favourite, his attempts to avoid the sort of war they wanted to fight, of which his manoeuvres in and around the Montague business were surely a part, were to leave them a far more complex and difficult set of problems than they had probably envisaged immediately after their triumphant return from Madrid, or indeed after the conclusion of the 1624 Parliament. On this view, Great Britain's Solomon remained gnomically Solomonic to the very end of his reign, and in so doing, went a good way towards causing the various crises that engulfed his son at the beginning of his.

Notes

1 Edward Elton, *A Plain and Easy Exposition upon the Lords Prayer in Questions and Answers* (1624); and *idem, God's Holy Mind touching Matters Moral which himself Uttered in Ten Words or Ten Commandments* (1625).

2 G. Ornsby (ed.), *The Correspondence of John Cosin* (2 vols, Surtees Society, vols 52, 55, Durham, 1869–72), I, pp. 59, 61: both letters from Petworth in Sussex from Montague to Cosin in February 1624–5.

3 Daniel Featley, *Cygnea Cantio, or Learned Decisions and most Prudent and Pious Directions for Students of Divinity delivered by our Late Sovereign of Happy Memory King James at Whitehall a Few Weeks before his Death* (1629), p. 5.

4 Daniel Featley, *Cygnea Cantio, or Learned Decisions and most Prudent and Pious Directions for Students of Divinity delivered by our Late Sovereign of Happy Memory King James at Whitehall a Few Weeks before his Death*, pp. 5–7.

5 T. Birch, *The Court and Times of James I* (1849), II, pp. 491, 498, letters to Mede from London, dated 21 January 1625 and 18 February 1625, respectively.

6 Thomas Gataker, *Discourse Apologetical wherein Lillies' Lewd Lies in his Merlin or Pasquil for the Year 1654 are Clearly Laid Open* (1654), p. 53.

7 This work (hereafter referred to as Crompton, *Austin*) was incorporated, with a separate title page, into the work on the same topic by Alexander Cooke; see Alexander Cooke, *Saint Austins Religion Wherein is Manifestly Proved out of the Workes of that Learned Father ... that he Dissented from Poperie .... Whereunto is Newly Added, Saint Austins Summes; in Answer to Mr. Iohn Breerely, Priest)* (1625).

8 The definitive account of Featley's career is now Gregory Salazar, *Calvinist Conformity in Post-Reformation England: The Theology and Career of Daniel Featley* (Oxford, 2022). For the Elton business, see Gregory Salazar, *Calvinist Conformity in Post-Reformation England: The Theology and Career of Daniel Featley*, pp. 59–69; also see D. Shuger, *Censorship and Cultural Sensibility: The Regulation of Language in Tudor and Stuart England* (Philadelphia, 2008); C. Clegg, *Press Censorship in Jacobean England* (Cambridge, 2001).

9 Cambridge University Library, MS Gg. 29, fo. 33^{r-v}; for another copy, see Cambridge University Library, Baker MS Mm 1. 43, pp. 513–14; also BL, Harleian MS 3142, part 10, headed 'Reasons for burning Mr Elton's book at St Paul's Cross'.

10 Elton, *God's Holy Mind*, p. 104.

11 Elton, *God's Holy Mind*, p. 122.

12 Elton, *God's Holy Mind*, p. 121.

13 Elton, *God's Holy Mind*, p. 114.

14 Elton, *God's Holy Mind*, pp. 36–7.

15 Elton, *God's Holy Mind*, pp. 38–9.

16 Elton, *God's Holy Mind*, p. 221.

17 Elton, *God's Holy Mind*, p. 117.

18 Elton, *God's Holy Mind*, pp. 118–19.

19 Elton, *A Plain and Easy Exposition*, pp. 123–4.

20 Elton, *God's Holy Mind*, p. 32.

21 Elton, *God's Holy Mind*, p. 95.

22 Elton, *God's Holy Mind*, p. 252.
23 Elton, *God's Holy Mind*, p. 68.
24 Elton, *God's Holy Mind*, p. 68.
25 Elton, *A Plain and Easy Exposition*, p.127.
26 Elton, *A Plain and Easy Exposition*, p. 17.
27 Elton, *A Plain and Easy Exposition*, p. 12.
28 Elton, *A Plain and Easy Exposition*, p. 79.
29 Elton, *A Plain and Easy Exposition*, p. 106.
30 Elton, *A Plain and Easy Exposition*, p. 39.
31 Elton, *A Plain and Easy Exposition*, pp. 46–8.
32 Elton, *A Plain and Easy Exposition*, p. 47.
33 Elton, *A Plain and Easy Exposition*, p. 48.
34 Featley, *Cygnea Cantio*, p. 3.
35 See P. Lake, 'Constitutional Consensus and Puritan Opposition in the 1620s: Thomas Scott and the Spanish Match', *Historical Journal* 25 (1982), pp. 805–25; *idem, The Moderate Puritanism of Samuel Ward (of Ipswich)*, Dr Williams Trust lecture, 2024; and T. Cogswell, 'England and the Spanish Match'. in R. Cust and A. Hughes (eds), *Conflict in Early Stuart England* (Harlow, 1989), pp. 107–33.
36 For Andrewes's anti-puritanism see P. Lake, *On Laudianism: Piety, Polemic and Politics during the Personal Rule of Charles I* (Cambridge, 2023), pp. 66–84; and L.-A. Ferrell, *Government by Polemic: James I, the King's Preachers, and the Rhetoric of Conformity, 1603–1625* (Stanford, CA, 1989).
37 The following paragraphs are based almost entirely on Dr Marshalek's magisterial article 'Putting the Catholics Back In: The "Rise of Arminianism" Reconsidered', *Historical Research* 97 (2023), pp. 238–58.
38 Daniel Featley, *Fisher Catched in his Owne Net* (1623) and George Abbot, *A Treatise of the Visibility and the Succession of the True Church* (1624). This was an extract taken from a tract of 1604 which had been unremarkable at the time, but which changing polemical circumstances had now rendered contentious.
39 Featley, *Cygnea Cantio*.
40 In Featley's words, he 'used the help and advice of Mr Cooke' to 'purge those errors and mend those faults' in Crompton's book: Featley, *Cygnea Cantio*, p. 11.
41 Richard Montague, *A Gagg for the New Gospell? No: a New Gagg for an Old Goose* (1624), p. 42.
42 Crompton, *Austin*, p. 98.
43 Crompton, *Austin*, p. 50.
44 Montague, *Gagg*, p. 246.
45 Montague, *Gagg*, p. 247.
46 Montague, *Gagg*, p. 249.
47 Crompton, *Austin*, pp. 74–5.
48 Crompton, *Austin*, p. 90.
49 Crompton, *Austin*, p. 89.
50 Crompton, *Austin*, p. 90.
51 Crompton, *Austin*, p. 86.
52 Crompton, *Austin*, p. 91.
53 Montague, *Gagg*, p. 250.
54 Montague, *Gagg*, pp. 251–2.
55 Montague, *Gagg*, p. 252.
56 Montague, *Gagg*, pp. 252–3.
57 Crompton, *Austin*, p. 74.
58 Crompton, *Austin*, p. 76.
59 Crompton, *Austin*, p. 102.
60 Crompton, *Austin*, p. 104.
61 Crompton, *Austin*, p. 107.

62 Montague, *Gagg*, p. 49.
63 Montague, *Gagg*, pp. 49–50.
64 Montague, *Gagg*, p. 41.
65 Montague, *Gagg*, p. 41.
66 Montague, *Gagg*, p. 48.
67 Montague, *Gagg*, pp. 47–8.
68 Montague, *Gagg*, p. 46.
69 Montague, *Gagg*, p. 325.
70 A. Milton, *Catholic and Reformed: The Roman and Protestant Churches in English Protestant Thought, 1600–1640* (Cambridge, 1995).
71 One can see here the outlines of the schemes for Church reunion that Montague pursued in the 1630s in a series of exchanges with Gregorio Panzani, the papal agent to the court of Henrietta Maria. See Milton, *Catholic and Reformed*, pp. 220–1, 227–8, 353–9, 362–6, 368–9, 372–3.
72 Crompton, *Austin*, p. 53.
73 Crompton, *Austin*, p. 55.
74 Crompton, *Austin*, p. 55.
75 Crompton, *Austin*, p. 59.
76 Crompton, *Austin*, p. 60.
77 Crompton, *Austin*, p. 59.
78 Crompton, *Austin*, p. 60–1.
79 Montague, *Gagg*, p. 74.
80 Montague, *Gagg*, p. 75.
81 Crompton, *Austin*, p. 191.
82 Crompton, *Austin*, p. 192.
83 Crompton, *Austin*, p. 193.
84 Montague, *Gagg*, p. 177.
85 Montague, *Gagg*, pp. 178–9.
86 Montague, *Gagg*, p. 179.
87 Montague, *Gagg*, p. 180.
88 Montague, *Gagg*, p. 183.
89 Montague, *Gagg*, p. 183.
90 Montague, *Gagg*, pp. 184–5.
91 Crompton, *Austin*, p. 11.
92 Crompton, *Austin*, pp. 11–13.
93 Crompton, *Austin*, p. 13.
94 Montague, *Gagg*, p. 107.
95 Montague, *Gagg*, p. 109.
96 Montague, *Gagg*, p. 110.
97 Crompton, *Austin*, p. 144.
98 Crompton, *Austin*, p. 142.
99 Crompton, *Austin*, p. 143.
100 Crompton, *Austin*, p. 145.
101 Crompton, *Austin*, pp. 144–5.
102 Crompton, *Austin*, p. 150.
103 Montague, *Gagg*, p. 157.
104 Montague, *Gagg*, p. 157.
105 Montague, *Gagg*, pp. 158–9.
106 Montague, *Gagg*, p. 169.
107 Montague, *Gagg*, p. 158.
108 Montague, *Gagg*, pp. 165–6.
109 Montague, *Gagg*, p. 165.
110 Montague, *Gagg*, p. 171.

111 Crompton, *Austin*, p. 150.
112 Crompton, *Austin*, pp. 151–2.
113 Crompton, *Austin*, p. 151.
114 Crompton, *Austin*, p. 150.
115 Crompton, *Austin*, p. 141.
116 Crompton, *Austin*, p. 116.
117 Crompton, *Austin*, p. 98.
118 Crompton, *Austin*, p. 89.
119 Crompton, *Austin*, p. 150.
120 Montague, *Gagg*, p. 325.
121 Crompton, *Austin*, sig. F^v.
122 Crompton, *Austin*, sig. F2^v.
123 T. Cogswell, *The Blessed Revolution: English Politics and the Coming of War, 1621–1624* (Cambridge, 1989); the analysis here and throughout is greatly indebted to Professor Cogswell's work.
124 Crompton, *Austin*, sig. F2^v–3^r.
125 Dr Williams Library, Mss. R.N.C. 38.34, nineteenth century transcripts of J. Quick, *Icones Sacrae Anglicanae*, pp. 187f, for the life of Crompton; for this incident, see esp. pp. 188–90. Unfortunately, the closure of Dr Williams has made it impossible to check these references.
126 See the entries in Laud's diary for 21 and 23 December, 1624, in *The Works of the Very Reverend William Laud, D. D.*, ed. J. Bliss (7 vols, Oxford, 1853), III, pp. 155–6.
127 Dr Williams Library, Mss. R.N.C. 38.34.
128 Featley, *Cygnea Cantio*, 'The printer to the reader', p. 40. Mylbourne hinted at the identity of the spy who had betrayed Elton and others of his friends to the authorities, and then boasted about having got Featley's anti-Montague tract of 1626, *Pelagius Redivivus*, banned, before high-tailing it to the north. When he claimed that the man had 'cousened' himself, Mylbourne in effect outed Cosin, through a heavy-handed pun.
129 Featley, *Cygnea Cantio*, pp. 4–5.
130 Featley, *Cygnea Cantio*, pp. 13–15.
131 Crompton, *Austin*, p. 84.
132 Featley, *Cygnea Cantio*, pp. 15–38.
133 Dr Williams Library, Mss. R.N.C. 38.34.
134 *Laud's Diary*, pp. 155–6.
135 Peter Heylyn, *Cyprianus Anglicus* (1668), pp. 123–4.
136 *Correspondence of John Cosin*, I, p. 40.
137 Dr Williams Library, Mss. R.N.C. 38.34.
138 Cogswell, *Blessed Revolution* and 'England the Spanish Match'.
139 At a similarly crucial moment, the duke was to repeat this equivocal performance at the York House Conference, where his refusal definitively to abandon Montague failed to satisfy his more godly allies like Warwick and Saye and Sele, who proceeded enthusiastically to join in the efforts to impeach Buckingham in the 1626 Parliament.
140 Dr Williams Library, Mss. R.N.C. 38.34.
141 Featley, *Cygnea Cantio*, p. 38.
142 Featley, *Cygnea Cantio*, p. 9, and Dr Williams Library, Quick Mss, 'Life of Crompton'.
143 See K. Fincham and P. Lake, 'The Ecclesiastical Policy of James I', *Journal of British Studies* 24 (1985), pp. 169–207.
144 In addressing Augustine's mistaken opinion about the necessity of baptism, Featley's account has James explaining that in 'vehemently oppugning those

heretics, *that agree with our Arminians* (to wit the Pelagians), who denied original sin in infants and consequently the necessity of baptism, [Augustine] was so far transported to urge the necessity thereof, that he excludeth all infants dying unbaptised from all hope of salvation' (Featley, *Cygnea Cantio*, p. 32). The phrase in italics was also italicised in Featley's text, thus flagging it as an interpellation into what was otherwise presented as James's *ipsissima verba*. In this way, Featley was (tendentiously) imputing to James an assertion of the same equivalence between Arminianism and Pelagianism upon which his own case against Montague turned. (See his *Pelagius Redivivus* of 1626.) Thus, even as he tried to recruit the dead king to his side in the Arminian debates, Featley was forced to admit that James had actually said no such thing, which only serves to emphasise just how sedulously James had, in fact, avoided the topic during the Elton/Crompton affair.

145 Featley, *Cygnea Cantio*, p. 2.

146 Featley, *Cygnea Cantio*, 'From the printer to the reader', p. 39. Mylbourne's memory clearly failed him about the date of the licence. Featley's account did not come out until 1629, when it marketed itself as James's 'swan song' containing pearls of wisdom on the study of theology from the dear departed king. Dedicated to Charles, in the context of 1629, Featley's tract formed part of a campaign, inside and outside parliament, to persuade the son to abandon the Arminians and return to a (Calvinist) version of the father's ecclesiastical policy. By wrapping himself in James's legacy, Featley sought to vindicate himself against those who had 'perhaps intended much evil against me'. He also took the opportunity to demonstrate his long-standing support for *iure divino* episcopacy (about which, he reminded the reader, he had preached two consecration sermons in Archbishop Abbot's chapel at Lambeth) and tore strips off Thomas Cartwright, Robert Parker, the sometime separatist and author of a notorious book denouncing the sign of the cross, and what he termed 'Martin's brood'. Beating up on a radical puritanism that Elton and Crompton had never espoused, enabled Featley to establish his anti-puritan credentials, while creating ideological space for his more accommodating attitude to the moderate puritanism of an Elton, a Crompton or a Stephen Denison, and allowing him (at least partially) to rehabilitate Elton (and to justify his decision to see Elton's book through the press) because of Elton's 'extraordinary painfulness in his pastoral function, even to the enfeebling of his body'. See Featley, *Cygnea Cantio*, pp. 4, 13, 16–17, 19. These tactics were typical of Featley's self-presentation going into the 1630s. See P. Lake, 'The Best Religion? The Revived Ambitions of the Reformed Conformist Establishment, 1637–1640' in E. Counsel and J. Griesel (eds), *Reformed Identity and Conformity in England, 1559–1714* (Manchester, 2024).

147 See N. Tyacke, *Anti-Calvinists* (Oxford, 1987), esp. the appendix on St Paul's Cross sermons; P. Lake, 'Calvinism and the English Church, c. 1570–1635', *Past and Present* 114 (1987), pp. 32–76.

148 For Hall, see P. Lake, 'The Moderate and Irenic Case for Religious War: Joseph's Hall's *Via Media* in Context' in S. Amussen and M. Kishlansky (eds), *Political Culture and Cultural Politics in Early Stuart England* (Manchester, 1994), pp. 313–34; for Sanderson, see *idem*, 'Serving God and the Times: The Calvinist Conformity of Robert Sanderson', *Journal of British Studies* 27 (1988), pp. 81–116; for Cotton, see D. Como, 'Puritans, Predestination and the Construction of Orthodoxy in the Seventeenth Century' in P. Lake and M. Questier (eds), *Conformity and Orthodoxy in the English Church, c. 1560–1660* (Woodbridge, 2000), pp. 64–87.

10

(THE LEGACY OF) JAMES'S COMMON CAUSE, 1624–1625

Kathryn Marshalek

An account of the reign of James VI and I cannot end with his death in March 1625. His political strategies and policy choices profoundly shaped the reign of Charles I. Scholarship has tended to draw a sharp line between the two early Stuart kings, in terms of their temperament, abilities and in the world-views which shaped their decision-making. The result of such a division has tended to work negatively in both directions – with James cast as an incompetent, increasingly senile, coward and fool and Charles as a virtuous and sincere defender of royal dignity, or, alternatively, James as a rational political actor operating under compounding structural issues and Charles as inflexible, duplicitous, with a tendency towards absolutism, unable to manage the balance in Church and state that his father had sustained.[1] The aim of this essay is not particularly to recover the reputation of either king, but to examine the continuity of the political situation between their reigns by emphasising that both James and Charles, whatever their personal in/abilities, were operating within a complicated international and interconfessional political framework, one that was made even more complex by the transitions that ensued after the end of what some scholars call Europe's Short Peace of the early seventeenth century.[2]

This continuity between their reigns is perhaps obvious, in that all monarchs are constrained or enabled by the choices of their predecessors, but the functioning of this continuity across 1624 and 1625 has been largely overlooked. Accounts of Charles's reign identify the later 1620s as a time of avoidable crisis, on a kind of high road to personal rule, while there has been a simultaneous tendency to disregard James as a driver of events in the final year of his reign, with an arguable overemphasis on the seizure of the initiative by Charles himself and by George Villiers, the duke of Buckingham. It is true that,

DOI: 10.4324/9781003319764-11

as James's choices across 1624 and early 1625 would constrain Charles's freedom to manoeuvre as king, Charles's choices as prince likewise constrained his father's political options across that same period. The return of prince and favourite from Madrid in October 1623 without a Spanish bride and with a settled determination to adopt an anti-Habsburg foreign policy forced James to grapple with long-standing domestic demands for a military intervention on the Continent. Here calls for the forceful recovery of the Palatinate – the lost patrimony of his son-in-law, the Elector Frederick V – from the emperor, Ferdinand II, and the duke of Bavaria, intersected with calls for the pursuit of a more aggressive Protestant cause, a cause grounded in a 'conception of the unity of the Reformed Church and the struggle between the Reformed Church and the papal Antichrist', wherein the king of Spain might be discerned as the temporal arm of antichristian Catholicism.[3]

But despite this, and particularly during the 1624 Parliament, James demonstrated a sophisticated ability to adapt and shape both his domestic and foreign policy in a way that opened up the field of political options which had been decidedly narrowed upon Charles's return from Madrid. Confronted with the parliamentary calls to break with Spain and turn to war, James repeatedly made it clear, first, that he was willing to turn back to Spain for a negotiated restoration of the Palatinate; second, that he was not willing to break without sufficient means to support a military intervention; and third, that any war which might follow the breach would not be grounded in religion. His refusal to entertain an anti-Habsburg (much less an anti-Catholic) foreign policy without concrete assurance that he would be backed by parliamentary funds pushed Charles and Buckingham into a position of active mediation between the Commons and the king – managing both the Commons' leveraging of the power of the purse against their demands to break with Spain *and* James's leveraging of his control over dynastic and foreign policy to force the Commons into a vote of supply. James did eventually agree to break the treaties, notably after the Commons agreed to give three subsides and three fifteenths. While James resisted a confessional gloss on this policy shift, the Commons attempted to Protestantise the king's foreign policy by forcing him to accept a petition for religion, having made that petition, as James himself understood, 'a condition *sine qua non*, though [they] not say it plainly' to the completion of the promised subsidy bill.[4] After further mediation by the prince and favourite, James accepted a moderated version of the petition, which not only called for the proper enforcement of the anti-Catholic penal statutes, laws which had lain sleeping during the Spanish negotiations, but also solicited James to declare that 'no treaty whatsoever, for marriage or otherwise', would again allow for the connivance at these statutes.[5] He accepted the petition in late April, and, after the House assigned a day for the collection of the first subsidy and fifteenth, James issued a proclamation ordering all Catholic priests and Jesuits to depart the realm by 14 June, upon the threat of severest penalty.[6]

While he indulged the anti-Catholic petition to secure supply, James also made it clear that, in addition to requiring financial assistance from his parliament, he would also need to 'call into his assistance many princes' of Catholic Europe to counter the 'ambition of the house of Austria'.[7] Across the early spring of 1624, the mercenary commander Count Ernst von Mansfelt was darting between London and Paris, proposing his services for the pursuit of a broad-based anti-Habsburg common cause – a joint league between England, France, Venice and Savoy which would fund an army to march 'up into Germanie for the recovering' of the Palatinate and would support the deliverance of the Valtelline corridor 'out of the Sp[aniard's] clawes'. A Spanish-backed Catholic revolt in the Valtelline, a critical Alpine pass in North Italy, against their Swiss Grison rulers had spurred French intervention in the region, where the duke of Savoy and the Venetian doge were likewise interested in toppling Habsburg control and restoring access to the valley pass. French support for this common cause was to be secured through a match between Charles and the sister of Louis XIII, Henrietta Maria – negotiations for which had begun in February, when Henry Rich, Lord Kensington, was sent as extraordinary ambassador to Paris. While Kensington was persuaded that the French would make a match with 'no longeness in condiscions for our Catholickes', the concessions that might be demanded within a cross-confessional alliance would work at cross purposes with the confessional cause within which many MPs clearly viewed the breach with Spain.[8]

James had regained, then, considerable strategic latitude in the face of Charles's and Buckingham's anti-Habsburg turn through the pursuit of conflicting policies – he had made his *sine qua non* for breaking the Spanish treaties and for intervening in the Palatinate the formation of a common cause league, a course seemingly incompatible with a domestic policy grounded in the renewed persecution of English Catholics. Yet, by the end of the session, this policy approach had left James in a satisfactory position: he had been voted supply, enough to fund military preparations until the proposed parliamentary session in November; he had broken the Spanish treaties without directly embroiling himself in a war with Spain; and, through Kensington's embassy, he had set the ground for a French Match, the terms of which, it did not appear, would require him to breach (or at least not egregiously so) his promises to enforce the anti-Catholic penal statutes.

While the Parliament of 1624 has, rightly, been treated as a watershed moment in both James's reign and in Charles's development as a political actor, much less attention has been given to the logic of, and consequences of, James's manipulation of domestic and foreign policy in the aftermath of this Blessed Revolution. Between the end of the parliamentary session and his death in

March 1625, James remained committed to the formation of a cross-confessional league for the narrow objective of the recovery of the Palatinate – a policy commitment which would require a tangle of barely compatible commitments to foreign and domestic audiences to sustain. In the short term, by continually postponing another parliamentary session, James was able to chart a narrow way between the domestic pressures of a transnational Protestant cause and the foreign pressures of a parallel Catholic cause. But, the long-term un/tenability of these entangled policies would become clear by June 1625, when Charles's French bride arrived in London just days before the young king opened his first parliament. The policy breakdown experienced by Charles in the first year of his reign can be attributed in large part to shifting circumstances of European geopolitics, but this essay suggests that James's reaction to those same circumstances, his attempt to work through compounding international and interconfessional constraints in the final year of his reign, profoundly limited Charles's freedom of action at his accession and, indeed, set up the tensions that would characterise his son's reign.

I

In the immediate aftermath of the 1624 parliamentary session, there remained some uncertainty over James's domestic policy course, in particular, his commitment to enforcing both the anti-Catholic penal statutes and the proclamation banishing Catholic clerics. As one Catholic priest observed, James 'did clearly shew that he wold never have made this proclamation if he co[u]ld otherwise have gotten the parliament to graunt him subsidies'.[9] Accordingly, some believed that, after the dissolution of the parliament, the king might revoke the proclamation before the day by which the clergy were ordered to depart.[10] But that day came and went, and, on 17 June, a London Catholic clergyman, one Father William Davies, was arrested.[11] The same day that Davies was detained, John Woodford, a secretary of the ambassadors in Paris, arrived in London with the proposed terms for the Anglo-French Match. With Woodford's arrival, it became clear that, despite Kensington's earlier assurances to the contrary, the French would ask for real concessions for James's Catholic subjects. Indeed, Louis hoped to 'obtain as many advantages for the faith as the Spaniards had', including an assurance that 'no harm shall be done to the Catholics' and that this liberty of conscience would be 'announced in parliament'.[12] This, as the papal nuncio in France maintained, would be necessary to secure the dispensation from Rome.[13]

Less than a month after the end of the parliament, and eight weeks after the king had accepted the Commons' petition for religion, it appeared that James would no longer be able to sustain this rather complex balancing act: the balancing of, on the one hand, the domestic demands of a transnational Protestant cause, and, on the other, the demands of an ideological 'inverse version of political reality' which would be recognisable to some contemporaries as a 'Catholic cause'.[14] Louis, under pressure, both from Rome and from a domestic faction of *dévots*, who would rather that he extirpate the Huguenots at home than enter into a league with English heretics, could not be seen to abandon confessional solidarity with the persecuted community of English Catholics. This confessional pressure on Louis was here transferred to James, with demands for visible concessions for Catholics which would be difficult to reconcile with the promises he had just offered his parliament.

These tightening knots of policy, however, were momentarily loosened with the unexpected arrival of Lord Kensington just days after Woodford. The ambassador carried with him moderated terms, formulated by the chief commissioner for the match, the marquis de la Vieuville, who apparently feared that 'upon Mr Woodfords report' of their 'stiffenes in the poynt of religion', James might break off the treaties with an 'inclination to looke backe to Spayne'.[15] As one English Catholic observer reasoned, if the French 'asketh the same condi[t]ions, or better, than Spaine', the king would 'rather matche with Spaine', who offered a larger dowry and the restoration of the Palatinate 'with out ware and bloudshedde'.[16] Here, James's threatened reversion to Madrid – something of a liability during the parliamentary session – seemingly worked in his favour. Kensington now brought word that the French only sought 'some handsome pretext to cover their honor with all against the calumnies of Spaine and other Jesuitically-affected persons, who' if 'nothing be obteyned in favor of the Catholiques', would 'exclude them' from 'the ordinary number of Christians'.[17] As Kensington now described, the French propounded these articles, 'not with any hope to obtayne them', but rather 'to make them the lesse blamable at Rome, where otherwise they wold bee acused to have done litle for the Catholicke cause'.[18]

Facing the pressures of a transnational Catholic cause, and the need to facilitate the papal dispensation, the French would ask James to make concessions, but with terms which Vieuville insinuated would 'not be pressed further in the execution'.[19] Most importantly, in contrast to the terms brought by Woodford, James would not be required to alter his confessional policy through a public article or through parliament, but rather might offer a private letter to Louis as security.[20] Such a formulation would enable James to maintain his conflicting policies – it presented a matrix of cross-promises that would allow him to press forward with the French Match and secure his common cause war effort without directly alienating the parliamentary body which would be necessary to continue to fund such an action.

While this formulation did not require the open abrogation of the anti-Catholic penal statutes, the maintenance of these cross-promises would be grounded in James's connivance at the law. The fate of Father Davies would provide an early demonstration of how James might manage his conflicting domestic and dynastic commitments. One week after Kensington's arrival at court, on 28 June, Davies was sent to Tyburn, but, 'when all was readie', a dramatic stay of execution arrived from the king.[21] That same day, James, understanding that other priests had already been 'arraigned and condemned', sent instructions to the Recorders of London that they were to 'stay the execution of anie priests' until they had 'given an accompt unto him and receaved his pleasure'.[22] The proclamation would stand, but, in practice, James had removed its bite.

James took a similar approach to the statutes exacting financial penalties against Catholic recusancy – namely, the collection of a 12d fine for absence at Church of England services, or, if unable to pay, the sequestration of two-thirds of the recusant's goods and lands. The proper enforcement of these statutes had formed part of the parliamentary petition for religion and James did indeed order his officers to proceed 'according to the lawes'. However, he directed that the 'execution' of those laws should be suspended until his 'pleasure were further knowne'.[23] This would make it appear that the law was being enforced – writs for the assessment of owed recusant monies and goods would be sent out – but would allow James to indicate his pleasure that the assessed penalties not be collected.

Balancing this impression both of enforcing the letter of the law and, equally, dispensing from its severities, proved difficult – made the more so by complaints of persecution from English Catholics which quickly made their way to Paris and Rome. By late June, English secular priests were flooding a transnational Catholic news circuit with accounts of the state's 'informants', busy 'above belief', and of the hundreds, if not thousands, of writs to seize recusant lands and goods which had already gone out.[24] In letters to Rome, English Catholics insisted that, unless 'mediation' was provided by Louis and his ambassador in London, the newly arrived Marquis D'Effiat, there was 'little hope' for relief.[25] These reports ramped up the pressure in Paris, in effect, by an appeal to a broadly constituted Catholic cause, that is, through claims upon confessional solidarity among Catholics, and a transnational obligation on their part to aid suffering co-religionists.

This pressure was seemingly effective. As the resident ambassador in Paris, James Hay, earl of Carlisle, discovered in late July, the 'state of the recusants in England hath bene (by some bodie's letters from thence) represented here under a bitter persecution'.[26] Louis apparently found the news of a 'great persecution against the Catholiques ... somewhat strange', and thought it reflected poorly on his honour that, while treating with Spain, James had 'take[n] away the lawes against them', and now 'in the like treaty', James 'proceed[ed] with that rigor'. Carlisle, in turn, emphasised that 'to take away the lawes' was not in the king's power 'without his Parlement', and that James could only 'exercise his grace against the penalty and execution therof'.[27] While this reliance on royal connivance was in line with the interpretation provided by Vieuville, Louis apparently now insisted that 'continued persecution may break off all negotiations'.[28]

On 4 August, Lord Kensington (newly raised to the peerage as earl of Holland) returned to Paris, authorised by James to complete the match upon the terms he had brought in mid-June – those terms conceived by Vieuville. Just the day before Holland's arrival, however, Vieuville fell from royal favour and was placed under house arrest. This court reshuffling, as Carlisle described, was 'like to give great hinderances and alterations to the pursuit of our negotiations here'. Carlisle suspected the French ministers, in particular Cardinal Richelieu, whose influence on the match negotiations rose with Vieuville's fall, would labour with all 'their wit and diligence by improving the conditions of the treaty to the advantage of the state and Rome'.[29] The English ambassadors were now told that, while the private letter from James 'assuring the indulgence for the Catholiques', would satisfy Louis, it would 'not satisfy the pope, and till he were satisfyed, there was little hope for getting a dispensation'.[30] Rather, the new commissioners, Henri de Schomberg and Henri-Auguste de Loménie, seigneur de Ville-aux-Clercs, who, alongside Richelieu, would negotiate the Anglo-French alliance, insisted that there would have to be a signed and sworn promise attesting to the concessions for Catholics.[31] Carlisle and Holland protested that, 'howsoever they qualified it *une escript particulier*', the act of 'signing and swearing' an oath 'made it an article'. The king, they emphasised, 'was engaged to his parliament to a quite contrary care', that 'no such article would be obtruded upon him'. The French commissioners, however, 'shrunk up the[ir] shoulders' and repeated that 'without such an oath … they could have no hope of any dispensation'.[32]

When this news arrived then in London, James insisted that he could not agree to any 'article nor goe further than the letter which was required' in Vieuville's formulation – 'the government and reason of state of his kingdome and people' would not 'permitt' it.[33] As the Venetian ambassador in London observed, the English Catholic issue would be 'the rock upon which the French alliance will either split, or the king will break with parliament, a rupture that would deprive him of the necessary subsidy'.[34] But this did not prevent James's own further manoeuvres. In late August, after extended discussions with the ambassador D'Effiat, James admitted some 'qualificcations or reformaccions in certane articles', including an agreement to sign a 'secret article' on behalf of the Catholics.[35] Carlisle and Holland continued their parallel negotiations in Paris, eventually coming to a form of the *escript particulier* which was thought to permit a 'double interpretation', so that its sense 'to the pope might include no lesse in effect' than what was demanded, but 'his Majesties sence to his subjects might contayne no such thing'.[36] With an eye towards Rome and towards Westminster, this was, again, an effort to construct terms that might allow, indeed, encourage, conflicting interpretations of James's policy.

Yet, as the buzz of dissatisfaction among those in England who identified as Roman Catholics continued to reach the Continent, James was forced into a more direct statement of his confessional policy. In late September, 'at the insistence [of] the French ambassador', James wrote to the chancellor of the Exchequer, Richard Weston, explaining that he had 'receaved information from sundry partes of this realme' that 'diverse under-sheriffs, and other inferior ministers' were not only assessing the recusancy penalties against Catholics, but were seizing their goods and 'sell[ing] away the goods of those recusants'.[37] James stressed that it was his 'expresse pleasure' that Weston 'taike notice of those complaints and give order that the sherriffs and their ministers abstaine from seezing the goods', making appraisements only and then redelivering the goods upon bonds.[38] In response to this order, local officials complained to the council over the 'false accusation' of their 'hastie sezinge' of recusants' goods, and pressed, rather that some of those recusant Catholics, 'soe rich in the attributes of the divell', might be 'made examples' of.[39] While the orders to Weston aggravated the under-officers who were now explicitly told to negate the effects of the law, James's instructions did little to quiet complaints of persecution. English Catholics balked at the notion that they were to celebrate the order. In the view of one secular priest, it was hardly effectual relief if they could keep their goods but would be 'bound to the king for so much money as they are prised', ready to be called upon 'for this debte when it shall please'.[40] Rather than rely on royal connivance at the law, some Catholics reportedly desired the ambassador D'Effiat to petition James for a '*supersedeat* under the public seal for non-execution', something 'entirely contrary to the laws and to the decisions and promises made to the parliament'.[41]

The looming prospect of parliament, initially adjourned to 2 November, was a central part of these claims and counterclaims around the treatment of English Catholics, who had to be mollified to secure the dispensation from Rome, but not given so much visible favour that the parliament would attempt, as it was now rumoured, to break the match. Either a 'breach of the promises made to parliament or a failure to stipulate the conditions for the Catholics would break off the marriage'. Facing pressure from all sides, James delayed the parliament until February, seemingly so that the body might 'accept the marriage as an accomplished fact, without question'.[42]

The religious issue, however, was not the only difficulty which had arisen in the Anglo-French negotiations. Rather, the common cause military alliance – the foundation of James's intervention on the Continent and the justification for the French Match (and the religious concessions he would make to secure that match) – likewise appeared at risk. In early October, James accepted Mansfelt's proposition for a military expedition for the recovery of the Palatinate, at the cost of £20,000 a month and levies of 12,000 foot and 2,000 horse.[43] On 5 October, Secretary Edward Conway sent a letter to Carlisle and Holland advertising that James had 'soe farr approved' of Mansfelt's propositions, but with 'reservation of this unmovable position': before James would 'put in execution anie thinge', the 'hand' of 'the French king must declare' his commitment to the action.[44] James demanded a categorical assurance, in writing, that the French would join in an offensive and defensive military alliance, joining the recovery of the Palatinate and the Valtelline together in a common cause.[45]

But, just as James attempted to secure the league under Mansfelt, the French negotiators pressed, again, for their own written and signed promises, now rejecting the form of James's letter which was to serve as effectual fulfilment of the secret article for English Catholics.[46] On 9 October, the English ambassadors reported that they were left singing 'a song to the deafe', for the French 'would not endure to heare of' the letter promising concessions to English Catholics endorsed only by James. Carlisle and Holland subsequently offered 'the same to be further signed by' Charles 'and a secretary of state', but this too 'would not serve the turne'. As the French continued to ratchet up the security required for the secret article, the commissioners apparently 'wondred much to see such stiffness' from the ambassadors – D'Effiat had apparently 'written to them' that James 'had accorded whatsoever they sought, both for matter and forme'.[47] The king's repeated willingness to bend, rather than to break, seemed to create an impression that James might be made to twist himself even further out of shape.

In turn, Carlisle and Holland reasoned that, if James were to bend further, that is, if he would 'come so thoroughly home to them in all and every point of their demaunds', then Louis should 'meet him by as franck and punctuall observances of those promises' made at the start of their treating – namely, a promise to enter a league, 'not only defensive but offensive for the Palatinate'. The commissioners answered that, as for an offensive league, they had 'never promised any till the marriage should be consummated, and then meant it not under writing'. There would be a 'reall and actuall performance', but to 'capitulate … in writing would cast rubs in the way of the dispensation'. The French insisted that it would 'highly offend the pope to hear they should enter into an offensive league with heretiques against Catholiques'.[48]

However, there were concurrent rumours that Pope Urban was willing to give 'carta bianca unto the princes of the League' concerning the Valtelline corridor, 'uppon condition that the Palatinat may rest as it doth'. The great danger, then, was that 'if advantage be not taken of this present conjuncture', then 'it may bee feared that' James would 'be left alone to recover the Palatinat with his owne forces' – precisely what he had attempted to avoid in forming a common cause.[49] Accordingly, while James was 'disinclined for the marriage without a joint agreement' for the Palatinate, he was convinced, in part, by 'the necessity of either allying with France or making her as his enemy', to 'consent to signing the marriage articles separately' and to rely upon Louis's royal promise that he would provide Mansfelt with financial 'support for six months, a passage for his English troops through France and a safe retreat in that kingdom in case of need'.[50] With this bare promise, on

10 November, the articles of the marriage were committed in Paris. Within days, arrangements were made for Mansfelt's payment; the governors of Calais and Boulogne were given order to prepare for the passing, lodging and potential retreat of Mansfelt's troops; and a call was made for 2,000 horse to be put at readiness.[51]

As preparations for war now progressed, there was a renewed threat that Mansfelt's forces might be drawn into a directly anti-Spanish version of this anti-Habsburg common cause. In late August, Spanish forces under the famed Marquis Spinola laid siege to the Dutch city of Breda. Conditions in the city quickly deteriorated, and, by October, some in England hoped that Mansfelt's newly contracted force would be sent to relieve this suffering front line of the European Protestant cause. Word from Madrid, however, indicated that if Mansfelt were to be 'sent to succor Breda', the Spaniards would interpret this as a 'breach of the peace', and would 'presently fall with' their armada 'upon some part of Ireland'.[52] King Philip, assuming that 'those great preperacons for warre' now underway were 'maynely bent aginst him, though covered with other pretexts', had begun to strongly 'arme himselfe'.[53]

This was an interpretation of English foreign policy that might be both feared in Madrid and endorsed at Westminster – that, as the seizure of the Palatinate formed only part of the usurpations underlying universal Habsburg monarchy, the forceful recovery of the Palatinate would form only part of a broader anti-Habsburg war, a war which would include Spain. But James had never fully committed to a war with Spain, particular one which, given the weak military agreement with France, he might be left to fight alone, or allied only with the Dutch. Accordingly, in mid-November, as Spinola's grip tightened around Breda, James clarified that Mansfelt's forces would 'do no harm to his friends and allies', among whom James expressly included 'the Catholic king [of Spain] and the infanta of Brussels'.[54] Mansfelt would only be directed to proceed 'against those who hold the Palatinate', meaning Ferdinand and the duke of Bavaria.[55] Despite the concurrent preparations of the navy, which, it was widely assumed, would be directed against the Spaniards in a revival of Elizabethan policy, James now made it clear that he had no intentions of entering into an Anglo-Spanish war at this conjuncture – a war which many MPs thought they had voted supply to fund – a war which might have rendered the dynastic alliance with the French palatable.

Exactly how unpalatable the alliance would prove, how much James would agree to swallow to push the match through, was not yet clear when the French commissioner Ville-aux-Clercs arrived in England to oversee the signing of the marriage treaty in early December.[56] There were, however, rumours that the conditions for English Catholics were 'as advantageous to the papists', as those which 'were agreed for the Spanish Match'.[57] Dudley Carleton predicted that 'the parlament will be but meanely satisfyed' if those rumours proved true.[58] On 12 December, James and Charles signed 'a confirmation of the articles of marriage', along with a separate 'French paper' under 'the title of Secret Escript'.[59] The long-fought-over secret article, the *escript*, granted James's 'Catholic subjects security of life and property without their being interrogated about the Catholic faith' – with Ville-aux-Clercs's intervention, James agreed, not to grant *faveur* to his Catholic subjects (as his ambassadors had negotiated in Paris), but *liberté*.[60] Further, Ville-aux-Clercs made it clear that he would remain in England after the signing and swearing to oversee the 'legal formalities' for the execution of what had been promised for the English Catholics.[61] This was a fresh insistence that James promptly perform the terms he had agreed to – pressure from the French ministers which was perhaps correlated with news from Rome that the dispensation was provisionally granted, but that the pope 'desired some pledge in the interests of religion' and would 'require some more explicit promise from this king'.[62]

Across the final week of December 1624, James made good on the secret article. 'In contemplation of the match', he issued a wave of royal orders reining in the enforcement of the anti-Catholic penal statutes. He ordered his judges and officers to 'forbeare … all manner of persecution against any the subjects Roman Catholiks for the exercise of ther religion'. James commanded that all prosecutions in the High Commission be stayed; that the 'penaltie of twelve pence imposed upon them by statute, for everie Sonday they goe not to church' go unexacted; and that the penalties which had been levied and paid into the Exchequer since Trinity Term now be returned.[63] All 'priests, Jesuites, fryers, and other Romaine Catholiques' presently imprisoned 'for several offences' made treasons, felonies, or offences of praemunire, by either Elizabethan or Jacobean statutes, were to be 'sett at liberty'.[64] The promises made to parliament in May 1624 to enforce the existing anti-Catholic penal statutes and to banish all priests and Jesuits had been replaced, just six months later, with royal orders indicating James's pleasure that English Catholics not be molested for the practice of their religion, that financial penalties for recusancy not be collected, and that nearly all imprisoned Catholics, both clerics and laity, be granted full liberty.

But, if reason of state – the securing of James's common cause – was supposed to warrant the cost of the match, the king's foreign policy was not proceeding in a manner that justified such a purchase price. James's order that Mansfelt 'not attack the dominions of the king of Spain in Flanders on his way through' to the Palatinate had come as something of a shock when reports reached Paris on 6 December. Louis, under a great deal of pressure at home and abroad, had just turned his back on a continental Catholic bloc in order to further his interests against Spain, and the altered commission for Mansfelt now 'filled everyone with disgust'.[65] On 17 December, Carlisle and Holland sent a panicked letter to Secretary Conway, begging for further instruction regarding James's foreign policy – his own ambassadors had seemingly been operating under the assumption that the moment had 'come to overthrow this Spanish monarchy, which so greatly disturbs the universal quiet and liberty'.[66]

Carlisle and Holland added that they were 'sorry' that James's refusal to enter into a war with Spain had come at 'this conjuncture', when the French 'affaires' were 'so fortunately successfull in the Valtelina'. By mid-December, reports out of Italy indicated that the French were edging towards a real victory in the Valtelline corridor – the marquis de Coeuvres, François Annibal d'Estrées, had advanced through the southern Rhaetian Alpine region and had 'reduced all the country of the Grisons to an acknowledgment of this kinges [Louis's] authority'. As Carlisle and Holland expressed, this series of quick victories meant that if 'any discouragement be given unto [the French], they may content themselves with the honour which they have purchased beyond the mountains and accepte of the conditions of accommodation as will be offered unto them'.[67] In other words, Louis might do exactly what James had attempted to prevent with his insistence on a sworn defensive and offensive alliance: the French might settle with Spain in the Valtelline and abandon the campaign for the Palatinate.

Compounding this problem, just as the marriage treaties were sworn in London, the French Huguenots began to stir around La Rochelle – one of the two remaining Protestant strongholds permitted by the Treaty of Montpellier after the unsuccessful revolt led by the duke of Rohan in 1621–1622. In early January 1625, Rohan's brother, the duke of Soubise, captured several royal ships in the port before the city and seized the Île de Rhé, off the coast of La Rochelle. As a result, 'all men' were 'eger and sharpe against those of the Religion'. As one English observer in Paris remarked in early January, 'the affaires here ... have taken a new face within these few dayes' – there was no longer speech of 'recovering the Palatinat and Valtelin', but only of 'going against those of the Religion'.[68] While Louis assured the English ambassadors that the 'insolencies' of Soubise would 'alter nothing in the resolutions he had taken for the publique good', he now refused to allow Mansfelt to make his passage to the Palatinate through France, as had been agreed (but not as a sworn article) in November. He suggested, rather, that the count should put ashore at Bergen-op-Zoom, the closest port city to Breda, or some other port in Holland or Flanders.[69] While various excuses were made, the real 'reasons for this change' appeared clear: 'they did not want so many English in their country, who would only reinforce the Huguenots'.[70] English (Protestant) soldiers marching through France, combined 'with such a large number of Huguenots', could leave Louis in some 'danger'.[71]

James did what he could to counteract this interpretation, insisting that, despite their shared confessional interests, he found Soubise's enterprise 'a bad action'. James assured Louis that the rebels would 'get no help here', and indeed, he was 'ready to supply ships to punish' Soubise 'and if necessary to take la Rochelle'.[72] This was an attempt by James to slip free from the demands and assumptions of a transnational Protestant cause, but Louis's continued refusal to allow Mansfelt to pass through France threatened to push James closer to the centre of that cause: the besieged city of Breda. To force Louis into a reconsideration, James, in turn, refused to allow the count to make his landing in the Low Countries.[73] This set off a diplomatic back-and-forth that James could not afford to entertain – at least not for long. Mansfelt and his pressed soldiers were now sitting at Dover with no direction. They were ill-provisioned and his men were daily reduced, either dead of disease or 'run away'.[74] Something had to give, soon, 'or the action on which the worlds eye is would vanish and come to nought'.[75] Under pressure, on 25 January, James consented to Mansfelt's passing through the Low Countries, but was careful to reconfirm that he was not to make 'anie hostile attempt' upon the 'dominions or lawfull inheritances, and possessions of our deere brother the kinge of Spaine'.[76] They were 'by no meanes to goe neare Breda'.[77]

The count made landing at Flushing on 2 February. His English forces were 'in bad condition' and it was not thought that he 'could force his way through a hostile country with this army'.[78] Mansfelt required more money – money which would 'not easily be obtained' unless James acted in 'conformity with the wishes of the parliamentarians'.[79] Given the sweeping concessions he had just granted to the English Catholics, James could not risk opening the parliament before the bride made her own landing in England. Parliament was now deferred until 15 March, as James attempted to gain time to clear the remaining obstacle to the marriage: the papal dispensation.[80]

On 3 February, the dispensation arrived in Paris.[81] When the terms were handed over to Carlisle and Holland, Ville-aux-Clercs admitted he was 'ashamed to reade' them, but professed that 'they were such conditions as the pope had limited the dispensation unto, and they were bound to present them'.[82] There were several key alterations, the most controversial being that Louis was to take an oath to the pope, based on a *public* oath by James and his ministers, to uphold the toleration of the English Catholics. This was a step that James had long resisted as impossible to square with his promises to parliament. Carlisle and Holland urged James to reject the 'presumptuous and unseasonable demandes' of the dispensation 'with a sharpe, stoute nega-tive' – to admit any of these terms would be 'to enter into a new treaty, to the losse of tyme, hazard to the whole business, and to give them courage and appetite to presse for more'.[83] Carlisle suggested that inflexibility at this con-juncture would not lead to a 'break' but would rather 'facilitat and secure the marriage'.[84] But whether the French would now press the terms of the dispen-sation to the point of a breach remained unclear. Ville-aux-Clercs had been heard to say that 'if these nue conditions were refused' in London, it would only 'cost another jorny to Rome' – then they would see 'who shall have it worst by the delay, eyther France or England'. This was, perhaps, spoken as 'a threatening', presuming that James would 'graunt any thing rather then deffer a weekes time'.[85]

This threatening, however, carried the weight of truth. Delay would prove costly for James. Mansfelt had just landed at Flushing, in desperate need of money which could not be supplied without calling parliament, and parliament could not be called before the match was secured. As one English Catholic priest observed in late February, there was 'not anie great probabilitie for [Mansfelt] to doe anie thing either for the releaving of Breda or the recoverie of the Palatinate' – the money 'which our hot headed puritaynes gave for the recovering of the Palatinat' in the last parliament had all been spent, and 'that enterprise' was 'as farr from atchiving' its goal 'as it was before they began', perhaps even 'further' off, considering that the French now seemed to gather 'together on this syde', the side of the Catholic cause, for the 'peace of Gods church'.[86]

For, while Mansfelt's forces languished off the Dutch coast, Coeuvres's army in North Italy moved from strength to strength, 'working miracles in the Valtelline'.[87] In early February, the French had encountered the Spaniards at Campo, and 'put [them] to flight'. This victory, and the 'faintness' of the Spaniards on that occasion, gave the French (and their Italian allies) 'courage' not only to retake the Valtelline but to aim at the territories of Spanish-allied Genoa and Milan. To 'stopp the course of these proceedings', the pope now entreated the Spaniards to 'treate an accommodation' – for that purpose, Urban appointed his nephew, Cardinal Francesco Barberini, to travel to France as papal legate. It was rumoured that Barberini's legation was to 'procure the two crownes of France and Spaine to joyne with the emp[eror], the pope, and Bavaria in an universal extirpation of heretiques'.[88] Given the fresh revolt of the Huguenots, there was a reasonable threat that Louis might flinch at this critical point. For James then, a dispensation-induced delay of the marriage would not only threaten the success of Mansfelt's campaign by delaying expected parliamentary funding, but it would also open a window for Barberini to negotiate a peace between Spain and France in North Italy, effectively destroying the foundation of James's common cause. In a contest of who would 'have it worst by the delay, eyther France or England', the winner, or rather, the loser, was evident.

Still, James was resistant to the terms of the dispensation. When news arrived on 21 February, the king's 'offended patience expressed it selfe much att the severall novelties mixed in with the olde articles'.[89] He declared that he had already 'condescended unto all that was possible for him to yield unto'. James's 'earnestness' in the business had 'perhaps perswaded that kings ministers to think that hee will swallow all things' – he had, indeed, 'passed by' Louis's 'receding from some articles and pressing of others more violent than those of Spaine'; he had passed 'by all his councell'; and he had put 'off his parliament twice' in order to push the match through. In return, the French had treated him 'worse than Spaine' with these 'unjust and unlaw-full demands'.[90]

Despite this high language, James would again be drawn to compromise. Fresh couriers from Paris arrived soon after the initial dispatch, bringing 'from the mouth of some of that kings ministers a discourse intimating qual-ifications, and a new way of fast and loose upon the mixture of the articles and propositions'.[91] On 27 February, D'Effiat met with James, Charles, and Secretary Conway – they engaged in a meeting that lasted from eight in the morning to eleven at night.[92] Louis had provided his own 'sense' of the terms, which he thought would give '*commun contentement*'.[93] It was emphasised that the distance between the signed articles and the terms of the dispensation was not so great, as the Latin apparently appeared more harsh than the French translation.[94] The greatest obstacle was understood to be the request from Rome for the publicisation of the *escript particuler*. Louis here clarified that what had already been sworn by James would not now be requested '*en autre forme, ni d'etre mis en autre lieu*'. While Louis would never desire any-thing from James '*qui puisse blesser ses affaires*', there was a suggestion that James might extend his favour if he found it expedient.[95] This gentle nudge towards flexibility was followed by a reminder of the urgency of Mansfelt's expedition: the freshly arrived couriers not only brought Louis's interpreta-tion of the terms, but also the money owed for the transport of the French horses for Mansfelt's force.[96]

Again and again, James would prove himself flexible on the religious terms in order to push forward seemingly the one policy on which he would not bend – the necessity of the Anglo-French alliance to his common cause, and the necessity of that common cause to any anti-Habsburg war that he would fight. On 1 March, James's own 'explanations' of the terms of the dispensa-tion were dispatched to Carlisle and Holland. While the king had been 'resolved' to 'stick absolutely to the negative concerning the noveltyes putt into the dispensation', he had now reconsidered.[97] The article insisting that the toleration promised in the *escript* be 'known and assured' would not be granted, but if the current form was not enough, '*ne suffit*', they would look for '*autre remede*' to give the pope '*les asseurances requises*'.[98] These 'expla-nations' offered by James were not changes to the sworn articles, but they allowed for the phrasing to be 'strengthened and made more advantageous for the Catholic faith and the Roman Church'.[99] To shrink the distance between the pope's demands and the sworn articles, James would again encourage a double interpretation of his policy.

How sustainable that double interpretation might be, however, was under question. As the Venetian ambassador in London observed, the 'words of the pope's articles' were so 'different from the king's interpretation', that if the nuncio had 'express orders', he might not 'hand over the dispensation with-out fresh negotiations and commands from Rome'.[100] And if Pope Urban might be found ill-satisfied with the terms, so, it seemed, would be many of James's subjects – the rumoured demands, that the 'pope will have a free and absolute toleration of that religion in these kingdoms', had led to some alarm.[101] The political observer John Chamberlain remarked that he would be 'sory to see us brought so low as to accept whatever is imposed'.[102]

Against a backdrop of this growing discontent with the rumoured terms, on 3 March, James again postponed parliament, pushing the opening back to late April. To prevent any further blocks, when James's generous 'explanations' were dispatched to France, they were sent with instructions that Louis was to be given only three days to agree to 'an act under his hand and seale' promising that with the arrival of Buckingham or another proxy, the marriage would 'be solemnized' according 'to the articles agreed on'.[103] By 11 March, the ambassadors and commissioners had come to an agreement in Paris. James and Charles would not be required to 'sign any more', but they would 'be bound to observe' the previously sworn *escript*, and Louis would offer a signed promise that, within thirty-one days of the proxy's arrival, the marriage would be celebrated.[104]

Through a series of cross-promises and compromises, James had secured the match with France, and it seemed, at least for a moment, that his hard-fought foreign policy might work. As Carlisle described on 14 March, any further delay would be to the 'infinite prejudice' of the king's 'endes and the affaires of those of our religion both here and in other partes', but a quick conclusion of the match would allow James to 'secure himselfe and his allies' and 'advance his just ends'.[105] If Buckingham quickly travelled as proxy, he might 'prevent' the legate Barberini's 'artifices' and hold Louis to his 'present good resolucons'.[106] Instead of settling with Spain in the Valtelline, the French might be drawn to invade Genoa, cutting the 'kinge of Spaynnes purse' in Europe; the Hollanders might find victory in the West Indies, where the 'bottome' of Philip's 'purse' would be cut; and if Breda could hold out a while longer, the Spaniards would be underfunded and occupied, leaving Mansfelt a fit opportunity to march east and recover the Palatinate.[107] James had constructed a narrow path through the diplomatic briars – a path built upon a great deal of contingency and conflicting commitments. James, however, would not be the one charting that path. He died, less than two weeks later, on 27 March 1625.

II

In the first weeks of his reign, Charles I would attempt to unpick some of his father's knotted policies – working to complete his Blessed Revolution, but from seemingly a worse position as the result of James's common cause policy, the logic of which Charles could not entirely escape. Days after James's death, Carlisle and Holland were informed that their 'former directions concerning the marriage' held firm.[108] Buckingham, in an 'extremity of sorrow', would no longer travel as proxy, but orders for a French replacement to participate in the rites on Charles's behalf were quickly issued.[109] Charles hoped that the solemnities might be performed and that Henrietta Maria might arrive in England by the 'ende of May att furthest, and if it were possible[,] before the 17th', the day set for the opening of the new king's first parliament.[110]

While Charles would work within the Anglo-French common cause his father had constructed, he now attempted to turn the direction of that cause onto a more directly anti-Spanish course – a course not unlooked for by his domestic audience or his foreign allies. On 19 April, Charles gave the order that 'the restraint laid upon Mansfelt by our late king of glorious memory for not going to Breda died with him'. Mansfelt would now have 'as much scope' as necessary 'to take his next and best waies for recoverie of the Palatinat', and if that meant passing through the dominions of the king of Spain or the archduchess of Austria, his forces were permitted to 'make their waie by armes'.[111] Charles now did what James had consistently refused to do; he gave occasion to break the peace with Spain. For a domestic audience who envisioned the recovery of the Palatinate as only one part of a broader anti-Habsburg cause – a broader Protestant cause – and for those who saw Breda as the suffering front line of that cause, this was an entirely overdue policy shift.

Yet the logic of James's French Match for Charles, the foundation of his anti-Habsburg common cause, meant that the breach with Spain could not be made entirely compatible with the pursuit of a Protestant cause. On 1 May, the day the marriage was to be solemnised in Paris, Charles, in a show of 'favour and clemency towards his Catholics subjects', signed a series of 'mandates, submitted unto him' by D'Effiat, which would be sealed 'and thereafter enforced', if not immediately, in 'deference to Parliament', then 'soon after' the session was concluded.[112] Charles promised to 'publish generally and to every one' his desire that all his officers 'desist from molesting Catholics on account of their religion'; to command that his archbishops 'abstain from any proceedings whatsoever against the Catholics', including the 12d fine for recusancy; and he promised that the lord treasurer would revoke 'all the written obligations to pay', which had already been issued to recusant Catholics.[113]

While Charles reconfirmed his father's promises on behalf of Catholics at home, on 4 May, English forces, combined with the prince of Orange's army, endeavoured to relieve the besieged city of Breda, the suffering front line of the Protestant cause. The attempt failed. By the 7th, the situation was 'given over as desperate', and on 26 May, Breda was rendered to Spinola.[114] In the aftermath, a 'scornfull, insolent picture' began to circulate on the Continent: a depiction of 'Breda's funerells', with Mansfelt riding 'before the coffin bareheaded on an asse, the English forces vanishing in smoke, and all the kings, princes and states of the new league riding after in mournfull heavines'.[115] Frederick V followed 'upon an asse, and his wife upon a mule', followed by their '7 children with theyre hatts in their hands'.[116] Breda had fallen, and, it seemed, there was little hope for success in the Palatinate.

While Mansfelt would now 'take his army to Germany', he lacked 'in effect all things necessary for the field'.[117] He could not be provided for, as Mansfelt's treasurer could not 'find a merchant to give him money, seeing that he only ha[d] bare promises from England'. With parliament 'postponed and the six months for the payment' from France 'hav[ing] nearly expired, with nothing done', he could find no creditors.[118] It was hoped that Henrietta Maria would have arrived before 17 May, but her journey was delayed, and, accordingly, so was the opening of parliament – a delay which 'occasion[ed] the most pernicious results'.[119] 'The expenses are great and cannot be borne without the help of parliament'.[120] By mid-June, it was feared that, 'without help', Mansfelt's force would 'dissolve within a week'. The 'whole affair' now seemed to be 'a failure'.[121]

On 12 June, Henrietta Maria landed at Dover. Six days later, Charles opened the first parliament of his reign. The tensions of the 1625 Parliament – the rise of a vocal opposition across the short session; the reluctance of the Commons to grant further supply for a war they had seemingly demanded a year earlier; the evident difficulty that Charles faced in adapting to his new role – are not entirely comprehensible without a consideration of the political situation and policy course that Charles had inherited from James. Any account of this parliament is entering *in medias res*, in the middle of a half-completed policy turn, a turn initiated by Charles as prince, resisted and altered by James, and now taken up again, in a distorted form, by Charles as king. Accordingly, to treat the 1625 Parliament as a blank slate for the new king is to draw a dividing line between the reigns of James and Charles that contemporaries were not willing to make. Charles would spend much of the session defending (and attempting to retroactively reshape) James's common cause, while dealing with the consequences of his father's entangled promises, the long-term unsustainability of which Charles was now forced to confront.

By the opening of the session, the entirety of the subsidies granted in 1624 had been spent, along with 'much more of the revenues of the crown', on the 'great engagements for the recovery of the Palatinate'. Charles now urged the House to grant speedy supply so that he might 'perfect a work which [his] father ha[d] so happily begun'.[122] Charles, however, would soon discover that his anti-Spanish turn, and the naval force he was assembling at Plymouth for such a purpose, would not be enough to justify James's common cause and placate the parliament – not enough to have them overlook that Breda had fallen, that the Palatinate was no closer to recovery, that Mansfelt was now languishing in the field, and that Catholics had been granted liberty at home.

This last point would prove one of James's most difficult legacies. Try as he might, Charles could not draw a line under his father's reign, partly because he perpetuated James's cross-promises to Paris and to Westminster. Just the day before the opening of parliament, Charles assured the French ministers in London, 'with an oath', that what had been promised in favour of the Catholics would be performed – though, he added, it may be 'necessary to temporise' during the session.[123] On 20 June, the parliament was informed, conflictingly, that Charles had 'privately, and now publicly' resolved for his officers to 'go forward with the old course of law'. The following day, the marriage was publicly pronounced, and, before the French ministers, Charles again submitted to the contract his father had condescended to – a contract entirely incompatible with the assurances now offered to parliament.[124]

By 22 June, the Commons had turned to debate the growth of popery which had been allowed by James's connivance at the unenforced anti-Catholic penal statutes, the connivance demanded by the promises Charles had just reaffirmed. The former petitions for religion from 1621 and 1624 were now re-examined, along with Charles's voluntary protestation, offered in response to their 1624 petition, that he would not allow toleration of English Catholics for the sake of a foreign Catholic bride.[125] As John Chamberlain described, the Commons latched onto this promise the king had made 'when he was Prince that he wold never contract any mariage with conditions derogatorie to what we professe'. Now there was a great 'desire to understand what hath passed in that point'. The secrecy surrounding the exact terms granted to Catholics by the French treaty, the keeping of those terms 'close', had only made the parliamentarians 'suspect the more'.[126] It became clear, early on, that the Commons would again tie their vote of subsidies to religious redress – they were willing to grant supply, but Charles would be asked, first, to 'give retribution and recompense to his people', by which was meant 'the enforcement of the laws against the Catholics'.[127]

An eventual offer of two subsidies and no fifteenths was agreed upon, with some in the Commons voicing a reluctance to grant even that, and certainly no more, as there had been yet 'no reckoning' for their 'former grant'.[128] They had 'yet no account' of the thousands of men, who along with hundreds of thousands of pounds, had been 'expended without any success of honor or profit'.[129] 'Many thousand men' had 'perished and been lost' in the Mansfelt expedition, and for what?[130] James's common cause had accomplished little, and at great cost. Charles, through the mouth of Sir John Coke, attempted to raise the amount of supply by offering a defence of his father's policy. Recounting (and refashioning) the events of the last year of James's reign, Coke explained that their former grant of three subsidies had 'inhabled us only to stand uppon our guard', and to 'proceed no further', changing 'our ague into a fever whilst wee suff[e]red the growing monarch', the king of

Spain, 'to enjoy, besides al[l] his own estates ... both the Valteline and the Palatinate'; to 'translate the Electorate' to the duke of Bavaria; and to 'range the Low Countries'.[131] Accordingly, 'to make a balance to that power', James negotiated a 'strong confederacy' with European powers, the fruits of which first appeared in 'the army beyond the Alps', in the Valtelline, and 'in Mansfeld's army'.[132] There might, it was noted, be some 'objection ... taken from the event of those troops'. It was 'true that the change of the design caused some delay and impeachment of that good effect which was hoped' – the change, James's refusal to employ Mansfelt against Philip or the arch-duchess, had allowed for the fall of Breda – but the employment of Mansfelt had 'not been altogether unprofitable', for the 'appearance of that army kept divers princes of Germany from declaring themselves for the Emperor'.[133] And, despite reports to the contrary, Coke assured the House that Mansfelt's 'armie stand[s] on foote', ready to counter 'the progress of the Catholic league'.[134] The common cause was alive and well, they were assured.

And further preparations were now in hand, namely the fleet, raised at the cost of above £200,000, plus an additional £93,000 for the ordnance and men. This sum was compared to their fresh gift of two subsidies, which would 'amount but to 160,000*l*'.[135] In other words, their subsidies 'now granted' were 'spent' before they were 'received'.[136] This was in addition to the continued monthly payments of £20,000 to Mansfelt, along with another £40,000 per month to support a newly arranged league with Denmark.[137] Kings, like 'good chess-players, fortifie everie drawght with a second, third and fowrth' – the first moves, completed under James, secured their affairs at home, provided aid for their Dutch allies, and formed the 'confederate armies' under Mansfelt. The fourth move, 'which susteineth all the rest', was this unlaunched fleet.[138] Further supply would hold the common cause together, enable the fleet to launch, and would position Charles to win the board.

But James's common cause policy was not one that Charles's first parlia-ment appeared keen to fund. When it became clear the offer of two and none would not be raised, Charles ordered a short recess. They would meet again at Oxford in just under three-weeks' time. He held them over with his infor-mal acceptance of their petition for religion. On 11 July, Charles indicated that his answer to their petition would be 'real and not verbal'. They would 'shortly have a particular satisfaction in that point, and in the meantime', the king would 'command a strict execution of the laws'.[139]

Yet, during the recess which followed, Charles continued to grapple with the consequences of his father's cross-promises. Just the day before he prom-ised his parliament to enforce the anti-Catholic penal statutes, he swore to do the opposite before the French ministers, assuring them that what had been promised for his '*sujets Catholiques Romains*' in contemplation of his mar-riage would be performed in '*entier effect*' – an explicit reconfirmation of James's letter to this effect, signed in December 1624, and Charles's own promises sworn in early May.[140] The French ministers now took pains to hold Charles to his word. At their insistence, on 13 July, Secretary Conway issued a letter of favour for a Jesuit, Alexander Baker. It was not exactly a pardon, as this had already been granted, but rather a release of the £50 that was being demanded for Baker's surety and a note for the 'expedition' of the matter.[141] On 17 July, Conway issued a number of similar letters, executing the king's connivance at the law, including a letter reprimanding two Dorset JPs who had searched the home of a convicted recusant, Mary Estmond, and seized some 'books and other things' from her.[142] Such favour for Charles's Catholic subjects would be the expected fruit of the cross-confessional alliance with France.

And, indeed, that would be a primary focus of debate for the final twelve days which the parliament sat. The day they readjourned at Oxford, on 1 August, as the 'first bud put forth', a complaint was raised against a 'pardon given to a Jesuit' – the letter of favour for Alexander Baker.[143] The 'pardon' was found offensive for a number of reasons, but predominantly so because of the date of issue: the day after Charles had promised his 'answer' to their petition for religion would be 'real and not verbal'. Accordingly, this action was 'held [as] an ill comment on that text', their petition, and 'an unhappy performance of that promise', generating 'wonder' in some and 'fear generally in all'.[144]

But there was still the matter for which they had been carried over: adequately supplying Charles for the war effort.[145] In a short speech on 4 August, Charles pressed the 'impossibility' of 'go[ing] through with so many great affairs as were now in hand without further help'.[146] The fleet, in particular, could not be set out without another £40,000. As a 'cordial and restorative' to 'sweeten' this request for additional supply, Charles indicated that they would soon receive a full answer to their petition for religion.[147] This sweet coating (perhaps not as sweet as Charles intended) did not make the pill easier to swallow. That they had been brought to Oxford, during a plague, it should be noted, to request £40,000 *after* they had agreed to two subsidies was seen as a bad turn – in terms of precedent and as a comment upon the crown's finances. But the continuation of James's foreign policy also left a bitter taste. In 1624 they had given three subsidies and three fifteenths for the 'queen of Bohemia, for which she is nothing the better'.[148] 'What has been therein done worthy of that intention?'[149] 'Nothing has been done. We know not our enemy. We have set upon and consumed our own people'.[150] They had given and James had not pursued the war they expected; they had given and it had come to nothing. Now, they were asked to give more.

Robert Phelips, a key parliamentary undertaker of Charles's and Buckingham's patriot coalition in 1624, now became the voice of opposition to Charles's course – the policy he had inherited from his father. Phelips emphasised that when the treaties with Spain were broken, they had desired 'three things': first, that Charles 'would link himself in such an alliance as might agree with us in religion'; second, that they 'uphold' their neighbours' safety; and third, that they 'maintain the religion in the kingdom' and that the 'laws might have their life'.[151] 'How those' intentions 'were kept' was only too clear – 'little' was 'being done for support' of their allies abroad, while, at home, the 'papists did still increase, their priests and Jesuits gr[e]w more bold'.[152] All their treating had not helped Frederick and Elizabeth, nor the Dutch, and it had come at an (unclear) cost. 'What the Spanish articles were we know. Whether those with France be any better is doubted. There are visible articles and invisible. Those we may see, but these will be kept from us'.[153] They could all feel the effects of the French Match – they might not know the exact terms of the *escript particuler*, but they could see the effects of James's cross-promises, of Charles's connivance granted to men such as Baker.

And so, rather than debate further supply, for the next several days, grievances of religion continued to be the Commons' focus. On the 6th, a Dorset MP brought forward the letter that had been sent from Conway to two JPs of his constituency, reprimanding them and ordering that they 'forbear the execution of law' against a 'suspect[ed] papist', Mary Estmond. Upon the 'reading of this letter the House was much moved'.[154] They 'did not much dispute it', but 'did much resolve it in the consideration of their thoughts, that at that time' the 'law' had been 'controlled in favor of such persons', while the faithful 'ministers of justice' had received an 'increpation for their duties'.[155]

All of this cast a shadow upon Charles's answer to their petition for religion, delivered by Buckingham two days later, on 8 August. Buckingham declared that 'all' of their 'desires' were granted and that the anti-Catholic penal statues would be put in execution and 'strictly followed'.[156] While the duke claimed that Charles did not intend his answer to their petition to be a 'wheel to draw' on his other 'affairs and designs', Buckingham then outlined their present needs and, again, defended James's policy course.[157] 'If you look upon the change of the estate in Christendom' since the end of the 1624 Parliament, you could not 'think it less than a miracle'. At that time, the king of Spain 'went conquering' – he had become 'master' of the Valtelline, had broken 'Germany into pieces', and 'was possessed of the Palatinate'. Now, the Valtelline was 'at liberty', war had been 'proclaimed beyond the Alps', the princes of the union were 'revived', and France was 'engaged against Spain' and had 'confederated with Savoy and Venice' for that purpose.[158] Buckingham defended James's common cause, noting that Charles would be made 'chief of the war' by these various wars of diversion – the common cause would force their enemy to 'spend his money and men in other places', while strengthening and enabling their allies. And as for the question of 'where is the enemy?', Buckingham answered that, if they made the fleet 'ready to go',

Charles would have them 'name the enemy' themselves. 'Put the sword into his Majesty's hands', Buckingham declared, 'and he will employ it to your honor, and the good of the true religion'.[159] Their petition for religion had seemingly been answered in full, as had lingering questions about Charles's foreign policy. But this foreign policy – the pursuit of (a more directly anti-Spanish version of) James's common cause – remained incompatible with the confessional policy to which Charles had just committed.

This apparent incompatibility remained at the centre of parliamentary attention. The morning after Buckingham's speech, and the morning after the king had answered their petition for religion, the Commons sent up yet another petition to the Lords, now against the royal favour recently shown to Catholics. This petition emphasised the fact that, on 11 July, Charles had given them 'an assurance of real performance of those things for which' they had humbly begged, and then, the very next day, had granted his favour to Baker, 'a known and notorious Jesuit', and four days after that, to Estmond, a convicted recusant. All of this, the petition declared, tended to the 'prejudice of true religion', the king's 'dishonor', the 'discouragement' of parliament, the 'discountenancing' of ministers of justice, the 'grief' of 'good people', and to the 'animating of the popish party'.[160]

Caught between – and now caught out in – his cross-promises, on 10 August, Charles issued an ultimatum: either give further supply or go home.[161] There were indeed some MPs who would give, both because they would continue the war effort, now on the brink of collapse without funding, and because Charles had provided religious redress. More than one man argued they should supply in respect of the king's 'answer to our petition for religion'.[162] One MP, previously against giving, even turned to support further supply on the 11th, offering the penetrating (if perhaps resentful) observation that 'we would have bought this answer for religion' with supply.[163]

Yet, the opposition held. When the House gathered on 12 August, it was widely understood this would be their last day. Christopher Sherland offered a final and decisive speech against giving. He acknowledged the 'lines drawn' by some men between Charles's answer to their petition and the grant of supply, but questioned, essentially, whether or not they were (again) being deceived.[164] He was as 'glad of it', the king's answer, 'as any member of the House', but 'who knows what will be the execution of it?' 'Nay, have we not cause to fear the worst?'[165] Charles had promised at the end of the London session that they would see his answer to their petition in practice, and everyone knew exactly how that had turned out – pardons to Jesuits and protections for papists at the behest of the French. Why had they any reason to believe the king would *now* oversee the enforcement of the laws?

This speech, offered at the end of a parliament which failed to pass a subsidy bill before being dissolved, offered a fit conclusion to the session and an interpretative key to the issues which plagued Charles's first parliament and set the tone for his reign. Sherland's speech was about promises made and broken. This included Charles's recent promises, in answer to their petition, seemingly betrayed by the immediate favour shown to Baker and Estmond, but this sense of betrayal also extended to deeper-rooted promises. More than once in the 1625 session, Charles was reminded of his own voluntary protestation, offered in the 1624 Parliament when he was prince of Wales, that he would not allow any marriage to obstruct the execution of the laws against Catholics. This too was a promise broken, as were nearly all of James's assurances and declarations. All surety had been crushed by the terms of the French marriage and the requisite papal dispensation. And as Charles defended his father's foreign policy and requested supply for the perfecting of that policy, it had become clear that these promises would continue to be broken – the Anglo-French alliance demanded it, the continued pursuit of James's common cause demanded it.

Here, at the start of his reign, Charles was caught in a policy problem created, in large part, by James's reaction to the international and interconfessional political conjuncture brought on by Charles's and Buckingham's bride-less return from Madrid. Having broken the Spanish treaties with some parliamentary persuasion, James was confronted with both domestic calls for a Protestant cause war and an inability to recover the Palatinate without continental (Catholic) allies. His attempt to meet these competing demands across the final year of his life arguably provides a fit illustration of the nature of James's kingship. Here, he emerges as a skilful, and necessarily slippery, political operator, whose greatest strength was, perhaps, his ability to keep his options open and to preserve his freedom to manoeuvre in the face of domestic and foreign pressures which threatened to constrain the exercise of his royal will. In the short term, the Anglo-French Match, the formation of a common cause league, and the restrictions James placed on Mansfelt's commission were all effective tactics to satisfy the push towards a military intervention on the Continent, while simultaneously rejecting the anti-Spanish and broader confessional glosses which might be placed upon that war.

While James's political manoeuvring afforded him significant tactical latitude in the aftermath of the Blessed Revolution, there was a fundamental difficulty in translating his common cause into a long-term strategy, namely because that cause was built upon unstable cross-promises and was, arguably, sustained by James's ability (and willingness) to hold those conflicting policies together in tension. While points of stress were clearly discernible under James, he was able to paper over the cracks inherent to his course of action by repeatedly delaying parliament – a body which was both essential to the maintenance of his common cause and, as he understood, held confessional interests incompatible with that policy. The repeated delays, however, only compounded the tension. And, by the time of the 1625 Parliament, it was Charles who was left to deal with the consequences of James's common cause: English

Catholics were living with near impunity, Breda was lost, Mansfelt's forces were on the edge of dissolution, the French on the verge of settling in the Valtelline, and the Palatinate no closer to recovery. Charles now attempted to pursue the anti-Spanish war that the patriot coalition and their parliamentary undertakers thought they had put into motion in 1624, but arguably from a worse starting position as a result of James's manoeuvring – both in terms of the circumstances of European geopolitics and in terms of the domestic support of, and trust in, the regime's policy course. This early erosion of trust in Charles, a problem which would profoundly shape his rule, is revealed, then, to emerge out of the policy choices and political strategies employed by James in the final year of his reign.

Notes

1 For variously polarized accounts: D. H. Wilson, *King James VI and I* (1956); D. Hirst, *Authority and Conflict: England 1603–1658* (Cambridge, MA, 1986); C. Russell, *Parliaments and English Politics, 1621–1629* (Oxford, 1979); P. Croft, *King James* (Basingstoke, 2003); L. J. Reeve, *Charles I and the Road to Personal Rule* (Cambridge, 1989); K. Sharpe, *The Personal Rule of Charles I* (New Haven, Conn., 1992); M. Kishlansky, 'Charles I: A Case of Mistaken Identity', *Past and Present* 189 (2005), pp. 41–80.
2 See, for example, the AHRC-funded research network, 'Europe's Short Peace, 1595–1620', under the leadership of Noah Millstone.
3 S. Adams, 'The Protestant Cause: Religious Alliance with the European Calvinist Communities as a Political Issue in England, 1585–1630', (PhD, Oxford, 1973), p. 2.
4 M. Questier, *Dynastic Politics and the British Reformations, 1580–1630* (Oxford, 2019), pp. 416–17.
5 Proceedings in Parliament, 1624, available digitally on *British History Online* (hereafter, PiP, 1624), NRO, FH/N/C/0050, fo. 47^{r-v}; *LJ*, III, pp. 289–90.
6 For a full account of 1624 Parliament, see T. Cogswell, *The Blessed Revolution: English Politics and the Coming of War, 1621–1624* (Cambridge, 1989), chs 4–7.
7 PiP, 1624, HRO, 44M69/F4/20/1, p. 80; TNA, SP 14/166, fo. 107^r.
8 BL, Harleian MS 1581, fo. 26^v [Kensington to James, 26 February 1624].
9 M. Questier (ed.), *Stuart Dynastic Policy and Religious Politics, 1621–1625* (Camden 5th Series, 34, 2009, hereafter, *QSDP*), p. 269 [Smith to Rant, 23 May/2 June 1624].
10 *QSDP*, pp. 96–7.
11 *QSDP*, p. 271 [Colleton to Rant, 18 June 1624].
12 *CSPV 1623–1625*, p. 340 [Pesaro's report, 3/13 June 1624]; for the arrival of this news in London, see *CSPV 1623–1625*, p. 372 [Valaresso's report, 25 June/5 July 1624].
13 *CSPV 1623–1625*, p. 352 [Pesaro's report, 10/20 June 1624].
14 Questier, *Dynastic Politics*, p. 6.
15 TNA, SP 14/168, fo. 55^v [Nethersole to Carleton, 25 June 1624].
16 AAW, B 26, no. 88 [Missenden to Rant, 18 July 1624].
17 TNA, SP 78/72, fo. 373^r [Carlisle to Conway, 21 June 1624].
18 Bodleian Library, Oxford, MS Clarendon 96, fo. 92^r [Kensington to Charles, 14 June 1624].
19 TNA, SP 78/72, fo. 373^r [Carlisle to Conway, 21 June 1624]. Cf. *CSPV 1623–1625*, p. 378 [Pesaro's report, 15 June/5 July 1624].

20 TNA, SP 78/73, fo. 6ᵛ [Carlisle and Holland to Conway, 7/17 August 1624].
21 AAW, B 26, no. 95 [Colleton to Rant, 1 August 1624]. See also TNA, SP 14/168, fo. 88ʳ [Locke to Carleton, 29 June 1624].
22 TNA, SP 14/168, fo. 83ʳ [Conway to Recorder of London, 28 June 1624].
23 TNA, SP 14/171, fo. 27ʳ [Conway to Weston, 6 August 1624].
24 *QSDP*, p. 272 [Colleton to Rant, 18 June 1624]; AAW, B 26, no. 72 [Colleton to Rant, 20 June 1624].
25 AAW, B 26, no. 72 [Colleton to Rant, 20 June 1624].
26 TNA, SP 78/72, fo. 361ᵛ [Carlisle to Conway, 22 July 1624].
27 TNA, SP 78/72, fos 365ᵛ–6ʳ [Carlisle to Conway, 23 July 1624].
28 *CSPV 1623–1625*, p. 407 [report by Pesaro and Morosini, 23 July/2 August 1624].
29 TNA, SP 78/73, fo. 1ʳ⁻ᵛ [Carlisle to Buckingham, 6 August 1624].
30 TNA, SP 78/73, fo. 7ʳ [Carlisle and Holland to Conway, 7/17 August 1624].
31 TNA, SP 78/73, fo. 66ᵛ [Holland to Conway, 18/28 August 1624].
32 TNA, SP 78/73, fo. 66ʳ⁻ᵛ [Holland to Conway, 18/28 August 1624].
33 TNA, SP 78/73, fo. 35ʳ⁻ᵛ [Conway to Carlisle and Holland, 12 August 1624].
34 *CSPV 1623–1625*, p. 435 [Valaresso's report, 3/13 September 1624].
35 TNA, SP 78/73, fos 112ʳ, 114ʳ, 116ʳ [Conway to Carlisle and Holland, 31 August 1624].
36 TNA, SP 78/73, fo. 106ʳ [Carlisle and Holland to Conway, 29 August/8 September 1624].
37 *QSDP*, p. 298 [Musket to More, 23 September 1624]; TNA, SP 14/172, fo. 83ʳ [James to Weston, 24 September 1624].
38 TNA, SP 14/172, fo. 82ʳ [James to Weston, 24 September 1624].
39 TNA, SP 14/173, fo. 92ʳ [Staffordshire JPs to Council, 22 October 1624].
40 AAW, A XVIII, no. 73, p. 385 [Musket to More, 14 October 1624].
41 *CSPV 1623–1625*, p. 455–6 [Pesaro's report, 1/11 October 1624].
42 *CSPV 1623–1625*, pp. 455–6 [Pesaro's report, 1/11 October 1624].
43 TNA, SP 14/173, fo. 8ʳ [King James to the Council of War, 3 October 1624]. See also *CSPV 1623–1625*, p. 450 [report of Pesaro and Valaresso, 24 September/ 4 October 1624].
44 TNA, SP 78/73, fo. 225ʳ [Conway to Carlisle and Holland, 5 October 1624].
45 *CSPV 1623–1625*, p. 454 [Pesaro's report, 1/11 October 1624].
46 TNA, SP 78/73, fo. 229ʳ [Carlisle and Holland to Conway, 9/19 October 1624].
47 TNA, SP 78/73, fo. 229ʳ [Carlisle and Holland to Conway, 9/19 October 1624]..
48 TNA, SP 78/73, fos 229ᵛ–30ʳ [Carlisle and Holland to Conway, 9/19 October 1624].
49 TNA, SP 92/11, fo. 47ʳ [Wake to Conway, 29 October/8 November 1624].
50 *CSPV 1623–1625*, p. 479 [Pesaro's report, 29 October /8 November 1624].
51 TNA, SP 78/73, fos 295ᵛ, 300ʳ [Carlisle and Holland to Carleton, 12/22 November 1624]; SP 78/73, fo. 318ᵛ [Carlisle and Holland to Carleton, 15/25 November 1624].
52 BL, Harleian MS 1580, fo. 58ʳ [Aston to Buckingham, 1/10 December 1624].
53 BL, Additional MS 72278, fo. 148ʳ⁻ᵛ [Chandler to Trumbull, 9/19 December 1624].
54 *CSPV 1623–1625*, p. 494 [Pesaro's report, 12/22 November 1624]; see TNA, SP 81/31, fo. 57ʳ [James I, declaration on employment of forces, 26 January 1625].
55 *CSPV 1623–1625*, p. 494 [Pesaro's report, 12/22 November 1624].
56 McClure, *LJC*, II, p. 589 [Chamberlain to Carleton, 4 December 1624].
57 BL, Additional MS 72255, fo. 157ʳ [Beaulieu to Trumbull, 3 December 1624].
58 TNA, SP 14/176, fo. 27ʳ [Dudley Carleton to Sir Dudley Carleton, 4 December 1624].

59 TNA, SP 14/176, fo. 66ʳ [list of documents signed by the King's stamp in his presence, 12 December 1624]; also TNA, SP 78/73, fo. 362ʳ [Conway to Carlisle and Holland, 23 December 1624]; *CSPV 1623–1625*, p. 523 [copy of the marriage articles, enclosed]. For the full text of the marriage articles, see BL, Harleian MS 354, fos 93ʳ–7ʳ.

60 *CSPV 1623–1625*, p. 523 [copy of the marriage articles, enclosed]. For the change in phrasing, later debated, see TNA, SP 14/214, fo. 95ʳ [Conway Minute Book, 20 January 1625]; SP 78/74, fo. 49ʳ [Conway to Carlisle and Holland, 31 January 1625]; SP 78/74, fo. 84ᵛ [Buckingham to Goring, undated, February 1625].

61 TNA, SP 78/73, fo. 362ʳ [Conway to Carlisle and Holland, 23 December 1624]; *CSPV 1623–1625*, p. 521 [Pesaro's report, 17/27 December 1624].

62 *CSPV 1623–1625*, p. 529 [Pesaro's report, 24 December 1624/3 January 1625]; A. F. Allison, 'Richard Smith, Richelieu and the French Marriage. The Political Context of Smith's Appointment as Bishop for England in 1624', *Recusant History* 7 (1964), p. 190.

63 TNA, SP 14/177, fo. 12ʳ [James to Conway, 24 December 1624]; SP 14/177, fo. 33ʳ [James to Abbot, 26 December 1624]; SP 14/177, fo. 43ʳ [proposed warrant to the treasurer and chancellor, 29 December 1624]; SP 14/177, fo. 46ʳ [copy of James to Ley and Weston, 29 December 1624]; SP 14/177, fo. 47ʳ [Conway to Williams, 30 December 1624]; SP 14/177, fo. 48ʳ [note of orders for restitution of all moneys paid by recusants since Trinity term last, 30 December 1624]; SP 14/177, fo. 49ʳ [Conway to Coventry, 30 December 1624].

64 TNA, SP 14/177, fo. 35ʳ [James to Williams, 26 December 1624].

65 *CSPV 1623–1625*, pp. 513–14 [Morosini's report, 6/16 December 1624].

66 TNA, SP 78/73, fo. 354ʳ [Carlisle and Holland to Conway, 17 December 1624]; *CSPV 1623–1625*, p. 514 [Morosini's report, 6/16 December 1624].

67 TNA, SP 78/73, fo. 355ʳ⁻ᵛ [Carlisle and Holland to Conway, 17 December 1624]. See also BL, Additional MS 72332, fo. 87ʳ [Woodford to Trumbull, 31 December 1624]; TNA, SP 78/73, fo. 370ʳ [Carlisle and Holland to Conway, 29 December 1624].

68 TNA, SP 78/74, fo. 1ᵛ [Woodward to Windebank, 3/13 January 1625].

69 TNA, SP 78/74, fo. 3ᵛ [Carlisle and Holland to Conway, 4 January 1625].

70 *CSPV 1623–1625*, p. 558 [Contarini's report, 10/20 January 1625].

71 *CSPV 1623–1625*, p. 560 [Morosini's report, 13/23 January 1625].

72 *CSPV 1623–1625*, pp. 560 [Morosini's report, 13/23 January 1625], 563 [Pesaro's report, 14/24 January 1624].

73 BL, Additional MS 72255, fo. 165ʳ [Beaulieu to Trumbull, 27 January 1625]; TNA, SP 14/181, fo. 92ʳ [Sir John Ogle to Conway, 14 January 1625]. For a sense of James's continued commitment to Mansfelt's landing in France, see Conway's minute book from 17 to 23 January: TNA, SP 14/214, fos 95ʳ–6ʳ.

74 BL, Additional MS 72255, fo. 165ʳ [Beaulieu to Trumbull, 27 January 1625]; BL, Additional MS 72276, fo. 137ʳ [Castle to Trumbull, 2 January 1625].

75 TNA, SP 14/182, fo. 63ʳ [Ogle to Beecher, 23 January 1625].

76 TNA, SP 14/214, fo. 97ʳ [Conway Minute Book, 25 January 1625]; quoted: TNA, SP 81/32, fo. 57ʳ [James I, declaration on employment of forces, 26 January 1625].

77 TNA, SP 81/32, fo. 56ʳ [Conway to commissioners, 26 January 1625].

78 *CSPV 1623–1625*, pp. 580 [Morosini's report, 4/14 February 1625], 581 [Contarini's report, 7/17 February 1625].

79 *CSPV 1623–1625*, p. 568 [Pesaro's report, 21/31 January 1625]. For Mansfelt's need for money, see for example, TNA, SP 84/122, fo. 16ᵛ [Dudley Carleton to Sir Dudley Carleton, 6 January 1625].

80 See: TNA, SP 84/122, fo. 70ʳ [Cottington to Carleton, 24 January 1625]; SP 99/26, fo. 17ᵛ [Conway to Wake, 26 January 1625].

81 For its arrival, see *CSPV 1623–1625*, p. 580 [Morosini's report, 4/14 February 1625].
82 TNA, SP 78/74, fo. 60ʳ [Carlisle and Holland to Conway, 14 February 1625].
83 TNA, SP 78/74, fo. 61ʳ [Carlisle and Holland to Conway, 14 February 1625].
84 BL, Harleian MS 1580, fo. 207ᵛ ['Carlisle concerning the treatie of the match with France'].
85 TNA, SP 78/74, fo. 66ʳ [Goring to Conway, 16/26 February 1625].
86 AAW, B 47, no. 49 [Champney to More, 23 February/5 March 1625].
87 *CSPV 1623–1625*, p. 582 [Senate deliberation read to Wake, 9/19 February 1625]; TNA, SP 99/26, fo. 26ᵛ [Wake to Conway, 4/14 February 1625].
88 TNA, SP 99/26, fo. 38ʳ [Wake to Conway, 18/28 February 1625].
89 BL, Additional MS 35832, fos 185ʳ [Conway to Carlisle and Holland, 23 February 1625], 183ʳ [Conway to Carlisle and Holland, drafted 21 February 1625, sent 1 March 1625].
90 BL, Additional MS 35832, fos 183ʳ, 184ʳ [Conway to Carlisle and Holland, 21 February 1625, sent 1 March 1625].
91 BL, Additional MS 35832, fo. 187ʳ [Conway to Goring, 23 February 1625].
92 TNA, SP 14/184, fo. 80ʳ [Conway to Buckingham, 27 February 1625].
93 BL, Kings MS 135, fo. 408ʳ [Ville-aux-Clercs to D'Effiat, 11/21 February 1625].
94 BL, Kings MS 135, fos 409ᵛ–11ʳ [Ville-aux-Clercs to D'Effiat, 11/21 February 1625].
95 BL, Kings MS 135, fo. 412ʳ [Ville-aux-Clercs to D'Effiat, 11/21 February 1625].
96 BL, Kings MS 135, fos 413ʳ–14ʳ [Ville-aux-Clercs to D'Effiat, 11/21 February 1625].
97 TNA, SP 78/74, fos 88ʳ–9ʳ [Conway to Carlisle and Holland, 1 March 1625].
98 BL, Kings MS 135, fo. 522ʳ [Avis du Roy…].
99 *CSPV 1623–1625*, p. 615 [Pesaro's report, 11/21 March 1625].
100 *CSPV 1623–1625*, p. 616 [Pesaro's report, 11/21 March 1625].
101 BL, Additional MS 72255, fo. 166ʳ [Beaulieu to Trumbull, 25 February 1625].
102 McClure, *LJC*, II, p. 603 [Chamberlain to Carleton, 26 February 1625].
103 TNA, SP 78/74, fo. 88ᵛ [Conway to Carlisle and Holland, 1 March 1625].
104 Quoted: *CSPV 1623–1625*, p. 619 [Morosini's report, 15/25 March 1625]. See also TNA, SP 78/74, fo. 107ʳ [Goring to Conway, 11 March 1625]; SP 78/74, fos 126ᵛ–7ʳ [Carlisle to Conway, 14 March 1625].
105 TNA, SP 78/74, fo. 127ᵛ [Carlisle to Conway, 14 March 1625]; SP 78/74, fo. 119ʳ [Carlisle to Buckingham, 14 March 1625].
106 TNA, SP 14/185, fo. 154ʳ [Morton to Conway, 21 March 1625]; SP 99/26, fo. 65ᵛ [Conway to Wake, 24 March 1625].
107 TNA, SP 78/74, fos 119ʳ–20ᵛ [Carlisle to Buckingham, 14 March 1625].
108 TNA, SP 14/214, fos 104ᵛ–5ʳ [Conway Minute Book, 30–31 March 1625].
109 Quoted in TNA, SP 14/214, fo. 104ᵛ [Conway Minute Book, 30 March 1625]; SP 78/74, fo. 182ʳ [Conway to Carlisle and Holland, 13 April 1625] for the dispatch of the power of proxies.
110 TNA, SP 78/74, fo. 184ᵛ [Conway to Carlisle and Holland, 14 April 1625].
111 TNA, SP 84/126, fo. 219ʳ [Conway to Carleton, 19 April 1625].
112 H. B. Tomkins (ed.), *The Manuscripts of Henry Duncan Skrine, Esq.: Salvetti Correspondence* (HMC, 11th report, appendix, part I, 1887), p. 12 [6/16 May 1625]. For the planned solemnization of the marriage, see TNA, SP 78/74, fos 213ʳ–14ʳ [Carlisle and Holland to Conway, 28 April 1625].
113 *Salvetti Correspondence*, p. 13 [6/16 May 1625]. See TNA, SP 16/2, fo. 7ʳ⁻ᵛ [Charles to Ley, 1 May 1625]; SP 16/2, fo. 5ʳ [Charles to Williams, 1 May 1625]; and draft: SP 16/2, fo. 2ʳ⁻ᵛ [Charles to Williams, 1 May 1625].

114 TNA, SP 84/127, fo. 36^v [Carleton to Conway, 7 May 1625]; SP 84/127, fo. 55^v [Carleton to Conway, 10 May 1625]; SP 84/127, fo. 128^r [Carleton to Conway, 29 May 1625].

115 BL, Harleian MS 389, fo. 458^r [Mead to Stuteville, 14 June 1625]. Reported also by English Catholics, see: AAW, B 47, no. 197 [Richard Wariner to Rome, 28 June 1625]; QSDP, p. 373.

116 AAW, B 47, no. 197 [Wariner to Rome, 28 June 1625].

117 CSPV 1625–1626, p. 46 [Contarini's report, 9/19 May 1625]; TNA, SP 84/127, fo. 72^r [Carleton to Conway, 14 May 1625].

118 CSPV 1625–1626, p. 78 [Contarini's report, 6/16 June 1625].

119 Quoted in CSPV 1625–1626, p. 62 [Pesaro's report, 20/30 May 1625]. For the delay of parliament, see TNA, SP 16/3, fo. 21^r [Williams to Conway, 3 June 1625]; SP 16/3, fo. 30^r [Morton to Buckingham, 4 June 1625].

120 CSPV 1625–1626, p. 62 [Pesaro's report, 20/30 May 1625].

121 CSPV 1625–1626, pp. 85 [Contarini's report, 13/23 June 1625], 78 [Contarini's report, 6/16 June 1625].

122 PiP, 1625, pp. 20–30 [LJ 436, p. 10].

123 CSPV 1625–1626, p. 98 [Pesaro's report, 24 June/4 July 1625]; BL, Kings MS 136, fo. 358^r [Ville-aux-Clercs and Chevreuse to Louis, 20/30 June 1625].

124 PiP, 1625, p. 37 [HLRO, Manuscript Minutes, fo. 10^v]; AAW, A XIX, no. 56, p. 166 [Ward to Rant, undated, June 1625].

125 PiP, 1625, p. 242 [Bedford MS 197, fo. 9^v].

126 McClure, LJC, II, p. 626 [Chamberlain to Carleton, 25 June 1625].

127 CSPV 1625–1626, p. 97 [Pesaro's report, 24 June/4 July 1625]. Cf. BL, Additional MS 72331, fo. 105^v [Wolley to Trumbull, 24 June 1625].

128 For supply: PiP, 1625, pp. 508 [Negotium, p. 55], 276 [HLRO, MS 3409, fo. 147^v]. Quoted: PiP, 1625, p. 507 [Negotium, p. 53].

129 PiP, 1625, p. 278 [Bedford MS 197, fo. 17^v].

130 PiP, 1625, p. 507 [Negotium, p. 53].

131 TNA, SP 16/4, fo. 34^v [Sir John Coke's report of a message from his Majesty, 8 July 1625].

132 PiP, 1625, p. 351 [Bedford MS 197, fo. 32^v]; and TNA, SP 16/4, fo. 34^v [Coke's report, 8 July 1625].

133 PiP, 1625, p. 351 [Bedford MS 197, fo. 32^v].

134 TNA, SP 16/4, fo. 35^r [Coke's report, 8 July 1625].

135 PiP, 1625, p. 351 [Bedford MS 197, fos 32^v–3^r].

136 PiP, 1625, p. 347 [CJ 806, p. 25].

137 PiP, 1625, p. 351 [Bedford MS 197, fo. 33^r].

138 TNA, SP 16/4, fo. 35^v [Coke's report, 8 July 1625].

139 PiP, 1625, p. 525 [Negotium, p. 120].

140 AAW, A XIX, no. 36, p. 113 [engagements of Charles I in favour of Catholics, granted 25 May, signed 10 July].

141 BL, Kings MS 136, fo. 409^v [Chevreuse to Conway, 12/22 July 1625].

142 PiP, 1625, pp. 665 [HLRO, Main Papers, HL, Conway to Drake and Gollop, 9 August 1625], 414 [Bedford MS 197, fo. 52^v], 415 [ILT, Petyt 538/8, fo. 141^{r-v}].

143 PiP, 1625, pp. 529 [Negotium, p. 135], 376 [Bedford MS 197, fo. 40^r].

144 PiP, 1625, p. 530 [Negotium, p. 137].

145 As expressed by John Coke: PiP, 1625, p. 388 [Bedford MS 197, fo. 44^r].

146 PiP, 1625, p. 386 [Bedford MS 197, fo. 42^v].

147 PiP, 1625, p. 534 [Negotium, p. 149].

148 PiP, 1625, p. 394 [Bedford MS 197, fo. 45^r].

149 PiP, 1625, p. 538 [Negotium, p. 161].

150 PiP, 1625, p. 394 [Bedford MS 197, fo. 45ʳ].
151 PiP, 1625, pp. 396 [Bedford MS 197, fo. 47ʳ], 541 [Negotium, p. 171].
152 PiP, 1625, p. 541 [Negotium, p. 171].
153 PiP, 1625, p. 396 [Bedford MS 197, fo. 47ʳ].
154 PiP, 1625, p. 415 [ITL, Petyt 538/8, fo. 141ʳ⁻ᵛ].
155 PiP, 1625, p. 549 [Negotium, p. 194].
156 PiP, 1625, pp. 552 [Negotium, p. 205], 157 [*LJ* 479, p. 80].
157 PiP, 1625, p. 160 [*LJ* 481, p. 84].
158 PiP, 1625, pp. 161 [*LJ* 481, p. 85], 434 [ITL, Petyt 539/8, fo. 158ᵛ].
159 PiP, 1625, p. 166 [*LJ* 484, p. 89].
160 PiP, 1625, pp. 154–5 [*LJ* 478–9, p. 79].
161 PiP, 1625, p. 442 [*CJ* 813, p. 53].
162 PiP, 1625, pp. 444–5 [*CJ* 814, pp. 54–6].
163 PiP, 1625, p. 467 [HLRO, Historical Collection 143, fo. 3ʳ].
164 PiP, 1625, p. 566 [Negotium, p. 265].
165 PiP, 1625, pp. 478 [ITL, Petyt 538/8, fo. 154ʳ], 566 [Negotium, p. 265].

INDEX

For Product Safety Concerns and Information please contact our
EU representative GPSR@taylorandfrancis.com Taylor & Francis
Verlag GmbH, Kaufingerstraße 24, 80331 München, Germany